BRINGING BUII

BRINGING BUILDINGS BACK

From Abandoned Properties
to Community Assets

A GUIDEBOOK FOR POLICYMAKERS AND PRACTITIONERS

Second Edition

ALAN MALLACH

NATIONAL HOUSING INSTITUTE

Montclair, New Jersey

Published by the National Housing Institute

The National Housing Institute (NHI) is an independent nonprofit research and education organization
driven by a belief in the ability of all neighborhoods
to be healthy and thriving. NHI serves the needs of
practitioners and policymakers fighting poverty and
revitalizing distressed communities.

Distributed by Rutgers University Press,
New Brunswick, New Jersey
Printed in the United States of America.

The paper meets the requirements of the American
National Standard for Information Sciences—
Permanence of Paper for Printed Library Materials,
ANSI Z39.48-1992

Library of Congress Cataloging-in-Publication Data

Mallach, Alan.
Bringing buildings back : from abandoned properties
to community assets : a guidebook for policymakers
and practitioners / Alan Mallach. — 2nd ed.
    p.   cm.
  Includes bibliographical references and index.
  ISBN 978-0-8135-4986-6 (pbk. : alk. paper)
1. Housing rehabilitation—United States—Handbooks,
manuals, etc.   2. Housing—Abandonment—United
States—Handbooks, manuals, etc.   3. Community
development, Urban—United States—Handbooks,
manuals, etc.   4. City planning—United States—
Handbooks, manuals, etc.   5. Land use, Urban—
Environmental aspects—United States—Handbooks,
manuals, etc.   I. Title.
HD7293.M258   2010
307.3'4160973—dc22   2010030894

CONTENTS

PREFACE TO THE SECOND EDITION

Since *Bringing Buildings Back* was first published in 2006, the world it described has radically changed. The year 2006 was the high water mark of the greatest real estate boom in the history of the United States, a boom that affected not only Wall Street bankers and real estate speculators but also, in different ways, the thinking of state and local officials, planners, community development practitioners, and millions of ordinary citizens. Even those who decried the subprime mortgages and out-of-control prices that were the most visible manifestation of the boom were subtly influenced by the climate it engendered, not least in their perception of the future of older cities and towns, their neighborhoods, and their problem properties. It was a moment of almost boundless optimism about American cities: billions were being invested in urban downtowns and neighborhoods into which thousands of young people and empty nesters were moving, not only in strong markets like Boston and San Francisco but also in less thriving communities like St. Louis, Oakland, or Pittsburgh.

Writing early in 2010, it is hard to believe that that era ever existed. Housing prices have collapsed, and millions of American households have already lost their homes through foreclosure, with many millions more likely to share the same fate over the next two or three years. City and state governments across the country are trying desperately to avoid bankruptcy, while laying off thousands of workers. Housing starts have slowed to a trickle, while thousands of brand new homes and condominiums go begging. Hundreds of neighborhoods have been destabilized by foreclosures and the vacant, abandoned properties that have followed in their wake.

These changes have made the contents of this book even more relevant to policymakers and practitioners. Four years ago Sunbelt cities like Las Vegas, Miami, or Stockton, California, considered discussion of abandoned properties largely irrelevant to their reality. That is no longer the case today, as they grapple with collapsing house prices and massive foreclosures. States and cities are exploring the creation of land banks, following the lead of the Genesee County Land Bank Authority, which has demonstrated how effective an aggressive land banking strategy can be. As states, cities, and counties figure out how to use their federal Neighborhood Stabilization Program funds, they are taking a closer look at the tools and strategies described in this book to use those funds most effectively.

At the same time, there is much that is new about today's scene that no one would have predicted five years ago. The Neighborhood Stabilization Program itself is new. For all its limitations, it has spurred a wave of creativity on the part of local governments and community development organizations as they try to deal with the abandoned properties in their neighborhoods. The dynamics of abandonment and its relationship to mortgage foreclosure have changed, raising new legal and procedural issues and fostering new and often difficult relationships between community stakeholders and mortgage lenders.

This second edition of *Bringing Buildings Back* contains a new chapter that directly addresses the issues that have arisen as communities across the country try to stabilize their neighborhoods in the wake of the foreclosure crisis. As does the rest of the book, it looks at both the fundamental "big picture" issues and the technical and practical questions that have emerged since the onset of the crisis. It tries to help the reader understand the concept of neighborhood stability and how that relates to the economic forces affecting a neighborhood, city, or region. It also considers such specific questions as how to deal with vacant properties while they are in the midst of the often protracted foreclosure process, how to work with the growing number of investors buying distressed properties, and how to plan for the most productive reuse of the properties being acquired with Neighborhood Stabilization Program funds. As in the first edition, the new material does not seek simply to provide technical guidance to practitioners; it also suggests creative ways of thinking about local policies, strategies, and actions. Ultimately, no strategy for dealing with problem properties is about just the properties themselves; it is about how to build stronger, healthier neighborhoods, towns, and cities.

The difficulties facing our communities and our nation today are great and can easily appear daunting. Yet just as it was a mistake to be overly optimistic in 2006 and to fail to recognize that we were seeing a bubble rather than sustainable growth, it would be wrong to be too pessimistic in 2010. From the wreckage of the housing bubble and foreclosure crisis we have a real opportunity to rebuild our towns and cities on a sustainable basis, rooted in realistic values and solid economic reality. Cities, towns, nonprofits, and others across the country have already begun that work.

Cities and towns large and small across the United States are confronting the problem of vacant land and abandoned properties, ranging from scattered vacant lots or boarded single-family houses on residential blocks to hulking industrial buildings and gutted tenements. These properties do serious harm to their communities, diminishing property values and discouraging investment, increasing crime, raising the risk of fire, and imposing burdensome costs on the municipalities that must bear the expense of securing and demolishing such structures and providing the added police and fire services needed to protect the public.

Abandoned properties, however, also represent opportunities. Sensitive, carefully planned reuse strategies have enabled towns and cities throughout the country to find new uses for abandoned buildings and lots, reviving neighborhoods at risk and providing new housing opportunities, parks, and open space. States have devised new tools to help cities gain control of properties from owners who have abandoned them. Local governments and nonprofit organizations have crafted new strategies to help owners maintain their properties, keeping them in productive use rather than allowing them to deteriorate and become a drain on the community.

Efforts to prevent abandonment and to redevelop abandoned properties have been going on for decades; as people have come to better understand the close relationship between property abandonment and the many other issues affecting their communities, however, they have focused on addressing this issue directly, rather than as an outgrowth of other strategies or programs. Through the work of the National Vacant Properties Campaign, this issue has been placed in the national spotlight.[1] Some states, including New Jersey, Michigan, and Indiana, have enacted laws designed to help cities gain control of abandoned properties, while a range of cities large and small, from Chicago and Philadelphia to Lima, Ohio, and Davenport, Iowa, have begun to confront the problems posed by abandoned properties in their midst.

Deciding what measures to take, however, can be daunting to a local official or a community development corporation. A comprehensive abandoned property

1. The National Vacant Properties Campaign is a joint project of numerous organizations, led by Smart Growth America, the Local Initiatives Support Corporation, and the International City/County Management Association. Further information can be obtained from its web site, www.vacantproperties .org.

strategy must not only be grounded in a thorough understanding of the complex legal issues involved but also take into account local economic constraints and market opportunities, address the difficult social issues associated with neighborhood change, and, in considering alternative uses, confront the multifaceted questions of site layout and physical form. As increasing attention has been given to addressing the problems of abandoned property, the demand for useful information and technical assistance, from understanding the basic issues involved to identifying specific good practices that can be replicated in other communities, has grown.

Discussions with policymakers and practitioners as this book was being written made it clear that what was needed was not an overview of the subject, or a compilation of so-called best practices, but something more substantial: a book that would provide the big picture as well as the details needed to apply the principles in the field. This book has been written to respond to this demand and to provide an understanding of the strategic issues, as well as specific technical and programmatic information, at a level of detail that will make it useful to anyone involved in framing policies to address the issue of abandoned properties—at the state, local, or neighborhood level—or trying to effect change in a city or neighborhood. We hope that readers will find it easy to navigate and will not be intimidated by its length.

After an introduction that offers a broad overview of the abandonment phenomenon, the book has been organized into three parts, each of which corresponds to one stage of the abandonment cycle:

- *Preventing abandonment.* The best strategy for dealing with abandonment, in many respects, is to prevent it from happening in the first place by understanding the causes of abandonment in the community and developing strategies and programs to keep buildings in productive use.

- *Taking control of abandoned properties.* Successful reuse of an abandoned property requires placing it in the hands of someone willing and able to put it to productive use. This can be accomplished either by taking control of the property or by motivating the owner to reclaim the property by putting it back to use. Taking control encompasses not only applying legal tools to take title to properties but also minimizing the period between abandonment and reuse, maintaining the properties in the interim before turning them over to the most appropriate entity for redevelopment.

- *Fostering sustainable reuse of abandoned properties.* The long-term strength of a community depends not only on abandoned properties' being reused but also on making sure that their reuse provides the greatest benefit—socially, economically, and physically—to the community.

Each of these parts is divided in turn into chapters, each of which addresses a specific topic or concern that can contribute to building the community's strategy.

Each chapter, in turn, is divided into subchapters treating more specific questions and issues.

Illustrations of good practices from the field, showing how a particular entity, such as a city, a community development corporation, or a neighborhood organization, successfully tackled a specific problem are added throughout. A reference guide at the end of each part offers relevant background reading. Contact information and web sites for agencies mentioned in connection with the good practices described are available on the National Housing Institute web site, www.nhi.org.

The book does not, however, aim simply to provide technical guidance but is designed to encourage creative thinking about the underlying issues and overarching policy concerns associated with any strategy that attempts to solve abandoned property issues and put a community on the path to long-term sustainability. This is particularly important when a community sets about dealing with the reuse of its abandoned properties. No one from the outside can prescribe how a community should reuse its vacant properties or what specific uses are most appropriate. The last part of the book, therefore, is more conceptual, even visionary, than practical: it is not about what to do but about how to think about what to do, and how to frame the vision and direction most appropriate for the community. For example, by raising issues such as how a city can rebuild its real estate market and how neighborhood planning can support an abandoned property strategy, this part of the book aims to encourage the reader to think about the larger issues—the use and reuse of the city's land and buildings and the ways in which the city addresses the need to be competitive in today's marketplace—that must drive a successful abandoned property strategy.

For that reason and more, this guidebook is far more than a compilation of so-called best practices. Although good practices are identified and described throughout the book, the guidebook's greatest value lies in the framework, interpretation, and analysis that it offers. Simply describing a practice or policy without explaining why it may be effective, or the circumstances that will make it more or less effective, is rarely useful.

Clearly, interpretation and analysis include opinions. Readers may well disagree with some of the opinions offered in this book. Many issues that arise in dealing with abandoned properties are matters of disagreement, and some are highly controversial, such as the municipal practice of bundling tax liens for sale to investors or the conditions under which a city may decide to demolish rather than preserve an abandoned building. The positions taken in this guidebook reflect my personal experience as a practitioner and researcher as well as the knowledge gleaned from the interviews and research I carried out in the course of writing this book. While deeply appreciative of the thoughts, suggestions, and insights of the many individuals who contributed to this project, I take full responsibility for the opinions and judgments expressed in these pages.

ACKNOWLEDGMENTS

This book, even more than most, could not have been written without the help of far more people than I can ever fully acknowledge. Hundreds of people gave generously of their information, their ideas, and their time to this project, through formal interviews and informal contacts in person, over the phone, and by e-mail. Many people shared not only formal reports but also working papers, memoranda, and drafts that were invaluable.

There are many individuals whom I would like to thank, however, for their help as well as for their own sustained involvement with the issues I seek to address. Frank Alexander, Don Chen, Frank Ford, Jim Kelly, Dan Kildee, Lisa Mueller Levy, Kermit Lind, Charleen Regan, and Joe Schilling all made valuable contributions to this book, and, if they look closely, will have little difficulty finding them in its pages.

While writing this book, I was also deeply engaged in working on a project to reform New Jersey's abandoned property laws, an effort which was not only successful but also added greatly to my understanding of the issues addressed in these pages. Much of that understanding came from working with and learning from a host of partners, including Keith Bonchi, Wayne Meyer, Pat Morrissy, Hannah Shostack, and the staff of the Housing and Community Development Network of New Jersey—in particular Diane Sterner, its indefatigable executive director.

The research, writing, and publication of this book were made possible with funds from the Fannie Mae Foundation and the Ford Foundation. Stephanie Jennings at the Fannie Mae Foundation, with her colleagues Kris Rengert and Sheila Maith, and George McCarthy at the Ford Foundation were consistently supportive. Publication of the second edition was made possible by support from the Fannie Mae Corporation.

The assistance of Nichole Brown, David Holtzman, and Alana Lee at the National Housing Institute was invaluable. I am particularly grateful to Harold Simon, the institute's executive director, for his steadfast encouragement and sage counsel. Finally, as always, my deepest gratitude goes to Robin, whose companionship and support sustained me in this effort, as it has in my many other projects over the years.

BRINGING BUILDINGS BACK

CHAPTER 1

Understanding Abandonment

This chapter offers an introduction to the dynamics of property abandonment in America's towns and cities. It attempts to answer four basic questions:

- What is an abandoned property?
- How widespread is the problem of abandoned properties?
- Why are properties abandoned?
- Why are abandoned properties a problem?

With an understanding of the dynamics involved in these issues, readers will be able to engage more profitably with the strategies and programs discussed in the rest of the book.

A. What Is an Abandoned Property?

An abandoned property is not the same as a vacant property. A property that is vacant for a few days or weeks before someone moves in, or is awaiting rehabilitation, is not abandoned. Conversely, a property that is not entirely vacant may still be an abandoned property. An apartment building whose owner has stopped providing services to the remaining tenants and is no longer paying taxes or utility bills should be considered abandoned even if a handful of tenants still live in the building.

An abandoned property is a property whose owner has stopped carrying out at least one of the significant responsibilities of property ownership, as a result of which the property is vacant or likely to become vacant in the immediate future. The ownership of real property carries not only rights but also responsibilities, of which paying taxes and municipal charges is only one. Others include maintaining the property in conformity with relevant codes and ordinances and keeping it from becoming a nuisance to the community. In many cities where property values are rising, owners are paying taxes on buildings that are sitting empty and unsecured, magnets for crime and disease. A vacant property on which taxes are being paid is an abandoned property if the owner allows it to become a nuisance to the neighbors.

A property can become a nuisance for many different reasons. It may be a site of criminal or drug-related activity, a health hazard, or, if unsecured, a safety risk to local children; or it may simply diminish the property values and the quality of life of its neighbors. Any of these factors may offer grounds for legal action against the property owner. The principle that a property should not be allowed to become a nuisance, and that, if it does, government can step in and solve or "abate" the nuisance, is a basic principle of law in the United States. Although state laws generally define nuisances, few states have provided a clear legal definition of what constitutes an abandoned property. One of those is New Jersey (see box), whose standard is an expansive one which recognizes that many different conditions may lead to a property's being considered abandoned.[1]

Abandoned properties take many different forms. The apartment buildings that were abandoned in New York City and other big cities in the 1960s and 1970s are only one example. At least four types of abandoned buildings are widely found in America's towns and cities, each with its own distinct "triggers" leading to abandonment:

- *Multifamily rental properties,* from New England three-unit triple-deckers to large apartment buildings in New York City

- *Single-family homes,* often formerly owner-occupied, such as Phila-delphia row houses or detached houses in Midwestern or Southern cities

- *Commercial or mixed-use properties,* from older neighborhood commercial areas to obsolete 1950s highway shopping strips

- *Industrial properties,* widely known as brownfields, which raise particular issues because of the reality or perception of environmental contamination

The types of properties most likely to be abandoned vary from city to city, depending on the character of the city's real property stock and the economic factors affecting the community. In Philadelphia, Pittsburgh, or Flint, Michigan, where most of the residential stock is single-family houses, these are also the most commonly abandoned properties. Abandoned buildings in New York City have usually been older apartment buildings and tenements. Vacant former industrial properties or brownfields, while present in almost all American cities, are most common in the older industrial cities and towns of the Northeast and Midwest. Abandoned commercial properties are found not only in once-thriving neighborhood shopping streets in older communities but also in many big city downtown areas and in roadside commercial strips.

Vacant lots are another category of abandoned property. Many older cities contain vast areas of vacant land, former sites of buildings that were first abandoned and then torn down. Although vacant lots are often seen as less of a problem than

---

1. The New Jersey definition applies only to buildings, not to vacant lots.

A Legal Definition of Abandoned Property

Sections 4 and 5 of the New Jersey Abandoned Property Rehabilitation Act (N.J.S.A. 55:19-81 and 82):

4. Except as provided in Section 6,* any property that has not been legally occupied for a period of six months and which meets any *one* of the following additional criteria may be deemed to be abandoned property upon a determination by the public officer that:

(a) The property is in need of rehabilitation in the reasonable judgment of the public officer, and no rehabilitation has taken place during that six-month period;

(b) Construction was initiated on the property and was discontinued prior to completion, leaving the building unsuitable for occupancy, and no construction has taken place for six months as of the date of a determination by the public officer;

(c) At least one installment of property tax remains unpaid and delinquent on that property as of the date of a determination by the public officer; or

(d) The property has been determined to be a nuisance by the public officer in accordance with Section 5.

5. A property may be determined to be a nuisance if:

(a) The property has been found to be unfit for human habitation, occupancy or use;

(b) The condition and vacancy of the property materially increases the risk of fire to the property and adjacent properties;

(c) The property is subject to unauthorized entry leading to potential health and safety hazards; the owner has failed to take reasonable and necessary measures to secure the property; or the municipality has secured the property in order to prevent such hazards after the owner has failed to do so;

(d) The presence of vermin or the accumulation of debris, uncut vegetation or physical deterioration of the structure or grounds have created potential health and safety hazards and the owner has failed to take reasonable and necessary measures to remove the hazards;

(e) The dilapidated appearance or other condition of the property materially affects the welfare, including the economic welfare, of the residents of the area in close proximity to the property, and the owner has failed to take reasonable and necessary measures to remedy the conditions.

*Section 6 provides exceptions for properties in seasonal use and properties for which a buyer of a tax lien on the property is keeping taxes current and moving to foreclosure in a timely fashion.

abandoned buildings, they can still cause serious harm, particularly if illegal dumping or the accumulation of debris creates health or safety hazards for the property's neighbors.

B. How Big Is the Abandoned Property Problem?

Counting abandoned properties is a difficult proposition, and comparing results from different states and cities is even more difficult. Some communities count abandoned buildings, whereas other estimates are based on abandoned dwelling units. Residential properties are counted differently from industrial properties, and hardly anyone counts vacant storefronts or commercial buildings. Some communities count vacant lots, but a vacant lot can be anything from a 12- by 75-foot sliver in the middle of a block to a former industrial site covering many acres.

By any account, however, abandoned buildings and vacant lots are widespread, not only in the nation's large cities but also in thousands of small cities, towns, and villages throughout the United States. A few examples illustrate the extent of the problem:

- An analysis by the author using 2000 U.S. Census Bureau data for the nineteen cities with over 100,000 population showing the greatest population decline estimated 185,000 abandoned residential units, or an average of nearly 10,000 per city.[2]

- A survey by the city of St. Louis in 2000 found nearly 13,000 vacant abandoned residential units, despite the city's having demolished over 7,000 units between 1991 and 2000. In twenty out of the city's seventy-nine neighborhoods, more than 10 percent of all housing units were abandoned.

- A 2001 Philadelphia survey found more than 27,000 abandoned residential structures, more than 2,000 abandoned commercial buildings, and 32,000 vacant lots.

- Detroit contains more than 45,000 abandoned residential and commercial buildings, although the city has demolished more than 28,000 houses since 1989.

The most severe abandonment problems, however, are not in the largest cities but in cities of less than 100,000 population, such as East St. Louis, Illinois; Highland Park, Michigan; and Camden, New Jersey. More than 10 percent of the properties in these cities have been abandoned.

Although abandonment may be at its worst in the older industrial cities of the Northeast and Midwest, it is a national phenomenon. Cities as diverse as Covington, Kentucky, Durham, North Carolina, and Fresno, California, as well as hundreds of smaller communities throughout the South and West, are grappling with this problem. Thousands of homes and stores are being abandoned in the small towns and villages of America's plains and prairie states. Even in the nation's fastest-growing cities, such as Las Vegas and Houston, properties are abandoned as people and money move to the periphery and older inner-city neighborhoods are neglected. Each affected community has its own pattern of abandonment, whether it is the storefronts and office buildings of a once-vibrant downtown, the factories that once employed the town's workers, or the houses in which the workers once lived.

2. See the appendix to this volume, which illustrates the wide range of available estimates as well as the different definitions used.

C. Why Are Properties Abandoned?

In agrarian societies, abandonment was often triggered by ecological factors, such as soil exhaustion or climate change. Today, abandonment usually reflects economic and demographic shifts within American society, ranging from inner-city disinvestment to the migration patterns that are depopulating Western prairie towns. It most often occurs when an owner concludes, rightly or wrongly, that the potential losses from continuing to occupy or maintain the property exceed the potential benefits. While economic reasons are by far the most important, abandonment is often exacerbated by exploitative practices, such as predatory lending and real-estate speculation.

Abandonment links location, physical obsolescence, and market obsolescence, made worse by exploitation. Location is largely self-explanatory; the other terms are defined as follows:

- *Physical obsolescence* occurs when the physical condition of the building is such that it cannot continue to be used productively without new investment that exceeds the potential market value of the property.

- *Market obsolescence* occurs when the size or layout of the building is such that, given its location and physical condition, it is no longer attractive to potential buyers or tenants. Examples include old industrial properties, small, single-family row houses in cities such as Philadelphia and Baltimore, and so-called "grayfields," 1950s shopping strips that no longer reflect consumer preferences. Many such properties may be adaptable to other uses and thus reclaimed from abandonment.

Location, as always in real estate matters, is the most important factor, because it dictates whether the owner can justify rehabilitating or replacing the property to overcome problems of physical or market obsolescence. A rational landlord will not invest money in a building unless she expects a return on that investment through either greater cash flow or future appreciation. Location can drive abandonment even without obsolescence. In Flint, Michigan, hundreds of single-family houses built in the 1950s and 1960s, identical to those selling at respectable if not stellar prices only a few miles away, have been abandoned because the location is perceived as undesirable.

The decline in real estate demand that leads to property abandonment often reflects the lack of local or regional economic growth. In many parts of America's Midwestern "Rust Belt," entire cities and regions are in economic decline. In the Buffalo and Pittsburgh metropolitan areas, more people are leaving than arriving, and the supply of houses substantially exceeds the demand. Even where net regional growth is limited or nonexistent, newer and more affluent parts of the region may be growing, drawing population away from the region's inner core. While Pittsburgh is losing population and suffering from massive property abandonment, Cranberry Township, ten miles away, is booming.

Different types of properties in the same location are affected by different market conditions. In some areas, owner-occupied properties may be abandoned, but rental properties are not. Although home buyers may not see the area as attractive, its apartments may still command high enough rents to support landlords, particularly if the area contains a large pool of Section 8 vouchers.[3] The opposite could also happen, but it is less likely. Some commercial strips have high levels of abandonment even where nearby residential areas are healthy, because their residents, in today's automobile-oriented society, no longer find the local stores competitive with others that they can easily reach in their cars.

All of these conditions are aggravated by practices such as predatory lending or speculative "flipping" of properties, which can cause properties to be abandoned—as a result of either foreclosure or misuse—even when abandonment might not be inevitable on market grounds. Other factors, such as landlords' or homeowners' having inadequate information, the complexities of tax and estate situations, and the poor functioning of inner-city real estate markets, also add to abandonment risk.

All of these factors can give rise to events leading to abandonment, which can be referred to as abandonment triggers. Although the number of potential events is large and cuts across all property types, as shown in table 1.1, each property type typically is most subject to a small number of principal abandonment triggers:

- The decision to abandon *rental property* is most heavily driven by negative cash flow, often made worse by the difficulties of owning and operating inner-city rental property. Some landlords attempt to improve cash flow by "milking" a property, cutting back on maintenance and repairs and ceasing to pay property taxes, a few years before completely abandoning it.

- Abandonment of *single-family owner-occupied properties* often takes place after the death or relocation of the owner. It is closely associated with a weak market in the area, reflected in low resale prices and the length of time that properties stay on the market. Abandonment of owner-occupied property is exacerbated by fraud and predatory lending associated with refinancing or home improvement loans, practices that can trap low-income families in substandard properties they cannot afford to maintain or trigger foreclosure after borrowers have defaulted on extortionate loan payments.

3. The federal Section 8 program provides low-income tenants with vouchers that permit them to rent an apartment at a "fair market rent" set by the government, with the tenant paying 30 percent of his or her gross income and the government paying the balance of the rent. Because fair market rents are set on a regional basis, they may be considerably more than a low-income tenant without a voucher can afford to pay and so represent an attractive proposition for an inner-city landlord.

TABLE 1.1 Abandoned Properties and Abandonment Triggers

Property type	Abandonment triggers
Multifamily rental property	Inadequate cash flow or income base (i.e., rents too low to cover costs) Inadequate cash flow or excessive cost base (i.e., mortgage payments, taxes, and insurance) Deterioration; need for major repairs inadequately supported by cash flow or market value Difficulty in obtaining financing Excessive liens, or liens that exceed market value Management and maintenance difficulties (e.g., tenant/landlord problems and crime) Neighborhood change Perception of market trends
Single-family homes	Household transition (e.g., death or relocation) Deterioration; need for major repairs not supported by market value Low market value Neighborhood change Market imperfections Lack of information about market and resources Excessive liens Fraudulent transactions and predatory lending
Commercial and mixed-use properties	Loss of commercial vitality (e.g., in inner-city neighborhood or substandard arterial highway shopping strip) Inadequate cash flow Deterioration or need for major repairs Difficulty in obtaining financing Excessive liens, or liens that exceed market value Crime
Industrial properties (brownfields)	Building configuration or location no longer suitable for prior use Environmental remediation costs and uncertainties High capital cost of redevelopment Legal obstacles Difficulty in obtaining financing Excessive liens, or liens that exceed market value

- Abandonment of *commercial* or *retail property* is largely a function of shifts in consumer preferences and buying power, which leave owners unable to find tenants for retail properties. Small city downtowns and neighborhood shopping streets have been particularly hard hit, but abandonment is also widespread in older highway strips, whose shoppers have moved on to other commercial districts, such as malls or "big box" stores.

- Abandonment of *industrial properties,* or brownfields, reflects the obsolescence of many older industrial facilities, particularly multistory buildings served by railroads or canals rather than highways. It is made worse and sometimes triggered directly by the costs and uncertainties associated with real or perceived environmental contamination.

Two factors that are often underestimated in property abandonment are inadequate information and limited owner property management capacity. Abandonment is a decision made on the basis of the information available to an individual at that point. Markets, particularly in inner-city areas, are far from perfect, and many owners may not have the information to make the most rational decision about the future of their properties. Many landlords contemplating abandonment may be poor managers or be unaware of resources available to help them upgrade their buildings or manage their cash flow. Many homeowners facing potential foreclosure may abandon their homes because they are unaware of the legal remedies available to them. A factory owner may not realize that environmental cleanup costs may be modest and that many states offer public funds for that purpose. Better information, training, and advice can all help reduce abandonment and put buildings back into productive use.

Finally, *transactional abandonment,* arising from legal disputes, estate and inheritance issues, or bankruptcy, can result in even valuable buildings' being abandoned. Some buildings in areas where property values are rising may be owned by speculators who continue to pay the taxes on the property while allowing it to deteriorate, indifferent to the harm it is causing its neighbors.

Understanding the dynamics of abandonment makes it possible to prevent many properties from being abandoned in the first instance and to develop rational strategies for the productive reuse of those that are abandoned.

D. Why Is Abandonment a Problem?

Any property abandonment is wasteful, but when it takes place in a community where people live, work, and raise families, the harm it does goes far beyond the waste of resources.

Among the most visible costs of property abandonment are the following:

- *Effect on neighboring property values.* The presence of abandoned properties in a neighborhood significantly diminishes the value of adjacent occupied properties. A Philadelphia study found that the presence of a single abandoned property on a block reduced the value of the other properties on the block by an average of nearly $6,500. Where properties are physically connected, as in row houses, abandoned properties can cause direct physical damage to attached occupied homes.

- *Effect on public safety.* Abandoned properties are frequently used as venues for criminal activity, including prostitution and drug trafficking.

Strategies to eliminate or reduce abandonment can also reduce crime in the area.

- *Effect on public health.* Abandoned properties are sites of infestation by rats and other vermin and are often used as illegal dumping grounds for construction debris and garbage. Abandoned industrial sites may create further health hazards by exposing neighborhood residents to environmental contamination and toxic materials.

- *Effect on fire safety.* Abandoned buildings increase the risk of fire that can spread to nearby occupied homes, particularly in high-density urban areas.

- *Effect on taxpayers.* Substantial costs may be imposed on local taxpayers to secure, clean, or demolish abandoned properties, to take legal control of properties, and to cover the costs of the added police and fire services they demand. Over the past five years, the city of St. Louis has spent $15.5 million, or nearly $100 per household, to demolish vacant buildings. Detroit spends $800,000 per year just to clean vacant lots.

The presence of abandoned properties, particularly in large numbers, undermines the well-being of the community and affects how it is perceived by both residents and outsiders. The sight of abandoned properties, whether boarded row houses or the shells of old industrial buildings, affects the morale of nearby residents, fostering social isolation, discouraging community engagement, and breaking down the community's social controls. When abandoned properties constitute as little as 3 to 5 percent of the buildings in a neighborhood, abandonment may begin to feed on itself as property owners see the abandoned properties in their midst as harbingers of further neighborhood decline.

Of all of the factors blighting the lives of the people who live in troubled inner-city communities, abandoned properties may be the single most destructive, not least because they aggravate many of the other problems faced by such communities. Neighborhoods would still have crime and fires if they contained no abandoned properties, but probably to a far lesser extent. Older cities would still have fiscal problems if no properties were abandoned, but those problems would be less severe and more easily solved. In many different ways, property abandonment significantly exacerbates the social and economic problems faced by communities across the United States.

Preventing Abandonment

1

Introduction: Thinking Strategically

The best strategy for dealing with abandoned properties is to prevent them from being abandoned in the first place. The financial and social cost of keeping a property in use is often far less than the cost of restoring the property to productive use once it has been abandoned.

Abandonment may sometimes be all but inevitable, given local economic and social conditions. Nevertheless, effective local strategies can significantly reduce the number of properties that are lost, under a wide range of conditions. Abandonment prevention, therefore, should be part of any community's overall revitalization strategy.

The most effective abandonment prevention strategies share some common features. They are, or should be:

- solidly grounded in the realities of property ownership and economic conditions in the community;

- linked to larger strategies to improve the neighborhoods in which abandonment is taking place;

- based on effective partnerships between the public and private entities with a stake in the outcome.

Strategies that do not take into account local economic conditions and the needs of property owners are likely to be ineffective and may even backfire. A program to provide financial assistance to struggling property owners will be ineffective and potentially wasteful if the terms of the assistance do not truly stabilize the owners' financial condition. A code enforcement program which puts pressure on landlords without offering them financially realistic ways of addressing their buildings' deficiencies can hasten rather than prevent abandonment.

First, as Paul Brophy and Jennifer Vey put it, "Know your territory."[1] Knowing your territory requires gathering information, understanding what it means, and using it effectively. Using information in turn requires understanding the social

---

1. Paul Brophy and Jennifer Vey, *Seizing City Assets: Ten Steps to Urban Land Reform* (Washington, DC: Brookings Institution/CEOs for Cities, 2002). This publication offers a good introduction to strategic thinking about abandoned property issues.

and economic forces affecting properties in the community. Some of the critical questions include:

- What types of property are being abandoned in the community?

- Where are the at-risk properties located?

- What are the market conditions in the neighborhoods or districts where properties are at risk?

- What are the particular abandonment triggers at work in the community?

Market dynamics are particularly important not only because they affect owners' behavior but also because they establish the framework within which public policies can be applied. To understand a neighborhood's real estate market, one must understand not only the prices that real estate commands—both sales and rental properties—but also the character of the activity taking place: who is buying and for what purpose. A market that appears strong may be driven by speculative buying, which may be an indicator of future instability rather than solid appreciation.

Equally important are lending patterns—including refinancing and home improvement loans—in the neighborhoods where properties are being lost. Increased subprime lending in many neighborhoods has led to more foreclosures, which have led in turn to the abandonment of many formerly owner-occupied homes. Understanding those patterns can help public officials and community development corporations (CDCs) to develop programs to prevent those losses.

There is no substitute for actually talking to the people—the landlords, homeowners, and lenders—who ultimately make the decisions that lead to a property's being abandoned. A neighborhood is a dynamic, changing system. The forces in a neighborhood that affect abandonment are not the same today as they were five years ago, and will not be the same five years from now. Knowing one's territory is not a single action but an ongoing process. Only by gathering and analyzing data over time and by tracking the forces affecting the community can trends and problems be identified before they get out of control.

Second, abandonment prevention must be part of a larger strategy for improving both the neighborhood and the community as a whole. Abandonment is as much about what is going on in the neighborhood as about the condition of a single building, and as much about expectations as about today's reality. A property owner who expects that the neighborhood will continue to deteriorate may walk away from a break-even or marginally profitable property, whereas one who expects that the neighborhood will improve may put up with a short-term negative cash flow in anticipation of greater returns down the road.

The best long-term strategy to prevent abandonment and preserve existing housing is to improve the quality of life and build a stronger housing market in affected neighborhoods. Such a strategy may not only bring about improvement in the present but also build hope for the future.

Third, it is important to understand that no one entity alone can make abandonment prevention strategies work effectively. Although local government wields substantial legal powers to enforce codes and abate nuisances, it is often poorly equipped to give property owners the support they need to preserve their properties and less able to track the changing dynamics of neighborhoods than are CDCs or civic organizations. Conversely, CDCs and neighborhood organizations lack the resources and often the technical capacity of local governments, especially in larger cities. Where local governments, CDCs, social service providers, neighborhood organizations, and private lenders have formed partnerships for abandonment prevention or housing preservation, those partnerships have been far more effective than the efforts of any of these agencies operating alone.

Strategies for preventing abandonment tend to fall into two broad categories:

- *Strategies to improve the economic viability of at-risk properties.* These include financial assistance, tax relief, and other activities that enhance the stability of the property. They rely on the desire of the owner to maintain her property if it is economically possible to do so. Strategies that are effective in working with owner-occupants are very different from those appropriate for absentee landlords and owners of nonresidential property.

- *Intervention or regulatory strategies.* These include code enforcement, nuisance abatement, and receivership. They are employed when the owner is unwilling to maintain her property or needs to be motivated to do so.

Regulatory strategies by themselves can lead to uncertain results because many owners, particularly in distressed neighborhoods or weak market areas, may lack the resources—or may find it economically unproductive—to remedy their buildings' deficiencies. If the city does not offer assistance to help the owners of properties targeted by enforcement, it can foster abandonment rather than preservation. The most effective approach should combine providing assistance to those in need, using regulatory powers to act against property owners who fail to respond to incentives, and intervening directly in critical situations to preserve properties through receivership or other means. The approach should link financial and regulatory tools through a system that brings together local government, the courts, residents of the affected neighborhoods, CDCs, and other community-based organizations.

This part of the book describes the elements of an effective abandonment prevention strategy and the ways each element can be most effectively used.

CHAPTER 2

Property Information and Early Warning Systems

A successful strategy for dealing with problem properties begins with a good information system, one that provides information about individual properties as well as neighborhood conditions and trends. An effective information system not only tracks conditions and identifies problem properties but also serves as an "early warning system" for spotting potential problem properties and areas before it is too late to handle them effectively.

Before the development of computer-based tools, a detailed, regularly updated property information system was beyond the reach of all but a few unusually well-funded and determined organizations. Today, the widespread use of computerized data systems and inexpensive handheld devices to gather data in the field, coupled with geographic information systems (GIS) that enable data to be organized spatially in different ways, make it possible for any community to establish and maintain a property information system. In most cities, many of the elements of the system may already be in place but not yet organized into a workable whole.

The observations and recommendations here are not designed to serve as a technical guide; they do not include specific information on computer hardware, software, or similar matters. Other sections of the book describe how property information systems can be used to help implement specific programs, such as code enforcement or property maintenance.

A. Designing the Information System

A *property information system* is a system that tracks information about specific properties, whereas a *neighborhood information system* tracks information for a larger area, which can be a resident-defined neighborhood, a census tract, a cluster of city blocks, or a single block. The two systems reinforce each other. While a system that provides information on individual properties can be very useful on its own, a system that combines property information with neighborhood-level information such as census data, real estate market trends, and crime statistics is even more valuable for planning and program development. Information about area-wide trends, such as an increase in subprime lending or a decline in the number or value of houses being sold, can be even more important to an abandonment prevention strategy than information about individual properties.

The community's information system should meet the following general criteria:

- It should include both individual property and neighborhood-level information.

- It should cover all properties within the municipality, although, if resource or other constraints dictate, the system can be phased in neighborhood by neighborhood.

- It should provide enough information, and the right kind of information, about each property and about the neighborhood to be useful for both overall strategic planning and specific activities.

- It should be organized to present information in a variety of different forms, such as maps, tables or lists, and data aggregated or disaggregated to a variety of different areas, depending on the needs of different users.

- It should be regularly updated.

- It should be flexible and user-friendly, so that it can be used by anyone concerned with property conditions in the community.

- One entity should have overall responsibility for designing and maintaining the system as well as for coordinating training and technical support for users. This can be an entity within municipal government, although in many cases—for reasons of both technical capacity and staff resources—it is most effectively housed in a local college, university, or research center.

Every effort should be made to design a system that satisfies all of these criteria. In some respects, a system that is inadequate in some important respect—one that contains outdated information or is difficult to access or use—may be worse than no system, as it may create the illusion that the problem is being addressed when it is not.

The specific contents of the system may vary depending on the resources of the community and on the underlying data capabilities of the many different agencies and departments that contribute data, such as taxation, code enforcement, and public safety agencies. Three critical elements must be defined:

- The categories of information that can be included in the system

- The specific information, by category, that is most useful as an indicator for tracking or addressing problem property issues

- Potential sources for each category of information

These elements are summarized in tables 2.1 (neighborhood information) and 2.2 (property information). Many of the elements in the two systems overlap,

TABLE 2.1 Neighborhood Information Indicators

Data category	Indicators	Data source
Tax sales	Properties sold at tax sale as percentage of total privately owned properties Increase or decrease from preceding year	Municipal or county tax collection office
Tax arrears and liens	Number of properties in tax arrears	Municipal or county tax collection office
Property characteristics and conditions	Properties by type and use Properties in public ownership as percentage of total properties Number and location of brownfield sites Percentage of properties that are owner-occupied Number and percentage of abandoned properties by type (prior use, whether abandoned building or vacant lot)	Municipal planning or community development office Census data Survey
Code enforcement and nuisance abatement	Number of complaints Number of citations Number and type of nuisance abatement actions Number of utility shut-offs	Municipal building or inspection department Public utilities
Residential sales	Number of sales Sales price change from preceding year Days on market change Characteristics of buyers	County clerk or Multiple Listing Service Sample surveys
Home mortgage transactions	Number of conventional home mortgages made Change from preceding year	Home Mortgage Disclosure Act (HMDA) data
Property improvement activity	Number and value of building permits issued Number and amount of home improvement loans	Municipal permitting office HMDA data
Rent levels	Distribution of rental units by rent level and number of bedrooms Change from preceding year	Landlord reporting under landlord registration ordinance Census data
Crime statistics	Number of major crimes per capita Crime rate change from preceding year	Municipal police department
Fire statistics	Number of fires as percentage of structures Change from preceding year	Municipal fire department
Population and demographic statistics	Social and economic characteristics of population School enrollment trends Temporary Assistance for Needy Families (TANF) and other social service demand trends	Census data School district Social service agencies

TABLE 2.2 Property Information Indicators

Category	Indicator	Data source
Property baseline information	Use(s) Structure type Number of floors Square footage Zoning	Municipal records or survey
Property tax status	Tax arrears (duration and amount) Tax liens (number and amount)	Municipal or county tax collection office
Other municipal liens	Utility liens (number and amount) Nuisance abatement liens	Municipal or county tax collection treasurer, or finance department
Nuisance abatement actions	Nuisance abatement actions by type Receivership status	Municipal buildings or inspection department
Code violations	Complaints Citations Court actions arising from uncorrected violations	Municipal buildings or inspection department
Vacancy and abandonment	Number of utility shut-offs Mail stops and forwarding Visual evidence of neglect	Public utility U.S. Postal Service Surveys or citizen reports
Crime	Crime reports at address Crime reports on block	Municipal police department
Improvements	Number and type of building permits issued Value of permits	Municipal permitting agency
Conveyances	Change in ownership Price of conveyance Nature of mortgage financing, if any	County clerk or Multiple Listing Service

as the same information—such as taxpayers in arrears or code enforcement complaints—is important to both. Nearly all of the information in these tables is a matter of public record, although its accessibility varies widely from town to town and state to state.

Much of this information—such as tax delinquencies or code violations—may already be entered into computers in the normal course of business by the agency responsible. Police departments, in particular, following the lead of New York City's CompStat program, often have highly sophisticated data systems for tracking criminal activity, although they may not be using them to full effect. As a result, the first step in setting up the information system is to identify what data is already being gathered by different agencies and organizations and taking the necessary measures to integrate it into an information system. Although all of the data shown in the tables is potentially useful, it may not all be necessary, depending on the resources available to develop the system and, even more important, the uses to which the system is going to be put.

Depending on how the data is being gathered, the compatibility of the computer systems being used by different agencies, and the degree of cooperation and trust between these agencies, the process can be either straightforward or excruciatingly difficult.[1] Once the necessary data linkages have been established, keeping the data up to date is largely a matter of designing the system so that new information from the various sources on which it relies is automatically incorporated into the property information system. Subsequently, updating the system should require only occasional special attention.

B. Using Information Systems

The development of a property or neighborhood information system must be justified as a tool for planning, analysis, and action rather than merely an elaborate, high-tech record-keeping system. Before investing time and money in designing and setting up such a system, those involved should ask the following questions about how the system will be used:

Who are the potential users of the system? Many potential users may exist for an information system. As a general rule, the greater the number of different users, the better. Potential users, in addition to municipal officials and university researchers, should include neighborhood organizations and CDCs, social service organizations, potential home buyers, developers, lenders, and businesspeople.

What are the capacities of the potential users of the system? Potential users are likely to vary widely in their technical skills and familiarity with data resources. The system design must recognize that many important users are likely to be relatively unsophisticated: it should allow users to access and manipulate information without high levels of technical skill.

What will the system be used for? Although the best systems are flexible and can be adapted to a wide range of uses not originally anticipated, the system *must* be usable for its primary intended purposes from day one. The number of potential uses is vast and can range from property-specific interventions—such as foreclosure prevention or outreach to offer home improvement loans—to large-scale neighborhood planning activities.

1. Privacy and liability are important concerns in designing an information system. Protecting individual or privileged information is a broad public policy issue and may also be a specific legal issue, depending on the laws of the particular state. Some states may impose potential liability on entities that provide property data to the general public, as the Texas "slander of title" statute does. Such statutes permit property owners to seek damages if inaccurate information provided by a public agency affects their ownership of or ability to convey their property.

GOOD PRACTICES

Many American cities have property information systems, some of which have been developed by an organization outside the municipal government—often a local university. Two good systems are found in Los Angeles and Minneapolis.

The Los Angeles system, known as Neighborhood Knowledge Los Angeles or NKLA, was developed by a team at the University of California, Los Angeles. It provides the following information for each property:

- Code complaints
- Nuisance abatement actions
- Building permits
- Property tax status (delinquency)
- Utility liens

The NKLA system is designed for interactive use. A user can find the full range of information for a particular building or find specific information for all the buildings in a particular area, such as all the buildings that are tax delinquent within a particular city block. Information can be obtained in tabular or map form.

The Minneapolis Neighborhood Information System (MNIS) was developed by Neighborhood Planning for Community Revitalization (NPCR), a consortium of colleges that works with communities in the Twin Cities area. The system not only includes property information but also integrates it with other community information, including census, crime, and education data. It is used by the municipal government and by NPCR staff in their ongoing work with neighborhood organizations.

One of the most valuable uses of an information system is as an *early warning system* that flags particular factors or combinations of factors that should trigger specific interventions, such as

- recurrent code violations associated with a particular property;
- recurrent criminal complaints or activities associated with a particular property;
- accumulation of liens on a property in excess of market value;
- increases in the number of tax-delinquent properties in a particular area.

In Minneapolis, the NPCR staff work with city officials, CDCs, and members of the city's eighty-eight neighborhood councils to train people to use the information system to analyze issues and answer questions posed by the neighborhood councils.

Rochester, New York, established the NBN Neighborhood Institute to provide training and information in many different areas to citizens engaged in that city's Neighbors Building Neighborhoods initiative. Programs have included training residents to use the city's Information Management System to track neighborhood change and in the use of GIS mapping software.

For a system to be effective as an early warning system, it must not only be able to identify the relevant factors but also provide timely information on them to the individuals or organizations responsible for taking action.

Another valuable use of a neighborhood information system is to evaluate real estate market conditions, as discussed in chapter 17, by tracking such key variables as housing price trends and vacancy rates. This information makes it possible not only to design cost-effective strategies for revitalization but also to adjust them regularly to reflect changes in market conditions.

Early in the design process, system designers should find out from potential users how they expect to use the system. By so doing, designers can also establish what training or technical support users will need to use the system effectively. This step is particularly important if key users, such as code enforcement staff or neighborhood council members, are likely to be inexperienced in using information systems.

The information system should be accessible through the Internet so that users in different locations can have easy access to the information. If the system includes information that may be subject to confidentiality restrictions, such data should be protected by passwords without limiting public access to the rest of the information in the system. (The Minneapolis and Los Angeles systems described in the box contain only information that is a matter of public record.)

To ensure that an information system is used effectively, users must understand the potential of the system and know how to make it answer their questions. This is as true for users within local government as for those in CDCs and neighborhood organizations. The organization responsible for designing and maintaining the system should offer formal courses and training sessions, as well as ongoing technical support, to enable users to take full advantage of the tools the information system offers.

CHAPTER 3

Improving the Economic Viability of At-Risk Absentee-Owned Properties

Rental properties owned by absentee landlords account for a large proportion of the properties abandoned in older cities, ranging from scattered single-family row houses in cities such as Philadelphia and Baltimore to large apartment buildings in cities like Jersey City and New York.[1] Their loss destabilizes neighborhoods while depleting the stock of affordable rental housing in those neighborhoods, little of which is being replaced by new construction. Many older apartment buildings in inner-city neighborhoods, moreover, are architecturally distinctive and prominently located. If these buildings are abandoned, their loss disproportionately affects the community as a whole.

Rental property owners are a diverse body of individuals with varied motivations. Some owners are engaged in short-term speculation; others are trying to build solid assets for themselves and their families. Although some property owners may care little about their holdings or the effect of their actions on their community, many others want to maintain and improve their properties or sell them rather than abandon them. Incentives and assistance to owners, by improving the economic viability of their properties, can often extend a property's useful life by years or decades.

This chapter discusses two general strategies for assisting absentee owners. The strategies fall into two general categories:

- Programs to reduce the cost of owning and operating property and improve cash flow

- Programs to improve the efficiency of the landlord's operations, including training and technical support

Programs that address the cost of owning and operating property include loan programs, tax relief, and insurance assistance.

---

1. Despite the widely held perception that rental housing is made up of apartment buildings, more than 50 percent of all rental units in the United States, and 70 percent of all private market rental units occupied by low-income households, are in one- to four-family properties. These properties are almost all owned by individuals (rather than corporations or partnerships), many of whom are part-time rather than full-time landlords.

The Community Preservation Corporation, operating in New York and New Jersey, is a nonprofit corporation supported by ninety banks, insurance companies, and public sector entities to provide short- and long-term financing for affordable multifamily rental housing. Through 2003, CPC had provided over $3.5 billion in financing for over ninety-six thousand units. Although CPC finances new as well as existing housing, the organization fills a particular niche by offering loans for small and medium-sized apartment buildings.

A. Loan Programs

The most important way in which the public sector can intervene to reduce landlords' costs and help increase the economic viability of their properties is by providing cost-effective loan programs that allow landlords to refinance or consolidate existing debt and to improve their properties, at a minimum bringing them up to code. *To be effective, a loan must either reduce the landlord's carrying costs or increase the value or the cash flow of the property without substantially increasing the landlord's cost.* Loan programs must offer low interest rates and long terms or amortization periods.

Many loan programs, including public sector programs in New York and Chicago, use public funds, sometimes combined with private funds, to offer low interest rates. This use of public funds is a highly cost-effective way to preserve affordable housing.[2] Many different public funds can be used for this purpose, including the federal HOME and community development block grant (CDBG) programs, and, where permitted by state law, tax increment financing (TIF).

Simplicity is critical in successful loan programs to small landlords. The owners of small multifamily buildings often lack specialized training or sophisticated investment or financial skills and see the requirements of federal and state housing programs or tax-exempt bond financing as onerous and complicated. Many landlords would rather forgo valuable resources than get enmeshed in what they see as endless red tape. *The program must be simple to administer, funds must come in quickly, and ongoing reporting requirements, such as income certifications, must be kept to a minimum or avoided entirely.*

---

2. A 2000 study by the Federal Reserve Bank projected that a blended public and private loan program of rehabilitation and refinancing assistance for at-risk apartment buildings could have a dramatic effect on the viability of thousands of endangered properties, at an average public sector cost of only $5,000 per unit.

GOOD PRACTICES

The Chicago Neighborhood Improvement Program (also known as the TIF Neighborhood Investment Fund) uses tax increment financing (TIF) in selected neighborhoods to provide grants to homeowners and to absentee owners of properties of five or more units. Because the funds are repaid through the increase in property tax revenues within the neighborhood as a whole, they can be provided as grants. The maximum grant is $5,000 per unit or $50,000 per property.

In order to encourage use of state funds to preserve multifamily housing, the New Jersey legislature eliminated all affordability and income certification requirements on loans and grants made from the state housing trust fund for moderate rehabilitation of rental properties of thirty units or fewer in low-income census tracts (New Jersey Statutes Annotated 52:27D-320[f]).

Local officials setting up a loan or grant program for absentee landlords must anticipate potential hostility and even outright opposition. Not only are many landlords suspicious of government intentions, but many civic associations and politicians may see such a program as rewarding slumlords. Where pursuing such a program, a solid case for the cost-effectiveness of the program, as well as its benefits to tenants—not just landlords—must be made.

B. Tax Relief

Local government can improve the economic viability of at-risk properties by providing relief from property taxes, which often represent a significant part of a landlord's operating costs. Tax relief should be offered as an incentive for a landlord to improve the property, not just hold on to it. Simply abating the taxes on the increased value of improvements, however, may not have enough effect on the landlord's bottom line to secure the viability of the property, given that the landlord may be incurring substantial rehabilitation costs. To have the greatest impact, the municipality should offer not only an abatement—or deferral—of taxes on the improvements but also a reduction of the prior real estate taxes, as New York City does. Politically, however, it may be more difficult to gain support for actions that abate not only potential future tax receipts but some portion of current tax revenues as well.

Tax abatement programs must be simple and self-administering. The abatement should be offered wherever possible as of right, or else through a straightforward administrative procedure. Property owners should know exactly the extent of tax relief they can expect if they carry out improvements to the property and should

GOOD PRACTICE

New York City's J-51 program provides two tax abatement options for moderate and gut rehabilitation of multifamily buildings:

- For affordable housing, up to thirty-four years of abatement (thirty years full and four years phase-out) for the improvements, and abatement of existing real estate taxes by 6 percent of the cost of the work for twelve years

- For other projects, up to fourteen years of abatement (ten years full and four years phase-out) for the improvements, and abatement of existing taxes by 4 percent of the cost of the work for twelve years

not be placed at risk of being arbitrarily refused the abatement. The municipal governing body should adopt an ordinance setting forth the policies and criteria governing the program but should not act on individual building applications. Under an as-of-right procedure, any project that meets explicit formal criteria automatically receives the tax abatement. Criteria may include the following:

- The minimum and maximum number of units

- A minimum level of capital investment in improvements

- The affordability of the units

- The location of the project[3]

- Evidence that the owner is current with property taxes and other municipal charges

The city should establish the relevant criteria, put them in writing, and disseminate them widely among property owners and other interested parties.

Local officials considering enacting tax abatement programs must understand relevant state laws. Some states grant cities broad discretion to tailor tax abatements to local conditions, whereas others grant such discretion only to home rule or charter cities. Still other states allow cities little or no discretion, limiting them to abatement formulas explicitly written into state law.

C. Insurance

Another factor that directly affects the cost of operating multifamily properties is the cost of insurance, which has historically been high in inner-city areas and has risen sharply since 2001. Although local entities have little leverage to obtain

3. New York City does not grant full abatements to projects in Manhattan below 110th Street.

reduced insurance premiums, statewide organizations in a number of states have established insurance pools that have resulted in reductions of 10 to 30 percent in premiums for their members. Even where such pools exist, small landlords in most cities are unlikely to be familiar with them. If insurance costs are seen as a problem in a community, local officials or CDCs may want to explore whether pools exist in their state which local landlords could join, or the possibility of using their expertise to help create a pool at the city or state level.

D. Training and Technical Assistance for Landlords

Many small landlords lack the skills and know-how to operate their buildings in the most cost-effective and responsible way, particularly those who own only a few units of rental property in small one- to four-unit buildings. If shown ways to manage their properties more effectively and improve the physical and financial condition of the properties, they may both hold on to their properties longer and become more responsible and effective landlords. Skills that can be imparted through training, small-group discussions, and one-on-one technical support include:

- building maintenance skills;
- budgeting and financing;
- tenant selection, tenant relations, and dealing with problem tenants.

Some cities have prepared manuals and guidebooks for landlords. All of these activities can be integrated into an overall landlord support strategy, designed to build a network of engaged property owners and support services.

Although manuals and formal training can be useful for some people, many landlords, particularly those with little formal education or limited English language skills, may not respond to written materials or training programs. The best

The city of St. Louis publishes a manual titled *Inforent: A Landlord's Guide to Managing Rental Property.*

The Borough of Rochdale, an English industrial city of some 200,000 population, has created the Landlord Accreditation Scheme, under which rental property owners who adhere to a code of good practice become eligible for a wide range of support services, including assistance with property improvements, ongoing advice and information, and regular landlord forums and training activities.

programs are those that combine training with one-on-one, on-site technical support, provided, where possible, by individuals with experience managing residential real estate, such as retired landlords and property managers.

Training and technical support services should be offered not only to landlords who run afoul of the code enforcement process but to any landlord in the community who can benefit from the service. The organization running the program should reach out to landlords of buildings that are at risk, encouraging them to participate in the programs before they get into trouble. Because landlords who find themselves in court are likely to be in particular need of assistance, it is important that support services be provided either by the court itself or by local government or a qualified private organization in tandem with the court.

Program staff should make an effort to identify "bad apples"—landlords who, because they lack either the motivation or the necessary skills and resources, should not be in the business of owning and operating rental housing. The difficult part of the process is not getting these owners out of the business but ensuring that the properties are taken over by a more responsible landlord—either another private owner or a CDC—rather than abandoned. Such an effort requires cooperation between the support program, the city's code enforcement arm (to provide regulatory pressure on problem landlords), and prospective replacement landlords.

The Cleveland Housing Court employs housing specialists who provide training through landlord-tenant clinics as well as one-on-one advice to landlords seeking financial resources to correct code violations.

The property information system (see chapter 2) should be designed to make possible the identification of buildings whose owners are potential candidates for training and technical support. For example, it should allow users to identify properties with a history of code violations or police complaints or a pattern of falling behind on taxes or utility bills. That information can then be directed to program outreach workers for follow-up.

Owners of nonresidential property can also benefit from support programs. Similar programs to help business owners improve the efficiency and productivity of their operations can both preserve jobs and reduce abandonment of nonresidential buildings in urban areas. Support programs are particularly effective with small and medium-sized manufacturing facilities, which are still a significant economic presence in many inner-city communities. Many of these enterprises are at risk of disappearing but can be preserved and made more efficient and more competitive with solid technical support.

CHAPTER 4

Preventing Abandonment of Owner-Occupied Housing

The loss of owner-occupied housing through abandonment is as serious a problem as the abandonment of buildings by absentee landlords. It is particularly acute in cities where, historically, large numbers of working-class and moderate-income residents have owned their own homes but where the local economy or particular neighborhood conditions have undermined the economic stability or prospects of those homeowners. The loss of owner-occupied housing destabilizes neighborhoods. It not only removes buildings but also erodes a critical part of the community's social fabric.

Owner-occupied housing is most often abandoned either because of an owner's inability to make mortgage payments or pay property taxes—a condition often created or exacerbated by predatory lending or selling practices—or because of market failure or low demand for housing in the area. Although the same forces generally affect all owner-occupied housing, two sectors within the homeowner population—elderly homeowners and owner-occupants of two- to four-unit properties—are at particular risk.

A. Loss of Property through Inability to Pay

Many communities, particularly neighborhoods in struggling older industrial cities, suffer from high levels of homeowner foreclosure. Particularly high foreclosure rates in lower-income and minority communities are increasingly associated with subprime lending, an industry prone to abusive and fraudulent practices which victimize unsophisticated homeowners.[1] Subprime lending is most widely associated with refinancing and home equity loans, both of which can burden a lower-income homeowner to the point that she is unable to maintain her payments. In many cities, the practice of "flipping," where investors buy substandard houses at discount prices, perform no more than cosmetic repairs, and sell them at inflated prices to home buyers, makes matters worse. The victimized buyer finds

---

1. Subprime lending is a legitimate, although widely considered questionable, sector of the lending industry. Subprime lenders lend to higher-risk borrowers who do not meet the credit requirements of conventional lenders, charging higher interest rates to reflect the higher risks associated with the loans. Many subprime lenders are subsidiaries of conventional lenders.

herself with an all but valueless asset, committed to make monthly payments that she cannot readily afford.

Foreclosure in itself does not always lead to abandonment. If the property is in good condition and the real estate market in the area is strong, the house may be quickly reoccupied by another homeowner. In areas where real estate values are low and market demand limited, however, foreclosure dramatically increases the risk of abandonment. The owner losing the property must usually vacate it, and the entity taking title to the property, be it the municipality, a lender, or a tax lien purchaser, is unlikely to have the ability—or in many cases the will—to fix up the property and put it back on the market.

Owners often abandon their properties even before the foreclosure takes place. For a poorly informed consumer, the "lawyer letter" from the lender's attorney, threatening foreclosure, may be enough to prompt her to abandon her home, even though the lender may be less than eager to actually take title to the property. In fact, even though the owner may have fled, the lender may never follow through with the foreclosure to the point of taking title, with the result that the property is left in an ownerless legal limbo.

Preventing the abandonment of property taken by lenders or tax lien buyers, and getting it quickly back on the market, is a widespread problem. Such properties, once taken, are often neglected and may deteriorate to the point where they are fit only for demolition. The most effective abandonment prevention strategy is two pronged, consisting of short-term foreclosure prevention efforts to address the specific needs of families at risk of losing their homes and a longer-term strategy to address predatory lending practices and reduce the role of subprime lenders in the local market.

Foreclosure Prevention

The goal of foreclosure prevention is to enable the owner to remain in the house and either regain the financial stability needed to keep the home or ultimately to sell it in an orderly fashion, on the owner's timetable. Key elements include:

- working with lenders and homeowners to prevent mortgage foreclosure;
- a tax foreclosure prevention program to enable elderly homeowners to remain in their homes;
- programs to address predatory lending and property flipping;
- partnerships with lenders and tax lien buyers to ensure that foreclosed properties are not abandoned and return quickly to the market.

The most important players in foreclosure prevention are generally nonprofit organizations, including CDCs and counseling agencies, such as the organizations that are part of the NeighborWorks America network. Although government usually does not provide such services directly, it too has a critical role to play by

Twin Cities Habitat for Humanity operates a foreclosure prevention program in partnership with other organizations in Minneapolis. Since 1993, the program has assisted nearly two thousand families at risk of foreclosure with counseling, advocacy with mortgage lenders, and, as a last resort, deferred loans to enable families to correct their mortgage delinquency.

The Minneapolis–St. Paul area has a comprehensive network of services for lower-income homeowners, including foreclosure prevention programs, as a result of a strong history of cooperation between local government, community-based nonprofit organizations, and key foundations. The work of this network is coordinated by the Minnesota Home Ownership Center.

The Housing Bureau for Seniors in Washtenaw County, Michigan (Ann Arbor) runs a property tax foreclosure prevention program, offering counseling, intervention with government agencies, and loans and grants to help elderly homeowners avoid losing their homes.

providing nonprofit organizations with financial support, using its influence with lenders and others to obtain their support for the program, and providing financial assistance to homeowners to enable them to keep their homes and stabilize their financial situation.

Where foreclosure prevention efforts are focused on preventing loss through tax foreclosure, the cooperation of the governmental entity with control over the tax foreclosure process is critical to the success of the effort. State laws vary widely, however, in the discretion they give local tax officials to offer alternatives that may enable struggling homeowners to avoid tax foreclosure. Depending on state law, municipalities may be able to offer installment payment plans, pull properties from tax sale or foreclosure lists, and structure forbearance programs, including deferring the collection of back taxes until the property is sold.

Predatory Lending

Predatory lending and property flipping, practices that burden lower-income homeowners with unsustainable costs, often substantially in excess of the value of the property, enormously increase the risk of foreclosure and abandonment. Predatory lending is a part of the subprime lending industry and is characterized by a wide range of abusive practices, including targeting particularly vulnerable homeowners, using deceptive or illegal marketing tactics, and charging excessive interest rates and fees or enforcing other unreasonable loan terms. Predatory lenders often extend credit based on the borrower's collateral even though they know or expect that the borrower cannot afford to make the payments on the loan.

GOOD PRACTICES

The State of Pennsylvania has enacted two creative programs, one regulatory and one providing financial assistance, to keep lower-income homeowners from losing their homes:

1. Act 6 (41 P.S. §101 et seq.) protects homeowners whose principal loan balance is $50,000 or less. The act provides for notice requirements, caps on attorney's fees charged by lenders, and the ability to make past-due payments and stop the foreclosure up to one hour before the bidding at the sheriff's sale.

2. The Homeowners' Emergency Mortgage Assistance Program (HEMAP), enacted in 1983, provides loans to homeowners suffering financial hardship through no fault of their own, to bring delinquent payments current and provide monthly assistance for up to two years, to a maximum of $60,000 per household.

Four strategies are being used to combat predatory lending on a systemic or preventive basis:[2]

1. Policy changes. A number of states have enacted laws to limit predatory lending practices. State laws may also permit municipalities to enact local laws barring predatory lending or otherwise penalizing entities that engage in predatory practices, as Chicago and Cleveland have done. Such laws may include provisions such as the following:

*   Limiting interest rates and fees that a lender may charge

*   Barring lending to borrowers without regard to their ability to pay

*   Requiring refinancings to provide a net tangible benefit to the borrower

*   Prohibiting excessive prepayment penalties and balloon payments

Some statutes also contain disclosure requirements and provisions requiring that counseling be provided to prospective borrowers. Among the better state statutes that combat predatory lending are those of Georgia, New Jersey, and North Carolina.

2. Public-awareness campaigns. Efforts to make potential borrowers aware of the risks of predatory lending, including ads, videos, and brochures, are being mounted in many communities around the country. In addition to providing writ-

---

2. An excellent resource is Christi Baker et al., *A Practitioner's Guide to Combating Predatory Lending* (see the references at the end of part 1).

ten and visual materials, which may seem impersonal and tend to have limited impact, an effective campaign should also engage organizations that are likely to reach high-risk borrowers, such as churches, social clubs, and neighborhood organizations.

3. *Consumer education.* A growing number of communities are mounting efforts to increase consumer financial awareness and help consumers learn to manage their money, plan their financial future, and make rational investment and borrowing decisions.

4. *Market competition.* Ultimately, perhaps the most important local strategy to combat predatory lending is to beat such lenders at their own game by offering homeowners affordable home improvement and refinancing loans on reasonable terms, and aggressively marketing loan programs within the communities most often victimized by predatory lenders. Local governments and CDCs, working with conventional lenders, community development financial institutions (CDFIs), and state housing finance agencies, can develop competitive loan products by combining modest amounts of public funds with conventional or CDFI loan capital, particularly where banks are already offering home improvement loan products under Community Reinvestment Act (CRA) agreements. Local governments and CDCs have rarely aggressively marketed home improvement loans, having traditionally assumed that "if you offer it, they will come." Competing successfully with predatory lenders requires that CDCs market their competitive products as aggressively as the predatory lenders do.

B. Loss of Property through Market Failure

Weak market demand contributes significantly to the abandonment of owner-occupied homes in many areas, particularly inner-city neighborhoods. In such areas, the supply of houses often vastly exceeds the demand. As a result, owners moving out of a community may simply walk away from their homes, as do the heirs of owners who have passed away and left behind an unmarketable house. Many elderly inner-city owners die without leaving a will, or leave the property to multiple parties or with unclear title. Such properties are at high risk of being abandoned and require considerable effort on the part of local government or a CDC to clear title for any future reuse.

Although low demand is exacerbated in cities such as Philadelphia or Baltimore by the small size and limited amenities of the traditional working-class row house, the same problems can exist even where the houses themselves may be acceptable by contemporary standards, as is the case in many neighborhoods of Flint, Detroit, and other Midwestern cities. Preventing abandonment of owner-occupied houses in those areas, therefore, depends on creating and maintaining a market for those houses, or *market correction*. Partnerships between local government, CDCs, Realtors, and lenders can often enhance market activity in inner-city neighborhoods.

While some neighborhoods clearly lack market demand,[3] in the sense that far fewer people want to buy homes than to sell them, in others market demand is depressed by a series of external factors:

> In low income neighborhoods, where prices are lower to begin with, fewer homes are represented by brokers, and those brokers present not only have less information about other sales, but have less incentive to get more, because the higher-price sale (with the higher commission) may be the less legitimate one. Fewer sales are advertised in the newspaper, because the cost to do so will make a sizable dent in an already modest commission. . . . [H]ousing markets in these areas are often extremely opaque: no one has a clue about what is going on or why.[4]

In addition to low overall levels of market activity, inner-city property markets suffer from limited broker activity coupled with large numbers of informal, often cash, transactions; an absence of meaningful comparable sales; inconsistent and unreliable appraisals; and a lack of accurate property information. Furthermore, because inner-city transactions are more likely to require buyers to satisfy property tax and other arrears and make repairs to meet municipal certificate of occupancy requirements, the transaction costs of inner-city sales relative to the value of the property are likely to be substantially higher. All these factors make inner-city property markets highly inefficient, increasing the risk that a house that some buyer might actually want will remain unsold and ultimately abandoned.

Where the real estate market citywide, or in a particular neighborhood, is being unduly constrained through market inefficiencies that lead to abandonment, a local government or nonprofit entity can pursue a variety of strategies. Market-building programs, however, are not easy to implement. They are labor-intensive, in that efforts must be undertaken house by house and are therefore difficult to bring to scale. They are likely to require substantial grant support, generally from

3. A more extensive discussion of building housing markets for cities and neighborhoods appears in chapter 15. The discussion here focuses on increasing effective demand by correcting inefficiencies in the local market.
4. Ada Focer, "The Price Is Wrong," *Shelterforce* 23, no. 3 (2001).

The City of Rochester, New York, created Rochester City Living, Inc., to help market housing and attract buyers to the city. Among other services, it buys advertising space in the local newspaper, which it offers free to brokers listing houses selling for $30,000 or less.

LiveBaltimore, a nonprofit organization established to build the residential market in Baltimore, has established a "Preferred Real Estate Professional" program under which it singles out and promotes real estate brokers and agents actively willing to market city property. To earn the designation, the individual must take a course sponsored by LiveBaltimore and pay a fee.

government or foundation sources, over and above the return that can be realized from transactions. As a result, there are few good practices to cite in this area. The strategies suggested below are presented as ideas for community stakeholders to explore. Cool Space Locator, Inc., an outstanding program that works to correct inefficiencies in the *nonresidential* property market, is described in chapter 15.

Market correction efforts can have a significant effect on the fate of a neighborhood. They are particularly appropriate activities for organizations already engaged in homeownership counseling or foreclosure prevention, and can often enhance these other missions. These ideas should be seriously explored by such organizations as well as by CDCs and local government agencies.

Community Brokerage

Few active, well-staffed, and sophisticated real estate agencies have offices in inner-city neighborhoods or are familiar with inner-city properties. Because suburban properties generally sell for much higher prices, they lead to higher commissions for the same or less work, discouraging brokers from focusing on urban markets. One solution is to establish a real estate brokerage firm within a city or neighborhood that focuses on marketing local properties for which demand potentially exists but which are not being effectively marketed by the area's existing real estate firms. Setting up such a firm is likely to require public sector or foundation support, at least in the initial stages.

State laws generally require that any firm assisting third parties to buy and sell real estate be headed by an individual licensed by that state as a real estate broker. To create a firm, therefore, an entity pursuing this strategy will have to either find an individual with the qualifications to obtain such a license or find someone already licensed as a broker to serve as the responsible broker.

Alternatively, if the local real estate industry is supportive, an organization can work to make existing brokers more responsive to the urban market, as in Rochester and Baltimore. As area boards of Realtors become aware of the problems of urban markets, they may become increasingly willing to work with CDCs and local governments to help become part of the solution rather than the problem.

Presale Improvement Programs

The condition and appearance of properties offered for sale in urban neighborhoods is frequently an impediment to their sale. A property that has been occupied for decades by a financially constrained or elderly homeowner may have suffered from deferred maintenance or a lack of attention to cosmetic matters. Two approaches should be considered:

- Work with people placing houses on the market, perhaps in conjunction with a community brokerage strategy, to make minor repairs and cosmetic improvements to enhance the marketability of the house.

- Offer an improvement package, including potential home-buyer incentives offered by the local government as well as assistance in finding reliable contractors, to prospective home buyers.

Senior Citizen Outreach

In many older neighborhoods and cities with weak real estate markets, many homeowners are senior citizens. In Wilkes-Barre, a small city in northeastern Pennsylvania, nearly 40 percent of the owner-occupied homes are owned by individuals over sixty-five. In Pittsburgh, over one-third of the homes fall into the same category. This condition reflects both weak market conditions in the past and the risk of large-scale homeowner abandonment for the future.

Abandonment following either the death or relocation of an elderly homeowner is particularly widespread, arising from a number of different factors, separately or together:

- The owner dies without leaving a valid will.

- The property is left to multiple heirs, without clear assignment of responsibility for disposition of the property.

- The heirs do not live nearby and have little or no interest in the property.

- The property needs substantial repairs to be marketable.

- Title to the property is unclear.

- The property is subject to excessive liens or judgments.

Abandonment of homes following the passing of elderly homeowners is often preventable if the homeowner takes appropriate steps in anticipation of that eventuality. Owners may be unlikely to do so, however, without the intervention of some outside entity. Nearly half of all lower-income adults over fifty do not have a will.

Local governments, CDCs, and social service organizations serving the elderly should work to reduce obstacles to the successful conveyance of homes now owned by elderly homeowners. They can help owners make wills under which a single heir or an executor has clear responsibility and authority for disposition of the property, or help make sure that the title being conveyed is a clean one. A proposal currently being considered in Pennsylvania would authorize courts to grant CDCs a limited letter of estate administration for the purpose of authorizing the CDC to sell houses left in limbo if the owner dies without leaving a valid will. Other forms of intervention may also be possible if initiated by an organization known to and respected by the area's elderly population.

C. Owner-Occupied Multifamily Housing

Owner-occupied two- and three-family properties require special attention. Properly maintained by a capable homeowner, such properties allow the owner to reduce her own housing costs—often dramatically—while providing affordable rental housing to others. Where such housing is common, as in many New England cities, a program to upgrade the rental units and provide the owners with the support they need to be effective landlords can provide benefits to both owners and tenants and prevent potential abandonment.

Many older cities have neighborhoods where large, older single-family houses are difficult to sell as single family homes, in part because they are uneconomical for that use. They are often illegally converted into multifamily housing and later abandoned after being "milked" by an absentee owner for a few years. A program to convert those houses into owner-occupied two-family housing, coupled with training and support to the homeowner, may be able to keep such houses in productive use.

CHAPTER 5

Enforcement and Intervention

Financial and other assistance will rescue only some of the properties at risk of abandonment. The ability of government to enforce building condition and maintenance standards, and address nuisance situations that affect building residents and their neighbors, is a critical part of any abandonment prevention strategy. Local governments throughout the United States are granted broad powers to require owners to maintain their buildings and grounds in sound condition and to step in and take action where the property owner fails to do so. These powers can motivate property owners to take advantage of assistance programs to improve their properties.

Enforcement tools are powerful but often crude. Code enforcement carried out without sensitivity to the economic realities of the community can hasten rather than prevent abandonment. Although there are cases in which it is better to board and vacate a building than allow continued use in its present condition, that option should be seen as a last resort.

Abandonment represents the failure of an enforcement strategy. The goal of enforcement programs is to improve the condition of buildings so that they can remain in use, providing decent housing to their residents and being good neighbors to those living around them. Enforcement strategies should be framed and carried out with this goal clearly in mind and integrated with policies that help property owners comply with enforcement orders.

This section focuses on code enforcement and nuisance abatement strategies.[1] The line between the two is not always clear. We define code enforcement narrowly to refer to procedures that use the legal system to compel property owners to comply with housing codes, including those governing fire safety and health. Nuisance abatement applies where government or third parties intervene directly to address nuisance conditions associated with a particular property.

1. Receivership, which may be seen as a specific type of nuisance abatement, is discussed in the next section.

A. Code Enforcement

Every state in the United States authorizes local governments to enforce standards of habitability for existing residential property. These statutes vary widely. Some states have established state codes that may be enforced by local officials, while others give broader discretion to local government to set and enforce codes. In some states, enforcement is a local matter, while in others it is a state responsibility that may be delegated to or shared with local government.

In principle, code enforcement is straightforward. Government officials inspect properties and serve notice on owners when violations are found. The owners either correct the violations or are taken to court, where they may be punished until the violations are corrected. In practice, the situation is far more complicated. An effective code enforcement system must address three critical elements:

- Effective targeting of resources
- Effective ongoing management of the system
- Integration with other abandonment prevention strategies

Targeting

The resources available to any municipality for code enforcement are always inadequate. There are never enough officials to inspect all of the properties in the city regularly, let alone follow up systematically to ensure that all violations are corrected. Given such limited resources, all inspection programs are selective in some fashion. The question is whether the selectivity is rational and designed to maximize improvement in people's living conditions and preserve sound residential buildings, or whether it is driven by complaints or the pressures of politicians or other officials. Not all violations are of equal weight. An inspector should not devote the same amount of time to making a struggling homeowner repaint a peeling side porch as to compelling a landlord to upgrade a dangerous electrical system in a rental building.

Rational targeting can take different forms, the most important of which are described below. As with any other form of selective enforcement of a police power, it is essential that the criteria for selection not be arbitrary or discriminatory, and that they further substantive public policy goals.

Targeting by Geographic Area. The most straightforward form of targeting, which is widely used, is to select certain neighborhoods for systematic enforcement efforts. Target neighborhoods may be selected on the basis of the extent of problems or the number of complaints, or they may be areas designated for neighborhood revitalization, with code enforcement integrated into a larger improvement strategy.

Although a code enforcement agency can undertake neighborhood targeting on its own, its effectiveness is significantly enhanced if other city departments—

GOOD PRACTICES

The City of Phoenix, Arizona, targets code enforcement activities in two types of neighborhood: Neighborhood Fight Back areas, which are the focus of short-term mobilization of residents and municipal services to stabilize the area, and Neighborhood Initiative Areas, where a more comprehensive revitalization effort is under way. Inspections in other parts of the city are conducted through a complaint-based enforcement system.

Atlanta trains neighborhood residents to be "neighborhood deputies." Volunteers patrol the neighborhood; when they observe potential code violations, they send a notice to the owner and occupant of the property. They follow up to see if conditions are corrected; if not, they refer the matter to the city for formal enforcement.

such as police and public works—and residents, CDCs, and neighborhood organizations are also engaged. Many neighborhood residents are deeply concerned about the condition of their neighborhood and are willing to volunteer time and energy to help rid their neighborhood of blighted properties, if they believe their contribution is part of a sustained effort. As one Atlanta city council member pointed out, "The $80,000 it takes to run Neighborhood Deputies [see box] would pay for just two housing inspectors, while the program is able to put what amounts to hundreds of code enforcers on the street."

Targeting by Building Characteristics or Ownership. Code enforcement can identify certain types of housing for priority treatment, where there is a rational basis for doing so. Rental property, particularly multifamily housing, is significantly more likely to contain code violations than is owner-occupied single-family housing. Many cities target rental housing through ordinances that require landlords to obtain occupancy permits for rental housing. The occupancy permit typically requires that the landlord register with the municipality and provide contact information for emergencies or legal notices and that the property pass a housing code inspection. While some municipalities require inspection only when the unit is first placed in service, or when a new tenant occupies the property, other municipalities require annual inspections. Occupancy permit ordinances may be limited to buildings above a minimum number of units (such as four or more) and may exempt rental units in owner-occupied properties.

A useful complement to code enforcement, and a way of keeping landlords accountable, is a landlord registration or licensing ordinance, a requirement that owners of rental property register—usually on an annual basis—with the municipality. In addition to the name and address of the owner, landlord registration ordinances generally require the following information:

- The name and contact information for a local agent, particularly if the owner lives outside the immediate area

- The name and contact information of an individual authorized to make emergency repairs

- The name and contact information of the primary mortgagee, if any

Ordinances may also require the owner to provide information about the property, such as the number and type of units, the type of heating fuel used, and rents charged. Landlords who fail to register may be fined and liens placed against their properties for unpaid fines. New Jersey, which requires owners of rental properties with three or more units to register with the state, bars the courts from issuing eviction judgments on behalf of landlords who are not registered.[2]

Code enforcement can be used to target properties at greatest risk of deterioration and ultimate abandonment by linking enforcement to the municipal property information system, tracking such conditions as

- tax delinquency;

- unpaid sewer, water, or other utility bills;

- nuisance or criminal complaints;

- tenant complaints.

Buildings meeting thresholds with respect to these conditions can be flagged, and code enforcement directed toward them. Linking code enforcement to a property information system also improves the ability to track the results of enforcement efforts.

Targeting Enforcement by the Nature of the Violation. Given their limited resources, most code enforcement agencies implicitly "triage" violations—that is, they devote the bulk of their resources to the violations that they consider the most serious or urgent. It may be difficult, however, to justify legally an explicit policy of citing certain violations but not others. One way to address this issue is by undertaking targeted enforcement "sweeps" with respect to specific violations that affect health and safety, particularly in absentee-owned multifamily buildings.

Managing the System

In many municipalities, code violations may be found but not remedied, while owners continue in business unhindered. Inspectors are only one part of an over-taxed system, which includes overloaded courts and prosecutors who may not

---

2. N.J.S.A.46:8–33. This statute provides that the case is then continued for ninety days, during which the landlord may register. If the landlord fails to register during the ninety-day period, the case against the tenant is dismissed.

regard housing code matters as a priority. There are many different points where the system can break down after a violation has been found or a complaint made:

- Violation notices are not properly entered or served on the owner.
- Follow-up visits are not made in a timely fashion.
- Cases are closed (violations are found to be corrected) without justification.
- Cases are not referred to the prosecutor in a timely fashion.
- The prosecutor fails to act in a timely fashion.
- The court fails to act in a timely fashion.
- Fines or penalties are imposed but not enforced.

A management information system which tracks each complaint and each violation cited, and which links the code enforcement agency with the relevant parts of the legal system, is an essential basis for an efficient, accountable code enforcement process. There is no justification today for the antiquated record-keeping systems still used by many municipal inspection agencies.

Other elements are equally important:

The wider community must be engaged in making the process work. The entire community has a stake in maintaining building quality. The best way to ensure both efficiency and accountability in the system is to have a pool of individuals—independent of City Hall—to monitor the process. The pool can be created by the municipality (although this is unlikely), by a court, or by one or more CDC or community-based organizations. Their presence both supplements the limited resources of the code enforcement agency and increases its accountability.

Adequate legal resources must be dedicated to code enforcement. Enough dedicated legal staff must be provided to ensure that all cases referred for prosecution are pursued in an aggressive and timely manner. Although in a small town code enforcement matters may be handled effectively by a part-time attorney, or as part of a full-time attorney's duties, in a larger community this responsibility should be a full-time job, so that the attorney develops the necessary expertise and devotes the necessary attention to it.

Code enforcement must be directed to a judicial forum in which it is taken seriously and given priority. In systems where the same court hears code violations, violent crimes, and complex business litigation, code violations routinely go to the bottom of the judicial docket. A number of states have created housing courts for their largest cities to provide a forum in which matters such as code enforcement are given priority. Housing courts are most effective when the judges are specialists who are specifically elected or appointed to that court, rather than assigned from the pool of judges in the general-purpose court for that location. Other jurisdictions, such as Detroit, have created administrative enforcement procedures that can provide for more effective enforcement than often overtaxed courts.

The Cleveland Housing Court has established a well-deserved reputation as a court that uses its judicial powers effectively to solve the housing problems that come before it. Other well-regarded housing courts have been established in Boston and in Pittsburgh.

The Cleveland Housing Court works closely with a network of forty to fifty code enforcement advocates, employed by nonprofit organizations and supported by a combination of public and private funds, who track complaints and violation notices to ensure that code matters are dealt with properly. The court also employs a pool of housing specialists, who work with landlords who come before the court as a result of code violations and help them obtain financial and other assistance to bring their properties into compliance.

The city of Detroit has created an Office of Administrative Hearings (OAH) to take action on blight violations involving both occupied and vacant properties. The OAH hears matters relating to property maintenance, such as failure to register rental property, rat infestation, and failure to maintain the exterior of buildings. The OAH can impose fines of up to $10,000 and take a variety of collection actions, including garnishment of wages and placing liens on affected properties.

Managing the system requires the ability to know the outcomes of the system. Despite the powerful effect of code enforcement on their housing stock, few cities track enforcement outcomes in any systematic fashion, or know whether their efforts lead to improved housing conditions or abandonment. Once a complaint has been disposed of, little effort is made to monitor the building over time to see whether the city's intervention led to a positive or negative outcome for the building, its residents, and its neighbors. Property information systems offer local officials and community leaders the opportunity to assess the effect of code enforcement on the community's housing stock. This opportunity should be pursued wherever possible.

Integrating the System with Other Abandonment Prevention Strategies

Even where code enforcement strategies are well designed and well managed, their effectiveness depends ultimately on the relationship between the costs imposed by enforcement and the economics of the affected property. Although effective enforcement may lead some owners to improve their properties, it may lead others to abandon theirs, often only after stalling for months or years while milking the last few dollars out of the building.

If code enforcement is to maximize property improvement and minimize abandonment, it must be integrated with complementary strategies and programs. Willing but financially constrained owners should be given assistance to improve their properties, as described earlier. Where owners are unwilling or unable to take advantage of those resources, the municipality—or a qualified third party—should be prepared to step in and take action, either making repairs or starting a process designed to transfer control of the property to a more capable entity. Such programs are described in the sections below dealing with nuisance abatement and receivership.

Even where such programs are available, they may not be used effectively unless they are closely linked to the enforcement process, as with the Cleveland Housing Court's housing specialists. The link may be through the court system, within the code enforcement agency or another arm of municipal government, or through a third party, such as a CDC. Any partner agencies or organizations must be routinely notified of code violations so that they have the necessary information to do their part of the job. In cities that have separate housing courts, it is important that the courts link enforcement and assistance for owners whose cases come before them. The link, however, must be made before the case goes to court: inspectors should be empowered to make owners aware of possible sources of assistance so that they have an opportunity to avoid court proceedings.

B. Nuisance Abatement

A nuisance is a condition that adversely affects the heath, safety, or well-being of the residents or neighbors of a property. The nuisance may arise from the physical condition of the property or from activities within it. The property may be occupied or vacant.[3] Many nuisance abatement programs have been established principally to address nuisances arising from criminal activity, such as drug dealing or gambling, which are not only illegal but also clearly affect the quality of life in the surrounding community.

Under the laws of most states, if an owner refuses to correct a physical condition that is causing a nuisance, the municipality can enter the property and make repairs needed to preserve it. Nuisance abatement procedures, however, can lead to the abandonment of the property rather than its improvement or preservation. Many state laws permit the owner to abate a nuisance by vacating the building rather than repairing it, a choice that many owners are likely to make. Under what conditions a municipality can order a building repaired rather than demolished, or whether the municipality can have the building restored to sound condition rather than vacated and demolished if the owner fails to act, is an important issue that remains a gray area (see chapter 12).

3. Chapter 12 discusses nuisance abatement as a strategy for dealing with properties that have already been abandoned.

Nuisance abatement actions taken against properties used for criminal or other improper activities also run the risk of creating negative consequences. In many cases, the chosen remedy is to have the building vacated and closed. An ordinance in Albany, New York, like many ordinances in effect elsewhere, provides that the landlord can be penalized by losing the use of her property for up to one year. In an inner-city residential area, property vacated as the result of such an order is unlikely to be reopened. The property may be abandoned, vandalized, and stripped, thus becoming a greater nuisance than it was before.

Undoubtedly it is sometimes preferable to vacate a building than to allow illegal activities or dangerous conditions to persist. Those may not, however, be the only alternatives. If the municipality has an integrated strategy for addressing problem properties—and the authority to do so under state law—other options may be available, such as placing the property in the hands of a receiver or an administrator with the power to abate the nuisance while keeping the property in use, as discussed in the following section. Another option may be to take the property through eminent domain in order to convey it to a qualified third party who will rehabilitate and maintain it.

Recapturing Nuisance Abatement Costs

Because municipalities have limited discretionary funds for making repairs on problem properties, the ability to recapture the cost of those repairs from the owner is an important tool for preserving at-risk property. State laws vary widely on this matter. In many states, the municipal lien for repairs is a priority lien, which can be foreclosed in a manner similar to foreclosure for nonpayment of property taxes. In some states, however, such liens are subordinated to preexisting liens on

GOOD PRACTICES

Ohio law provides that when a municipality makes repairs to a property in order to abate a nuisance, the cost is added to the taxes on the property and is due in full on the next tax installment date (R.C. §715.261[B]1).

The New York State Multiple Dwelling Law permits a municipality to sue the owner of a building for expenses incurred by a municipality in demolishing an abandoned building or the expenses of a receiver in remedying a building that has been deemed a nuisance.

New Jersey gives the municipality recourse against any asset of the owner of the property to collect on a lien for repairs, boarding, or demolition. Owners include any partner in a partnership or any owner of a 10 percent or greater interest in the ownership entity, if it is any other business organization or entity recognized by law (N.J.S.A. 55:19-100).

the property. In a few states, the municipality has the right to go after other assets of the property owner to collect the funds owed.

In states where state law limits the ability of the municipality to recapture its expenses, changing the law should be a priority for those engaged in dealing with abandoned and problem property issues. State law should provide municipalities with the option of placing a priority lien on the property and providing for fore-closure if it is not paid within a short period, such as sixty days, or seeking a judgment against other assets of the owner. For these purposes, the term *owner* should include any individual or other entity with a greater than 10 percent interest in the property, whether through a partnership, corporation, or other entity, such as an LLC. Furthermore, in states where the county, rather than the municipality, is responsible for tax foreclosure, state law should provide that the lien can either be added to the property taxes due or be foreclosed directly by the municipality, at the municipality's option.

CHAPTER 6

Receivership

Receivership is a powerful tool for preserving distressed residential property. It is explicitly directed toward improving and stabilizing the property and does not depend on the uncertain response of the property owner. It is based on ancient legal principles under which a receiver could be appointed by a court, in the words of *American Jurisprudence,* "to protect property, rents, or profits for those ultimately entitled to them." The use of receivership to protect the rights of residential tenants to decent habitation and to preserve buildings from further deterioration has been generally accepted in American law since the 1960s.

The basic principle of rental receivership is straightforward. If a property has deteriorated to the point where the health, safety, and welfare of the tenants are endangered, a receivership petition can be brought to a court within the jurisdiction. Almost every state which contains large cities authorizes receivership of distressed rental properties, including Arizona, California, Connecticut, Delaware, Illinois, Indiana, Maryland, Massachusetts, Michigan, Minnesota, Missouri, New Jersey, New York, Ohio, Oregon, Texas, and Wisconsin (see tables 6.1 and 6.2). The scope and effectiveness of state statutes, however, varies widely.

All states that permit receivership give municipalities the power to bring a receivership petition, and various states also permit petitions to be brought by a tenant or group of tenants, organizations representing the tenants, or local nonprofit organizations. If the court finds that the petition has merit, it may appoint a receiver who takes control of the property from the owner, collects the rents, and applies the proceeds to restore the property to sound condition. In some states, the receiver can borrow money to improve the property and place a lien on the property for the amount borrowed. State laws also vary with respect to the end of the receivership. In some, the receiver is discharged when the conditions have been remedied, while elsewhere the owner must petition to regain control of the property.

Receivership is not widely used. Legal obstacles often arise from the inadequacy of state statutory provisions, and practical obstacles include uncertainty about financial exposure and the difficulty of finding qualified receivers. Strategies to overcome both obstacles are discussed below. They are worth pursuing, as the use of receivership can significantly enhance a community's efforts to deal with problem properties.

TABLE 6.1 Grounds for Receivership Action under Selected State Laws

State	Grounds for receivership
Arizona	Property is designated as "slum property" that has deteriorated or is in a state of disrepair *and* manifests one or more of the following conditions: (1) structurally unsound features; (2) lack of adequate water or sewer facilities; (3) hazardous electrical or gas connections; (4) lack of safe, rapid egress.
Connecticut	Property manifests one or more of the following conditions: (1) housing code violations; (2) notice of termination of fuel oil or bottled gas delivery; (3) lack of heat, running water, electricity, light, or adequate sewage disposal facilities; (4) other conditions dangerous to life, health, or safety; (5) infestation of rodents, vermin, or other pests.
Illinois	Building fails to conform to the minimum standards of health and safety as set forth in the applicable municipal ordinances.
Indiana	Building meets any one of the following conditions: (1) is in an impaired structural condition that makes it unsafe to a person or property; (2) is a fire hazard; (3) is a hazard to the public health; (4) is a public nuisance; (5) is dangerous to a person or property because of a violation of a statute or ordinance concerning building condition or maintenance; (6) is vacant and not maintained in a manner that would allow human habitation, occupancy, or use.
Maryland	Building has defects *including but not limited to:* (1) lack of heat, light, electricity, or hot and cold running water; (2) lack of adequate sewage disposal facilities; (3) infestation of rodents in two or more dwelling units; (4) structural defects presenting a serious and substantial threat to physical safety; (5) any condition presenting a health or fire hazard.
Massachusetts	Building manifests any violation of the sanitary code.
Minnesota	Building violates any of the following: (1) any applicable state, county, or city health, safety, housing, building, fire prevention, or housing maintenance code; (2) landlord obligations under state law; (3) an oral or written agreement, lease, or contract between landlord and tenant.
Missouri	Building violates any provisions of the housing code applying to the maintenance of the buildings or dwellings which the code official in the exercise of reasonable discretion believes constitutes a threat to the public health, safety, or welfare.
New Jersey	Building (1) violates state or municipal codes in a manner that endangers health and safety; or (2) demonstrates a pattern of recurrent code violations, shown by four citations in the previous twelve months or six in the two years preceding filing the complaint, regarding which the owner has failed to take appropriate action.
New York	Building represents a nuisance. Nuisance is defined broadly to include conditions dangerous to human life or detrimental to health, overcrowding, and environmental and physical deficiencies.

TABLE 6.1 Grounds for Receivership Action under Selected State Laws, *continued*

State	Grounds for receivership
Ohio	Building is a public nuisance. Nuisance is defined broadly as any menace to the public health, welfare, or safety, including a wide range of conditions such as structural and sanitary deficiencies, fire hazards, and lack of habitability, or hazardous conditions resulting from inadequate maintenance, dilapidation, obsolescence, or abandonment.
Texas	Property is not in substantial compliance with municipal ordinances regarding (1) fire protection; (2) structural integrity; (3) zoning; or (4) disposal of refuse.

A. Elements of a State Enabling Statute

Although a receivership petition can be brought on the basis of common-law principles, it is clearly better to act with explicit statutory authority. Furthermore, in those states where a statute exists, action must take place within its parameters. The first step in a receivership strategy is to become familiar with the applicable state law. Unfortunately, many state statutes lack important features necessary for effective receivership. This section covers the key areas governed by state laws, the ways in which state laws vary, and what provisions make a statute most effective. Because some states have no receivership laws and others rely on laws that are largely unchanged since the 1960s or 1970s, advocating for the enactment or revision of state receivership statutes can be a productive activity for state organizations advocating on behalf of lower-income communities or housing issues.

Bringing a Receivership Action

All receivership statutes permit specified government officials, such as code enforcement or health officers, to bring receivership actions. Most statutes also allow tenants to bring actions, and some also provide that third parties, such as neighborhood organizations or CDCs, can bring receivership actions.

Few municipalities, however, have shown a commitment to use receivership statutes except in isolated cases; and tenants may be uncertain of their rights or intimidated by landlords. To be effective, *the statute should grant appropriate third parties with a clear interest in the matter, including nonprofit entities such as CDCs and housing corporations, the ability to bring receivership actions.*

Grounds for Receivership

State laws vary widely in the grounds for establishing a receivership. The most narrowly drafted statutes are those of Texas and Arizona, where receivership is

TABLE 6.2 Key Features of State Receivership Statutes

State citation	Parties authorized to bring receivership petition	Parties eligible for court appointment as receiver	Power of receiver to borrow
Arizona A.R.S. §33-1903*	State, county, city, or town	Real estate licensee specializing in property management, or attorney specializing in real estate law	Implied. May "exercise all other authority" of owner except for sale of property.
California Health and Safety Code §17980.7	Municipality, tenant, or tenant association or organization	An entity with the "capacity and expertise to develop and supervise a viable . . . plan for the satisfactory rehabilitation of the building." Specifically authorizes nonprofits and CDCs to be receivers.	Yes. If receiver is a nonprofit entity or CDC, it may also apply for grants for rehabilitation.
Connecticut Sec. 47a-14a	A majority of the tenants	Court has full discretion.	No
Connecticut Sec. 47a–56a	Municipal board of health or equivalent authority	Court has full discretion.	Municipality may advance funds to a receiver and place a lien on the property. No provisions for receiver's borrowing from other sources.
Connecticut Sec. 7-606	Municipality in which a neighborhood revitalization zone has been created	Court has full discretion.	No
Delaware Title 25, Chapter 59	Tenant or group of tenants	The State Division of Consumer Protection or a successor agency	May be implied.†

Lien status of funds borrowed by receiver	Provisions for owner's regaining control	Provisions for sale of property to third party
Receiver's lien has priority over some liens but not over prior recorded mortgages and tax liens.	Court may terminate on its own motion or on motion of any party when all violations have been cured or appointment "is no longer warranted."	None
May become a lien on the property with court approval. Statute does not provide for priority of receiver's lien.	Receiver discharged after conditions remedied. Court may retain supervision of owner for eighteen months after discharge of receiver.	None
NA	Statute implies that role of receiver ends when specific conditions that triggered receivership have been corrected.	None
Lien available only to municipality advancing funds	Receiver is automatically discharged after condition is remedied if all costs have been covered, but otherwise owner must make receiver whole in order to obtain discharge.	None
NA	Receivership is terminated after court finds that property complies with all state and local codes.	None
NA	Receiver may be discharged after conditions have been remedied, the building is code compliant, and the costs of the receivership have been covered.	None

continued

TABLE 6.2 Key Features of State Receivership Statutes, *continued*

State citation	Parties authorized to bring receivership petition	Parties eligible for court appointment as receiver	Power of receiver to borrow
Illinois 65 ILCS 5/ Sec. 11-31-2	Appropriate official of any municipality	At discretion of court[‡]	Receiver may issue notes and certificates.
Indiana IC 36-7-9	Municipal official or person designated by municipal official	Not-for-profit housing corporation or "any other capable person residing in the county"	Yes, with court approval
Maryland[§]	Tenants	At discretion of court	Yes, at discretion of court
Massachusetts Title XVI, Chapter 111, §127I	Affected occupants or a public agency	Court has full discretion.	Yes. Receiver may also seek financial assistance from state with court approval.
Michigan Sec. 125.534	Municipal enforcing agency	The municipality, a proper local agency, or any competent person	Yes
Minnesota §504B.385	State, county, or local agency; tenant or housing-related neighborhood organization	Person, local government unit, or agency. State agency or court can adopt regulations authorizing neighborhood organizations to act as administrators.	Yes, but court must find that borrowing will lead to building's long-term economic viability. May seek federal, state, or municipal grant funds.
Missouri §441.500	County, municipality, local housing corporation, or neighborhood association	Code enforcement agency, lienholder, local housing corporation, neighborhood association, licensed attorney or real estate broker, or "any other qualified person"[‖]	Yes, with court approval

Lien status of funds borrowed by receiver	Provisions for owner's regaining control	Provisions for sale of property to third party
Receiver's borrowing is superior to all prior liens except taxes.	Not specified	None
Receiver's borrowing has priority over all liens other than municipal liens.	Not specified	None
Yes, at discretion of court. Priority status of lien not specified.	At discretion of court, pursuant to petition by person with property interest or at court's initiative	With court approval, pursuant to Rule 14-300 governing judicial sales of property
Receiver's borrowing has priority over all liens other than municipal liens. Any state funds obtained by receiver also become liens on the property.	None	None
May become a lien against property, but priority not specified	At the discretion of the court	None
No, but if administrator obtains municipal funds for the property, those funds become a special assessment on the real estate affected.	Administrator discharged after violations are corrected. Court retains jurisdiction over landlord for one year.	None
Receiver's borrowing has priority over all liens other than taxes, municipal assessments, and any mortgage recorded prior to October 1969.	Receiver discharged after all conditions are corrected and all costs paid. Owner or lienholder may apply for discharge after conditions have been corrected by covering receiver's costs.	None

continued

TABLE 6.2 Key Features of State Receivership Statutes, *continued*

State citation	Parties authorized to bring receivership petition	Parties eligible for court appointment as receiver	Power of receiver to borrow
New Jersey N.J.S.A. 2A:42-114	Municipality, tenant, organizations representing tenants, nonprofit community service entities, and lienholders	Mortgage holder or any qualified entity, as determined by court or by New Jersey Department of Community Affairs	Yes
New Jersey N.J.S.A. 54:5-53.1#	Municipality	Collector of taxes or other municipal official	No
New York Multiple Dwelling Law Sec. 309	Municipality	Commissioner or chief executive of municipal department or bureau of real estate	Limited**
Ohio §3767.41	Municipality, neighbor, tenant, or nonprofit housing corporation	Entity with "the capacity and expertise to perform the required work." May be lender, nonprofit housing corporation, or other qualified property manager.	Yes
Oregon Ch. 105.420	City or county	A housing authority, urban renewal agency, not-for-profit housing corporation, or city or county agency	Yes
Texas Sec. 214.003	Home rule municipalities	Nonprofit organization with demonstrated record of rehabilitating residential properties (exceptions made for historic properties). Lienholders have right to request appointment as receiver.	No, but if costs of rehabilitation exceed cash flow, receiver retains control of property until made whole.

Lien status of funds borrowed by receiver	Provisions for owner's regaining control	Provisions for sale of property to third party
With court approval, may receive priority over all other liens and mortgages except municipal liens††	Owner must file petition, pay all costs and obligations of receivership, pay all municipal liens, and post a bond against future code violations. Court must find that reinstatement is in the public interest.	Receiver may request judicial sale at any time after one year from date of receivership. Sale must "promote the sustained mainte- nance of the build- ing as sound afford- able housing."
No	Receivership may be terminated when all property taxes in arrears have been paid or collected from rents.	None
Lien is superior to all liens except taxes and assessments.	Receiver discharged after all conditions are corrected and all costs paid. Owner or lienholder may apply for discharge after conditions have been corrected by covering receiver's costs.	None
Receiver's borrowing is a first lien superior to all other liens, with court approval.	Owner must "establish, by a prepon- derance of the evidence, that the benefits of not selling the building and the property outweigh the benefits of selling them."	Receiver can sell the property to third party after court hearing if owner fails to meet burden of proof under statute.
Receiver's borrowing is prior and superior to any lien other than governmental lien, as long as lender has not initiated foreclosure proceedings prior to appointment of receiver.	Owner or interested party must pay the costs and obligations of the receiver- ship and must show the court that it "will manage the property in conformance with applicable housing codes."	None
NA	If income exceeds costs of rehab, property is returned to owner. Otherwise, receiver retains control until made whole.	Court can order sale of property if receiver has been in control for three years and owner has failed to assume control or make receiver whole.

continued

TABLE 6.2 Key Features of State Receivership Statutes, *continued*

State citation	Parties authorized to bring receivership petition	Parties eligible for court appointment as receiver	Power of receiver to borrow
Wisconsin Ch. 254.595	Municipality, tenant or class of tenants, or any other person or class of persons "whose health, safety or property interests are or would be adversely affected" by building conditions	A disinterested person	Yes
Wisconsin Ch. 823.23	First- or second-class city in which property is located	Either (1) a housing authority, redevelopment corporation or authority, or community development authority; or (2) a nonprofit corporation whose primary purpose is housing improvement. If no one fitting these descriptions is available, then "any competent person."	Yes, but receiver may first give existing lender opportunity to lend the money needed.

Note: Statutes have not been reviewed for all fifty states. The absence of a state from this table does not necessarily mean that it does not have a receivership statute.

*The Arizona receivership statute can be triggered only if (in addition to the building's being in disrepair) the landlord has failed to comply with the state's landlord registration provisions.

†The statute provides that "in no case shall the Court permit repairs which cannot be paid out of the future profits of the property," which can be construed to imply the possibility of borrowing by the receiver (against the future profits, as distinct from current cash flow).

‡Court may waive bond requirement for receiver if it finds that the receiver is "especially qualified for the appointment."

§While the underlying authority for receivership is provided by the statute cited in the table, the specific provisions governing receivership (including provisions typically found elsewhere in statutes) are set forth in Maryland Court Rules, particularly Rule 3-722. Furthermore, with the exception of the definition of the defects and conditions that can trigger a receivership action, the above-cited statute explicitly provides that any of its provisions can be superseded by a local law enacted by a county or by the city of Baltimore.

Lien status of funds borrowed by receiver	Provisions for owner's regaining control	Provisions for sale of property to third party
Yes, but lien does not have priority status	At discretion of court	Receiver may sell property "at the request of and with the approval of the owner."
Yes, but superior to mortgage only if lender is given notice and lender has not initiated foreclosure proceedings prior to appointment of the receiver	Receivership is terminated when owner, interested party, or receiver shows court that (1) the abatement has been completed; (2) all the costs have been paid, or a lien filed; and (3) owner or interested party will manage the property in conformance with applicable codes.	None

‖Lienholders of record and local housing corporations, and, if there is no local housing corporation, local neighborhood associations, must be given (in that order) the right of first refusal to act as receiver. The right of first refusal is offered only to local housing corporations established before 28 August 2001.

#This statute applies only to properties for which the municipality holds a tax sale certificate as a result of a municipal tax sale. While the principal purpose of the statute is to further the municipality's ability to collect back taxes on the property, its provisions also require the municipality taking possession "to remove or remedy any violations of the standards of fitness for human habitation as are set forth in the State or local housing or health codes."

**While the New York statute explicitly calls for the receiver to place a lien on the property "for costs incurred in connection [with the receivership]," it does not provide explicit authority to the receiver to borrow funds. Since the receiver can only be the municipal agency, it appears that the intent of the statute is to provide security for *public* funds being used in connection with the receivership, rather than funds borrowed from private lenders.

††New Jersey law also allows receivers' liens recourse against other assets of the owner of the property; N.J.S.A. 55:19-100.

permitted only under extremely limited conditions. At the other end of the spectrum is the Minnesota statute, which not only permits receivership for any violation of any applicable code but also permits receivership for any violation of a landlord's obligation, either statutory or as embodied in an agreement between landlord and tenant. Although the Arizona and Texas statutes are too narrow, one could argue that the Minnesota language is too broad and open to abuse.

The statute should be drawn broadly enough to provide the courts with flexibility to address the wide variety of conditions that arise with respect to distressed rental property but not so broadly that it can be invoked for minor violations. Although this possibility may be unlikely in practice, landlords and their representatives may raise it as a concern. The best approach is to define the grounds for receivership broadly but to provide clear language authorizing the courts to dispose summarily of petitions that fail to provide adequate substantive grounds for the proposed action.

Appointing Receivers

Although some statutes are silent on this point, implying that the court can appoint anyone it deems appropriate, most specify who can be a receiver, either by setting qualifications for receivers or by defining the entities eligible to be receivers. Some states limit eligibility to government officials, whereas others provide preference for local housing corporations or CDCs. Too much discretion for the court, particularly in cities with powerful ward politics, risks unqualified appointments, but defining the qualifications too narrowly may make it difficult to find receivers.

The statute should provide clear language requiring that the receiver be fully qualified but should give the court broad discretion within those parameters. The receiver should combine property management capabilities with the ability to undertake substantial improvements, beyond routine maintenance or repair. The statute should encourage the court to consider CDCs and other experienced housing development entities as receivers, particularly in states with a strong housing corporation or CDC infrastructure. The specialized skills of such entities in raising rehabilitation funds and carrying out major improvements are invaluable in many receivership situations.

Borrowing Money and Placing Liens on Buildings under Receivership

The financial condition of many distressed rental properties, and the extent of improvements that many buildings need, often make it impossible for a receiver to finance the improvements on a "pay as you go" basis from rent collections. Many buildings need substantial capital investment to be restored to sound condition. Unless the receiver can borrow money for capital improvements, the receivership may be unsuccessful, and the building may end up being vacated and abandoned.

The ability to borrow is all but meaningless unless the loan can be secured with a lien on the property. Except for public agencies or foundations using grant funds—both rare—lenders will not lend money to a receiver unless the loan is secured. If the building already has liens on it, the lender will demand a priority position; that is, a lien that takes precedence over other mortgages already on the property. *The statute should provide clear language authorizing the receiver to borrow funds for improvements and place liens on the property, which should take precedence over all preexisting liens other than municipal liens.* To ensure that the funds will be used appropriately and that the priority is justified, the statute may require the receiver to obtain court approval for any priority lien. Even with lien priority, it may require some effort to make lenders comfortable with the idea of lending to an entity that does not actually hold title to the property.

The statute should also provide that the receiver be eligible to receive any public grant or loan funds—such as housing rehabilitation funds—that might be available to an owner of similar property. Some states have established special

The California statute authorizes the court to retain jurisdiction for up to eighteen months after the end of the receivership and to require reports from the owner and the governmental enforcement agency on a schedule set by the court.

The New Jersey statute sets high standards for an owner to regain control. In addition to paying all costs of the receivership and all municipal liens, and assuming all obligations made by the receiver, the owner must post a bond which is forfeited in the event that future major code violations are not quickly corrected. The court must also find that the reinstatement of the owner is in the public interest and may impose additional conditions as it determines necessary to protect tenants and neighbors.

programs to assist receivers with public funds. Valuable as such programs are, they are constrained by the limited resources available to state agencies and are not a substitute for the ability of the receiver to borrow funds from nongovernmental sources.

Restoration of Owner's Control of the Property

Many state laws are silent on the critical issue of when and how the owner can regain control of a property that has been placed in receivership. By definition, receivership means that the owner has demonstrated an inability to maintain the building in a decent and responsible fashion. Prudence dictates that provisions for restoration of the owner's rights be carefully designed to ensure, to the extent feasible, that the circumstances that led to the receivership will not recur.

Despite the logic of this position, most statutes set no standards for the owner's regaining control and do not provide for any oversight of the owner's subsequent behavior. Under many state statutes, once the property has been restored to sound condition, there is a presumption that the receivership is terminated and the owner gets the property back. This approach raises a serious risk that the process of decline that preceded the receivership will resume and ultimately lead to either to a reinstatement of the receivership or to the building's abandonment.

The statute should require that prior to regaining control the owner pay outstanding taxes, as well as costs incurred by the receiver, and assume responsibility for the receiver's liens, if any. The court should also be given discretion to require the owner to post a bond with the court or the municipal enforcement agency that may be forfeited in the event of future violations.

The Ohio statute provides that the receiver can initiate the sale of the building and provides that "if the owner or any interested party objects to the sale of the building and the property, the burden of proof shall be upon the objecting person to establish, by a preponderance of the evidence, that the benefits of not selling the building and the property outweigh the benefits of selling them" (Ohio Revised Code, §3767.41(I)(2)).

The New Jersey statute permits the sale of a property after a year from the beginning of the receivership if the owner has not regained control of the property during that period. The statute provides a variety of options for the sale at the discretion of the court, including open-market sale, negotiated sale to a qualified not-for-profit entity, sale for the purpose of conversion to cooperative or condominium ownership, or, with respect to one- to four-family buildings, sale to an owner-occupant (N.J.S.A. 2A:42-134).

The statute should give the court continuing jurisdiction and permit the court to require regular reporting by the owner and monitoring of the owner's management and maintenance of the property by the entity that brought the receivership action or the former receiver. If the owner fails to carry out her responsibilities, the court should have the power to reinstate the receivership summarily, rather than have to go through the process de novo.

Sale of the Property

Because in many receivership cases the owner may have little or no interest in regaining control of the building, the question of what eventually happens to the property is a critical one. Surprisingly, only New Jersey and Ohio address this issue, with the Ohio statute taking the position that sale of the property to a third party is to be preferred, as a matter of public policy, over restoring it to its owner.

The statute should provide for a judicially supervised sale of the property if the owner fails to regain control within a reasonable period. Although constitutional principles require that the property be sold at fair market value, it does not follow that it must be sold at auction to the highest bidder. The court should have broad authority to authorize the sale of the property on a negotiated basis, with the value determined by appraisal, in the manner most likely to ensure that the property will be appropriately owned and operated.

Provisions for sale of the property should include language authorizing the court, once the proceeds have been distributed, to extinguish any remaining liens on the property. Without such language, the buyer of a property in a post-receivership transaction may be unable to get clean, insurable title to the property.

B. Practical Obstacles to Receivership

Even in states with a sound receivership law, the financial and operational complications of receivership may deter many cities and nonprofit organizations from using it, particularly as a strategy to restore buildings to long-term stability rather than fixing isolated emergency conditions.

The financial uncertainties inherent in any activity involving control of distressed buildings are substantial, for a variety of reasons:

- It is difficult to anticipate what improvements are needed and how much they will cost.

- It is difficult to establish a predictable rent roll because of nonpaying tenants, evictions, turnover, and the length of time that apartments may be off the market because of needed renovations.

- The cost of improvements may exceed the market value of the property, particularly in weak market settings.

In the worst cases, it may be impossible to make the necessary repairs—particularly if substantial structural or system replacement is required—without having to vacate the building. When this happens, a receivership can turn into a major rehabilitation project and may require substantial public subsidy.

The financial uncertainties of receivership demand that those involved go in with a realistic understanding of the difficulty of bringing buildings back into sound condition and that potential fallback financial resources be identified in advance. Flexible funds should be available to make possible successful receivership in cases where cash flow and the ability to carry conventional debt will not in themselves cover the cost of restoring the building to sound condition, but the building nonetheless should be preserved. *State and local governments should consider using public funds to create revolving receivership loan funds that willl provide what is needed over and above what can be financed through conventional sources.*

Although not every building can be preserved, *it will almost always cost more to restore a building to productive use once it has been abandoned than to keep an occupied building in use through repairs and improvements.* Using public funds to preserve existing housing is almost always more cost-effective than using the same funds to rehabilitate a vacant building or to build new housing on the site of a demolished building.

These points highlight the importance—and the difficulty—of finding qualified receivers. Taking over a building that contains sitting tenants and also needs major improvements is a difficult task. It requires a highly skilled property man-

The city of Cincinnati, Ohio, has established a pilot receivership strategy. Using federal funds, it will reimburse receivers for legal fees and project management and provide up to 75 percent of the repair costs, to a maximum of $50,000 per building.

ager as well as someone well versed in both the financial and technical aspects of housing rehabilitation. These skill sets are not often combined in the same individual. The best receivers are not likely to be municipalities, or even, in most cases, experienced rental property managers, but rather organizations with substantial experience both in property management and in the rehabilitation of affordable housing. A municipality serious about pursuing a receivership strategy should recruit CDCs with a solid record in both areas to become receivers. Receivership must not be seen, however, as a roundabout route to substantial rehabilitation. Receivers must clearly understand their mission, including its limitations.

Resources for Further Information

Baker, Christi, et al. *A Practitioner's Guide to Combating Predatory Lending.* New York: Local Initiatives Support Corporation, and Washington, DC: Neighborhood Reinvestment Corporation, 2003. Available online at www.nw.org/predatorylending

Baltimore Neighborhood Indicators Alliance. *Healthy Neighborhoods Initiative Evaluation Report.* Baltimore, MD: Baltimore Community Foundation, 2003.

Culhane, Dennis P., et al. "An Economic Analysis of Housing Abandonment." *Journal of Housing Economics* 7, no. 4 (1998).

Dubin, Robin A. "Maintenance Decisions of Absentee Landlords under Uncertainty." *Journal of Housing Economics* 7, no. 2 (1998).

Federal Reserve Banks of New York and Philadelphia. *Preserving Multifamily Rental Housing: Improving Financing Options in New Jersey.* New York and Philadelphia: Federal Reserve Banks of New York and Philadelphia, 2000.

———. *Preserving Multifamily Rental Housing: Noteworthy Multifamily Assistance Programs.* New York and Philadelphia: Federal Reserve Banks of New York and Philadelphia, 2001.

Hillier, Amy, Dennis Culhane, Tony E. Smith, and C. Dana Tomlin. "Predicting Housing Abandonment with the Philadelphia Neighborhood Information System." Unpublished paper, Cartographic Modeling Laboratory, University of Pennsylvania, 2001. Available from authors at Meyerson Hall Room G-12, 210 S 34th Street, Philadelphia, PA 19104.

Housing Council. *Residential Foreclosure Action Plan.* Rochester, NY: Housing Council, 2000.

Lind, Kermit, et al. *Public Nuisance Abatement and Receivership: A Guide to Implementing Ohio Revised Code §3767.41.* Cleveland, OH: Community Advocacy Clinic, Cleveland-Marshall College of Law, 2001. Although specific to the Ohio statute, this guide is useful for any organization planning receivership actions.

Listokin, David, Lizabeth Allewelt, and James J. Nemeth. *Housing Receivership and Self-Help Neighborhood Revitalization.* New Brunswick, NJ: Center for Urban Policy Research, Rutgers University, 1985. Although in many respects out of date, this remains the only full-length book available on the subject of receivership.

Local Initiatives Support Corporation. *GIS Mapping for Change: Using Geographic Information Systems for Community Development.* New York: Local Initiatives Support Corporation, 2002.

Mardock, Lori. *Predicting Housing Abandonment in Central: Creating an Early Warning System.* Minneapolis, MN: Neighborhood Planning for Community Revitalization, 1998. Available from http://npcr.org

Neighborhood Planning for Community Revitalization. *Building Community: The First Five Years of NPCR*. Minneapolis: Neighborhood Planning for Community Revitalization, 1999.

Neighborhood Training and Information Center. *Preying on Neighborhoods: Subprime Mortgage Lenders and Chicagoland Foreclosures*. Chicago: Neighborhood Training and Information Center, 1999. A great deal of additional valuable material on predatory lending and related issues is available from http://ntic-us.org

Orr, Steve. "Fraud Leaves City Homes Empty." *Rochester Democrat and Chronicle*, December 15, 2002. A detailed look at how fraudulent transactions and flipping affect urban property.

Rolland, Keith L. "Pennyslvania Launches Broad-Based Response to Foreclosure Problem." *Cascade* 56, Winter 2004. A publication of the Federal Reserve Bank of Philadelphia.

Ross, H. Laurence. "Housing Code Enforcement and Urban Decline." *Journal of Affordable Housing* 6, no. 1 (1996).

Sarbanes, Michael. "Neighbors Plow Field of Nightmares." *Shelterforce* 80 (March–April 1995). Discusses self-help nuisance abatement strategies in Baltimore.

Sternlieb, George. *The Tenement Landlord*. New Brunswick, NJ: Urban Studies Center, Rutgers University, 1966. After nearly forty years, this is still the best study on the behavior of owners of urban multifamily property.

Taking Control of Abandoned Properties

2

Introduction

Despite the best preservation efforts, abandonment will always remain a problem. Local officials and concerned citizens must learn to manage the abandonment process, treating abandonment not as a permanent condition but as a transition between the property's former use and its future reuse, and developing the ability to control, directly or through regulatory means, the abandoned property inventory. To do so, local government must focus on three central tasks:

- Minimize the length of time properties remain abandoned.

- Minimize the harm to the community from abandoned properties.

- Create the conditions needed to bring abandoned properties back into productive use.

Minimize the length of time properties remain abandoned. Abandoned buildings have a substantive negative impact on the community. The longer a building sits vacant, the more it deteriorates and becomes a target for arson and vandalism. This deterioration not only affects the neighborhood's quality of life but also materially increases the cost of future rehabilitation and the likelihood that the building will have to be demolished rather than rehabilitated. The ability of a municipality to reduce the period that a property lies abandoned and move it toward reuse depends on the city's ability either to take title expeditiously to abandoned properties and convey them to third parties for reuse or to compel owners to take appropriate action. While cities should press owners to act responsibly, experience has shown that such efforts cannot substitute for action by local government. *The ability of the city to gain physical and legal control of properties is a critical part of a successful abandoned property strategy.*

Substantial obstacles impede all such efforts. Perhaps most important are those affecting tax foreclosure, because it is a tool so widely used by local government. Tax foreclosure laws, which vary widely from state to state and even within states, often result in time-consuming procedures that in the end may not give the municipality clear, marketable title. At its best, tax foreclosure is a limited tool, particularly in cities with improving market conditions, where owners speculating on the future may allow their properties to fall into disrepair but still pay their taxes. New and powerful tools to supplement tax foreclosure are emerging around the country, strengthening the hand of local governments and community groups.

Minimize the harm to the community from abandoned properties. In many cities, particularly weak market cities where the supply of older buildings exceeds the demand, many properties remain abandoned for extended periods, demanding attention if they are not to become serious threats to a neighborhood's health and safety. Although some municipalities may look the other way, most attempt to manage the community's abandoned building inventory, undertaking lot cleaning, boarding, and demolition, often at considerable expense and with mixed results.

Many municipalities have one set of policies to deal with the properties they own and another to deal with abandoned buildings still in private ownership. While most municipalities accept responsibility for maintaining the properties they own, their policies governing privately owned vacant buildings vary widely. Effective strategies to induce owners to take better care of their properties are critically important in preventing the responsibility from ultimately devolving onto local government. At the same time, the municipal government is rightly seen as the ultimate protector of its citizens' interests. If the owner does not take responsibility, government may have no choice but to intervene.

Although some municipalities attempt to maintain vacant buildings for rehabilitation, large-scale demolition is becoming increasingly popular as a strategy to deal with abandoned properties, reflecting the feeling that a vacant lot demands less maintenance and does less harm to the community than a vacant building. Carried out in an unplanned fashion, however, demolition may lead to the loss of valuable buildings and undermine the neighborhood's physical fabric. Moreover, local officials often underestimate the cost and difficulty of keeping vacant lots from becoming nuisances in their own right. Demolition should be part of a larger strategy rather than an end in itself.

In some cities, however, the combination of the negative effects associated with abandoned houses, the sheer magnitude of the problem, and the apparent lack of viable alternatives make large-scale demolition a realistic response to a very real crisis. In some cities, particularly those like Pittsburgh or Buffalo, where there is little growth in the region as a whole, there may never be a use for many of the buildings that currently sit abandoned. Some cities have begun to develop protocols, based on planning and historic preservation criteria, to determine which buildings should be demolished and which should be preserved, even if they have to be stabilized and mothballed for rehabilitation at some future date.

Create the conditions needed to bring abandoned properties back into productive use. Without a reuse strategy, policies to deal with abandoned properties are little more than holding actions. Conversely, without the ability to gain control of abandoned properties, a reuse strategy may be little more than empty rhetoric.

The acquisition, maintenance, and disposition of the abandoned property stock must be linked from the start with the reuse strategy, so that management activities will help ensure its success.

The fundamental condition for an effective strategy is a solid framework of cooperation between all the parties involved in the acquisition, disposition, and reuse of properties. Because reuse is generally carried out by private entities—developers and CDCs as well as individuals—who design their projects to fit the plans being developed by the city and by neighborhood organizations, the city must work closely with those entities to tailor its acquisition efforts to their plans. CDCs and neighborhood organizations can also become the municipality's partners in the management of abandoned properties, taking on a wide range of responsibilities for the acquisition and maintenance of properties as well as their ultimate reuse.

An aggressive abandoned property strategy is costly and not without political and legal uncertainties. Property acquisition is expensive, even when the costs are limited to transaction costs, and maintenance or demolition of large numbers of properties can cost even more. Many municipalities are reluctant to engage with abandoned properties because of potential environmental concerns, liability, and the uncertainty of future reuse. These difficulties cannot be ignored, but they can be managed through careful planning and organization. Municipalities must bear in mind that the cost of *not* undertaking such a strategy is likely to be greater in the long run, in terms of lost rateables, reduced property values, crime, and human misery.

The next four chapters deal with property acquisition and disposition through the tax foreclosure process and through other means. The three subsequent chapters deal with addressing the physical conditions of abandoned properties.

CHAPTER 7

Making Tax Foreclosure Work

Tax foreclosure, the taking of title to properties on which the owners have failed to pay property taxes or other obligations to the municipality, school district, or county, is usually the single most important tool in any municipality's property acquisition toolkit.[1] Although not all owners who have physically abandoned their properties stop paying property taxes, many do, particularly in weak market cities, making the properties potentially subject to tax foreclosure by local government.[2] The number of properties that can be taken this way is often substantial, and, since the municipality is not actually paying for the property, the costs—even with the transaction costs involved—are likely to be far lower than for most other acquisitions. The actual number of properties that a municipality may obtain, however, depends not only on the number eligible for foreclosure but also on the competition for properties from prospective buyers outside local government. The degree of municipal control over the process varies from state to state.[3]

Tax foreclosure is based on the principle that a lien resulting from an owner's failure to pay property taxes and other government charges has priority over all private liens, whenever they may have been incurred. As a result, when a municipality or county or a third-party buyer of a tax lien properly forecloses on the lien, any private liens, such as mortgages, are extinguished, and the municipality gets the property unencumbered and free of liens. Depending on state law, there are two fundamentally different procedures by which tax foreclosure takes place:

- In a *single enforcement proceeding,* the municipality holds a sale of the properties which are tax delinquent. The owners are given some period after the sale to redeem their property, but if they fail to do so, absolute title to the property vests in the successful bidder at the sale.

---

1. While the discussion here refers to the effects of unpaid property taxes, other unpaid obligations to a municipality or county, such as utility bills or special assessments, may trigger a similar legal procedure. This discussion also pertains to other liens having the same status under state law.

2. Although this text often refers to the "municipality," the information here is also relevant to states in which the county rather than the municipality carries out tax foreclosures.

3. This section is a brief overview of an extremely complex issue. For further information, consult Frank Alexander's *Renewing Public Assets for Community Development* and his article "Tax Liens, Tax Sales, and Due Process" (see references at the end of part 2).

• In a *two-step proceeding,* the municipality holds a sale of the tax liens on the property. Buying a tax lien does not give the purchaser title to the property, but rather conveys the right to foreclose on the property through a separate proceeding in the future. The owner has the right to redeem the property up to the second proceeding, and in many cases for some time after the second proceeding. More than half of the states in the United States use a two-step process.

While tax foreclosure is a powerful tool, there are many significant problems associated with it.

1. Protracted time period. A two-step proceeding will, as a rule, take substantially longer than a single proceeding. The length of time involved in either case will also depend on the time allowed by each state's statutes for various actions to take place. Those periods include the following:

• The length of time taxes must be delinquent before a sale can take place

• The length of time the owner can redeem after the tax lien sale in a two-step proceeding, before the holder of the lien may bring the foreclosure action

• The length of time the owner can redeem after the foreclosure

These time periods are generally set by state statute. Further delays are inevitable in the procedures that the municipality or the courts must carry out to effectuate the tax sale and the foreclosure. It is rare for a municipality to gain title through tax foreclosure in less than eighteen months to two years from the point at which the owner stopped paying taxes. In less efficient systems, the process can take five years or more.

2. Notice to parties. The United States Supreme Court, in its *Mennonite* decision, held that

> in a property tax foreclosure procedure notice must be given to every party holding a legally protected property interest whose name and address can reasonably be determined by diligent efforts. The notice must be of the kind designed to inform these parties of the proceedings. Notice by publication in a newspaper will not be adequate notice except in very rare circumstances. Notice by mail sent to the best available address will usually be required.[4]

This standard, which substantially exceeds the requirements of most state laws, requires a municipality to expend substantial time and money to comply. If the municipality follows a less demanding state standard and fails to follow the *Mennonite* rule, the title that it obtains at the end of the foreclosure process will not be insurable and will not be accepted by responsible buyers.

4. *Mennonite Board of Missions v. Adams,* 462 US 791 (1983).

3. Jurisdiction. Property taxes are levied to support both municipal and county government. The responsibility for tax foreclosure may lie with one or the other, depending on the provisions of the state statute. In some cases, responsibility may lie with state government itself, while, in a few areas, even the school district may have some say in the process. In most Southern and Midwestern states, county government handles foreclosures, while in most Eastern states it is a municipal responsibility. In one major city, both the municipality and county have the power to foreclose on their respective liens independently on the same properties. Although some municipalities and counties have established working agreements to ensure that both jurisdictions' interests are served, serious conflicts can arise, particularly between a city seeking to gain control of properties for redevelopment and a county more concerned with maximizing the income from the sale of tax liens.

4. Third-party purchasers. Most tax foreclosure statutes are written not to further urban revitalization but to enable municipalities to recoup lost tax revenues. Many statutes encourage acquisition of tax liens or title by third parties, who pay the municipality the taxes due in return for the opportunity either to collect the taxes from the owner with interest or to become the owners of the property. Under the laws of some states, such as New Jersey, the municipality is required to offer the lien to third parties. In others, such as Connecticut, the municipality retains discretion to sell or retain the tax lien. All in all, twenty-nine states either permit or require the sale of tax liens. Under such legal schemes, the county or municipality obtains the lien, and the right to foreclose and take title, only if no outside party purchases it.

Nongovernmental buyers of tax liens have often shown themselves to be dangerously irresponsible buyers. Attracted by the fact that the cost of buying the lien or title is often well below the apparent market value of the property, they have bought liens on inner-city properties, including many abandoned buildings, as a speculative investment, blocking efforts by municipalities or community organizations to get control of these properties for constructive use. They make little effort to maintain or improve the properties and often do not even bother to take title to properties that turn out to have little resale value.

This problem has been aggravated in recent years when financially strapped municipalities and counties securitize tax liens or sell them in bulk to purchasers. Although this practice raises more money for the municipality in the short term, it can lead to significant long-term problems for the community. In Pittsburgh, thousands of inner-city properties have fallen under the control of investment companies or speculators with no interest in the community's well-being, and often without the ability to take action to improve the properties. These liens may make it impossible for anyone else to gain title to the properties, instead tying them up for years while they continue to deteriorate.

Even taking into account the desperate fiscal situation of many older cities, selling bulk tax liens is almost always a bad idea and should be resisted wherever possible. The harm it does to the city's future will usually far outweigh the short-term financial benefit.

A. Statutory Reform: Getting the Tax Foreclosure Law Right

The Threshold Issue

The threshold issue that every engaged stakeholder must address with respect to tax foreclosure is the underlying state statute. State law establishes the rules by which the local jurisdiction responsible for tax foreclosure must carry out the process. While some state laws give local government some discretion, most provide a strict road map that the municipality must follow.

The first step in developing a strategy for using tax foreclosure to address abandoned properties must be a careful review of the state statute, along with the political climate for potential statutory reform. Those responsible for developing the strategy must ask:

- Do existing state statutes give the community the tools it needs to use tax foreclosure as an effective abandoned property acquisition strategy?

- If not, does the support exist for changes in the statutes to make such an effort realistic?

The best legislative strategy should emerge from balancing the answers to those two questions. Legislative efforts are time-consuming and uncertain. If the statutory defects are minor and the legislative climate doubtful, it may be more efficient to work with the existing legal tools. If the statutes are a serious impediment, however, it may be worthwhile to build a coalition for law reform, recognizing that years may pass before results are visible. The uncertainties of the legislative process raise both substantive and strategic issues.

Legislative Strategy

Experience in a number of states has shown that reform of tax foreclosure laws is often feasible, particularly if the issues are clearly defined and a strong base of support built. Abandoned property is a good organizing issue. Nobody is likely to be openly in favor of abandoning properties or against their being reused and returned to the tax rolls. Even though there may be powerful interest groups opposed to specific provisions of a bill, they may not want to be seen as being in favor of perpetuating blight or blocking the reuse of abandoned properties. As a result, it is often possible to negotiate successfully with such interest groups.

Unless the underlying tax foreclosure statute is so flawed (as was the case in Georgia) that nothing short of total rewriting will do, it may be better to focus on changing the way abandoned property is treated than to seek a wholesale change in the statute. First, from a public policy standpoint it is easy to distinguish

GOOD PRACTICES

Georgia and Michigan have recently enacted fundamental changes to their tax foreclosure laws. Georgia enacted a completely new tax foreclosure law, providing for a highly expedited judicial foreclosure process, in 1995 (O.C.G.A. 48-4-75 through 81). This law has substantially reduced the period for gaining title, which now takes only eighteen months to two years, and ensures that the county receives clean and marketable title. Michigan went to a similar one-step process in 1999, including an accelerated fore-closure process for abandoned properties (Public Act 123 of 1999, amend-ing the General Property Tax Act, M.C.L. Sec. 211).

Enactment of these two statutes has made possible important abandoned property initiatives, including land bank programs in Atlanta and Macon, Georgia, and the establishment of a major land reutilization strategy in Gene-see County, Michigan, focusing on the city of Flint.

between an abandoned property, which has been neglected by its owner and is doing harm to its neighbors, and an occupied property, which may be owned by an elderly woman having difficulty keeping up with her taxes. A change that is clearly limited to cracking down on the former while continuing to protect the latter may be far more politically palatable to many legislators and potential supporters. Second, abandoned properties are less likely to involve substantial financial inter-ests. As a result, if the scope of the reforms is limited to abandoned property, it may be easier to gain the support of key interest groups such as bankers or tax officials with a stake in the existing system.

Focusing on abandoned property issues makes it possible to build a broad coalition of support, including local government organizations, community development advocates, business leaders, and advocates for low-income com-munities and individuals. All of these organizations recognize that they share an interest in helping local government deal more effectively with abandoned prop-erties. Moreover, even in a state legislature in which urban interests are only a small minority, it may be possible to gain the support of suburban and rural leg-islators, who will see such reform as benefiting the cities without being inimical to any of their core interests.[5]

5. While abandoned properties can be considered principally an urban issue, the problem is far from being exclusively urban. Many rural areas and small towns have significant abandoned property problems. Even in affluent communities, moreover, isolated—but seemingly intractable—abandoned properties are often a major concern. Suburban and rural legislators may well have abandoned prop-erty issues in their districts as well.

The New Jersey Housing and Community Development Network, a state-wide CDC association, began to explore ideas for legislative reforms dealing with abandoned properties in 2001. This led to the introduction, with bipartisan support, of the Abandoned Properties Rehabilitation Act in June 2002, a "toolkit" bill that included major changes in the tax foreclosure law dealing strictly with abandoned properties, as well as other reforms. Over the next year, while many changes were made to satisfy the concerns of different parties (including the state judiciary, the League of Municipalities, the Bankers Association, and the Tax Collectors and Treasurers Association), the strength of the support coalition ensured that the substance of the bill remained intact. The bill was enacted into law and signed by the governor in January 2004.

Building the coalition, and building support in the legislature, takes time and effort. It also requires that one organization, preferably with both visibility and credibility in the state capital, take the lead and organize the effort. This can be a state municipal league, a statewide association of CDCs, or a business organization. If the impetus is coming from a single city, that city's leadership must enlist the support of its counterparts in other cities in the state as well as that of statewide organizations. In the end, unlike many other issues of concern to urban communities, this is likely to be a winnable issue in many states.

The Substance of Legislative Reform

This section describes the types of legal changes that may be necessary and appropriate, as a guide to analyzing the issues associated with each state law. The specific provisions of any legal reform clearly depend on each state's statutory scheme as well as on its underlying laws regarding local government.[6]

1. Ensuring that the tax foreclosure procedure, if carried out correctly, leads to clear, marketable, and insurable title. One of the principal problems with the old Georgia statute was the fact that, even if carried out properly by the entity conducting the foreclosure, its procedures failed to ensure that the buyer of the property received clear and marketable title. This failure reflected the absence of a judicial process in the statutes, inadequate notice requirements, and lack of a

---

6. Different states address local government matters very differently. While some states have a single body of laws that governs all local jurisdictions, others make distinctions between categories of town and city, including many that grant broad discretion to home rule or charter cities while giving less discretion to other jurisdictions.

clear termination of the right of redemption. These deficiencies, in turn, made the statute worthless as a tool for redevelopment. Where other statutes suffer from similar defects and result in tax foreclosure procedures that generate questionable title, remedying them must be a clear priority for reform. Such reform, however, can be achieved only by revising the entire tax foreclosure process, rather than by making changes narrowly tailored to abandoned property.

2. *Clarifying jurisdiction and eliminating jurisdictional conflicts.* The law should ensure to the extent possible not only that the responsibility for tax foreclosure is clearly defined but also that where foreclosure responsibilities are housed in county government, a city's interests are adequately addressed. It should include provisions, for example, under which a city can place a "hold" on properties that it needs in order to prevent them from being sold to third parties, or provisions permitting a county that takes properties to pass title to the city. Alternatively, the law could give cities above a certain size the right to take direct responsibility for tax foreclosures within their boundaries. Since this would require the city to establish the machinery for tax foreclosure from scratch, it is generally preferable to allow the county to retain jurisdiction while seeing that the city's interests are protected. This is not an issue in states in which municipalities already are the local government entity responsible for tax foreclosure.

3. *Changing tax foreclosure from a two-step procedure to a single enforcement proceeding.* The single most significant time savings in taking title to property through tax foreclosure can be achieved by changing the system from a two-step proceeding to a single proceeding. This change can be achieved only by revising the entire tax foreclosure process.

4. *Reducing the period that taxes must be delinquent, particularly with respect to abandoned properties, before initiating tax sale or tax foreclosure proceedings.* Each tax foreclosure law specifies the length of time that taxes must be delinquent before the tax sale or foreclosure action can be carried out. Under New Jersey law, properties that are tax delinquent as of the eleventh day of the eleventh month of the fiscal year are subject to tax sale. Georgia requires that taxes be in arrears for a year before the judicial proceeding leading to foreclosure can be brought. *When dealing with abandoned properties, the shorter the period the better.* If the property is abandoned, even a single quarter of delinquency should be enough to trigger foreclosure.

5. *Reducing or eliminating the period during which the owner of an abandoned property is permitted to redeem after the foreclosure, or imposing additional obligations as a condition of redemption.* Tax foreclosure laws vary widely with respect to the length of time after the foreclosure during which the owner can still redeem the property by paying the taxes, interest, and penalties due. By the time the foreclosure takes place, the owner has already received repeated notice and been given ample opportunity over many months or years to redeem prior to foreclosure. There is, therefore, no compelling fairness or due process reason to permit redemption *after* foreclosure. Once an abandoned property has been foreclosed,

the redemption period should be minimal. In 1988, the Ohio legislature passed legislation for the city of Cleveland and Cuyahoga County that shortened the redemption period from five years to two weeks.

It is not unreasonable to impose additional requirements on owners of abandoned property as a condition of redemption. New Jersey law provides, with respect to tax foreclosures of properties on a municipal abandoned property list, that no redemption is permitted after the foreclosure action is instituted unless the owner either

1. posts cash or a bond equal to the cost of remediating the conditions because of which the property was determined to be abandoned . . . or

2. demonstrates to the court that the conditions because of which the property was determined to be abandoned . . . have been remedied in full (N.J.S.A. 55:19-58c).

Restoration of the owner's property once tax foreclosure has begun should be linked to the owner's readiness to take full responsibility for the property.

6. *Permitting municipalities to retain liens, or to carry out foreclosures, without the requirement that properties be offered for sale to third-party purchasers, or to establish conditions of sale.* The statute should give the municipality or the county discretion to determine whether it wants to offer the lien or the property for sale to third parties, to retain it for the use of the municipality or county, to convey it upon foreclosure to an appropriately qualified third party, or to designate a qualified third party, such as a CDC, to act as the agent of the municipality or county for purposes of tax foreclosure. The heavy hand of state law should not force a municipality to let properties go into the hands of outside private parties when it is not in the public interest to do so.

7. *Providing for consistent treatment of other municipal liens.* Municipalities place liens on properties not only for nonpayment of taxes but also for nonpayment of utility bills and special assessments, such as for sewer lines or sidewalks; and for nuisance abatement actions, ranging from yard cleaning and removal of debris to building stabilization or demolition. Treatment of such liens varies widely from state to state. Although they are generally given priority similar to that of tax liens, the procedures for collecting, and if unsuccessful, foreclosing are not always clear. State legislation should provide that such liens may be collected and foreclosed in tandem with property tax liens by being added to the outstanding taxes due, but the law should also provide that other liens can be foreclosed independently of tax liens by the municipality creating the lien. This ensures that the municipality can collect on the lien where the owner is current on taxes but delinquent on a nuisance abatement or other lien, or where the county rather than the municipality is responsible for foreclosing on tax liens.

8. *Providing a statutory definition of abandoned property.* Any legislation that creates a special tax foreclosure track for abandoned properties should contain a

Maryland House Bill 743, enacted in 2000, created a procedure known as a special tax sale in the city of Baltimore. Under this procedure, the city can package vacant properties in a tax lien sale specifically for purchasers who commit in advance to foreclose expeditiously and then redevelop the properties, and can set minimum bid prices that are less than the full amount of the payments in arrears. If the purchaser fails to comply with the conditions of the sale, including foreclosure by a certain date or the completion of improvements, the property can revert to the city. This is a highly creative way of addressing the problems of the tax sale system while continuing to operate within its framework. A similar procedure was created in New Jersey in 2004 under the Abandoned Properties Rehabilitation Act (N.J.S.A. 55:19-101).

New York City established its Third Party Transfer Program under legislative authority granted by Local Laws 37 and 69 of 1996 enacted by the New York State legislature. These laws established an expedited single enforcement proceeding for tax foreclosure of multifamily buildings containing four or more units. A not-for-profit corporation established for this purpose, rather than the city, takes title to the properties through foreclosure and conveys them to for-profit or nonprofit entities designated by the city after the four-month redemption period permitted by the law.

statutory definition of abandoned property. The definition should be broad and as clear as possible to minimize potential questions of interpretation. The New Jersey Abandoned Properties Rehabilitation Act provides a comprehensive, self-executing definition (see page 3). Although the facts of specific cases will inevitably be disputed, either in administrative hearings before the public officer making the determination or in subsequent court proceedings, a clear statutory definition will provide the public officer or the courts with the ability to resolve such disputes expeditiously.

B. Managing Foreclosure

Assuming the state statute provides the municipality or county with the necessary authority to carry out tax foreclosures consistent with local priorities, managing the system raises specific issues that must be addressed by any city or county seeking to utilize the statutes to best effect. Although the conduct of tax foreclosures is conceptually straightforward, the devil is indeed in the details. Any jurisdiction that plans to use tax foreclosure as a strategic property acquisition tool must establish and maintain systems for the management of the process. The following are recommendations for good management of the system:

- Tax foreclosure is a legal procedure and must be supervised by an attorney. Most of the tasks, however, actually devolve onto the attorney's paralegal staff. The attorney and, even more important, the paralegal staff must be specialists, fully versed in the details of the law, since even minor defects in the procedure—particularly with respect to the *Mennonite* notice requirements—can render the entire process worthless. *If a tax foreclosure results in defective title, the only recourse is usually to begin all over again.* Assuming that the volume of tax foreclosure activity is substantial, the paralegal staff assigned to tax foreclosure should devote their full time to this task.

- In a large city, it may be possible to assign a full-time attorney and one or more paralegal staff within the municipal or county attorney's office to tax foreclosure. If the municipal or county attorney's office cannot dedicate staff to this effort, either because of limited volume or because of the structure of the office, it is better to hire an outside specialist firm rather than risk that the process be mishandled by inexperienced staff.

- A number of jurisdictions have found that it is better to place tax foreclosures under the supervision of a line department engaged in redevelopment or revitalization activity rather than have it administered by the municipal or county attorney. Where the tax foreclosure process is supervised by a line department, it becomes far easier to integrate tax foreclosure with other acquisition activities being carried out by the city and with the reuse strategies being pursued by the city and its CDC and developer partners.

- Interdepartmental coordination is critical. Where city government is responsible for tax foreclosure, the coordination process is internal, but where the county has that responsibility, coordination must be intergovernmental as well. To the extent that the legal system gives the city or county discretion within the process, that discretion must be exercised in a way that is both internally consistent and in keeping with the city's redevelopment or reuse priorities. Where the county handles tax foreclosures for a city which seeks to use the process as a redevelopment tool, a formal intergovernmental agreement between the city and county should be executed, setting out clearly how the county will ensure that the city's interests are addressed. Information or review systems should be established to ensure that all relevant entities share information and participate in the process.

In many cities, the number of properties eligible for tax foreclosure is so large that simply working through the backlog can take many years. In such cases, it is important to have systems in place to set priorities for tax foreclosure that reflect the priorities of the city and its partners. Close communication between the city, CDCs, neighborhood associations, and others involved in reuse planning is essential.

- A reliable, usable property information system that combines information on tax delinquency and other liens with other property information is critical. It should enable users—including interested citizens—to track the status of eligible properties through the entire process.

- A common cause of delay, over and above the time frames mandated by statute, is the lag between filing foreclosure actions in court and the issuance of a judicial order. Many courts are understaffed and do not consider tax foreclosure to be an urgent matter. It is important to educate the courts—at the highest level possible—about the importance of tax foreclosure for community revitalization and about how time-sensitive it is. One approach is for the mayor or key civic and business leaders to arrange a meeting with the local presiding judge.

Finally, tax foreclosure must be fully integrated into the overall management of the abandoned property strategy. A single, coordinated process in which the same people supervise tax foreclosure and other acquisition strategies, such as eminent domain or gift programs, is the most effective approach to property acquisition. The acquisition process, in turn, should be closely linked to the disposition process, which in turn should be even more closely tied to the ultimate strategy for reuse of the properties being acquired and conveyed.

CHAPTER 8

Other Property Acquisition Tools

A. Building a Property Acquisition Strategy

A municipality seeking to foster redevelopment cannot rely on tax foreclosure alone to assemble the properties it needs. The process is often slow and time-consuming; moreover, many important properties may never become available through tax foreclosure. In cities with strong real estate markets, or where speculation has created the illusion of market demand, owners or lienholders of abandoned properties may continue to pay taxes on properties while allowing them to deteriorate. Often, the owner may not consider the building itself to have value but may want to hold on to the property in the hope of benefiting from future redevelopment. To develop a property acquisition strategy that can support serious revitalization goals, a municipality must utilize property acquisition tools beyond tax foreclosure.

Property acquisition activities are generally designed to further one of three basic revitalization strategies:

- To obtain a specific outcome with respect to a specific property, such as restoring a historically or architecturally valuable building, or reusing a strategic site

- To assemble a site made up of multiple properties for redevelopment of a larger area

- To assemble scattered problem properties within a neighborhood in order to carry out a rehabilitation or reuse strategy targeting those properties

Some goals for a particular property may be achievable without acquisition. Cities should never spend their own money to achieve goals that can be achieved by having the property owner spend hers. Where the goal is to secure the rehabilitation of a specific building, it is usually preferable to motivate the property owner to rehabilitate the property than to spend public funds to acquire it and reconvey it to another entity for rehabilitation. Even tax foreclosure, although nominally free, involves both transaction costs and considerable expenditure of time and energy. Tools that local government can use to motivate property owners to improve their properties are explored in chapters 5 and 12.

The most effective strategies involve partnerships between the city and CDCs and other neighborhood-based organizations. Some acquisition methods may work better for CDCs, whereas others may be better handled by a municipality. In some cases, property owners may prefer to deal with a CDC rather than with local government, particularly when exploring a gift or bargain sale.[1] In other cases, a CDC or a developer can move more quickly and be more flexible than local government. A strategy for property assembly that is being carried out jointly by a municipality with CDCs or developers, using the municipality's legal powers and resources as necessary, is likely to be both faster and more cost-effective than unilateral action by the municipality. Where the municipality is unwilling to become actively engaged in property acquisition, CDCs should develop strategies that they can carry out either without governmental support or with such limited governmental involvement as the municipality is willing to provide.

Effective acquisition strategies will use a property information system to identify, for each area or property targeted for acquisition,

- the reuse goal for each property (i.e., rehabilitation, infill, or assembly into a larger site);
- the strategy that can best achieve the goal for each property;
- the entity that should appropriately take responsibility for action.

The choices of an acquisition strategy and responsible entity require close attention to the circumstances of each property. A CDC that has a close relationship with a bank that has taken title to a number of abandoned properties in its neighborhood may be able to negotiate a better deal for those properties than the municipality. Conversely, if the same CDC has been engaged in a dispute with a particular property owner, the owner should be approached by the city rather than the CDC.

A tracking system should follow the progress of each parcel. The more participants, and the more parcels being acquired, the more important a computerized tracking system becomes. The system should be updated regularly and should be accessible to all participants so that they can monitor one another's progress and make sure that steps are taken sequentially and without undue delay. *While the tracking system should be integrated into the city's larger property information system, access to its contents should be controlled to ensure that sensitive or proprietary information is not inadvertently made inappropriately available.*

1. The term *bargain sale* is used to refer to a real estate transaction from which the seller receives part of the market value of the property in cash and takes the balance as a charitable deduction. The bargain sale is widely used as a property acquisition tool by nonprofit organizations, particularly with respect to acquisition for open space and environmental protection purposes. The value of the charitable deduction is the same whether the recipient is a governmental body or a private nonprofit entity.

This section addresses four means by which abandoned property can be acquired:

- Eminent domain
- Voluntary conveyances
- Buying liens
- Acquisition as an outcome of other intervention, such as nuisance abatement or receivership

While the first can be used only by governmental entities, the others are available to both governmental and nongovernmental bodies.[2]

B. Eminent Domain

Eminent domain, sometimes referred to as condemnation, is government's most powerful property acquisition tool. Coming from ancient English legal traditions, eminent domain is the power of government to take property from its owner against the owner's will when it is needed for a public purpose. Although historically the use of eminent domain was generally limited to traditional governmental functions, such as creating roads or public parks, two fundamental elements were added to eminent domain law by Title I of the Federal Housing Act of 1949, which stipulated that

- the redevelopment of blighted areas was determined to be a public purpose for which eminent domain could be used; and
- properties could be taken for redevelopment through eminent domain and then resold to another private entity to redevelop, rather than be used solely by the government.

This reinterpretation of eminent domain, which was and remains highly controversial, was upheld by the United States Supreme Court in the landmark *Berman v. Parker* decision in 1954 and recently affirmed in its 2005 *Kelo v. New London* decision. All use of eminent domain for neighborhood revitalization and elimination of blighting influences such as abandoned properties stem from this seminal legislative act and Supreme Court decision.

If the first principle of eminent domain is that the property must be taken for a public purpose, the second principle, enshrined in the Fifth Amendment to the

2. The highly publicized delegation of eminent domain authority from the Boston Redevelopment Authority to the Dudley Street Neighborhood Initiative is the exception that proves the rule. Few if any other states have language similar to that of the Massachusetts statute that permitted an administrative delegation of eminent domain to a nongovernmental entity, and efforts to create such statutes are likely to be strongly opposed by local governments. Even in Massachusetts, the statutory authority to delegate has never been used except on this one occasion.

United States Constitution, is that private property shall not be taken for public use without just compensation. To take a property through eminent domain, the city must pay the owner a fair market price, which must be determined through a process that is fair to the property owner.

Municipalities seeking to use eminent domain to acquire abandoned properties and convey them to a third party for reuse or redevelopment must understand

- the conditions under which eminent domain may be used;
- the procedures that must be followed to obtain title to property through eminent domain; and
- the basis on which compensation will be determined.

Within the overall framework set by the United States Constitution, the use of eminent domain is governed by state statutes. Where an eminent domain law fails to provide a municipality with adequate tools to address abandoned property issues, legislative reform may be an option. Although legislative attempts to broaden eminent domain powers may trigger strong opposition, legislation limited in its scope to abandoned property or—as with a Maryland statute enacted in 1999 specifically for the city of Baltimore—limited to a particular local jurisdiction may be more successful.[3]

Conditions under which Eminent Domain Can Be Used

The key question is whether the state statute permits eminent domain to be used against abandoned and other individual blighting properties *as such*, or whether it permits eminent domain to be used against abandoned properties only in the framework of a larger redevelopment project or other legal exercise of the power. A number of states and the District of Columbia have enacted statutes that permit *spot blight* eminent domain, under which municipalities may use eminent domain to take blighted properties whether or not they are part of a redevelopment area. Spot blight eminent domain is the best way of using eminent domain as part of an abandoned property acquisition strategy, since it permits the municipality to target the abandoned properties directly. It is particularly valuable where the municipality is trying to target scattered abandoned properties in an otherwise viable neighborhood, a situation in which the use of the redevelopment power—and the designation of the area as blighted—might well be excessive and inconsistent with sound planning practice.

---

3. The use of eminent domain for redevelopment has certainly been subject to abuse, particularly in states where the laws permit its use for economic development without regard to whether the areas being taken meet "blight" criteria. The controversy that has followed the Supreme Court's *Kelo* decision has led to efforts to roll back eminent domain powers in a number of states. The use of eminent domain against abandoned properties, which are arguably ipso facto a source of blight or a nuisance, is likely to remain a viable option in the great majority of jurisdictions, whatever may happen with respect to other uses of the power.

Virginia statutes explicitly authorize spot blight eminent domain, providing as follows: "An authority, or any locality, shall have the power to acquire or repair any blighted property, as defined in '36-49, whether inside or outside of a conservation or redevelopment area, by exercise of the powers of eminent domain . . . and, further, shall have the power to hold, clear, repair, manage or dispose of such property for purposes consistent with this title" (Code of Virginia '36-49.1:1).

In 2002 the District of Columbia enacted the Quick Acquisition of Abandoned and Nuisance Property Act (§42-3171.01-03), providing for spot blight acquisition and disposition of abandoned and deteriorated properties. In addition to authorizing eminent domain, the act authorizes other means of property acquisition, including gift, donation, assignment, and voluntary sale, and prescribes procedures for the negotiated disposition by the District of properties acquired under the act.

A Maryland statute, enacted for the city of Baltimore, not only authorizes spot blight eminent domain but also permits the city to use eminent domain to acquire occupied properties on any city block on which more than 70 percent of the properties are abandoned and in need of immediate demolition.

Where state law does not permit spot blight eminent domain, the municipality may have to use its powers under the state's urban renewal or redevelopment statute to acquire abandoned properties *for any purpose that will require subsequent reconveyance to a nongovernmental entity.*[4] This requirement can pose major procedural obstacles to an effective acquisition strategy, because the use of eminent domain under redevelopment law usually requires that the municipality undertake extensive studies and develop a redevelopment plan for the area, procedures that are not only time-consuming and potentially expensive but clearly out of proportion to the objective, if the municipality's goal is to acquire scattered abandoned properties for rehabilitation or infill.

A strategy developed by Jersey City, New Jersey, to resolve this problem, which may also be appropriate for other municipalities, is described in the accompanying box.[5] Despite the option offered by the Jersey City approach, a munic-

4. Although they may have somewhat different meanings to the lay public, the terms *urban renewal* and *redevelopment* are generally legally interchangeable, *urban renewal* having largely gone out of favor among state and local governments.

5. Although New Jersey enacted legislation permitting spot blight eminent domain in 1996, the language of that act made it all but impossible to use. These provisions were substantially amended in 2004 in order to make it a more effective tool.

The city of Jersey City, New Jersey, completed an inventory of abandoned properties and then created a single "vacant buildings redevelopment area" in which the area was defined as: "those Vacant Building Study Area properties that were recommended to the Municipal Council by the Planning Board to be declared an area in need of redevelopment."[6] The properties are scattered throughout the city (Vacant Buildings Redevelopment Plan, adopted August 18, 1999, amended September 8, 1999).

The plan itself set the objective of the project as "to redevelop or rehabilitate each individual property in accordance with land use, density and design standard objectives and criteria for the surrounding environment." While commendable, some doubt exists whether this redefinition of what constitutes a redevelopment "area" would survive a legal challenge.

ipality seeking to initiate an abandoned property strategy in a state that lacks statutory spot blight eminent domain authority should explore the prospects for legislative reform.

Eminent Domain Procedures

State statutes lay out detailed procedures for use of eminent domain, which have often been further clarified by state court decisions. These procedures, which involve notice, appraisal, and the obligation of the municipality to negotiate with the owner in good faith, must be followed rigorously to avoid the risk of the entire proceeding being invalidated.

A critical issue for a municipality seeking to use eminent domain as part of its property acquisition strategy is whether state statutes authorize what is known as "quick-take" eminent domain. State statutes generally lay out the process by which the property owner can challenge the municipality's determination of fair market value. Under New Jersey law, which is representative, the amount must first be reviewed by a board of condemnation commissioners appointed by the court. If either party objects to the commissioners' findings, the proceedings are set aside, and the matter goes to court for a trial de novo. The court's decision can then be appealed. Such a process can take many years, and if the municipality cannot take title until the award has finally been determined, the entire procedure may be of questionable value. Under a quick-take statute, the municipality

---

6. The term *area in need of redevelopment* was substituted for the traditional term *blighted area,* still used in many states, in an amended New Jersey state redevelopment law adopted in 1992. The statute makes clear that the two are legally equivalent.

is able to obtain title at the *beginning* of the process and can move forward with the resale or reuse of the property while the value of the property is disputed.

The downside of a quick-take procedure is that if the municipality takes the property, and a court subsequently awards the owner a sum substantially larger than the one the municipality had proposed, the municipality is legally obliged to come up with the difference. In the case of a major site assembly, such as for a large sports facility, the difference can be millions of dollars. While this downside is less significant with respect to most abandoned properties in inner-city neighborhoods, municipalities using eminent domain extensively should maintain acquisition reserve funds to protect themselves against potential cost shocks resulting from post-taking litigation.

Determining Compensation

Although the value of most individual abandoned properties may not be large, the number of properties involved in an area-wide redevelopment effort may be large enough that the sum may add up to a substantial investment. How abandoned properties are valued can therefore become a significant factor in the feasibility of a municipality's abandoned property strategy, particularly where the market value of a new or rehabilitated unit may well be less than the cost of rehabilitation or new construction.

The problem arises where a true property market does not exist, either in the area generally or with specific respect to the abandoned properties in the area. A market is created by arm's-length transactions between private buyers and sellers. When an appraiser determines market value, for example, for a typical house in a typical suburban area, she looks at recent real estate transactions, identifies similar transactions, and makes adjustments as necessary to compare those transactions with the property being appraised.

When this approach is applied to abandoned inner-city property, it often yields highly irrational results. To begin with, there are often few, if any, truly comparable transactions. In a low-value neighborhood, few private parties buy abandoned properties. Those transactions that exist are unlikely to be bona fide transactions but rather cases of flipping or other questionable or related party transactions. In other cases, the only buyer of record for abandoned properties in a distressed area may be the city, in which case appraisers may determine market value by treating the municipality as the market.

The problem is greatest in low-value areas where the market value of a new or rehabilitated unit is less than the cost of rehabilitation, or of demolition and new construction, a disparity sometimes referred to as the *appraisal gap* or *market gap*. Such areas are widespread in many of America's older cities, as well as in struggling towns and villages away from the nation's faster-growing regions. In such locations, any construction or rehabilitation of abandoned properties requires that capital subsidies be provided to fill the appraisal gap.

GOOD PRACTICE

Recently enacted New Jersey legislation attempts to address the issue of appraisal directly by establishing a statutory guideline for appraisal of abandoned properties being taken through spot blight eminent domain. The law reads as follows:

The fair market value of the property shall be established on the basis of an analysis which determines independently:

a. The cost to rehabilitate and reuse the property for such purpose as is appropriate under existing planning and zoning regulations governing its reuse or to demolish the existing property and construct a new building on the site, including all costs ancillary to rehabilitation such as, but not limited to, marketing and legal costs;

b. The realistic market value of the reused property after rehabilitation or new construction, taking into account the market conditions particular to the neighborhood or subarea of the municipality in which the property is located; and

c. The extent to which the cost exceeds or does not exceed the market value after rehabilitation, or demolition and new construction, and the extent to which any "as is" value of the property prior to rehabilitation can be added to the cost of rehabilitation or demolition and new construction without the resulting combined cost exceeding the market value as separately determined. If the appraisal finds that the cost of rehabilitation or demolition and new construction, as appropriate, exceeds the realistic market value after rehabilitation or demolition and new construction, there shall be a rebuttable presumption in all proceedings under this subsection that the fair market value of the abandoned property is zero, and that no compensation is due the owner.

(N.J.S.A. 55:19-102, enacted January 2004)

Common sense dictates that, when a property requires either major rehabilitation or demolition and construction to have any productive use, and if that productive use has a market value less than the cost of the rehabilitation or demolition and new construction, then the "as is" value of the property is a negative number, or at most, zero. Few appraisers, however, know enough about inner-city housing markets, or about real-world development costs, to reach this conclusion.

Local officials should educate appraisers about the marketplace realities and the cost of development in the neighborhoods where property acquisition and revitalization activity is under way. The city should also explore working with state or local appraisal associations to develop guidelines for appraisers to use to establish the market value of abandoned properties in low-value areas. Finally, cities may want to explore legislative reform, perhaps along the lines of the New Jersey legislation described above. This legislation should substantially narrow the scope of the problem, and, through subsequent court decisions, create clear rules for realistic determination of market values of abandoned properties.

C. Voluntary Conveyance

Voluntary conveyance is a transaction in which the owner willingly sells the property for market value, at bargain sale, or at nominal cost such as $1. Many owners of abandoned properties are eager to be relieved of the responsibility, and some may even be willing to donate their properties to the city or a CDC. Voluntary conveyance should be used wherever possible, as it tends to be speedy, involves low transaction costs, and avoids the potential political and legal complexities of tax foreclosure or eminent domain.

There are reasons why voluntary conveyance can only be part of a larger acquisition strategy, rather than a strategy in itself. First, many owners have an unrealistic sense of the value of their property, particularly if they have invested substantial time and money in the property over the years. Second, particularly in low-value areas, the amount of the liens on many properties may exceed the value of the property. In such cases, the owner may not be able to sell for a reasonable price without incurring financial hardship and may indeed prefer that the city take the property through eminent domain, to extinguish any liens in excess of the property's market value.

Gift Property Programs and Bargain Sales

Voluntary conveyance may make it possible to acquire properties at less than market value. A property owner in a low-value area gains substantially by donating property to a municipality or a CDC. Aside from being relieved of responsibility for the property, the owner can deduct the value of the property from her federal income tax obligations. The municipality gains the property with a minimum of cost and aggravation. A *bargain sale* is a variation of the above in which the owner sells the property to a governmental or nonprofit entity for a price that is significantly below fair market value, taking a tax deduction for the difference. Depending on their financial situation, some owners unwilling to make a gift of a property may be willing to sell it at a bargain sale.

The municipality must resolve a number of issues before establishing a gift property program and inviting property owners to offer the city their properties:

- *The city must establish that it has clear legal authority to accept property as a gift or to enter into below-market transactions.* While most states give local governments the flexibility to do so, some states may

The city of Covington, Kentucky, initiated its urban reclamation program by placing newspaper advertisements stating the city's willingness to purchase blighted, vacant properties and lots. City staff contacted owners directly to inform them of the availability of the program.

The city of Trenton, New Jersey, initiated a gift property program under which owners of vacant properties could offer their properties to the city as a gift. If the city accepted the property, it wiped out any municipal liens on the property. The city prepared and distributed a flyer describing the features of the program.

Both Trenton and Covington also used tax foreclosure and eminent domain as key elements in their acquisition strategies and did not rely solely on voluntary conveyance.

impose limitations or procedural hurdles on municipal property acquisition. In addition, some funding sources may impose restrictions on their use for below-market transactions.

• *The city must determine whether it has clear legal authority to extinguish municipal liens or forgive unpaid charges as part of a gift transaction.* For many owners, the principal attraction of donating their property to a municipality is the ability to wipe the slate clean of unpaid municipal obligations. For a gift program to be successful, the municipality must be able to forgive these liens. From a policy standpoint, forgiving the liens is of minimal concern, since it is unlikely that any of these funds would ever be collected.

• *Due diligence on the part of the municipality is critical.* Unlike tax foreclosure or eminent domain, a voluntary conveyance does *not* extinguish other liens, such as mortgages and judgments, on the property. The municipality must conduct a title search before offering to take a property. *Absent compelling reasons to the contrary, a municipality should never take a property that is not free of all liens other than municipal liens.* Similarly, particularly with respect to potential brownfields, the city should do enough environmental investigation to establish that the site poses no remediation issues, or, if it does, that the benefits of obtaining the property exceed the liabilities.

• *The city should never give the impression that it will take any property offered.* It must make clear that the program is discretionary and that the city will accept only those properties which—in addition to being free of nongovernmental liens—further the municipality's acquisition and re-development strategy.

While some owners may prefer for personal reasons to deed their properties to a CDC or community-based organization rather than the municipality, they gain no benefits from doing so. The tax benefits are the same whether the property is donated to the city or a CDC. A CDC, moreover, lacks the ability to extinguish the municipal liens. If a CDC is approached by an owner seeking to donate property subject to municipal liens, the CDC should explore whether the municipality is willing to take the property, extinguish the liens, and reconvey it to the CDC. The CDC can act as the municipality's agent in the transaction or can reimburse the municipality for its costs, at the municipality's option.

D. Buying Liens

Local governments or CDCs can also acquire abandoned properties by purchasing liens on those properties and foreclosing on them. These liens include both nongovernmental liens such as mortgages and municipal liens held by third parties. While lien buying offers the potential of acquiring properties at a cost substantially below market value, it also requires the lien buyer to enter treacherous legal territory. *Assistance from a competent attorney, well versed in this specialized area of the law, is critical.*

Mortgages and Other Nongovernmental Liens

Many lenders hold mortgage liens on properties whose owners have long since ceased making payments and which are now abandoned or distressed. While lenders could foreclose on these properties, they may have little desire to take title. As a result, they may be willing to sell their liens and their right to foreclose. In many cases, they may be willing to sell for substantially less than the amount of the liens to a municipality or CDC just to be relieved of the obligation to continue paying the property taxes.[7] The buyer of the lien can then foreclose on the property, usually through a sheriff's sale or similar procedure.

Even though selling their liens may be in their interest, lenders may be hard to negotiate with. Banks may be reluctant to write off any part of these liens, even though they may informally acknowledge that their true value is far less than their face amount. Moreover, in an era of constant mergers and reorganizations, where banks routinely sell paper to one another, it is often difficult to find the right entities with whom to negotiate, and even then it may be difficult to get their atten-

---

7. If the lender does not pay the property taxes, the municipality can take the property through tax foreclosure, a process which wipes out the entire value of the lender's mortgage.

Neighborhood Housing Services of New Haven, Connecticut, set up a program to recapture abandoned houses for affordable home ownership by purchasing liens, foreclosing, and rehabilitating the houses for sale to first-time home buyers. The investors were happy to settle for a small fraction of their initial investment in order to be rid of these properties. NHS's initial program included twelve properties at an average acquisition cost of $15,000 per house, as follows:

Payment to investors	$2,500
Payment to city	$10,000
Transaction costs	$2,500

Two-thirds of the cost went to pay off the more recent tax liens held by the city.

HANDS, Inc. in Orange, New Jersey, buys older liens on abandoned one- and two-family detached houses from lienholders, generally at a deep discount, and immediately forecloses, paying any subsequent lienholders what is due them. The organization then rehabilitates the properties and sells them to moderate-income home buyers.

tion. A CDC that has already established a relationship with a bank may be able to use such a relationship as a starting point for negotiating a lien sale.

Tax Liens Held by Nongovernmental Entities

Over half of the states in the nation sell tax liens to investors. Those buying tax liens, particularly bulk lien packages, often subsequently discover that the cost of foreclosure and paying off the outstanding taxes on some properties may exceed the value of those properties. As a result, they do not foreclose, often freezing the properties into financial limbo. As CDCs in New Haven, Connecticut, and Orange, New Jersey, have found, many tax lien holders are ready to sell, often at a substantial discount, if approached by a credible buyer with a serious offer. The prospective buyer must, however, invest time and effort to engage the lienholder's interest in order to initiate the process.

A CDC or other private entity buying tax liens must pay close attention to the potential impact of subsequent municipal liens on their own lien position. Under many state laws, a subsequent lien takes precedence over the prior tax lien.[8] If

---

8. If subsequent taxes are not paid on a property that has already had a lien sold at the tax sale in a given year, a new lien for the new unpaid taxes is created, which is sold at the next year's tax sale. This procedure can be repeated ad infinitum.

the holder of the old lien fails either to keep taxes current or to buy new tax liens at subsequent sales, the subsequent lien may be bought by another party, who could then foreclose and wipe out the CDC's interest.

E. Acquisition as an Outcome of Intervention

There are circumstances under which properties may change hands as an outcome of an intervention, such as nuisance abatement or receivership, that is not explicitly intended to lead to a change of ownership. While municipalities or nonprofit entities should not misuse these powers in order to gain title if the intervention in itself is not clearly justified, they should be vigilant for such opportunities that may legitimately arise.

Receivership

The use of receivership can lead to the property's sale, either to the receiver or to another qualified entity. The Ohio receivership statute, indeed, encourages such sales as a matter of public policy. While receivership is generally applied to occupied buildings, it has been used against abandoned properties as well. The Baltimore ordinance also permits a receiver to be appointed for the purpose of selling the property rather than solely for the purpose of rehabilitation. The property must be sold at auction unless the owner agrees to a negotiated sale. No other state law or local ordinance contains a similar provision.

The New Jersey vacant property receivership statute, N.J.S.A. 55:19-84 through 97, provides explicitly for sale of an abandoned property that has gone through rehabilitation by a receiver, in the event that the owner fails to meet the stringent statutory conditions for reinstatement. The receiver may purchase the property or sell it to a third party under court supervision if the court finds that "such conveyance will further the effective and timely rehabilitation and reuse of the property."

Nuisance Abatement

There is less precedent for conveying title as a product of nuisance abatement. In an unusual proceeding, however, the circuit court of Wayne County, Michigan (which contains Detroit), began in 2000 to award the county title to properties identified as nuisances whose owners had failed to repair or demolish them by the deadlines established by the court.

While the courts in most jurisdictions might not follow Wayne County's lead, a case can be made that at some point neglect of a property reaches a level where the right of ownership can reasonably be deemed forfeit. This is the principle behind the laws of forfeiture, under which properties used for criminal activities are taken from their owners by law enforcement authorities. Given the many harms that can be caused by abandoned properties, including fostering criminal activity,

Baltimore enacted a vacant building receivership ordinance specifically authorizing the receiver to sell vacant properties, either before or after rehabilitation, and to foreclose on a receiver's lien unless the owner takes responsibility for rehabilitating the building (IBC Sec.121 Baltimore City Revised Code). Maryland legislation delegates unusually broad powers to chartered counties, including the city of Baltimore.

Illinois and Missouri have enacted statutes that create a status for abandoned properties similar to receivership, called *possession,* under which a nonprofit entity can seek a court order giving it control of an abandoned property for the purpose of rehabilitation and reuse. In both cases, if the owner has failed to meet strict conditions for reinstatement of his or her rights, the statute authorizes the court to grant a deed to the nonprofit entity. These statutes are described in further detail in chapter 12.

it does not seem far-fetched to apply the same principle to them. Local officials may want to explore this issue with legal counsel in the context of the statutes and case law of their state.

F. CDC Property Acquisition Strategies

A CDC or a group of CDCs may have compelling reasons to pursue property acquisition on their own, separately from municipal acquisition efforts. Circumstances under which this approach may be appropriate include the following:

- The municipality is not engaged in acquiring properties for redevelopment either in general or in the areas where the CDC is active.

- Fiscal or capacity constraints, or competing demands from other sources, make it impossible for CDCs to obtain enough properties from the municipality to maintain a development pipeline or pursue other community goals.

Neither of these conditions is unusual. Some cities, for a variety of policy reasons, may not want to take properties at all, or may not want to pursue an aggressive acquisition strategy, even though they may take isolated parcels from time to time. Others may be willing to take properties through tax foreclosure but may not give CDCs access to the city-owned inventory. These obstacles may be citywide and affect the CDC sector generally, or they may be specific to a particular neighborhood or a particular CDC.

Even where a city and CDC are collaborating, there may be good reasons for a CDC to carry out property acquisition activities independently, in addition to obtaining city-owned properties. In some cases, the CDC may have greater access to particular properties or be able to work with particular owners more readily than the city. Given the length of time involved, having more than one entity work on acquisition—as long as their efforts are well coordinated—can increase the efficiency of the process. Finally, CDCs should not be totally dependent on the municipal government. Their ability to acquire properties on their own increases their credibility and the respect with which they are treated.

Tools

CDCs can use a number of the tools described above to acquire properties:

- Acquiring properties through voluntary conveyance, including conveyance by gift and bargain sale

- Purchasing "paper" from lenders and taking properties through sheriff's sale

- Purchasing tax title or tax liens and pursuing foreclosure actions to take the properties

- Where state law or local ordinances permit, using vacant property receivership statutes to rehabilitate properties and in some cases ultimately take title

CDCs, even more than municipalities, must exercise due diligence in all transactions, because they lack not only the powers that municipalities have to extinguish certain liens but also the municipality's leverage in negotiating with other lienholders or interested parties.

Financial Resources

Property acquisition does not come cheaply. Costs that must be covered include:

- transaction costs, including legal fees, title searches, environmental due diligence, and notice;

- the cost of up-front options, contract payments, etc., for transactions that do not require full up-front cash payment;

- the full cost of properties that must be acquired through 100 percent cash transactions;

- the cost of property taxes, insurance, and other fees on properties incurred while the CDC holds the property;[9]

---

9. In some states, a nonprofit tax exempt entity may not have to pay property taxes on vacant properties it holds. Since the property is not actually being used for charitable purposes, this is the exception rather than the rule.

GOOD PRACTICE

The PLAN (Predevelopment Loans and Acquisition for Nonprofits) Fund was established early in 2005 to support CDC property acquisition activities in New Jersey. Capitalized at $10 million, it provides credit lines of up to $500,000 for acquisition and land banking efforts by CDCs with solid track records, as well as more conventional predevelopment loans for specific projects. Developed by the Housing and Community Development Network of New Jersey, it is managed by the Reinvestment Fund in Philadelphia. As an inducement to raise capital for the fund, the New Jersey Housing and Mortgage Finance Agency has provided a 50 percent guarantee of loans made from the fund.

- The cost of maintaining the property, which may range from the modest cost of periodically cleaning and mowing a vacant lot to substantial costs associated with stabilizing and securing a vacant building.

Any CDC planning a property acquisition strategy must make sure that it has sources of financing adequate to acquire the property and carry and maintain it until it can be restored to productive use. CDCs, moreover, need to be able to have immediate access to cash as they negotiate specific transactions. Once an owner has agreed to sell or give the CDC an option, she is likely to expect cash within a matter of days or weeks, rather than the months it would take to line up financing at that point. CDCs planning large-scale acquisition activities need to obtain a credit line for acquisition which they can draw upon immediately for each transaction.

CDC acquisition financing is available from a variety of potential sources. National intermediaries, including the Local Initiatives Support Corporation (LISC), the Enterprise Foundation, and the Neighborhood Reinvestment Corporation, provide assistance to CDCs that are either members of their network or located in participating communities. Some local intermediaries and CDFIs provide predevelopment assistance, with varying degrees of effectiveness.[10] A growing number of organizations are now developing revolving funds specifically addressing this issue, such as the New Jersey PLAN Fund (see box above).

10. Many public agencies and CDFIs operate predevelopment loan funds for nonprofit developers which can be drawn upon, in theory, for property acquisition. Because these funds, however, typically require approval by the lender of each transaction, the CDC cannot apply for a loan until after it has entered into an agreement with the property owner. Given that months may elapse between the application and closing and cash disbursement, such loan funds are effectively useless for a CDC seeking to carry out a serious acquisition strategy.

Any such fund should offer acquisition credit-line financing. Under a credit-line agreement, the CDC and the lender agree on criteria for property acquisition, including the area in which properties will be acquired and the characteristics of the properties to be acquired. When the CDC acquires a property and requests money, documenting that the property meets the criteria, the funds are disbursed immediately, typically within forty-eight hours. Access to such credit lines can be limited to CDCs that have both financial stability and a record of demonstrated performance.

CHAPTER 9

Property Disposition

Municipalities rarely acquire abandoned property for their own use. As a rule, they plan to hold it only temporarily, with the intention of conveying the property to an entity that will reuse it. The process, therefore, by which local government disposes of the properties it acquires is as important as the process by which it obtains them. Although local officials often devote considerable time and energy to framing property acquisition policies, few pay equal attention to seeing that their property disposition policies effectively further the community's redevelopment goals.

Property disposition raises many policy questions:

- What procedures should be followed to ensure that the process is fair and consistent?

- Which properties should be conveyed, and to whom: to developers, CDCs, adjacent property owners, or other entities?

- What terms and conditions should be established for property disposition?

- What prices should be charged for properties under various circumstances?

The answers to these questions have significant policy consequences. A decision to maximize income through the sale of city-owned property to the highest bidder may offer short-term financial benefits but choke off development opportunities offering substantially greater benefits in the long run. Although cities constantly scramble for operating funds, disposition policies should still balance their immediate fiscal demands against long-term goals.

These issues are clouded by the widely recognized but rarely addressed issue of the pervasive role of politics in many cities' property disposition activities. In many cities, the sale of city-owned property is one of the few means by which politicians can reward supporters in the guise of furthering public policy. In some cities where city council members are elected by ward or district, a council member often becomes the de facto property disposition manager within her ward, as described in a recent book:

In Chicago city government the aldermen have a privilege to veto any city action within their ward. . . . Ward Three has 3,300 vacant lots owned by the city—over a third of such lots in all Chicago—but their sale, through various city programs, is subject to the aldermanic hold, which in [Alderman] Tillman's case is a tight grip.[1]

In another example, the mayor of one small Northeastern city, over staff opposition, committed more than fifty key vacant city-owned properties to an unqualified development corporation established by the politically influential pastor of a local church. That corporation's inability to move forward over the next few years, while other development was taking place in the area, significantly impeded progress in one of the city's highest-profile redevelopment areas.

Such practices are not harmless. They reflect badly on the city and its leadership and can cost the city millions in unrealized revenues and market appreciation. The cleaner and fairer the process by which property is sold, the more eager responsible developers will be to invest in the city, particularly in weak market cities without powerful competitive advantages. Developing a fair process which subordinates political considerations to policy objectives should be a priority for those developing abandoned property strategies.

A. Legal Considerations in Property Disposition

The opportunities and constraints imposed on a municipality by state law affect both the terms and the procedures of property disposition.

Terms of Sale

The customary rule is that when a governmental entity disposes of property, it must do so at fair market value. Most state laws, however, provide broad exceptions to that rule.

1. Urban renewal or redevelopment. Nearly all states provide an exception for properties sold within an area that has been designated an urban renewal or redevelopment area. The language of the New Jersey statute is typical:

[The municipality has the power to] lease or convey property or improvements to any other party . . . without public bidding and at such prices or upon such terms as it deems reasonable, provided that the lease or conveyance is made in conjunction with a redevelopment plan. ([N.J.S.A. 40A:12A-8[g]])

Similar language is found in most state statutes.

2. Sale for specific public purposes. Many states provide exceptions to public bidding or fair market price where the property is to be used for a public purpose, such as low- and moderate-income housing or social services. New Jersey

1. Alexander von Hoffman, *House by House, Block by Block* (New York: Oxford University Press, 2003), 137.

law, for example, sets specific uses for which a private sale for nominal consideration is permitted, including animal shelters, volunteer fire companies, and housing rehabilitation.

3. *Blanket exceptions.* A few states give local government full discretion to sell property on such terms as it deems appropriate. Connecticut law grants municipalities power to "convey such real and personal property or interest therein absolutely or in trust as the purposes of the municipality or any public use or purpose . . . require," without requiring any specific terms or conditions of sale.

In most cases, a municipality can find room in state statutes to establish a sound disposition strategy. In some cases, however, careful structuring of the program may be required to stay within the purview of the law. In others, legislative changes may be needed to implement an effective process.

Sale Procedures

State law may specify the process by which sales take place. Under New Jersey law, unless the transaction falls under redevelopment or one of the specific exceptions to the law, municipal property must be sold by public auction. The Baltimore vacant buildings receivership ordinance provides that the sale must be by public auction but permits the city to set qualifications for bidders to ensure that the purchaser is capable of rehabilitating the property. Massachusetts law, by comparison, grants discretion to the city council or town meeting, as the case may be, to set both terms and procedures of sale within the statutory framework established by Chapter 30B of the General Laws of Massachusetts.

The fact that under many state laws a municipality *can* dispose of property however it sees fit does not mean that it *should. Any private, noncompetitive, sale, particularly of a property with substantial present or potential value, is potentially subject to abuse.* There are strong public policy reasons, not least the need to maintain public confidence in the integrity of the process, for a municipality to establish a formal competitive process for property disposition even where it is not required to do so by law.

B. Framing Sound Property Disposition Policies

Setting sound policies for property disposition is a matter of matching the characteristics and location of the property with the disposition method most likely to achieve the reuse goals for the property itself and for the neighborhood in which it is located. Table 9.1 presents the principal criteria to be considered for each type of property and the disposition options likely to be available.[2] The clearer the goals for the neighborhood, the easier it is to establish a rational property disposition system.

2. Whether these options are available to a municipality depends on state law.

TABLE 9.1 Vacant Property Disposition Strategy Options

Category	Vacant land (including land containing buildings to be demolished)		Buildings potentially suitable for rehabilitation	
	Individual lot	Large parcel	Small building (one- to four-family residential)	Large building (multifamily or nonresidential)
Neighborhood criteria (these cut across all property-specific categories)	Level of market demand in area Level of home ownership in area Historic district Other neighborhood assets affecting development potential Proposed reuse(s) under neighborhood plan or redevelopment plan Goals and priorities of community association or neighborhood council Presence or absence of viable CDC in area Level of developer interest and activity in area			
Site criteria	Size and configuration Potential for combination with other sites to create larger assemblage Nature of adjacent properties and ownership	Size and configuration Nature of adjacent properties and ownership Presence of environmental concerns (as with brownfields)	Condition Presence of additional similar buildings in area with which to create rehabilitation package Architectural and historical amenities Suitability by type and location for owner occupancy Suitability for homesteading	Condition Reuse potential Architectural or historical quality and amenities Size and character relative to potential market demand Presence of environmental concerns (as with brownfields)

Disposition options			
Public auction Side lot sale to adjacent property owner Negotiated sale to CDC for infill development or greening activity (e.g., mini-park or community garden) Combination with other sites into package for negotiated sale through RFP to CDC or developer Conveyance to land bank for future site assembly	Negotiated sale through RFP or other procedure to CDC or developer Conveyance to public or nonprofit entity for open space use Conveyance to land bank for future redevelopment	Public auction (subject to prequalification) Sale to prospective owner-occupant (homesteader) Negotiated sale to CDC for rehabilitation Combination with other sites into package for negotiated sale through RFP to CDC or developer for rehabilitation Stabilization and conveyance to land bank for future reuse or assembly	Negotiated sale through RFP or similar process to CDC or developer Stabilization and conveyance to and land bank for future reuse or assembly

Based on these criteria, as well as on additional criteria that a city may want to specify, the city can construct a decision tree to make decisions about specific parcels. Figure 9.1 gives an example of a decision tree for individual vacant lots. It shows clearly how property disposition decisions must be tied to property reuse. The following discussion identifies key disposition issues for each of the principal land and building types shown in table 9.1.

Individual Lots

The bulk of many cities' vacant property inventory is made up of scattered building lots, many of which are too small by today's standards to accommodate new homes. These sites may offer little of the development potential of larger tracts even if located in relatively strong neighborhoods. The key issues in the decision tree are as follows:

1. *Is the site potentially part of a larger site with greater redevelopment or reuse potential?* Having a good GIS-based property information system is critical to answering this question. By looking at city-owned properties together with sites owned by other public bodies, tax delinquent properties, and other vacant or underutilized parcels, one can assess whether the opportunity for an assembly exists and whether it is likely to be feasible in terms of expenditure of time and money. Once that determination has been made, a decision can be made whether to tackle the additional acquisition needed for the assembly now, bank the property for future assembly, or dispose of the property. That decision should take into account the market conditions in the area and the potential reuse value of the assembled parcel.

2. *Is the site buildable under current standards, based on its size and configuration?* If the site is buildable and potentially suitable for infill development, additional questions must be answered before an option can be chosen:

- What is the market for an infill house in that location?
- Is additional density appropriate for the location?

Whether a house *can* be built on a particular site is a legal and engineering issue. Whether a house *should* be built on that site is a planning and economic issue. If the market in the area is such that a new house could not be built without capital subsidy, the city must decide whether that construction is an appropriate use of limited funds. If the neighbors consider the density of the area to be too high already, adding more units through infill may be inappropriate. Conversely, if the vacant lot is an unsightly gap undermining the aesthetic quality of the area, the additional expense of constructing a new house on the property might be justified.

If infill is appropriate for the site, the city may choose to sell the property to a CDC or a developer. In some cities, such as Minneapolis, new infill houses are in great demand in many neighborhoods, and developers compete aggressively for buildable city-owned sites. Elsewhere, nonprofit development companies such as

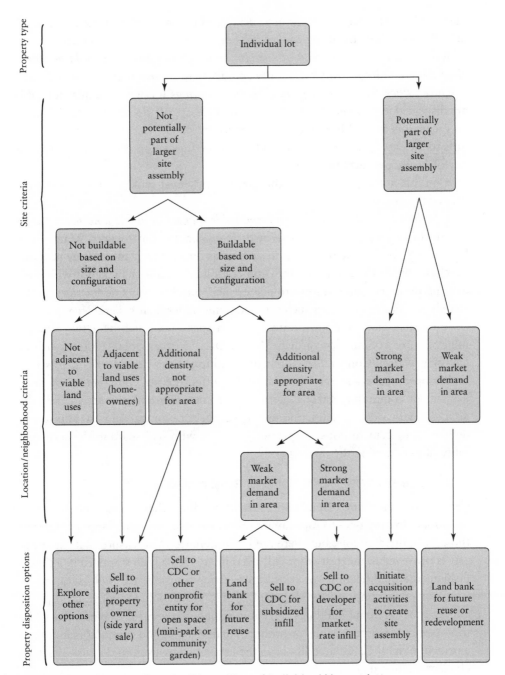

FIGURE 9.1. Decision Tree for Disposition of Individual Vacant Lots

Property type

Site criteria

Location/neighborhood criteria

Property disposition options

Individual lot

Not potentially part of larger site assembly

Potentially part of larger site assembly

Not buildable based on size and configuration

Buildable based on size and configuration

Not adjacent to viable land uses

Adjacent to viable land uses (home-owners)

Additional density not appropriate for area

Additional density appropriate for area

Strong market demand in area

Weak market demand in area

Weak market demand in area

Strong market demand in area

Explore other options

Sell to adjacent property owner (side yard sale)

Sell to CDC or other nonprofit entity for open space (mini-park or community garden)

Land bank for future reuse

Sell to CDC for subsidized infill

Sell to CDC or developer for market-rate infill

Initiate acquisition activities to create site assembly

Land bank for future reuse or redevelopment

the Cleveland Housing Network have developed the capacity to produce scattered infill houses efficiently, using capital subsidies in a cost-effective manner.

Where the city is disposing of sites for infill construction, it should establish clear design and construction quality standards to ensure that new houses will enhance rather than detract from their surroundings (design standards for infill are discussed in chapter 19). Construction of cheap, off-the-shelf, modular units on vacant lots in neighborhoods characterized by stately Victorian houses will add little to the city's present tax base while reducing future appreciation, robbing the city of future property tax revenues.

If infill is not appropriate for the site, the city must look to other alternative uses of the property.

3. Is the site located adjacent to responsible owners of viable land uses? Many vacant lots are in residential areas with many stable homeowners. Many cities have set up *side lot sale* programs in such areas under which adjacent owners can purchase the lot for a nominal sum and consolidate it into a single lot with their existing property. Some states provide explicit authority for side lot sales, while elsewhere cities can conduct such sale programs under their general legal powers.

Some sites may be appropriate for open space use, such as a playground, mini-park, or community garden. Many CDCs or other organizations, such as Detroit's Warren/Conner Development Coalition, have turned vacant lots into usable open space and recreation facilities, often linking construction of playgrounds or community gardens with other community-building activities in the area. As with side lot sales, the use of vacant lots for gardens or mini-parks demands adjacent responsible property owners who will share in the responsibility of maintaining the open space.[3]

Scattered Small Buildings Suitable for Rehabilitation

Criteria for evaluating disposition of small buildings that are suitable for rehabilitation, typically one- to four-family residential structures, are largely similar to those for individual lots, but there are key differences.[4] To ensure that the property is conveyed to an entity that will rehabilitate it to a high standard in a timely fashion, the qualifications of prospective buyers must be carefully scrutinized. CDCs or other nonprofit development entities are usually the most appropriate entities to rehabilitate buildings, except in strong market areas—particularly historic districts—where capable for-profit rehab developers and contractors may have emerged. Not all CDCs actually have the capacity, however, to do cost-effective, efficient, scattered-site rehab.

Another option is to establish a homesteading program and sell properties to families who will both rehabilitate and occupy them. Homesteading programs are

---

3. Uses of vacant properties for open space purposes are discussed in chapter 20.
4. An individual building that is slated for demolition is the functional equivalent of a vacant lot for property disposition purposes.

a high-risk undertaking, and many past efforts—particularly those restricted to lower-income buyers—have been less than successful. The program must be carefully designed to maximize the likelihood of success. The use of incentives to encourage people to buy and rehabilitate vacant properties is discussed in chapter 16.

Finally, many cities may find that they own some buildings which should clearly be rehabilitated by virtue of their historic or architectural character but lack feasible reuses under current market conditions. Rather than dispose of these buildings, the city may choose to hold them and stabilize them until market changes make reuse feasible. Stabilization is discussed further in chapter 13.

Large Parcels and Buildings

Large parcels and buildings represent the city's greatest redevelopment opportunities and demand the greatest care in both developer selection and reuse planning to ensure that the city gains the greatest long-term benefit from the sale of the property. Where a site has major development potential, an auction is rarely an appropriate way of disposing of the property, even if it appears to be the means by which the city can obtain the greatest immediate return.[5] The risks of the property ending up in the hands of an incapable or unsuitable developer, even if criteria are established for who may bid at the auction, are far too great.

The greater the development potential and developer interest, the greater the municipality's ability to impose conditions on potential developers competing for the property. A request for proposals (RFP) process, in which developers must present their plans for the reuse of the property, demonstrate their qualifications to carry out the project, and name the price that they are willing to offer for the property, should be seen as almost a threshold requirement for the disposition of such properties.

While some large properties offer great development opportunities, others may offer little or no short-run development potential. Many weak market municipalities, such as Detroit and St. Louis, contain vast amounts of vacant land and buildings for which no effective market exists at present. Depending on the city's assessment of future market potential, such properties must be land banked and held for future redevelopment, or attempts must be made to find viable nonmarket reuse options, such as open space.

The temptation, in a rising market, to sell such properties prematurely, or to sell to the first developer making an offer, should be resisted. Holding the property until the market is truly ready will result in both more money for the municipality and a higher quality of redevelopment on the property.

---

5. The greatest *immediate* sale revenue may not represent the greatest potential return for the municipality over time. A well-crafted development agreement can lead not only to a stronger redevelopment project—with greater long-term tax revenues flowing to the city—but also to a negotiated payment schedule that over time could yield the city substantially more than it would obtain at an auction.

C. Establishing Procedures and Setting Terms for Property Disposition

Within the framework the municipality establishes for property disposition, many decisions must be made about the process by which properties are conveyed and the terms of sale. Failure to address those issues can undermine even the best-conceived strategies. Procedures and terms of property disposition must be designed to achieve four objectives:

- Ensure that properties are placed in the hands of entities capable and willing to carry out reuse plans
- Ensure that the terms of sale make it feasible for the entities to carry out their reuse plans
- Protect the city's short-term and long-term interests
- Ensure that the city is recognized as an honest and competent player in the redevelopment process

Municipalities regularly disposing of properties should prepare a written manual setting forth the city's property disposition policies and procedures, which should be available both in hard copy and on the city's web site.

Procedures for Conveying Property

Redevelopment laws usually offer the municipality carte blanche to negotiate sole source contracts with developers in redevelopment areas. Without a competitive selection process, however, sole source negotiations with developers for city-owned properties are inherently suspect. Municipalities should use a competitive process for disposition of any city-owned property being offered to for-profit entities or which has substantial value or development potential, *whether or not such a process is legally required*. The competitive process need not be an auction. An RFP process or similar procedure, involving a written, widely disseminated solicitation clearly stating the criteria by which a developer will be selected, is usually the most appropriate process for disposing of properties with substantial value or development potential.[6]

Auctions are most appropriate in cases where the municipality is seeking broad public participation, where the sale of the properties may bring a substantial return to the municipality, and where the redevelopment or reuse issues are straightforward and do not raise significant issues of capacity or sensitivity. *Wherever permitted by law, the municipality should impose qualifications or per-*

---

6. There are many different approaches. One is a two-step process, under which a request for qualifications (RFQ) is issued, and a smaller number of entities are selected from that process and invited to submit a more detailed RFP. A variation is known as a request for expressions of interest (REOI), which falls somewhere between the RFQ and RFP in the amount of information required of applicants.

formance requirements on bidders at property auctions tied to the reuse goals for the properties being sold.

Imposing requirements on successful bidders is only the first step. Enforcing them is equally important and often much more difficult. Without a well-designed system for tracking properties, it can be hard for local officials to determine whether buyers are meeting their legal obligations. Even where local officials are aware of some buyers' failure to carry out their obligations, enforcing agreements and regaining title to properties—or imposing other sanctions—requires both will and a substantial expenditure of legal resources. There is no point in imposing requirements on bidders if the city does not intend to enforce them.

Noncompetitive disposition procedures should be limited to situations where buyers are either adjacent property owners or prequalified nonprofit entities, such as CDCs. Where a city is working in partnership with a CDC to redevelop a particular neighborhood, the city should make properties available to the CDC to carry out its plans. Depending on the CDC's capacity, the number of properties available, and the plan's provisions, the city and CDC should consider entering into a multiyear agreement for conveyance of city-owned property to the CDC. Such an agreement creates a "pipeline" for the CDC, enabling it to build its capacity and maintain a high level of productivity.

Where a municipality enters into a noncompetitive property disposition agreement with a CDC, it must first ensure that the CDC can reuse the properties in a timely fashion and then monitor the CDC's progress to ensure that it continues to do so for the duration of the agreement. If conditions change, and the CDC can no longer make progress, the municipality must be prepared to take corrective action to prevent loss of the city's assets.

Property Conveyance Terms

Properties are typically conveyed by a municipality under agreements that include monetary terms (consideration) as well as nonmonetary conditions.

Consideration. Conveyance of city-owned property generally involves monetary consideration, even if it is the familiar practice of sale at nominal cost, such as $1. Setting the consideration is a sensitive issue. Nearly every city is looking for revenue sources to support the general fund. By demanding excessive consideration, however, the municipality can place a burden on the buyer that may impede achievement of the buyer's—and the municipality's—objectives.

What is excessive will vary from case to case. A municipality should obtain a meaningful price for a property when it has significant value and where a substantial initial payment by the developer will not interfere with her ability to carry out the reuse of the site. In other cases, however, especially when the developer must incur substantial infrastructure or site remediation costs before construction and will not realize a return until many years down the road, a high initial price may undermine the feasibility of the project. In such cases, the municipality may want to negotiate a payment schedule keyed to construction phases or other milestones. That schedule may ultimately yield more to the municipality.

Other factors also enter into this equation, including the extent to which the municipality expects the developer to provide public benefits such as open space or affordable housing and the extent of any development incentives being offered. *A municipality negotiating with an experienced developer on a major project must have a negotiating team with experience and knowledge comparable to that of the developer's team, even if it has to hire expensive outside consultants for the purpose.* Failure to do so will almost certainly cost the municipality dearly in the long run.

Where the potential returns from a project are modest, the municipality should be willing to scale down its financial expectations. The value of the finished product is determined by the market, not by the municipality's wishful thinking. If a municipality sets excessive prices on vacant shells in weak market areas, the only buyers are likely to be those who will cut corners on rehabilitation in order to be able to sell the finished product for what the market will bear. Alternatively, a conscientious entity may buy the property for the inflated price, rehab it properly, and then be unable to sell it for a price that covers its costs. Either way, the municipality loses.

Another issue arises if the project requires capital subsidy to fill the appraisal gap. For example, a house may require $40,000 in capital subsidy based on zero land cost. If the municipality requires the CDC to pay $10,000 for the lot, the house will now require $50,000 in subsidy. Requiring such a payment is actually a device, not illegal but arguably improper, to make a de facto transfer of dedicated capital subsidy funds into the municipal general fund. It requires the CDC to obtain a larger amount of scarce capital subsidy resources for the same unit and ultimately reduces the number of units in the municipality that can be assisted with available funds.[7] *Where a project requires capital subsidy, the municipality should limit its demands to reimbursement for its direct costs associated with acquiring and conveying the property.*

Nonmonetary Terms. The agreement conveying property should establish terms that create the greatest likelihood that the city's redevelopment objectives will be achieved and effectively protect the city's interests in the event that they are not. Four elements should be present in the agreement:

- *A clear and specific definition of the use or reuse of the property that is the subject of the agreement.* The description should be highly

---

7. The statutes governing state and federal programs providing capital subsidies for housing development clearly stipulate that the funds must be used for affordable housing and cannot be used for general governmental purposes. A roundabout procedure which in essence requires a developer to obtain a larger amount of such funds in order to be able to pass part of them back to the municipality in the form of property acquisition costs may not technically be a violation of those laws, but it is clearly inconsistent with their intent.

specific. Recognizing that circumstances change, however, it should permit minor modifications to be made administratively, rather than by voiding the agreement or requiring city council action.

- *Clear standards governing the work to take place.* To the extent that the city is looking for anything beyond minimum code compliance, design guidelines and historic preservation guidelines should be set forth in the agreement or clearly incorporated by reference.

- *Realistic timetables for performance.* Timetables should be explicit, and demanding but not unrealistic. Unrealistic timelines, while looking good on paper, undermine the credibility of the entire process. The larger and longer-term the project, the more interim milestones should be built into the agreement to permit the municipality to monitor the developer's progress.

- *Clear and enforceable provisions governing nonperformance by the buyer.* The municipality must have effective recourse if the buyer fails to meet the terms of the agreement. While financial penalties, such as forfeiture of a bond, may be appropriate, the most effective means of enforcement is to incorporate an enforceable *right of reverter* in the agreement, under which the municipality can demand title back in the event of nonperformance. This provision can be enforced in the courts if the buyer fails to comply.[8]

By addressing these issues, the municipality maximizes the likelihood that the property will be developed appropriately and still protects its interests in the event that the developer fails to carry out its obligations.

D. Property Disposition by Other Governmental Entities

While most abandoned properties that fall into governmental hands come under municipal control, other entities, including state and county transportation departments, mental health agencies, and law enforcement agencies, often hold abandoned properties. They may include land or buildings acquired for projects that did not materialize, facilities no longer needed, or properties acquired through law enforcement proceedings such as forfeiture. They can range from a sliver of vacant land originally intended for a highway ramp to an abandoned mental institution covering hundreds of acres. All of these holdings within a city's boundaries should be included in its property information system and should be assessed to determine which are vacant, underutilized, or likely to become vacant in the near future.

---

8. Such reverter clauses must be carefully drafted to ensure that they do not inadvertently impede the developer's ability to obtain financing needed for the project.

Most non-local government agencies have little understanding of or interest in local redevelopment or revitalization efforts. Moreover, many state laws require state agencies to dispose of surplus properties at market value, or provide very limited exceptions to such a rule, rather than give agencies flexibility to work with local government or CDCs to maximize the value of their properties for redevelopment. There are, however, ways to obtain more flexible terms of sale:

- Even where state law requires that the transaction be at market value, it may allow the payments to be made over time, or deferred for some number of years, and may not require that interest be charged or that it be charged at market rate.

- Some states permit governmental agencies to convey property without consideration to quasi-governmental agencies, such as housing finance or economic development agencies, which are not subject to the same restrictions as line government departments.

The ability to obtain such terms depends on the municipality's or CDC's ability to convince the appropriate state agency that such flexibility furthers the revitalization of the community, and is therefore also in the state's interest. Where no flexibility exists, however, local officials and CDCs may want to explore the possibility of amending the state law to provide for below-market or negotiated disposition of state-owned parcels to local government or nonprofit entities for redevelopment activities.

CHAPTER 10

Setting Up an Abandoned Property Management System

A. Getting Everyone on the Same Page

Any municipality that plans to tackle its abandoned properties should create an *abandoned property management system*. The effectiveness of even the strongest legal tools and financial resources is easily undone by a fragmented, dysfunctional system in which different public agencies and private organizations are working at cross purposes. A well-organized system that brings together public and private entities to work toward common goals can enable a community to make the most of limited resources and legal tools.

Abandoned property management in most cities usually consists of separate functions handled by separate agencies, departments, or divisions. Responsibilities are often divided not only within the municipality but also between municipality, county, special districts, and authorities:

> The responsibility for vacant property in Philadelphia is divided among 15 public agencies. Anyone wanting to buy a property may spend weeks negotiating the maze of agencies just to apply. . . . Decisions made by one city agency can undermine those made by others. A single city block may contain homes owned by the Pennsylvania Horticultural Society, slated for demolition by the Department of Licenses and Inspections, included in a Redevelopment Authority urban renewal project, awarded an Office of Housing and Community Development grant for rehabilitation, and promised for a specific redevelopment plan by a council person.[1]

Getting all of the governmental agencies on the same page can be hard enough, but it is important not to stop there. Although government may have the legal responsibility, nongovernmental entities—such as CDCs, neighborhood councils, environmental groups, and crime watch organizations—are also engaged with abandoned properties in their communities. A management system that includes meaningful roles for these organizations will be far more effective at reducing blight and fostering sustainable reuse than one in which the municipality is the only significant player.

1. Mark Alan Hughes, "Dirt into Dollars: Converting Vacant Land into Valuable Development," *Brookings Review* 18, no. 3 (Summer 2000).

An abandoned property management system is an organized process linking all of the activities involved in dealing with abandoned properties, from acquisition through disposition, in a way that maximizes the use of public resources, minimizes the present harm caused by those properties to the community, and maximizes the city's redevelopment opportunities for the future. Such a system can only be created through conscious choice and effort.

B. Understanding the Issues

As a first step in organizing an abandoned property management system, officials must confront the way the different elements of that system are handled under the municipality's current structure. In a typical city, five to ten different agencies may be involved (see table 10.1).

It is not unusual, moreover, for two or more agencies to handle what appears to be the same function with respect to different categories of property. For example, the treasurer may take properties into the municipal inventory through tax foreclosure, while the city attorney may take properties into the same inventory through eminent domain. As in Philadelphia, different governmental agencies may control separate property inventories for different purposes. This fragmentation impedes efforts at assembly or strategic reuse.

Agency priorities are often at odds with one another. The treasurer may want to maximize municipal revenues through tax sales, while the redevelopment agency may want to use tax foreclosure as a tool to assemble properties for neighborhood revitalization. The department of inspections may recommend demolition for almost any vacant property, while the historic preservation commission may want the same buildings preserved for rehabilitation. The city solicitor may give tax foreclosure a low priority, thereby undermining the community development department's efforts to build a strategy to deal with abandoned properties.

These issues tend to be easy to understand but difficult to resolve. Establishing a system to deal with abandoned property issues is often stymied not only by the number of different entities involved but also by established bureaucratic territories, political and organizational alliances and rivalries, and the inherent tendency of governmental bodies to develop their own values and practices without regard to efforts at central direction. These issues must all be addressed if the city is to mount an effective strategy. There are a number of ways in which these issues can be approached.

Diagnostic Assessment

All changes from standard operating procedure exact a cost, if not in dollars, then in creative energy or political capital. Before embarking on a process of change, local officials should evaluate the situation in order to identify the most serious obstacles to carrying out the city's abandoned property strategy and the most effective—and least costly—ways to overcome them.

TABLE 10.1 Typical Distribution of Governmental Responsibilities in the Abandoned Property Management System

Functions	Responsible agency or agencies
Holding tax sales and selling tax liens	Tax collector, finance director, municipal or county treasurer
Acquiring vacant properties through tax foreclosure (foreclosing tax liens)	Municipal attorney, finance director, municipal or county treasurer
Acquiring vacant properties through other means	Municipal attorney, department of community development, redevelopment agency, parks and recreation department
Clearing and maintaining vacant lots	Department of public works, department of community development, department of parks and recreation
Boarding and maintaining vacant buildings	Department of public works, department of community development, department of buildings or inspections
Demolishing vacant buildings	Department of buildings or inspections, department of public works, department of community development, redevelopment agency
Preventing criminal activity in vacant buildings	Police department
Framing reuse or redevelopment objectives for vacant properties	Department of planning, department of community development, redevelopment agency
Designating priorities and allocating funds for rehabilitation or construction	Department of community development, redevelopment agency, city council
Disposing of municipally owned vacant properties	Department of community development, municipal or county treasurer

Note: This table reflects the patterns typically found in many different cities, not one particular city.

The following are diagnostic questions that should be asked about each function listed in table 10.1. Answering the questions honestly and in detail for each function will enable governmental bodies to identify problems that might be addressed through better coordination or reorganization.

- Where is each function performed?
- What is the mission of the organization performing the function, and how does that mission fit into the overall abandoned property strategy or priority of the city?
- Is the organization performing this function in a way that fully implements the overall strategy?

- Is the organization performing this function efficiently and in a cost-effective manner?
- What are the conflicts between strategies and priorities?
- Where is there excessive duplication or inefficient use of resources?
- What are the reasons for the conflict or duplication?

Conflicts in priorities, or inefficiency in use of resources, can arise for many different reasons, as the following examples show.

- The treasurer's office, eager to maximize revenues for the city budget, is packaging tax liens for bulk sale, preventing the city from acquiring properties that the redevelopment agency needs to carry out its redevelopment goals.

- The redevelopment agency, department of community development, and department of parks and recreation are all spending money to acquire property for their own projects or activities, spending far more money than if one agency was responsible for all property acquisition.

- The department of buildings is scheduling demolitions without input from other bodies, resulting in actions inconsistent with neighborhood reuse goals.

By revealing the nature and extent of the conflicts and inefficiencies in the system and the reasons they exist, the assessment should permit local officials to come up with effective ways of restructuring the management system to eliminate the problems.

The solution is likely to reflect a balance between a strategy that is optimal from an organizational standpoint and the realities of the political and organizational landscape. In a bureaucratic world where the number of departmental programs and the size of the departmental budget are the measure of a commissioner's importance, any reorganization will have its opponents. Many commissioners have their own political constituencies, which must also be taken into account.

The assessment may also identify areas where a particular practice is mandated by state law; or, conversely, the city may find that state law does not permit it to implement changes in practices that would further its strategy. This is often the case in home rule states with respect to municipalities that are not home rule cities. In such cases, the municipality may want to include a legislative strategy in its plans.

While a cautious approach may often be necessary, boldness is sometimes more appropriate. An ambitious reorganization plan, which may include creating a new land bank authority or similar agency, can be a dramatic and effective way for a new mayor or chief executive to demonstrate her commitment to change and her willingness to do what it takes to address a complex, demanding issue. A bold, high-profile strategy can often bring new energy and creativity to addressing a problem, in contrast to a cautious, risk-averse approach.

C. Interagency Coordination

One basic step any municipality can take is to create a body to coordinate the city's efforts across departmental lines. An interagency task force can be a good way to build coordination and information sharing. For such a task force to be effective, however, it should follow certain commonsense principles:

- The scope and importance of its mission should be clearly laid out by the city's chief executive, whether a mayor or city manager.

- The task force should be headed either by a senior staff person without line responsibilities but with the mayor's confidence, such as the city administrator or mayor's chief of staff, or by the individual heading the agency responsible for implementing the core features of the strategy.

- The task force should include representatives of all of the departments with a significant role in the system.

- Key individuals should be present at all task force meetings. While junior staff may be permitted to attend, commissioners should not send junior staff to represent them.

- The task force should meet on a regular schedule over an extended period.

- Minutes should be taken and procedures established to track performance over time.

- The task force should create smaller working groups involving only those entities directly engaged in a particular issue. Examples might include a working group on acquisition that involves the treasurer, the city attorney, and the community development director, or a working group on property maintenance made up of the director of buildings, the director of public works, and the city attorney.

Interagency coordination is most effective where not only is it structured according to the above principles but certain underlying conditions are also met:

- There is an underlying level of trust and cooperation between the participants

- All participants clearly understand that they must give priority to the effort

- The city's chief executive regularly reinforces the initial message about the importance of the effort

The city of Pawtucket, Rhode Island, established an organizational structure for its abandoned property strategy, including the following elements:

- Overall supervision by the city administrator

- Coordinating responsibility in the Department of Planning and Development

- An interagency task force under the supervision of the Department of Public Works, responsible for maintenance and securing of abandoned properties

The city simultaneously obtained stronger tools to address abandoned properties by pursuing a legal reform strategy with the state legislature.

Interagency coordination is a useful but not a powerful tool. Under the right conditions it can be effective, but it is unlikely to be as efficient as more far-reaching strategies, and it needs constant reinforcement to maintain its effectiveness. Agencies whose core mission is elsewhere are unlikely to give as high a priority to abandoned property issues as those setting the agenda would like, and they have to be repeatedly pressed to maintain their involvement. Indeed, interagency coordination is often used as a fallback strategy where political or other reasons make reorganization of governmental functions infeasible.

D. Internal Reorganization

Where possible, functions should be reallocated to link related activities and eliminate conflicts of mission or priority. Reorganizations can range from small adjustments in the division of responsibilities among departments to wholesale restructuring of relevant governmental functions.

Selective reorganization can address those changes most urgently needed or those that are feasible within political and bureaucratic constraints. The Trenton reorganization (see box below) reflected both considerations. Trenton did not carry out a comprehensive reorganization of its property-related functions for two reasons. First, most of the relevant functions were already housed in one department; and, second, for various reasons, the mayor was reluctant to pursue more extensive organizational changes.

The Livable City Initiative in New Haven, Connecticut, is an example of a more extensive and comprehensive reorganization of municipal functions. While the mission of the Livable City Initiative goes beyond abandoned properties, it brings

The city of Baltimore centralized all of its property acquisition activities in the Department of Housing and Community Development, and—reflecting the priority given property acquisition by the mayor—created the senior position of assistant commissioner for land resources to administer the city's activities in this area.

The city of Trenton, New Jersey, centralized property acquisition in a new Division of Real Estate in the Department of Housing and Development. Tax foreclosures were shifted from the city attorney's office to outside special counsel working under the direct supervision of the director of real estate. A second outside special counsel was retained by the department to handle eminent domain proceedings.

nearly all of the important municipal tools to deal with abandoned properties into a single agency, and—equally important—closely ties abandoned property activities to the larger mission of neighborhood revitalization and redevelopment.[2]

On occasion, when a municipality has wanted to broadly reorganize its efforts to deal with abandoned properties, it has created a land bank entity, often under explicit statutory authority. This approach is particularly useful where responsibilities are divided between the city and county, and the city does not exercise all the relevant authority itself. For that reason, many land bank authorities, such as those authorized by the Georgia statute, are joint city-county agencies. Land bank entities are discussed further in chapter 11.

E. Building Nongovernmental Organizations into the System

Nongovernmental organizations are important partners in making the system work. Their potential roles range from providing policy guidance in the design and operation of the system to the mundane role of assisting the city to maintain the vacant lots in its inventory. Table 10.2 provides an overview of the roles and responsibilities of nongovernmental organizations. The following are representative examples:

- If the city proposes to establish a land bank authority with certain neighborhoods targeted as priority areas, some of the members of the board of the authority should be from the target neighborhoods.

2. The Livable City Initiative, established in 1995, got off to a rocky start. In 1998 its loan practices triggered an outside investigation, which led to a reorganization and replacement of the executive director in 1999.

TABLE 10.2 Roles and Responsibilities of Nongovernmental Partners in an Abandoned Property Management System

System element	Potential partners	Roles	How nongovernmental partners should be involved
Overall policy and direction	Neighborhood councils and similar representative bodies	Providing input in policymaking and priority setting	Consultation on design and structure of management system Representation on boards (i.e., land bank authorities) and advisory bodies
Property acquisition	Neighborhood councils CDCs	Providing input into priorities for property acquisition	Reviewing lists of potential properties available for acquisition
Clearing and maintaining vacant lots	Neighborhood councils CDCs Youth and community service organizations	Cleaning and maintaining vacant lots	Contractual relationship Providing material and technical support for development of community gardens and mini-parks as interim uses
Boarding, maintaining, and stabilizing vacant buildings	CDCs	Boarding buildings Maintaining buildings Stabilizing buildings	Contractual relationship Maintenance agreements pending reuse of property
Preventing criminal activity in vacant buildings	Neighborhood councils Neighborhood and block watch organizations	Monitoring activity Monitoring other problem property issues Reporting activity to police department	Informal agreements Training

Framing reuse or redevelopment objectives	Neighborhood councils Neighborhood planning organizations CDCs	Developing neighborhood plans Identifying problem areas and reuse opportunities Providing input into municipal reuse or redevelopment proposals	Consultation on reuse or redevelopment objectives Technical assistance and support to develop neighborhood plans Involvement in integration of neighborhood plans into municipal planning and decision-making framework Participation on advisory boards
Designating priorities for reuse	Neighborhood councils Neighborhood planning organizations CDCs	Providing input into municipal priorities for reuse Proposing specific priorities based on organization's mission and business plan	Consultation on reuse or redevelopment objectives Integration of priorities set by neighborhood plans into municipal decisionmaking framework Participation on advisory boards
Disposing of city-owned properties	Neighborhood councils CDCs	Providing input on suitability of potential purchasers Proposing specific property dispositions based on organization's mission and business plan	Consultation on specific proposals for property disposition

In Connecticut, the city of New Haven's Livable City Initiative centralizes nearly all of the city's abandoned property responsibilities in one agency, as follows:

• Property Division: acquisition and disposition of real estate, including relocation, demolition, and leasing and marketing of property

• Neighborhood Services Division: outreach, property maintenance, coordination of "neighborhood sweeps" with other departments, and coordination with the City Planning Department to develop neighborhood plans

• Administrative Services Division: Financial and technical assistance to homeowners, neighborhood groups, and CDCs, including the HOME program, and coordination of efforts to develop green spaces and community gardens

• Building Division: enforcing the state building code, including issuing permits, and identifying buildings in need of demolition

• Code Enforcement Division: enforcing the state housing and zoning codes and administering the emergency repair program

• Legal Division: providing legal resources

• Neighborhood plans, particularly those developed through a strong participatory process, should be used to prioritize property acquisitions and to set reuse priorities. The city's planning staff should work closely with neighborhood organizations or CDCs developing neighborhood plans to make sure that the city provides solid, specific input on these issues.

• A wide variety of organizations, including CDCs, block groups, and youth groups can be enlisted to help maintain vacant lots and develop community gardens and mini-parks as interim uses for these properties through contractual agreements with the city.

• CDCs with rehabilitation and maintenance capabilities can be contracted to perform services on vacant buildings, including boarding and reboarding as needed, cleaning, and stabilization.

• Neighborhood and block watch organizations can be engaged to monitor criminal activity in buildings that are vacant, no longer effectively secured, or illegally occupied.

CDCs are often the city's most important partners in the reuse and redevelopment of abandoned properties. If a city has one or more CDCs with the necessary skills and financial resources to produce housing, through either new construction or rehabilitation, the city should engage them in the abandoned property strategy from the beginning. The process of engaging CDCs should include the following:

- Working with CDC staff to facilitate acquisition of properties needed by CDCs for their projects

- Prioritizing acquisition of properties that reflect CDC priorities in order to ensure that CDCs have access to a "pipeline" of properties for reuse

- Developing explicit terms for disposition of properties to CDCs that realistically further the reuse of those properties consistent with CDC and city objectives

- Regular interaction of senior city staff with CDC staff and community leadership to ensure consistency between CDC and city priorities and objectives

If local CDCs lack the capacity to contribute meaningfully to achieving reuse objectives, the city should explore ways—together with state CDC associations and national intermediaries such as LISC or Enterprise—to build CDC capacity within the community.

The relationship between the city and the CDCs must be one of partnership, rather than one in which the city dictates the mission and priorities. While local government is ultimately responsible for setting the overall direction and vision for the city, that direction should emerge from a process which reflects the vision and priorities of neighborhood organizations and CDCs and should be flexible enough to reflect changes in those priorities over time.

CHAPTER 11

Designing and Establishing Land Bank Entities

A. Using Land Bank Entities to Manage an Abandoned Property System

A land bank authority or similar entity exists for the explicit purpose of gaining control over the city's problem property inventory in order to make possible its timely and productive reuse.[1] Dedicated to reclaiming the public assets represented by vacant land and buildings, a land bank entity can be an effective vehicle by which local government can advance its abandoned property strategy, as well as a symbol of the community's commitment to dealing with its abandoned property problems.[2]

The mission of any land bank entity is to take title to, hold, and dispose of property. The creation of such an entity should reflect a decision by the municipality to embark on such an effort and a conviction that creating a land bank entity will materially advance its goals. Furthermore, since the structure and legal powers of a land bank entity must be tailored to local conditions and priorities, before creating the entity, the city should have a clear idea of both the impediments to the productive reuse of vacant or underutilized properties and the ways in which it will use the land bank entity to overcome them. Those strategies may call for substantial changes in local practices or state laws. State law reform, particularly in the area of tax foreclosure, has sometimes been linked to the establishment of local land bank entities. In some cases, land banks have grown out of state law reforms, while in others the creation of a land bank has provided the impetus for the reforms.

---

1. While many land bank entities are in fact authorities in the legal sense of a governmental or quasi-governmental entity established with a separate governing structure independent of general-purpose governmental bodies, they can in fact take a variety of legal and organizational forms. The term *land bank entity* is used in this section to describe any entity that carries out the land bank function, whatever its legal basis or organizational structure.

2. See Frank Alexander, *Land Bank Authorities: A Guide for the Creation and Operation of Local Land Banks,* prepared for the Local Initiatives Support Corporation and available at www.lisc.org/resources/vacant_abandoned.shtml. This publication, which provides a detailed guide to both the issues and the practicalities involved in establishing a land bank authority, is highly recommended. This section (and others) owes a great deal to Alexander's research and insights.

GOOD PRACTICES

1990 Georgia legislation authorized the creation of joint city-county land bank authorities with the authority to acquire, clear title to, and dispose of tax-delinquent properties, and to foreclose on tax-delinquent properties (Title 48, Sec. 4-61 through 4-65 [O.G.C.A. 48-4-61]). The effectiveness of these authorities was limited until the Georgia legislature passed a comprehensive reform of tax foreclosure laws in 1995, creating a judicial foreclosure process. The Fulton County/City of Atlanta Land Bank Authority has since become an important vehicle in returning vacant and underutilized properties to productive use, fostering affordable housing, and returning nontaxpaying properties to the tax rolls.

In Michigan, the Land Bank Fast Track Act, which authorizes the creation of county or multijurisdictional local land bank authorities, grants those authorities the power to initiate expedited quiet title and foreclosure actions, and provides a variety of tax and other incentives for land bank authorities, was enacted in 2004 (Act No. 258, Public Acts of 2003; M.C.L.124.751-124.774). The first such authority created under the act, the Genesee County Land Bank, is described further in the text.

The state of Kentucky also provides explicit authority to create land bank authorities, modeled closely on the Georgia statute (Kentucky Revised Statutes Title 65, Sec. 350-375 (KRS 65.350). Other land bank statutes are found in Missouri (V.A.M.S. Sec. 92.700-920) and Ohio (Ohio Revised Code, Chapter 5722).

The discussion here is designed to assist readers in exploring whether creating a land bank entity is appropriate for their community, and if so, how it should be organized in the following respects:

- Scope of operations
- Legal power and authority
- Governance and staffing

Since local conditions, needs, and statutory framework vary so widely, rather than proposing a single model, this discussion attempts to frame key questions and set forth alternatives to help a community build the model that best suits its needs.

B. Scope of Operations

The mission of a land bank entity is to take title to property, to hold the property, and to convey it to others. By definition, any land bank entity will have some responsibilities in each of those three areas. The scope of those responsibilities can vary widely.

Taking Title to Properties

Most land bank entities are established to enable local government to gain clear and marketable title to vacant or underutilized properties that may be blighting a neighborhood or standing in the way of needed redevelopment and revitalization, and to overcome the impediments to local government's ability to pursue that goal, including:

- lack of information about problem properties;
- inadequate internal procedures or capacity to carry out property acquisition;
- complications arising from multiple taxing districts and jurisdictions involved in property acquisition;
- difficulty clearing title to properties acquired through tax foreclosure or other means;
- cumbersome legal processes with respect to acquisition, particularly with respect to tax foreclosure.

While changes to state statutes may be needed to address some of these impediments, others, such as creating information systems or building internal procedures and staff capacity, can be addressed locally.

The key issue is how best to use a land bank entity to overcome these impediments. Table 11.1 shows how centralizing acquisition within a single entity with the capacity and legal powers to carry out efficient acquisition activities can overcome most of the impediments to a successful property acquisition strategy. *The purpose of creating a land bank entity is to overcome significant impediments in the property acquisition and disposition system.* Unless the impediments are clearly identified and the entity is carefully designed to address them, a community may find that it has created a new entity only to see the same problems persist.

Not all of these impediments exist in every jurisdiction. If no significant impediments exist, a land bank entity may not be needed. Where some parts of the system are effective, the land bank entity should build on those elements rather than replace them. In such cases, the land bank entity may actually be an extension of an existing organization, which is given new tools or resources. The formal processes involved in taking property through tax foreclosure, for example, are likely to remain the legal responsibility of an existing governmental agency, such as a municipal or county treasurer. If that agency is already performing its responsibilities adequately, the appropriate step might be to have properties taken by the treasurer conveyed to the land bank entity. If, however, the treasurer's office lacks the internal capacity to carry out its responsibilities, or lacks the ability or will to

TABLE 11.1 Impediments and Strategies in Property Acquisition

Impediment	Strategy
Lack of information	Create centralized property information system within single entity
Inadequate internal procedures	Establish dedicated high-quality staff and consultant team within single entity to conduct property acquisition
Multiple jurisdictions	Reform state statutes to eliminate inter-jurisdictional conflicts Frame interagency or interlocal agreements to permit coordinated property acquisition by single entity
Difficulty clearing title	Reform state statutes to ensure that acquisition procedures meet legal and constitutional standards Improve technical quality of acquisition activities to ensure legal standards are met
Cumbersome legal process	Reform state statutes to provide for a more expeditious process Establish single entity to carry out new expedited acquisition procedures

address statutory changes or to expand its property acquisition efforts, the land bank entity should be given the responsibility to conduct property takings, either in its own name or as the agent for a public agency, such as the county treasurer.

Some jurisdictions limit their land bank entity to taking properties through tax foreclosure, while others are permitted, and encouraged, to take property through other means. That choice should reflect local conditions. If the number of tax-delinquent properties is such that the community can achieve its objectives by focusing exclusively on those properties, or if existing mechanisms adequately address other properties, then it may be appropriate to limit the scope of the land bank entity to tax-delinquent properties.

This is generally not the case. Furthermore, even if at first the number of properties available through tax foreclosure is substantial, it may decrease over time, particularly if market conditions improve. In that situation, a land bank that uses tax foreclosure as its only acquisition tool will no longer function effectively. *Except where compelling reasons exist to the contrary, municipalities should give land banks the flexibility to acquire properties through all available means.* Most land bank entities acquire property through tax foreclosure, donation, or voluntary conveyance. Few, if any, utilize eminent domain, although municipal governments may convey properties acquired through eminent domain to land bank entities.

Baltimore and Houston represent contrasting approaches to property acquisition.

Baltimore, under its Project 5000, made a commitment in 2002 to take title to five thousand vacant properties within two years. While many properties are in areas slated for redevelopment, and some are earmarked for specific projects, the city recognizes that it will hold many of these properties in its inventory for several years. The city's goal is to gain control over its future redevelopment by gaining control of these properties, even when their future use is uncertain.

Houston, in establishing its Land Redevelopment Authority (known as LARA), limited its initial scope to a pilot program involving acquisition through tax foreclosure of long-term delinquent vacant land parcels in two target areas, representing roughly two hundred out of sixteen thousand potentially eligible properties citywide. This decision reflected an assessment of capacity and political support as well as the difficulty of obtaining the complex multijurisdictional agreements needed to get LARA up and running.

Other arbitrary limitations on the land bank's acquisition activities, such as authorizing it to acquire only vacant land and not structures, are counterproductive. While some cities have imposed such restrictions, largely because of potential liability concerns, other communities, such as Genesee County, Michigan, have found not only that the liability and maintenance issues associated with holding structures in inventory can be addressed, but also that buildings taken through tax foreclosure create valuable income-generating opportunities to support the land bank's operations.[3]

Holding Properties

All land bank entities hold properties. In some cases the mission of the land bank entity is to reconvey the property to a private entity as quickly as possible, while in others it may hold properties for an extended period before they can be sold. Some, therefore, will keep relatively few properties in inventory, and turn them

---

3. A little-appreciated dimension of the tax foreclosure process, particularly in states with efficient foreclosure procedures, is that, while the overwhelming majority of properties taken by the local jurisdiction have little or no immediate market value, a small percentage do have substantial value, including readily marketable houses and commercial buildings in good repair that have fallen through the cracks of the financial or legal system. By screening out these properties and selling them on the conventional real estate market, the Genesee County Land Bank Authority raises enough money to cover a substantial part of its operating budget.

over relatively quickly. Others will keep larger numbers of property in inventory for longer periods. The land bank should have a clear idea of which direction it is heading in before it begins operations. *If the land bank entity expects to maintain a substantial property inventory, it must build in the tools and resources it needs to do so responsibly.*

The factors determining whether a land bank entity should be organized to hold a substantial long-term property inventory are economic, physical, and political:

- The strength of the local real estate market and the local demand for land and buildings
- The number of properties available for acquisition
- The congruence between short-term developer interests and the city's larger goals
- The scope of the city's revitalization strategy

In a strong market city such as Boston or Minneapolis, where qualified developers are ready to build on any parcel that a land bank entity might have available, the land bank is unlikely to control more property than the private market can use. The land bank, therefore, should have no difficulty finding qualified buyers as quickly as properties become available.

In a weak market city the situation is very different. In cities such as Baltimore or Detroit, the number of properties potentially available to a land bank entity vastly exceeds the short-term market demand for land or buildings. Moreover, to the extent that demand exists, it may be for low-end uses that the city does not want to encourage.

In such cases, the land bank has two options. It can take large numbers of properties, recognizing that many will have to be held for years before they can be productively reused, or it can limit acquisition to a smaller number of properties that can be reused immediately.[4] The Genesee County Land Bank in Flint, Michigan, has made a commitment to take as many properties as it can in order to create an environment conducive to future productive reuse opportunities.

While maintaining a property inventory can impose significant costs, it is likely to be in the community's interest. Future opportunities for reuse of abandoned properties may offer significantly greater benefits to the community than those realistically available at present. Such future opportunities may come about for many reasons:

- Through assembly of larger parcels

---

4. No matter how committed it may be to the rapid conveyance of properties, the land bank will have to hold some of its properties for weeks, months, or years. The best-case scenario of property acquisition—the simultaneous closing in which one takes title to a property and simultaneously reconveys it to another party—is rare.

- Through improvements in neighborhood, city, or regional market conditions

- Through implementing comprehensive neighborhood revitalization strategies

By systematically assembling and holding properties, the land bank can position the city to take full advantage of these opportunities. Furthermore, if property values are increasing—or expected to increase—it will become harder rather than easier to acquire properties in the future. Gaining control over properties sooner rather than later permits a municipality to set a course for the future of the community which might become impossible later on.

Where future reuse opportunities may be significantly better than those currently available, then, the land bank should consider a long-term holding strategy. That does not mean that the land bank should hold *all* properties it obtains. Properties that can be conveyed without impairing the city's long-term goals should be disposed of. The tax foreclosure process routinely yields such properties, such as side lots or single-family houses needing no more than cosmetic repairs. A long-term holding strategy will, however, require the land bank entity to hold many of the properties it acquires.

Holding properties requires the ability to maintain them. The larger the inventory, and the longer properties are held, the greater the capacity needed by the land bank to carry out necessary maintenance tasks. A land bank entity with a substantial inventory should be prepared to carry out the following tasks:[5]

---

5. If the land bank entity takes title to occupied as well as vacant properties, responsibilities toward the tenants it inherits will demand that it perform additional tasks.

- Cleaning and mowing of vacant lots and grounds around vacant buildings

  - Cleaning, boarding, and re-boarding vacant buildings

  - Stabilizing vacant buildings slated for future rehabilitation

- Making repairs and cosmetic improvements to properties obtained in good or fair condition

  - Demolishing vacant buildings

  - Maintaining sidewalks in front of vacant land and buildings

Wherever possible, the entity should identify existing entities—governmental or nongovernmental—that can carry them out and enter into agreements with them to ensure that the job gets done. In some cases, the appropriate entity may be obvious, such as a municipal public works agency that already has crews that clean and mow city lots. Sidewalk maintenance and demolition are two areas where the land bank, if it retains responsibility for those tasks, should usually hire experienced contractors, who are likely to be found in any city or region.[6] Capable neighborhood-based organizations may be willing, for a reasonable fee, to perform repairs or maintenance on land bank properties. Such relationships can both strengthen the organization and reduce the need for the land bank entity to build its own capacity.

Nevertheless, the land bank may have to carry out certain tasks itself. First, in some areas it may be impossible to find adequate capacity in existing governmental or nongovernmental entities, particularly in smaller towns and cities. Second, it is critical that maintenance tasks be performed in a competent and timely fashion and that the results are visible to neighbors of the properties. The land bank entity has ultimate responsibility for performing these tasks. If it cannot find reliable partners to carry them out, it may have to take on the responsibilities directly.

Conveying Properties

The issues connected with conveyance and disposition of properties are addressed in chapter 9. The land bank entity's disposition activities may cover the full range of options described there or may be more limited, depending on the land bank entity's mission and the scope of its authority. Each community establishing a land bank entity must address these issues by answering key questions arising from the entity's mission:

What are the land bank's reuse objectives for the properties it holds? The objective may be simply to return properties to the tax rolls in the most efficient

---

6. If an existing city agency already has efficient systems in place to handle matters such as demolition or sidewalk repair, the land bank entity should establish a procedure to refer properties to that agency for action, so that it is not directly involved in contracting for those services.

manner, or it may be to increase the supply of affordable housing or implement neighborhood revitalization plans. The objectives may vary depending on the location of the property or the particular features of the land or building. Since a land bank entity is generally not an independent body but a vehicle for executing the policies of one or more governmental entities, it must take direction from the planning, housing, and community development officials of its parent jurisdictions.

To *whom should the entity convey properties?* The land bank should identify the potential purchasers who can best further its objectives. If its mission is simply to return properties to the tax rolls as quickly as possible, it may want to cast its net widely in order to find any prospective purchaser willing to take the property and restore it to some productive use. If its goal is to produce affordable housing, the entity may want to establish qualifications to ensure that the purchasers are capable of producing the housing the community needs, or that they represent the interests of the neighborhoods in which the housing is to be built. Maintaining flexibility is always important, however, to ensure that land does not lie fallow because the land bank entity has defined eligible buyers or reuse options too narrowly.

Ultimately, the success of the land bank entity will be measured by whether the parcels it conveys are redeveloped in a timely fashion in ways that are seen as desirable by the neighborhoods in which they are located. Success hinges on the ability of the land bank entity to establish and follow sound criteria for selecting buyers and to establish terms of sale that facilitate rather than hinder achievement of the buyer's redevelopment plans. The land bank must also make sure that the size and location of properties are well matched to buyers' capabilities and avoid committing too many parcels to organizations without the capability to develop them in a timely fashion.

What terms should govern the conveyance of properties? Once the land bank entity has clearly defined its objectives and identified appropriate purchasers for its properties, it must establish both monetary and nonmonetary terms for the conveyance of the properties that will enable the purchasers to reuse the properties in a timely fashion, consistent with the land bank's objectives.

Unless conflicts between short-term fiscal goals and long-term redevelopment goals are resolved at the outset, they can significantly undermine the land bank entity's effectiveness. Municipalities have a legitimate interest in obtaining short-term revenues, but that interest must be balanced against the need to promote long-term, sustainable redevelopment of urban property. The rules governing conveyance of property by the land bank must reflect this balancing process. *Those rules must be put in writing and formally adopted by the parties governing the land bank entity.*

C. Legal Power and Authority

Local government must have a legal basis for creating a land bank entity. Depending on the entity it wants to create, and the scope of responsibilities it wants to give that entity, that legal basis may come from one of three possible sources:

- The powers granted the municipality or county under general local government law
- Statutes permitting local governments to create public benefit corporations or authorities for various purposes
- Statutes specifically authorizing land bank entities

General Governmental Powers

Municipalities or counties in many states can create land bank entities within their existing governmental framework under general laws permitting them flexibility in organizing their governmental functions. Through the municipality's power to carry out internal reorganizations, the responsibilities governing acquisition, holding, and conveyance of property can be placed in a single administrative unit, such as a department of community development, or established as a separate line department of the city. The former path was taken by the city of Trenton, New Jersey, in the 1990s, when land banking functions were centralized in the Division of Real Estate of the Department of Housing and Development.[7]

---

7. This reorganization, although intended to create a land bank entity, took place through a number of steps over several years rather than as a single comprehensive reorganization, and the entity was never characterized as a land bank entity by city officials. In contrast to some land bank efforts that are clearly intended to be high-profile actions, the city chose to play down the extent to which this reorganization was leading to departures from previous practice.

Under this approach, the substance of the municipality's powers to deal with abandoned properties does not change. The change is in how those powers are exercised and how different elements of the land banking function are integrated with one another.

The effectiveness of this approach will vary from state to state. In many states, it may depend on whether the municipality is a home rule or charter municipality or whether certain powers—such as the ability to carry out tax foreclosures— may belong to designated officers under the state constitution or statute. Where responsibility for key elements of the process is divided by law between jurisdictions, an effective land bank entity may be difficult to create except through an interlocal agreement, as discussed below, that centralizes the relevant authority within one jurisdiction.

Statutes Permitting Local Governments to Create Public Benefit Corporations or Authorities

All states have laws permitting municipalities or counties to create different public benefit authorities for various purposes, such as redevelopment, housing, economic development, or parking. Some of these may have narrowly written powers and purposes; others may be broadly drawn. Some states provide cities with the power to create public benefit corporations to carry out various governmental functions or to delegate certain responsibilities of local government to those corporations. The utility of this approach will vary from state to state. Using such a statute may permit the city to create a land bank entity that can operate more independently than a line agency of municipal government and is more immune from political or bureaucratic pressure.

Statutes Specifically Authorizing Land Bank Entities

The most ambitious solution is to use an existing state statute or craft a new statute explicitly authorizing the creation of land bank entities and granting them appropriate legal powers. This is particularly important where no general statute provides clear legal authority for such an entity, or where the effectiveness of the land bank depends on an interlocal agreement between two or more jurisdictions.

Interlocal agreements are often critical to attempts to create a land bank entity to deal with tax foreclosed properties. Under the laws of many states, legal responsibility for different elements of the land bank process is divided between different jurisdictions, typically between a municipality and the county in which it is located. In others, such as Texas, the legal entitlement of multiple jurisdictions to property tax revenues, including the proceeds of tax foreclosures, requires their approval for any changes in the process and for the disposition of properties taken through the process.

In order for Houston to establish its Land Redevelopment Authority with the ability to dispose of properties taken through tax foreclosure, the city has had to

GOOD PRACTICES

The state of Texas permits cities to establish public nonprofit local government corporations for a variety of purposes. A housing finance corporation created under chapter 394 of the Texas Local Government Code could carry out the functions of a land bank entity *where the purpose of the land bank entity is to convey properties for reuse as affordable housing.*

While many state redevelopment statutes permit redevelopment agencies to operate only in areas that have been designated as redevelopment areas, the New Jersey Local Redevelopment and Housing Law (C.40A:12A-1 et seq.) permits an agency to operate in any area that has been designated "in need of rehabilitation," defined as an area in which

> (1) a significant portion of structures therein are in a deteriorated or substandard condition and there is a continuing pattern of vacancy, abandonment or underutilization of properties in the area, with a persistent arrearage of property tax payments thereon, or (2) more than half of the housing stock in the delineated area is at least 50 years old, or a majority of the water and sewer infrastructure in the delineated area is at least 50 years old and is in need of repair or substantial maintenance; and (3) a program of rehabilitation may be expected to prevent further deterioration and promote the overall development of the community.

This definition is likely to encompass any area in which a land bank entity would be active. A redevelopment agency can exercise any of its powers except for the power of eminent domain in "areas in need of rehabilitation." The broad powers of a redevelopment agency, coupled with the equally broad powers of the municipality to act in cooperation with the agency, appear to offer ample statutory basis for a municipality to use a redevelopment agency as a land bank authority.

execute interlocal agreements not only with the county and school district but also with a community college district and a hospital district. The Louisville–Jefferson County Land Bank Authority operates under an interlocal agreement between the city, Jefferson County, and the Jefferson County School District, to which the state of Kentucky is also a party. A well-drafted state land bank statute can provide clear parameters and statutory authority for the interlocal agreements needed to make the process work.

Local officials in states which lack explicit statutory authority for land bank authorities should consider seeking legislation, but only after addressing the question: *Can the municipality achieve its goals without new legislation, either by acting under its general governmental powers or by utilizing existing legislation not specific to land banking?*

The creative use of existing statutes should be investigated. Only if it is clear that there are areas, such as the ability to craft suitable interlocal agreements with other jurisdictions, which cannot be adequately addressed under existing law should new legislation be pursued.

If new legislation is needed, it may be possible to frame it as technical amendments to existing statutes, rather than legislation authorizing the creation of new entities. Skepticism about local government capacity and concerns over the proliferation of authorities and special districts may generate opposition to a bill authorizing municipalities to create land bank authorities, even from people who support the goals of the legislation. One approach would be to amend the state's redevelopment statute to enable redevelopment agencies to act as land bank entities. Amending the redevelopment statute might be easier than enacting a new law authorizing the creation of land bank authorities as such.

D. Governance and Staffing

Each community must determine how it wants the land bank entity to operate with respect to its governance and its staffing.

Governance

The fundamental choice is between a line entity in municipal government and an entity that is governed by a separate board of directors. In a line entity, the manager of the land bank reports to a senior municipal official, such as the director of community development, who reports in turn to the municipal chief executive.[8] Where a board of directors governs the entity, as with a land bank authority, the manager or director reports to the board, rather than to a line government official.

Placing the land bank within the line structure of city government should make it responsive to city policies and integrate it with other city operations. Where the land bank is part of a line department, however, it is likely that many of its actions—particularly property disposition—will require city council approval, raising potential political issues. Governance by a separate board of directors can insulate the land bank to some extent from such political pressures. Boards of directors vary widely in terms of their independence from municipal government, both in their membership and in the scope of their authority. While

---

8. In the Cleveland land bank program, the land bank manager reports to the director of the division of neighborhood development, who reports in turn to the director of the department of community development, who reports to the mayor.

some boards may be made up in whole or part of city or county officials, others include individuals outside government, although they generally owe their appointments to a city or county official. While the Fulton County/Atlanta land bank authority operates fairly independently, the Louisville–Jefferson County land bank authority is chaired by the director of the city's department of housing and acts in many respects as an arm of the department.

Staffing

Whether the land bank should have a separate, dedicated staff is both a practical and policy decision. If city departments have adequate competent personnel to carry out the operations of the land bank, there is a strong case to have them perform the work and not spend the extra money needed to hire dedicated employees. This view assumes, however, that the staff is committed to working together to carry out the mission of the land bank entity. If the staff is led by a strong leader within city government, who is herself committed to the land bank's mission, that is likely to be the case. Otherwise there is a serious risk that using city personnel rather than assembling a dedicated staff will compromise the land bank's mission. The situation may also change over time. If the land bank is dependent on city personnel, and therefore on the goodwill of the mayor or a senior member of her administration, policy or personnel changes in city government can disrupt long-term goals.

Scale is also a factor. City personnel may be able to handle the land bank's affairs as long as the volume of transactions is modest. As the land bank entity expands its operations, city staff may no longer be adequate to meet its needs, and it may have to hire dedicated staff to continue to operate effectively. Table 11.2 shows some examples of land bank governance and staffing.

Financial resources are critical. No matter where the staff is situated, if it is inadequate to carry out the land bank's mission, that mission will be compromised. Given the competition for limited general government revenues, a land bank program should be prepared to justify support by showing that its activities provide a significant return to the local treasury, either in the form of revenues from property sales or tax revenues generated from properties being placed back in productive use. At least some part of the revenues from land bank property sales should be retained by the land bank to cover its cost of operations.

Ultimately, governance and staffing should be driven by the organization's mission and the anticipated scope of its operations, with respect to both the volume of properties it expects to take and maintain and the question of whether it is designed to pursue a long-term strategy or simply act as a vehicle for the short-term transfer of property. The larger the scale of its operations, and the longer the time frame in which it will be acting, the more important becomes its need both for some degree of separation—if not outright independence—from the line functions of local government and for a dedicated staff of its own.

TABLE 11.2 Representative Land Bank Governance and Staffing

Land bank	Governance	Staffing
Fulton County/ City of Atlanta Land Bank Authority	Independent city/county authority. Four-member board, with two members appointed by city and two by county.	Land bank has own staff.
Cleveland land bank program	Land bank manager reports to director of neighborhood development division in department of community development.	Dedicated land bank staff within department of community development
Louisville–Jefferson County Land Bank Authority	Multiple-jurisdiction authority with four board members representing city, state, county, and school district, chaired by city's director of housing	Land bank staffed by city housing department
St. Louis Land Reutilization Authority	Subsidiary of St. Louis Development Corporation (SLDC), with three board members representing mayor, comptroller, and superintendent of schools	Utilizes staff of SLDC and city of St. Louis

CHAPTER 12

Getting Action on Privately Owned Properties

Acquiring properties costs the public sector money, takes them off the tax rolls, and often imposes maintenance burdens on public agencies poorly equipped for the role. While it is often necessary to take properties in order to restore them to productive use or eliminate blight, acquisition should be seen as a last resort. Alternatives that can bring results without government taking title to the property should almost always be encouraged.

Before a jurisdiction takes action against privately owned vacant properties, the purpose of the action must be clear. *Is action being taken to restore the property to productive use now, or to minimize the harm it is doing to its surroundings at present while deferring the question of reuse to the future?* This distinction is important, since localities have far stronger tools available to motivate property owners to minimize the harm caused by their properties than to compel them to restore their properties to productive use.

Two general approaches are possible when dealing with privately owned vacant properties. One is to motivate the property owner to take action; the other is for the public sector or a motivated third party to step in and take action short of taking title to the property. Powerful legal tools allow local government, CDCs, neighborhood organizations, or even concerned neighbors to take action when an owner has been given the opportunity to act and has failed—or refused—to do so. While these tools have traditionally been used to minimize harm, in recent years intervention strategies have emerged that focus on the rehabilitation and reuse of problem properties.

The effectiveness of these strategies is often closely tied to the strength of the real estate market in the community. The more valuable the property, the more likely that the owner will spend the money needed to maintain or even improve it. Similarly, the stronger the real estate market, the more likely that the city will be able to recover any costs incurred in taking action against privately owned properties.

A. Motivating Property Owners to Maintain or Improve Vacant Properties

Privately owned vacant properties blight thousands of inner-city communities, doing harm to their neighbors and impeding neighborhood revitalization efforts. Short of eminent domain, which may not be feasible, many of these properties are not readily available. Owners who believe that property values may be rising may pay the taxes on the properties to hold them for the future while ignoring the present harm they do. Tax sale certificates or liens held by faraway third parties may block action by the municipality and cloud the owner's title. Timely acquisition may be made infeasible by statutes that limit governmental action or impose extended delays. Under such circumstances, properties may sit for years before the municipality can take them, if ever. Without the ability to motivate private property owners to maintain or improve their properties, thousands of valuable properties will be lost and incalculable damage done to their neighbors' quality of life.

A strategy to motivate private property owners should incorporate three elements:

- Financial strategies, including penalties for owners who maintain abandoned properties and incentives for them to put the properties back into productive use

- Strategies that hold owners legally accountable for their property and its condition

- Information and technical assistance programs to help owners improve their properties

If owners are not held accountable for the condition of their properties, only the most conscientious may take the necessary steps to maintain and improve them. Many owners of abandoned properties, however, lack the skills or financial resources to deal with their responsibilities. Unless they are given assistance, or linked up with other entities with whom they can partner, they may be unable to move forward on their own.

Ultimately, however, owners will be most influenced by their assessment of the economic consequences of their behavior. If an owner sees her property as having little value, and if the city's ability to penalize her is limited, she is more likely to walk away from the property than to improve it or abate the nuisance that it has become. Although in areas with rising property values efforts to motivate owners are most effective, legal tools that enable local government to intervene directly, and if necessary, take title to the property, may still be needed.

Financial Penalties and Incentives

Vacant properties typically yield little in property taxes and impose disproportionate burdens on local government for public services, including police and fire calls. By lowering the property values of occupied buildings around them, they reduce the tax revenues available to the city from those properties. This situation provides strong grounds for arguing that a financial charge explicitly tied to the ownership of vacant property does not violate any fundamental constitutional or legal principles, as long as it falls within municipal powers as established by state law. There are a variety of ways in which local governments can establish such a charge.

Washington, DC, imposes a higher tax rate on vacant properties: $5 per $100 in assessed valuation, compared to $1.85 per $100 for other properties.

1. *Differential property tax rates.* Many states permit municipalities to impose different tax rates or assessment ratios on different categories of property.[1] In such cases, a municipality may be able to impose higher taxes on vacant properties, including vacant land and buildings. While Washington, DC, can establish its own rules for property taxation (see box), other cities must follow tightly written state rules. As a result, few cities can set a higher tax rate for vacant properties unless state law or regulations already explicitly permit it.

A well-known variation on this principle is the procedure, associated with the late nineteenth-century economist Henry George, of taxing land and improvements at different rates.[2] Taxing the land at a substantially higher rate than the improvements creates an incentive for putting the land to more productive use, since the taxes on the property as a whole will not increase in proportion to the added value. Differential taxation along these lines is used most notably in Pennsylvania.

2. *Fees.* Requiring owners of vacant property to pay a fee, tied to registering the property, both increases the property owner's accountability and imposes a cost on the continued ownership of vacant property. A fee has certain clear advantages over a differential property tax rate. It can be more precisely targeted, and it can be more easily waived at the city's discretion as an incentive for the owner to rehabilitate the property. In many states, municipalities have more leeway to impose fees than they have to tinker with the administration of the property tax. Furthermore, should a municipality need enabling legislation, statutory authority to levy a tightly defined fee is likely to be far easier to obtain than a major change to the state's property tax statutes.

Any municipality contemplating enacting a registration fee on the ownership of vacant or abandoned property must enact or adopt a clear definition of what properties are considered vacant for purposes of the fee and have in place a property information system capable of tracking which properties in the city meet the definition and are subject to the fee. If the city cannot reliably identify which

1. The amount of property tax due from any particular property is a function of two factors: the tax rate, meaning the percentage of assessed value that must be paid; and the assessment ratio, which is the ratio of assessed value to market value. Either can be adjusted.

2. The property tax is generally the sum of the separate taxes on the value of the land and on the value of the improvements (the buildings) on the land. In most cases, the value of the improvements is considerably more than that of the land. Henry George, it should be noted, believed that the improvements should not be taxed at all.

Wilmington, Delaware, has enacted an ordinance establishing a graduated annual registration fee for vacant properties, which increases with each year that the property remains vacant, as follows:

- $500 for properties declared vacant for one year

- $1,000 if a property is vacant more than one year but less than three years

- $2,000 if a property is vacant three years or more but less than five years

- $3,500 if a property is vacant five years or more but less than ten years

- $5,000 if the property has been vacant ten years or more, plus an additional $500 for each year in excess of ten years

If the fee is not paid, the city may place a lien against the property, which could ultimately result in the foreclosure of the property. The ordinance also gives the city the authority to grant a one-time, one-year waiver to allow the owner time to rehabilitate or sell the property.

properties are subject to the ordinance, not only will the ordinance be ineffective, but it might also be subject to legal challenge. As in Wilmington, fees unpaid by a specified date should become a municipal lien against the property subject to potential foreclosure.

3. *Liens.* Many municipalities place liens on properties when they act to abate a nuisance, as when they board a property. Municipalities should consider expanding this practice to include placing liens on abandoned properties if other municipal resources are being spent to protect neighbors, including fire or police calls and building inspections, if permitted under state law. Other issues dealing with state law and local government policy regarding municipal liens are discussed later in this chapter.

4. *Financial incentives.* Financial measures directed at the owners of abandoned property should not be punitive but should motivate the owners to improve the properties. For that reason, it is desirable to offer incentives along with financial penalties. Possible types of financial incentives fall into three categories:

- Direct financial assistance, through provision of grants or below-market loans

Albany, New York, offers up to $15,000 per building to owners of buildings in immediate need of repair to stabilize them for subsequent rehabilitation. The assistance comes in the form of a loan, but if the owner rehabilitates the property within eighteen months after receipt of the assistance, the loan is forgiven.

- Tax abatement
- Waiver or forgiveness of liens

It is harder to frame effective incentives for abandoned than for occupied buildings. Since the owner is receiving no income from the property, no cash flow is available to offset the cost of improvements. The cost of placing a vacant building back into productive use is often substantially greater than the cost of upgrading an occupied building. Finally, while occupied buildings should generally be preserved, that is not necessarily the case with abandoned buildings, particularly if their preservation will require substantial public funds.

With hundreds or even thousands of abandoned buildings sitting empty, most cities lack the resources to offer substantial incentives to more than a handful of property owners. It is, therefore, important to distinguish between incentives that can be offered with minimal impact on the city's finances, such as the waiver of tax or other liens that represent at most a hypothetical future revenue source, and capital grants for stabilization or rehabilitation, which require devoting limited cash resources to this use. The program in Albany, New York (see box above), offers a more substantial incentive, but because of limited funds it can be offered only to a handful of property owners each year. Programs that offer only a waiver of liens tend to reward the worst offenders, who have accumulated the largest amount of liens; moreover, for most owners, the size of such an incentive is modest. *The more aggressive the municipality is in putting liens on properties, however, the more leverage it has to use lien forgiveness as an incentive.*

Incentives should never be offered for activities that are part of the fundamental responsibilities of property ownership, including securing the property, keeping the property clean, and even demolishing it if it becomes a hazard to its neighbors. They should be used solely to motivate owners to go beyond their legal responsibilities and restore properties to productive use. Incentives should be calibrated to the market realities of the abandoned properties that a city wants to see rehabilitated. If the value of a restored property will be substantially more than the cost of rehabilitation, it is hard to justify offering financial incentives.

If large numbers of seemingly suitable buildings are sitting empty in a community where restored properties have substantial market value, it is likely that issues other than financial feasibility are involved. Those issues must be identified, and other strategies devised to address them. Conversely, if the market gap between the cost of rehabilitation and the subsequent value of the property is large, incentives may have to be substantial to be effective.

Holding Owners Accountable

Any strategy for motivating the owners of abandoned properties to maintain or improve them should begin with adopting absolutely clear standards of responsibility for property owners.

1. *Framing a vacant property owner accountability ordinance.* The core element of the strategy should be a vacant property owner accountability ordinance, which clearly establishes

- a clear definition of which properties are subject to the ordinance, perhaps following the New Jersey standard (see page 3);
- the obligations of owners of abandoned properties with respect to their properties;
- the time frames in which work must take place once the owner has been placed on notice in order to avoid penalties or municipal intervention;
- the outcome of the owner's failure to take action in a timely fashion;
- provisions for registration or licensing of the owners of vacant properties;
- any other reasonable provisions that the municipality may consider appropriate or necessary.

The ordinance should specify what the owner must do with respect to maintaining both the building and its grounds, and what standards of maintenance or workmanship must be followed.[3] It should specify what actions the municipality may take if the owner fails to act, and the consequences of those actions in terms of penalties, the possibility of court proceedings, where applicable, and the potential consequences of those proceedings. The ordinance should provide for civil or criminal penalties as determined by the municipal prosecutor.

Registration or licensing requirements are a particularly valuable starting point for making property owners understand that they are accountable for their properties, as well as a way of imposing a threshold financial cost on the ownership of vacant property. The registration should provide the city with contact information for the owner, or, if the owner lives a substantial distance from the community, for a local authorized agent. The ordinance should require annual

---

3. See chapter 13 for further discussion of boarding vacant buildings.

GOOD PRACTICE

The city of Chicago requires all owners of vacant buildings to register the building with the city within thirty days of the vacancy and amend the filing within twenty days of any change in the registration information. The owner must also provide the name of an authorized agent with an office or residence in Cook County, Illinois, for receipt of notices of code violations. The city can impose a fine of up to $500 per day for failure to register. (Title 13, chapter 12 of the Municipal Code, available online at www. cityofchicago.org/buildings/BuildingCode/VacantBuildingOrdinance.html)

registration renewal and timely notice to the municipality of changes in any relevant information. A registration fee should be set, and, if permitted by state law, unpaid fees should become liens against the property.

A number of municipalities have imposed additional requirements on the owners of vacant properties in response to local concerns. Chicago requires owners to carry liability insurance (see box below); other requirements may include provisions for security in buildings that are particularly vulnerable to vandalism, squatting, or illegal activity; requiring owners to provide information directly to neighborhood associations; and posting the name and contact information of the owner or authorized agent on the building.

2. Requiring affirmative steps. A number of municipalities have gone further and moved toward what can be called "affirmative accountability" for property owners. Under such measures, the owner must commit to take action by a date certain to rehabilitate or demolish the property. Failure can result in the municipality's imposing sanctions on the owner. Minneapolis's Chapter 249 list makes

GOOD PRACTICES

The city of Chicago requires the owners of vacant properties to maintain liability insurance coverage of at least $300,000 for residential properties and $1 million for commercial properties. The policy must contain provisions for notice to the commissioner of buildings if the policy lapses or is canceled.

A number of cities, including Dayton, Ohio, and Peoria, Illinois, post the name and contact information for the owner of a vacant building on the building. "We're basically calling it shaming," said the director of Dayton's building services department.

clear that the municipality does not consider it acceptable for vacant, boarded properties to remain in that condition indefinitely, even if they meet minimum standards of maintenance.

An alternative approach is to establish a regular cycle of vacant building inspections, with sanctions for violations of the municipal code. By making the inspection cycle predictable, this procedure has an effect similar to setting deadlines for action. Programs requiring affirmative steps by the owner should be linked to financial incentives and other support for the owner's efforts to improve the property, as in San Diego (see accompanying box).

3. *Assisting property owners.* Financial impositions and incentives, and ordinances establishing responsibilities and sanctions for nonperformance, will motivate many property owners but will have far less impact on those who lack the skills or information to deal responsibly with their properties. Many property owners have little idea how to go about rehabilitating a building, how to finance the rehabilitation, or how to find a reliable architect or contractor. Such owners need technical assistance in order to take advantage of any incentives that the city may offer.

Technical assistance, however, is often not enough. It will not turn a dentist or factory worker into a competent real estate developer or spur a distant or uninterested owner to respond. Where a city has community-based developers or CDCs with both the skills and the desire to do scattered-site rehabilitation, matching willing but unable property owners with CDCs to rehabilitate the owners' properties can be an effective option.

In the end, however, tools are still needed to permit the municipality, as well as other capable parties, to intervene to abate nuisance conditions and save properties that would otherwise be lost.

B. Nuisance Abatement: Intervention to Minimize the Harm from Vacant Properties

Nuisance Abatement by Local Government

Nuisance abatement is the principal way for municipalities to deal with the harms caused by abandoned property. Where nuisance conditions exist, state laws permit local governments to enter the property and take action to abate, or correct, the condition creating the nuisance. Such laws allow government to address conditions affecting the health, safety, and property values of nearby residents and property owners, ranging from mowing a lawn or removing trash from a front yard to carrying out structural repairs or demolishing a building. In most cases, the municipality can place a lien on the property for the cost of abating the nuisance. Such interventions are not only important in themselves but may motivate a property owner to take better care of her property to avoid having the municipality step in.

Municipal nuisance abatement programs are generally governed by state law, which determines under what circumstances a municipality can intervene, the pro-

In the city of Minneapolis, any vacant building can be boarded for no more than sixty days without penalty. Thereafter, unless the owner has removed the boards or taken out a permit to rehabilitate the building, the building may be placed on the city's Chapter 249 list. Putting a building on the list permits the municipality to demolish the building as a nuisance. It also requires the owner to obtain a code compliance inspection before beginning rehabilitation or selling the property, and to post a $2,000 deposit before taking out any building permits. The deposit is forfeited if the building is not rehabilitated within six months, a period which can be extended at the city's discretion to nine months.

In the 1990s, the city of Portland, Oregon, began conducting quarterly inspections of vacant properties, with fines of $50 to $100 assessed monthly as long as code violations remained outstanding. Portland's code treats any building that is vacant and boarded (by any entity) as out of compliance and subject to penalties.

The city of San Diego, California, requires the owners of vacant, boarded buildings to submit a statement of intent to bring the property into productive use. The statement must include the following:

- Expected period of vacancy
- A maintenance plan during vacancy
- A plan and time line for the lawful occupancy, rehabilitation, or demolition of the building

If the owner fails to make a diligent effort to implement the statement of intent, the city may impose a penalty of $250 for every ninety days the structure remains vacant.

The city actively assists property owners in dealing with their buildings, providing a matching grant program in certain neighborhoods, real estate and contractor guidance, and referrals to financial resources and nonprofit organizations and CDCs that can partner with property owners to rehabilitate the property. The program is managed by a full-time vacant properties coordinator in the Department of Neighborhood Code Compliance.

cedures it must follow, and the sanctions that can be imposed on property owners whose inaction has forced the city to act. Some state laws, however, may make things difficult for local officials, either because they do not clearly define what constitutes a nuisance or because they impose overly burdensome procedures on a municipality seeking to address a problem. State nuisance abatement law should

TABLE 12.1 Provisions of Model State Nuisance Abatement Enabling Statute

Section	Subject	Key features
1	Legislative findings	Clearly sets forth the harm that vacant or abandoned properties cause to health, safety, and property values of residents and owners, and the importance of providing a clear, expeditious means by which local government can address those harms
		Clearly recognizes that nuisance abatement is a strategy to address only short-term harms and that it should be seen as part of a larger strategy to address the problem of vacant and abandoned properties
2	Definitions	Provides a comprehensive, clearly written definition of what conditions constitute nuisance conditions
3	Legal authority	Provides clear legal authority to local government to act to abate nuisance conditions
		Provides similar authority to all appropriate local government entities (i.e., not only home rule or charter cities)
4	Standards	Gives local government the authority to set standards to govern owners' actions to maintain vacant properties and abate nuisance conditions
5	Process	Provides expeditious process for action, including notice to owner; time for owner to act; and ability of local government to act if owner fails to act
		Permits action to be triggered by local government on its own motion or by petition from neighbors or neighborhood association
		Requires timely local government response to petitions
6	Emergency process	Permits local government to carry out summary abatement actions where the condition poses an imminent threat to health and safety
7	Scope of actions permitted	Provides clear authority for local government to take a wide range of actions, including cleaning, boarding, demolition, and stabilization or repair, with the nature of the action taken to be at the discretion of the responsible local official
8	Liens	Authorizes responsible local official to place a lien on any property that is subject to a nuisance abatement action
		The amount of the lien includes all costs incurred by the municipality, including such items as municipal inspections and attorneys' fees

continued

TABLE 12.1 Provisions of Model State Nuisance Abatement Enabling Statute, *continued*

Section	Subject	Key features
		Provides that lien can be added to taxes due or separately foreclosed within sixty days after lien is recorded
		Gives local government recourse to other assets of owner for payment of municipal costs incurred
9	Sanctions	Provides that owner is subject to fine for allowing nuisance condition to come into being
		Provides for partial abatement of fine if owner corrects condition
		Allows fine to be added to lien on property

provide a clear definition of a nuisance that can easily be understood by property owners, neighbors, and public officials. The law should give local government broad authority to act to abate nuisances and provide an expeditious procedure, consistent with due process standards, for action. It should provide a clear procedure for local government to collect funds expended on nuisance abatement from the owner, whether through liens on the property or direct recourse against the owner.

Table 12.1 provides an outline of a model state nuisance abatement enabling statute.

Responsiveness to neighborhood concerns is a critical part of nuisance abatement. Nuisances are by their nature both visible and of urgent concern to neighboring residents and property owners. Residents not only want to see action but, in the interim, want to know that progress is being made. This is particularly important when abatement involves demolition or substantial repair, because there is often a delay between the decision to act and the beginning of work. Information technology not only can be used internally by managers to track progress toward resolving nuisance complaints but should also be used to provide citizens with up-to-date information on the status of complaints filed with the city.

Placing liens on properties that are the subject of nuisance abatement actions, enforcing them through foreclosure action, and prosecuting serious offenders are critical elements of a nuisance abatement strategy. Property owners should face consequences for their inaction on matters affecting the health and safety of their buildings' neighbors. Without effective enforcement, many property owners, particularly those who see little value in their properties, may come to see local government action as a convenience, sparing them the trouble of finding a contractor or a handyman. Key provisions of lien enforcement are the following:

GOOD PRACTICE

Under the Super Neighborhoods program in Houston, Texas, each designated neighborhood council can submit action requests to city departments, including requests for nuisance abatement, as well as other neighborhood improvements such as, park improvements or street widening. Each request is entered into the Super Neighborhoods database (SNAP), which provides for online tracking of the action request, including the following information:

- Location
- Nature of action requested
- Department to which request is made
- Result of department review of action request
- Status and comments
- Estimated start date for action
- Actual start date for action

The public can access the SNAP response tracking system from the web page www.houstontx.gov/planning/supernbhds/sn_links.htm by clicking on "SNAP response tracking."

- A lien should be placed on a property immediately after the action triggering the lien takes place.

- Detailed records of municipal expenditures in connection with each action, including time records, should be maintained to ensure that the lien includes all costs to which the municipality is entitled and can be defended if challenged by the owner.

- Where lien foreclosure separate from tax foreclosure is likely to lead to speedier results, abatement liens should be the subject of separate foreclosure proceedings. This approach is particularly important in cases where the lien is enforceable by the city but tax foreclosure is a county proceeding.

- Where permitted by law, the municipality should selectively bring legal actions to recover its costs against other assets of the property owner through in personam proceedings.[4]

---

4. Such proceedings are more complicated than in rem proceedings against a building. This strategy should therefore be used only in cases that have a strong likelihood of success and in which the

The residents of Baltimore's Butcher's Hill neighborhood were faced with the problem of a vacant house that had become a base of operations for drug dealers. Faced with the city's inability to respond effectively, the residents notified the owner that they would board the property if he did not do so within two weeks. When no action was taken, they boarded the property, using construction techniques specifically designed to keep the building secure, and then successfully took the owner to court to recover their costs (which totaled $340.15).

Finally, an aggressive strategy of placing liens against properties can also be used as a financial tool to encourage future positive action by property owners, by putting the city in a position to offer the waiver or suspension of all or part of the lien if the owner agrees to restore the property to productive use.

Self-Help Nuisance Abatement

If the neighbors of a nuisance property find that recourse to local government does not result in timely or effective relief, an alternative route is available through the common law remedy of self-help nuisance abatement. Under common law principles, neighbors whose health, safety, or quality of life is affected by a nuisance have the right, after notice to the owner, to enter the property and remedy the nuisance themselves. The neighbors can then file a civil action to have the owner of the nuisance property reimburse them for their money and time.[5]

It is always preferable to try to get local government to act to enforce codes. Self-help nuisance abatement, however, is an option if local government, by virtue of financial or managerial constraints, is unable to act in a timely fashion or to take the action appropriate to the circumstances.[6]

Self-help nuisance abatement must be approached carefully. Every step of the proceeding must be carefully documented. Even then, there is the risk that a

costs justify the action, such as the demolition of a substantial commercial property. A few successful proceedings of this kind, especially if well publicized, may significantly influence the behavior of other property owners.

5. See Erin Artigiani, *Revitalizing Baltimore's Neighborhoods: The Community Association's Guide to Civil Legal Remedies* (Baltimore, MD: Community Law Center, 1996).

6. In the Baltimore case (see box above), both circumstances applied. The city indicated that it might be four to six months before they could board the property; moreover, experience had shown that when the city boarded a property, it often did so in an inexpensive, corner-cutting fashion that provided no real barrier to forced entry.

vindictive owner will file a counterclaim against the neighbors for trespass or damage to the property, which can be bothersome even if ultimately dismissed. Some state courts may be less hospitable to self-help nuisance abatement than the Maryland courts were in the Butcher's Hill case. Moreover, since the action must be brought by the neighbors themselves and cannot be delegated to a community association or CDC acting on their behalf, it is inherently a limited remedy.

Self-help nuisance abatement can be a powerful tool, however, for calling attention to the abandoned property problem in a neighborhood. Used judiciously, it can help motivate other property owners in the area to act more responsibly and put pressure on local government to abate nuisance conditions in its jurisdiction. It can also empower the residents of a community to work together to address a common concern and thus is a potentially valuable element in a community organizing strategy.

How Far Can Nuisance Abatement Go?

Nuisance abatement remedies are generally held to extend only to abating the nuisance that is the basis for the complaint or code violation. Their purpose is to ameliorate a specific condition, such as accumulation of construction debris in a vacant lot, or drug dealers' use of a vacant building. In some cases, by addressing the short-term problem, they can be counterproductive in the long run, as when a building is demolished to abate a nuisance even though the building's rehabilitation might have contributed more to the long-term improvement of the neighborhood.

The extent to which nuisance abatement, or more generally, the municipal police power, can be used to compel an owner to restore a property to productive use is a difficult question. While a municipality can use its ordinances and incentives to try to induce owners to rehabilitate their properties, nuisance ordinances are widely held to stop short of the power to compel them to do so if there is a less expensive way to remove the nuisance. Since its purpose is to remove the nuisance, the law will generally permit the owner to remove the nuisance in the way she considers least burdensome. For that reason, ordinances such as those in San Diego or Minneapolis, while encouraging rehabilitation, ultimately give the owner a choice between rehabilitation and demolition.

In some circumstances a municipality may have the authority to compel an owner to rehabilitate the property rather than give her the unfettered choice to demolish or restore. One such circumstance is where the property has been designated a historic property or a key or contributing building in a historic district. The police power has been further extended in this direction by a recent North Carolina statute enacted specifically for the city of Greenville, which provides that "if the repair, alteration or improvement of the dwelling can be made at a reasonable cost in relation to the value of the dwelling (the ordinance of the city may fix a certain percentage of this value as being reasonable), [the public officer may serve an order] requiring the owner . . . to repair, alter or improve the dwelling in order to render it fit for human habitation."[7]

In other words, even if the rehabilitation may cost more than the demolition, as long it bears a reasonable relationship to the value of the property, the municipality may order the building rehabilitated rather than demolished. If the owner fails to comply with such an order, the municipality may step in and have the building rehabilitated.

In situations where the owner has failed to act, and explicit legal language provides no guidance, two key questions arise:

- Can the municipality take any action it deems to be in the public interest, including rehabilitation at whatever cost, or is it limited either to the most cost-effective action capable of abating the nuisance or to a cost/value calculus similar to that in the North Carolina statute?[8]

- Assuming the municipality has the power to go beyond the most cost-effective action and take more expensive actions that it deems necessary to further the public interest, can it pass the full additional cost on to the owner, as is generally permitted with respect to the costs of nuisance abatement?

The issue remains a gray area, one of balancing the historical, architectural, or other nonmonetary value of the building with the cost of rehabilitation and the resulting value of the property. While many properties might satisfy such a balancing test, under which an order to rehabilitate the property would be found legally acceptable, where state law, however, adequately provides for vacant property receivership, which is explicitly designed to address this issue, receivership is likely to be more appropriate.

C. Possession and Receivership: Intervention to Restore Privately Owned Vacant Properties to Productive Use

Many abandoned buildings should be preserved. They may be of intrinsic architectural or historical value or may simply contribute to the fabric of the block or the neighborhood. They may represent opportunities for valuable reuse options that cannot be replicated with new construction on a vacant site. *Vacant property receivership,* or possession, is intended to address this issue.[9]

---

7. North Carolina Session Law 2003-76, amending G.S. §160A-443.

8. The question of what truly abates the nuisance is not always a simple one. Demolition removes the building that was found to be a nuisance but leaves in its place a vacant lot, which can easily become a nuisance in turn. It can reasonably be argued that the only certain way of ensuring the abatement of the nuisance is to restore the building to productive use through rehabilitation.

9. Some state statutes, including Illinois and New Jersey, refer to this procedure as possession, presumably to differentiate it from rental receivership. The term is misleading, however, and risks being confused with taking or eminent domain.

GOOD PRACTICE

Baltimore uses vacant property receivership extensively. Under the city's ordinance, the city has designated community associations to bring receivership actions and act as receivers and has worked with the Community Law Center to create Save a Neighborhood, Inc., a nonprofit entity that works with neighborhood-based organizations to use receivership as a tool for neighborhood revitalization. A unique and highly effective provision of the Baltimore ordinance permits a receiver to sell the property *before* rehabilitation to a buyer with "the ability and experience needed to rehabilitate the property within a reasonable time." This provision makes it significantly easier for the buyer to borrow funds in order to rehabilitate the property. Under this provision, many properties have been conveyed to CDCs for rehabilitation.

Vacant property receivership has been used strategically in a number of Baltimore neighborhoods, including Patterson Park. Not only has it placed many properties into the hands of qualified entities but, in roughly half the cases brought, it has motivated property owners to take action to restore their properties rather than allow them to go into receivership.

Vacant property receivership applies the principle of receivership to vacant properties. Where permitted by law, entities may seek a court order requiring that a particular vacant property be rehabilitated. If the court finds the petition to have merit, the court may first give the owner, and in some cases lienholders, the opportunity to rehabilitate the property. If the owner or lienholder fails to do so, or fails to submit a credible plan to do so, the court may award possession of the property to the entity bringing the petition, or another qualified entity, for the purpose of rehabilitating the property and placing it back into productive use. Subsequently, the owner may regain control of the property by making the receiver whole or meeting other conditions set by the court. If the owner fails to regain control within some period, the receiver can either obtain title from the court or seek approval for a judicial sale of the property.

Vacant property receivership is not a simple process, since it significantly affects the owner's property rights.[10] To protect these rights,

- the owner must be given timely notice of the proceedings;

10. The legal interests of lienholders, in cases where the lien arises from a legitimate arm's-length transaction, should also be protected. A conservative approach should offer lienholders the same rights as the owner to take action, except when they have a substantial identity of interest with the owner.

- the owner must be given the opportunity to block receivership by committing firmly to rehabilitate the property;

- if a receivership order is entered, the owner must be given a reasonable opportunity at some point to regain control of the property.

The process by which vacant property receivership operates under the New Jersey statute is shown in figure 12.1.

The similar Missouri and Illinois statutes grant the power to bring a receivership action exclusively to nonprofit housing corporations or CDCs. The Baltimore ordinance and New Jersey statute treat the receivership power as an extension of the municipal police power. Under those laws, the power to bring a receivership action belongs to local government, which, however, can delegate that power to qualified entities. The New Jersey statute defines such an entity as follows:

> "Qualified rehabilitation entity" means an entity organized or authorized to do business under the New Jersey statutes which shall have as one of its purposes the construction or rehabilitation of residential or non-residential buildings, the provision of affordable housing, the restoration of abandoned property, the revitalization and improvement of urban neighborhoods, or similar purpose, and which shall be well qualified, by virtue of its staff, professional consultants, financial resources, and prior activities to carry out the rehabilitation of vacant buildings in urban areas. (N.J.S.A. 55:19-80)

Even though the power to pursue vacant property receivership may derive from municipal police power, most local governments are reluctant to use those powers. Few cities are equipped to engage in the extended process of rehabilitating abandoned property. The entities most likely to pursue vacant property receivership are nonprofit community-based developers. Ideally, the statute should permit such entities direct access to the courts. Failing that, as in New Jersey and Baltimore, language permitting local government to delegate its authority to qualified nongovernmental entities is essential.

Elements of a Vacant Property Receivership Statute

Vacant property receivership can be pursued only under explicit legislative authority or where an existing receivership statute can be construed to permit receivership of vacant as well as occupied properties. As of the beginning of 2005, at least three states and one city, using its broad home rule powers, had enacted legislation specifically focusing on vacant property receivership: Illinois, Missouri, New Jersey, and the city of Baltimore. A number of other receivership statutes apply to both occupied and vacant property, including those of Indiana and Ohio. In Massachusetts, the state attorney general's office has ruled that the state's receivership law can be used to deal with vacant properties.

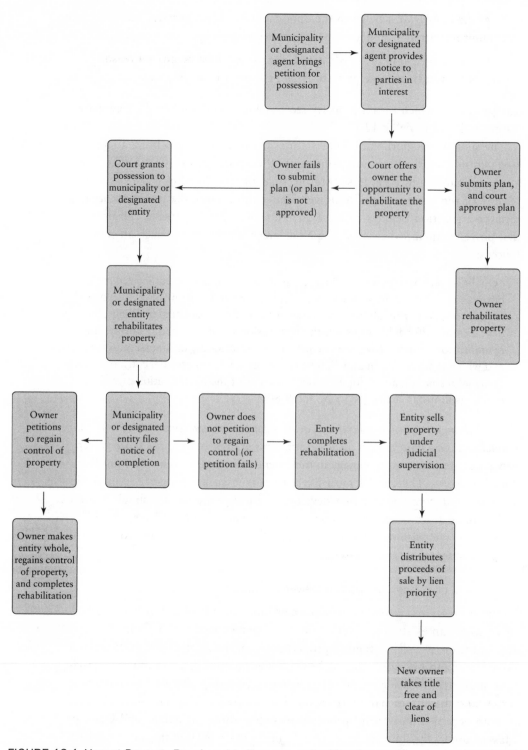

FIGURE 12.1 Vacant Property Receivership Process under New Jersey Abandoned Properties
Rehabilitation Law

The first step for any entity seeking to pursue vacant property receivership is to establish that it has the clear legal authority to do so under state law, either by using an existing statute or by enacting a new vacant property receivership law.[11] If the opportunity exists to draft a new statute, it should include the following provisions:

- A clear definition of which properties are subject to vacant property receivership. The definition must *not* set tax delinquency as a threshold for applying the law, as it is those properties whose owners are paying taxes while allowing the property to deteriorate that are most suitable for receivership.

- Direct access to the courts for nonprofit, community-based developers to utilize this remedy; alternatively, a straightforward process by which the municipality can delegate its authority to qualified nongovernmental entities

- Language protecting the interests of owners and lienholders while ensuring that those protections do not undermine the fundamental purpose of the legislation, which is to ensure that properties are rehabilitated and returned to productive use in a timely fashion

- Provisions governing the process by which the owner can regain control of the property to ensure not only that the receiver is made whole but also that the purpose of the receivership is achieved in full

- Authority for the receiver to take all steps necessary for the rehabilitation of the property, including legally standing in the owner's shoes for purposes of obtaining approvals and permits, and the ability to borrow funds for the purpose of rehabilitating the property, with lien priority given to funds borrowed for rehabilitation

- Language permitting the property to be reused for the most appropriate purpose, rather than being arbitrarily limited to specific reuses

- Authority for the receiver to sell the property, either before or after rehabilitation, through a judicial procedure that ensures that the purchaser of the property, which may be the receiver itself, gains clear title, free of liens and encumbrances

The key provisions of the four statutes or ordinances noted above are summarized in table 12.2. The New Jersey statute comes closest to serving as a model for advocates in other states to follow.

---

11. Few municipalities, even home rule cities, are likely to have independent authority similar to Baltimore's to enact such ordinances. An attempt by St. Louis to enact such an ordinance was overturned by the Missouri courts as exceeding municipal authority in 1967.

TABLE 12.2 Provisions of Vacant Property Receivership or Possession Statutes in Four States

Category	Baltimore	Illinois	Missouri	New Jersey
Statute or ordinance citation	Sec. 121 Baltimore City Revised Code: Vacant Building Receiver	310 LICS 50/ Abandoned Housing Rehabilitation Act	MRS Sec. 447.620 et seq.	N.J.S.A. 55:19-84 through 99
Which buildings are subject to provisions of the law?	Any vacant building, as defined in Sec. 115.4 of the Code, whose owner has failed to comply with an order to rehabilitate	Building must be a nuisance, vacant for at least one year, and tax delinquent for at least two years.	Building must be a nuisance, vacant for at least one month, and tax delinquent (no time period specified).	Building must be abandoned as defined in statute (i.e., it must have been vacant six months and meet one other statutory test). The court must find that the building should be rehabilitated rather than demolished.
Who can petition for receivership?	City building official or building official's agent (agent can be nonprofit entity)	Nonprofit organization whose purpose includes the improvement of housing	Nonprofit organization whose purpose includes provision or enhancement of housing opportunities	Municipal public officer or "qualified rehabilitation entity" acting as agent of municipality
Are owners or lien-holders given opportunity to rehabilitate the property?	Court may appoint owner or lienholder to rehabilitate property instead of appointing receiver.	If owner files a plan for the rehabilitation of the property, court shall give owner ninety days to rehabilitate property.	Burden is on owner to show that plaintiff should not be allowed to rehabilitate the property.	Owner can submit plan to rehabilitate property, which court can approve if it finds the plan to be "realistic and expeditious." If owner fails to submit plan, lienholders are given the opportunity.

Who can act as receiver?	At discretion of court	Entity bringing the petition	Entity bringing the petition	Municipality or qualified rehabilitation entity
Can receiver borrow for rehabilitation?	Yes	Not specified	Not specified	Yes
Does receiver's lien have priority status?	Yes, automatically	NA	NA	Yes, with court approval
What other powers does receiver have?	Receiver can manage the property for two years after rehabilitation. Receiver can foreclose on receiver's lien.	Receiver may enter into leases and other agreements in relation to the property.	Receiver may enter into leases and other agreements in relation to the property.	Receiver is deemed to have ownership interest for purposes of filing permit applications and receiving state grants or loans.
How can owner regain control of property?	Owner may file motion to dismiss receiver on payment of receiver's costs, fees, and expenses, but only after rehabilitation has been completed.	Owner can petition for restoration. Owner must pay receiver compensation as determined by the court and abide by all existing rental agreements entered into by receiver.	Owner can petition for restoration. Owner must pay receiver compensation as determined by the court and abide by all existing rental agreements entered into by receiver.	Owner can petition for restoration within thirty days after receiver has filed a notice of completion with court. Owner must complete rehabilitation, if applicable; pay all costs of municipality and receiver; and abide by all agreements entered into by receiver. Court may require owner to post bond against future code violations.

continued

TABLE 12.2 Provisions of Vacant Property Receivership or Possession Statutes in Four States, *continued*

Category	Baltimore	Illinois	Missouri	New Jersey
Under what conditions can receiver sell or gain title to the property?	If owner does not regain control, receiver can sell property at auction, or privately if owner and mortgagee consent. Receiver can sell property prior to rehabilitation to third party with "ability and experience needed to rehabilitate the property within a reasonable time."	If owner does not regain control within two years, a judicial quitclaim deed is granted to the receiver, subject to a requirement that the property be used for low- and moderate-income housing for at least ten years.	If owner does not regain control within one year, a judicial quitclaim deed is granted to the receiver. The conveyance extinguishes all interests and liens in the property except tax liens.	If owner does not petition within thirty days after notice of completion is filed, or two years after the initial order, receiver can seek court approval to sell the property or vest title in receiver. After distribution of proceeds of sale, all liens are extinguished.
What limitations are there on reuse of the property after rehabilitation?	Not specified	Property must be used for housing for low- and moderate-income households.	Not specified, but reuse as housing is implied	Any reuse that is "appropriate and beneficial." Reuse must be consistent with applicable redevelopment or neighborhood revitalization plans.

Implementing a Vacant Property Receivership Program

Any entity seeking to pursue vacant property receivership must have adequate resources in two critical areas:

- The legal resources to bring receivership petitions and defend them if they are contested by property owners or lienholders
- The technical and financial resources to successfully rehabilitate the buildings that become subject to receivership orders

The legal fees of a contested proceeding, along with costs such as title searches and notices, can be substantial. Similarly, no one should even contemplate bringing a receivership petition unless they are confident that they will be able to rehabilitate the property and ensure that it will be appropriately used after rehabilitation. To the extent that borrowing is necessary and justified by the economics of the project, the entity contemplating the receivership should identify potential lenders in advance.

Because of the resource demands of vacant property receivership, it may be more productive and cost-effective to use this tool strategically, by dealing with multiple properties in one neighborhood, as was done in Baltimore's Patterson Park, rather than with scattered individual buildings. In addition to meeting its specific goals, a strategic approach is more likely to prompt the owners of buildings in the targeted area to improve them rather than risk their going into receivership. Roughly half of the properties in Patterson Park for which receivership was sought were improved by their owners and never actually went into receivership.

The success of the Baltimore vacant property receivership program also reflects the effectiveness of an ongoing three-legged working relationship:

- The city of Baltimore, which has the legal power to bring receivership actions and create the legal basis for the receivership through code enforcement
- Save a Neighborhood, Inc., and the Community Law Center, which provided the legal resources to bring receivership actions and act as receivers on behalf of community associations
- Capable community development corporations, which rehabilitated the properties going into receivership

Vacant property receivership is but one of many tools, not a strategy in itself. It can be particularly useful, though, as it enables a municipality or nongovernmental entity to rehabilitate properties without having to take title as a condition for action. Where the municipality is reluctant to take title for whatever reason, or where the property is not subject to potential tax foreclosure, the ability to pursue vacant property receivership is a valuable asset.

CHAPTER 13

Maintaining, Securing, and Removing Abandoned Properties

One of the most vexing but unavoidable problems with abandoned properties is what to do with them after they have been abandoned but before they can be reused. Abandoned buildings and vacant lots, left unattended, are magnets for almost every ill that can afflict a neighborhood, from criminal activity to health problems and hazards for children. Unsecured vacant houses and poorly maintained vacant lots are public nuisances affecting the entire community.

While anyone who owns abandoned property has a moral as well as a legal obligation to maintain that property so that it creates as few problems as possible for surrounding residents and property owners, local government's obligations go further. As the guardian of public welfare, it must take responsibility not only for the properties it owns but also for privately owned properties which are causing harm to their neighbors.

Perhaps the most frustrating aspect of maintaining abandoned property is that the work never seems to end. A newly boarded house may have to be boarded again a month later. A lot can be cleared of trash, but new debris may accumulate within days. This never-ending cycle demands that properties be tracked on a regular basis, so that city staff can respond quickly and effectively to problems as they arise. This is another task for which a property information system is invaluable.

While there is little disagreement over the need to maintain vacant lots and secure vacant buildings, the question of whether to demolish or rehabilitate a property is often the source of considerable controversy, pitting neighbors against one another or historic preservation advocates against City Hall.

A. Maintaining Vacant Lots

Any city with abandoned property problems is likely to have thousands of vacant lots, created as abandoned properties are demolished. In 2001, Philadelphia contained 31,000 vacant lots; the much smaller city of Kansas City, Kansas, contained more than 4,400. As demolition outpaces the reuse potential of the vacant lots being created in many cities, those numbers are steadily growing. In Philadelphia the number of vacant lots increased by 19,000 between 1976 and 2001.

Vacant lots come in all sizes. Some may be large, but many, such as Baltimore's "alley lots," are single lots as small as twelve by sixty feet.

Vacant lots need to be maintained in two important ways:

- Growth of vegetation needs to be controlled.
- Trash, debris and junk need to be removed.

The removal of trash and debris is the more demanding task. While controlling plant growth can be done, for the most part, on a regular schedule, trash and debris appear unpredictably. A schedule for controlling plant growth can allow for some flexibility, but an abandoned car or a pile of illegally dumped construction debris must be dealt with quickly if it is not to become a nuisance.

Whether to fence vacant lots is a matter of disagreement. A sturdy, well-anchored chain-link fence is likely to significantly reduce illegal dumping, but makes it more difficult to gain access to the property for mowing or cleaning. Any fence, after all, that can be removed by the city's work crew can be equally easily removed by an unscrupulous contractor looking to unload construction debris.[1] Whether and how to fence vacant lots is a matter that each responsible agency or organization must decide.

The discussion below addresses a number of areas that can enable a municipality or other entity with responsibility for maintaining vacant lots do so in the most effective and responsive manner.

Finding Partners

Maintaining vacant lots, particularly when one may have responsibility for hundreds or thousands of lots scattered around a city, is labor intensive and difficult. Few cities can hire enough workers and equipment to do an optimal job of maintenance. Fortunately, since vacant lots are a matter of concern to many CDCs and neighborhood associations, many potential partners are available to complement the city's own efforts. Moreover, unlike tasks such as demolition, maintenance requires little in the way of specialized skills or equipment. Community partnerships may involve not only recruiting workers to assist with maintenance of vacant lots but also finding creative interim uses for vacant properties.

Potential workers who can be tapped to help maintain vacant lots include

- inmates in jails (short-term holding facilities) and minimum-security prisons;
- individuals assigned to perform community service by the courts;
- participants in youth employment programs, either after-school or summer programs;
- participants in "cleanup days," such as Earth Day events.

---

1. A locking gate can be built into the fence to facilitate access; this, however, makes the cost prohibitive except for a small number of large, or particularly visible, properties.

Although there is some cost associated with all of these workers, the cost is usually substantially less than the cost of hiring additional municipal employees.

While finding additional workers to supplement municipal work crews is valuable, finding community partners willing to take responsibility for lots in their neighborhoods is even more valuable. Competent neighborhood partners not only relieve the city of part of the burden—permitting it to concentrate its own resources where partners are unavailable—but also empower residents to take greater responsibility for their community. In contrast to many other activities associated with abandoned properties, maintaining vacant lots requires only modest skills and is for the most part neither hazardous nor particularly unpleasant.

Partners can be neighborhood-based or citywide organizations. The relationship between the city and its partners can range from informal ties with block groups to contractual agreements with professionally staffed CDCs, neighborhood councils, or citywide organizations such as Kansas City's Operation Brightside, Inc. (see box). The city gets valuable services at reasonable cost, and the CDC benefits by gaining a predictable revenue stream for its operations.

In addition to sharing responsibility for lot maintenance, neighborhood partners can serve as the city's eyes and ears. To facilitate reporting nuisance conditions, the city's information system should permit them to enter reports directly into the system.

Neighborhood organizations can create interim uses, such as community gardens, decorative green spaces, or playgrounds, to turn lots from problems into assets.[2] Putting properties to such interim uses requires both capability and a long-term commitment. Many successful interim use projects have come about through a two-tiered system by which a large organization, such as a CDC or citywide open space group (such as the Pennsylvania Horticultural Society in Philadelphia), provides the support that enables smaller neighborhood or block groups to maintain the open spaces being created.

While public funds are generally needed to support interim use projects, the cost is modest compared to the cost of accomplishing similar ends through direct governmental action. Projects such as Operation ReachOut SouthWest (see box on p. 170) moreover, can use a small amount of public funds to leverage major foundation or corporate support, as well as the time and energy of hundreds of neighborhood residents.

Using Information Systems

Vacant lot maintenance, which may involve large numbers of lots and frequent return visits, is particularly appropriate for inclusion in a geographically based management information system, as discussed earlier. The system's capabilities should include the following:

2. Open space reuse strategies for vacant properties are discussed in chapter 19.

Operation Brightside, Inc., is a nonprofit organization that implements cleanup, beautification, and environmental programming in Kansas City, Kansas. It contracts with the Wyandotte County–Kansas City government to help neighborhoods to maintain their environment. During 2002, its activities included the following:

- Assisting with 44 neighborhood cleanups
- Assisting with cleanup of 753 abandoned lots and properties
- Assisting with cutting vegetation on 784 lots and properties

Operation Brightside also maintains a number of vacant lots as beautification beds and provides recycled paint for exterior house painting and graffiti cleanup.

- The ability to enter complaints and reports about lots in need of cleaning or maintenance and the nature of the action required, and to display the information by geographical area and in list form

- The ability to enter reports from municipal inspectors and police officers and complaints from citizens and neighborhood organizations; the system should be set up to accept information by e-mail or through an interactive web site as well as through more traditional means

- The ability to display geographical information and maintenance requirements for each site, so that crew assignments can be scheduled for maximum efficiency

Since a well-trained, well-equipped crew does not typically spend a great deal of time at each site, travel time from site to site makes up a large part of their work day. Efficient scheduling to minimize travel time between sites can make a maintenance operation much more cost-effective. Similarly, by knowing in advance the particular maintenance or removal issues for each site on the schedule, supervisors can deploy their personnel and equipment more efficiently. Finally, the system should enable the community to track patterns of illegal dumping, a critical issue in vacant lot maintenance.

Fighting Illegal Dumping

Illegal dumping is the bane of urban vacant lot maintenance. As environmental regulations have made it more expensive to dispose of trash and debris legally, people have increasingly taken advantage of vacant lots as a convenient, inexpensive

Operation ReachOut SouthWest (OROSW) in Baltimore, Maryland, created an Open Space Management Program bringing together volunteers, community-based staff and equipment, partner organizations, and diverse funding sources to turn vacant land into attractive open space in a community of 21,000 in Southwest Baltimore. In its first year, the program turned 185 vacant lots—targeting high-visibility locations along gateway streets—into attractive green spaces and acquired over 40 lots for reuse as side yards and other uses. Many different partners came together to make this happen:

• Operation ReachOut SouthWest, a coalition representing the various neighborhoods within the community, provides overall guidance and policy direction.

• The Bon Secours of Maryland Foundation, a multiservice agency in the community, manages and raises funds for the program.

• Civic Works, a nonprofit youth service corps, carries out site improvements and major maintenance under the supervision of Bon Secours.

• The Community Law Center provides legal assistance on property issues.

• The Neighborhood Design Center and the Parks and People Foundation provide technical assistance in lot design and selection of landscaping materials.

• The city of Baltimore, through various departments, provides support services, including right of entry, drop-off and pick-up of dumpsters, and delivery of compost.

OROSW also engages hundreds of residents through "clean and green" competitions and other community-building activities. Although initially skeptical, the city has become much more supportive of the project as it has shown its effectiveness.

alternative.[3] This practice triggers health and safety hazards affecting nearby residents, particularly children, while imposing heavy costs on local government, including both the increased cost of lot maintenance and the cost of disposing of

3. Illegal dumping is not limited to inner-city lots. Indeed, it is a serious problem throughout rural areas, from the north woods of Minnesota to the desert around Las Vegas. Dumping on abandoned property sites, however, is a distinctly urban problem.

In Philadelphia, individuals convicted of illegal dumping can be fined up to $10,000, have the vehicle used for the illegal activity confiscated, and serve up to five years' prison time.

Wichita, Kansas, imposes fines of $250 for the first offense and $500 for the second offense, both with possible jail time. Fines are doubled for bulk illegal dumping and doubled again for dumping particularly large items such as furniture, appliances, and tires. The municipal court can impose community service requirements in lieu of jail time.

Los Angeles imposes a fine of up to $1,000 and jail sentences of up to six months per illegal dumping offense.

the trash and debris collected. The city of Wichita, Kansas, has estimated that illegal dumping, littering, and vandalism cost city taxpayers more than $1.6 million annually. *Public funds used to reduce illegal dumping can realize savings far exceeding the funds spent.*

While it is unlikely that illegal dumping can ever be entirely eliminated, it can be significantly reduced through a series of linked activities:

1. *Increase penalties.* Illegal dumping is not a victimless crime. Its victims are families and children living near sites where it takes place. The penalties for illegal dumping should be substantial and aggressively enforced.

2. *Simplify legal disposal of trash and debris.* In some cases, illegal dumping may be exacerbated by the lack of opportunities for residents, businesses, or contractors to dispose of their trash legally in a convenient and affordable fashion. In such cases, the city may be able to significantly reduce illegal dumping by creating drop-off facilities in convenient locations or by providing more frequent bulk trash pickups.

3. *Increase surveillance of vacant lots to deter illegal dumping.* Many communities encourage neighbors to report illegal dumping. Philadelphia encourages residents to call 911 with license numbers and vehicle descriptions; Portland, Oregon, Metro government offers an online form as well as a telephone number to report illegal dumping. Along with imposing tough penalties, Wichita created a media campaign, "Don't Trash Wichita," to encourage citizens to report violators and pursue other activities to fight trash and graffiti. Technology, including the use of surveillance cameras, has also been enlisted to help reduce illegal dumping.

An effective strategy should combine information, technology, enforcement, and community outreach. It should engage as partners the residents of the areas most affected, not only through approaches such as flyers and exhortations to report offenders but by making the residents part of the solution.

Q-Star Technology of Chatsworth, California, manufactures a surveillance camera specifically designed for detecting illegal dumping and graffiti. The camera senses motion up to one hundred feet away. When motion is detected, the system starts taking 35 mm photographs. A bright flash goes off, and a recorded message warns the intruder to leave the area and announces that a photograph is being taken. The cameras cost approximately $2,500 each.

The city of Compton, California, credits use of surveillance cameras with a dramatic decline in trash dumping by demolition contractors, which has saved the city roughly $250,000 per year in cleanup and disposal costs.

Los Angeles, using funds from a settlement with a nuisance property owner, installed a number of cameras in alleys and near abandoned buildings in south Los Angeles. While the images are considered admissible evidence in court proceedings, the cameras are generally considered more important as a deterrent than as a prosecutorial tool.

The key to an anti-dumping strategy is that illegal dumpers are almost always opportunistic, rather than determined, criminals. Thus, increasing even moderately the risk of apprehension and prosecution can have a significant deterrent effect. This is particularly true of construction or demolition contractors, among whom information tends to travel quickly. Even so, no deterrent effect lasts forever. However successful the strategy, dumping will recur if potential violators perceive that enforcement or surveillance efforts have effectively ended. The effort must be an ongoing one.

B. Securing Vacant Buildings

The issues associated with minimizing the harm done by vacant buildings are similar to those associated with vacant lots, although the specific techniques are different. An open, accessible abandoned building is inherently destabilizing to a neighborhood. The city must do everything possible to secure abandoned buildings from illegal entry from the moment they are abandoned until they are demolished or rehabilitated.

Establishing a Boarding Protocol

Every city where abandoned buildings are widespread should establish a protocol for cleaning and boarding vacant properties that includes the following provisions:

A partnership between the city and neighborhood organizations has significantly reduced illegal dumping in the Little Haiti neighborhood of Miami, Florida. The partnership includes increased maintenance by the city's Solid Waste Department as well as an increased police presence, use of surveillance cameras, and active community involvement. SIDE Watch, a group of neighborhood residents and police officers, uses late night and early morning surveillance to spot and apprehend illegal dumpers, while Communities United, a grassroots neighborhood organization, assists the city in disposing of trash by holding regular Saturday cleanups. Local Creole-language radio and TV programs publicize the names of illegal dumpers.

1. The city should take responsibility for cleaning and boarding abandoned buildings as follows:

- All city-owned properties
- Privately owned buildings posing an immediate health or safety hazard, particularly buildings vacated as a result of severe fire damage
- Privately owned buildings whose owner has been given notice under city ordinances and has failed to correct the problem

The city should place liens on all privately owned properties to cover the cost of boarding as well as related enforcement costs to the extent permitted by state law. As previously noted, once liens are placed on properties, foreclosure actions should be aggressively pursued.

2. All buildings should be thoroughly cleaned before boarding. If emergency conditions make cleaning infeasible, the building should be reopened and cleaned as soon as possible thereafter. Although cleaning abandoned buildings is a messy and unpleasant task, it is necessary to reduce fire and health hazards.[4]

3. Boarding services should be available around the clock. The most cost-effective approach is usually to have one or more municipal boarding crews, depending on volume, for nonemergency work, or work to be completed during normal business hours, and to maintain a contract with one or more private firms for emergency boarding at other times and to supplement the work of the city's crews.

---

4. It is substantially more difficult for a municipality to enlist the assistance of others to clean vacant buildings than to clean vacant lots. It is much more unpleasant and dangerous work, which volunteers are reluctant to do and which raises serious liability issues. In New Jersey, moreover, corrections officials, while encouraging cities to use prison inmate work details to clean vacant lots, for security reasons prohibit the inmates from going into vacant buildings.

4. City ordinances should set minimum standards for boarding by private owners to ensure that buildings are adequately secured.[5] The city should adhere to those or higher standards in its own boarding activities.

5. If the city encourages or requires alternatives to conventional boarding in specific circumstances, those alternatives should be clearly specified in municipal ordinances.

6. The city should carry out regular re-boarding where made necessary by illegal entry. As with vacant lots, a property information system can not only provide for an efficient re-boarding scheduling process but also identify "hot spots" where more aggressive security measures may be needed.

Alternative Approaches to Securing Vacant Properties

While most abandoned buildings can be boarded conventionally, boarding is not always effective, particularly with respect to buildings that for one reason or another are particularly attractive to intruders. In some cases, it may not be feasible because of the nature or condition of the structure.

Even where boarding is effective in its immediate purpose, moreover, it can become in itself a symbol of neighborhood decline. Boarding can hasten further abandonment in areas where abandoned properties are still few in number by creating a negative perception of the area. A sophisticated strategy for securing vacant buildings utilizes alternatives targeted to particular building types or locations.[6]

1. Fencing. Fencing may sometimes be preferable to boarding. If a building is slated for immediate demolition, as in the case of fire damage, it may be more cost-effective to fence the building, particularly if the damage makes it hard to board the structure effectively. Boarding is often ineffective with large industrial buildings, both because of the number of window and door openings and the high risk of break-ins. Fencing may be more appropriate. In extreme cases, it may be necessary to seal ground floor openings with concrete block or other, more permanent materials.

2. Prohibiting boarding. Where the community has reason to believe that the negative effects of boarding outweigh the positive effects, it may be appropriate to discourage, or prohibit, property owners from boarding their buildings. This approach may be particularly appropriate in relatively stable areas where break-in risks are low and the risk of negative effects from boarded buildings high: such areas may include stable but transitional neighborhoods as well as struggling, but still viable, commercial areas.

5. The City of Chicago Vacant Property Ordinance, Sec. 13-12-125(d), specifies the boarding standards that must be followed by private owners of vacant buildings in the city.

6. Another approach, worth noting if perhaps not actively recommending, is placing noxious repellents in the interiors of abandoned buildings. The Los Angeles County Sheriff's Office credits use of a New Zealand–made preparation, known for obvious reasons as SkunkShot, with reducing illegal occupancy of vacant buildings in the city of Compton.

The city of Mankato, Minnesota, has adopted an urban design manual that actively discourages owners from boarding buildings within the city's downtown and other designated conservation areas. Instead, downtown owners are encouraged to

- use first-floor windows as display space for local arts groups, school programs, or community organizations;
- offer meeting space for community organizations;
- keep furniture, lights, blinds and merchandise in retail windows.

The Property Maintenance Code of Philadelphia bars owners of vacant buildings from boarding their buildings where such buildings are considered a "blighting influence," as defined in the code, and requires them instead to maintain doors and "windows that have frames and glazing." Owners of already boarded buildings must remove the boards. The intent of this code provision is to maintain neighborhood property values and morale in at-risk areas (Property Maintenance Code, Sec. PM-306).

3. Aesthetic boarding. The idea of painting boarded doors and windows to make the building look more appealing was pioneered in the city of New York during the 1980s, when the boards on many apartment buildings were painted to give a crude impression of occupancy to the buildings. While New York City's program was widely derided at the time as a vain attempt to camouflage a disastrous situation, the idea, if well executed, may have value. The quality of the aesthetic treatment is critical. A crude or unattractive treatment that fools no one may be no improvement. An attractive, professionally executed treatment may help mitigate some of the harm of the abandoned property and discourage vandalism and break-ins.

C. Demolition and Stabilization

Building Triage: Demolish or Preserve?

Vacant buildings that appear to lack immediate reuse potential are increasingly being demolished. In recent years, a growing number of cities have dramatically ratcheted up the number of properties demolished and the amount of public funds spent for that purpose. Cities such as Chicago, Detroit, St. Louis, and Philadelphia spend millions of dollars annually demolishing thousands of abandoned buildings.

GOOD PRACTICE

The Chicago-based Neighborhood Service Company has pioneered artistic boarding projects, which they combine with building and yard cleanup and regular inspection and preventive maintenance. The boards are professionally painted to look like doors, windows, and storefronts. The goal is to preserve the buildings for future reuse and revitalization.

This company is partnering with the International City/County Management Association to carry out a pilot project involving seventy-five to one hundred properties in each of five cities to test the effectiveness of these methods to keep buildings secure on a cost-effective basis while stabilizing neighborhood property values.

Some abandoned buildings clearly should be demolished. Cities that have lost large numbers of people, with no realistic prospect of a return to anything like their population of forty or fifty years before, often have a vast oversupply of housing, much of it of little value. In Buffalo, many of the abandoned houses are poorly built frame structures from the 1910s or 1920s, often haphazardly added onto over the years. In Baltimore, many of the abandoned houses are "alley houses," row houses with less than one thousand square feet of floor space, with no front yard and little back yard, typically facing a narrow alley without room for parking and often without a sidewalk. These houses, whether or not structurally sound, are arguably obsolete by modern standards.

Many abandoned properties in the same cities, however, are not inherently obsolete or unusable, while there are many other cities, such as Chicago or Washington, DC, without an oversupply of housing, even in distressed neighborhoods. Many abandoned houses in Baltimore are roomy row houses physically similar to those selling for high prices in prestigious neighborhoods elsewhere in the city. Much of Detroit's abandoned housing stock is made up of solidly constructed detached houses from the 1920s, with generous front porches and ample lots, and many of Flint's abandoned houses are ranch and split-level houses in 1950s and 1960s subdivisions. While it may not be realistic to preserve all of these units in the hope of future demand, it is arguably inappropriate to write them off a priori, particularly in cities where population and housing demand are rebounding from past losses. In those cities, one could argue that the burden should shift to those who want to demolish, rather than to preserve, abandoned properties.

A series of basic questions can guide the decision whether to demolish or preserve:

- What is the quality of the building, and does it have particular architectural or historical value worth preserving?

TABLE 13.1 Criteria for Evaluating Whether to Demolish or Preserve Abandoned Buildings

	Demolish	Preserve
Quality of building	The building is obsolete by virtue of small size or physical character.	The building is attractive, of high quality, or of architectural or historical value.
Neighborhood fabric	The building is located in an area where the neighborhood fabric has largely been lost through incompatible land uses and demolitions.	The building is located in an area where the neighborhood fabric is still strong, and its physical presence contributes to that fabric.
Reuse potential of resulting lot	Demolition will facilitate a comprehensive rebuilding or revitalization strategy in the area.	Demolition will result in a potentially unusable vacant lot rather than an opportunity for redevelopment or revitalization.
Nuisance level of property	The nuisance impact of the building and the harm that it is doing in its present condition, in the absence of immediate reuse potential, outweigh the benefits of saving it for possible future reuse.	The reuse potential of the building, even if not immediate, outweighs the current harm that it does in its present condition, particularly if enhanced efforts are made to secure or stabilize the property.

- What is the existing fabric of the neighborhood in which it is located, and does the building's presence contribute to that fabric?

- What potential redevelopment or revitalization opportunities, if any, will the demolition of the building create?

- How severe is the nuisance impact or other harm from the building in its present condition, and does that impact outweigh the loss of the reuse potential of the building?

The nuisance impact of the building often drives decisions to demolish, especially on the part of political leaders more sensitive to immediate perceived benefits than to long-term outcomes. It should not be underestimated, especially on a block whose residents have been victimized by the use of an abandoned building as a crack house or an attractive nuisance for children to explore. If the building has significant reuse potential, however, the responsible local officials, in tandem with neighborhood residents, should evaluate alternatives to reduce the nuisance level of the building while preserving it for the future. *It is critical that the neighbors be involved in this process, since they are the ones most directly affected by the outcome.*

Table 13.1 illustrates criteria for choosing demolition or preservation for each of the four factors set forth above. These are not either/or absolutes. While the right decision in extreme cases will be clear, many situations will be far more uncertain.

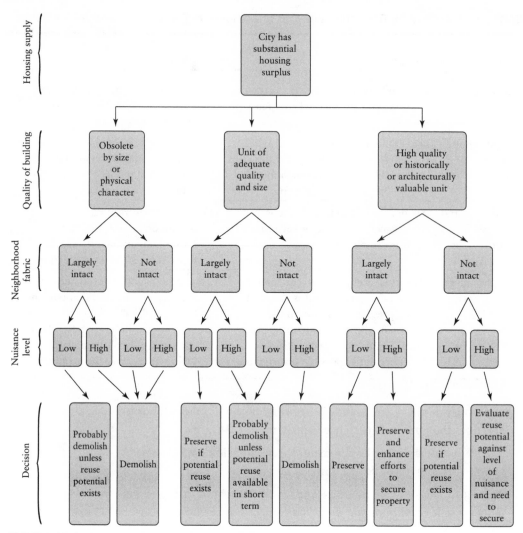

FIGURE 13.1. Property Demolition Decision Tree

Figure 13.1 presents a simplified decision tree which can be used as a triage model to help determine whether to demolish or preserve buildings.[7] As that figure shows, out of twenty-four hypothetical cases generated by the decision tree, the outcome is unequivocal for demolition or preservation in only eight cases. In the others, further judgment must be exercised before a decision can be made. The decision tree shows that it is almost always possible to come up with a threshold *predilection* toward either demolition or preservation, which may shift as one examines the issues affecting a particular building. Philadelphia has imple-

7. In the interest of simplicity, the third factor (reuse potential) has been left out of figure 13.1.

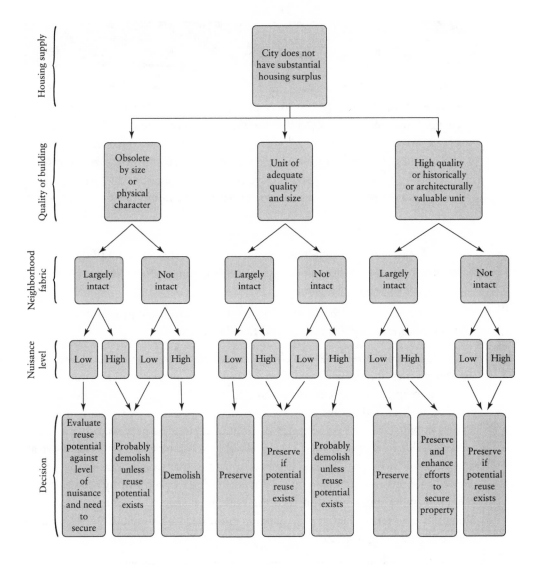

mented a similar process to determine which properties to demolish and which to preserve.

Further Demolition and Stabilization Issues

There are a number of specific issues that local government should address with respect to demolition and stabilization of abandoned buildings.

1. Demolition protocol. Every city should establish a protocol to guide all demolition activity. The city should take responsibility for demolishing the following types of abandoned buildings:

- City-owned properties

Philadelphia's Neighborhood Transformation Initiative uses several criteria to determine whether to demolish abandoned properties or preserve and encapsulate them for future rehabilitation. These criteria include the number of vacant properties on a block, the suitability of the property for the city's moderate rehabilitation program, and the strength of the real estate market in the area. Encapsulation is also used to preserve historically or architecturally significant structures for future rehabilitation.

- Privately owned buildings posing an immediate health and safety hazard, particularly those rendered unstable or incapable of being secured as a result of severe fire damage

- Privately owned buildings whose owners have been given notice to demolish under city ordinances and failed to do so

The legal procedure under which private owners may be required to demolish their properties should be established by ordinance and widely disseminated. If state law permits it, the city may want to establish a "fast-track" demolition process, as discussed below.

Except with respect to emergency demolitions, a review process, using a triage model similar to that described above, should take place prior to the authorization of any demolition. The practice widespread in many communities, by which demolition decisions are made by the city's building inspector or by the ward city council member in conjunction with the building inspector, is inappropriate and ultimately counterproductive. Participants in the decision should include, in addition to the building inspector:

- city housing and development, community development, or neighborhood revitalization staff;

- historic preservation officer or commission member;

- representatives of neighborhood councils or similar bodies.

Given the limited demolition resources available to most cities, the review process should also be used to prioritize demolitions.

The ordinance should establish technical standards for all demolitions, as follows:

- Removal of all foundations and footings[8]

---

8. Exceptions can be made if the reuse of the property is known in advance and will not be affected by allowing below-grade footings and foundations to remain.

- Removal of all demolition debris from the site

- Filling with clean soil

- Measures to ensure that removal of lead, asbestos, and petroleum product storage tanks is performed by qualified and licensed personnel

- Measures to minimize the problem of rodents and other pests, as well as dust, debris, or damage to adjacent properties from the demolition

- Measures to ensure that where the demolished building shares a common wall with another building, the common wall is properly rebuilt or reinforced

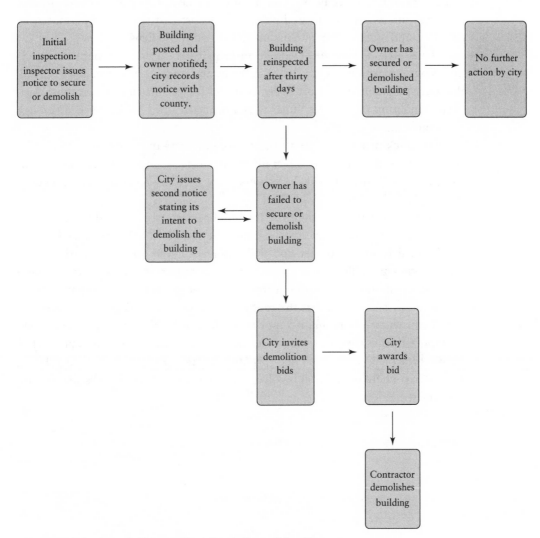

FIGURE 13.2. City of Chicago Fast-Track Demolition Process

The city should place liens on all privately owned properties to cover the cost of demolition as well as related enforcement costs, to the extent permitted by state law, and aggressively pursue foreclosure on those liens.

2. *Fast-track demolition.* Demolition of privately owned property except in emergency circumstances is a drastic remedy, and under many state laws is available only pursuant to a court order. Some states permit cities to establish fast-track demolition procedures under which properties can be demolished through an administrative process.

A fast-track process can be a valuable tool in a city that contains many buildings in need of demolition or generally unresponsive owners. The city must exercise great care, however, that the process is not used to short-circuit a thoughtful review.

3. *Stabilization or encapsulation.* If a building is to be preserved but cannot be reused or rehabilitated immediately, it must be stabilized or encapsulated so that it will not deteriorate further and will remain suitable for rehabilitation when that becomes possible in the future. The most important steps in stabilizing a building, in addition to securing it from unauthorized entry, are to ensure that it is structurally sound and that the roof is sound, without leaks or water seepage. A well-constructed building, if kept dry inside, can be preserved for many years.

Stabilization carried out soon after the building has been abandoned, when there is little or no damage to undo, is often no more expensive than demolition, particularly where demolition involves reconstruction of party walls shared with adjacent structures.

Resources for Further Information

Abandoned Houses Work Group. *Reclaiming Abandoned Property in Indianapolis.* Indianapolis, IN: Abandoned Houses Work Group, 2004.

Alexander, Frank. "Property Tax Foreclosure Reform: A Tale of Two Stories." *Georgia Bar Journal,* December 1995.

———. *Renewing Public Assets for Community Development.* New York: Local Initiatives Support Corporation, 2000. An excellent introduction to tax foreclosure and related issues.

———. "Constitutional Questions about Tax Lien Foreclosures." *Government Finance Review,* June 2000.

———. "Tax Liens, Tax Sales, and Due Process." *Indiana Law Journal* 75, no. 3 (Summer 2000).

———. *Land Bank Authorities: A Guide for the Creation and Operation of Local Land Banks.* New York: Local Initiatives Support Corporation, 2005. The definitive practical guide to establishing land bank authorities.

Allred, Christopher J. *Breaking the Cycle of Abandonment: Using a Tax Enforcement Tool to Return Distressed Properties to Sound Private Ownership.* Boston: Pioneer Institute, 2001.

Arsen, David. "Property Tax Assessment Rate and Residential Abandonment: Policy for New York City." *American Journal of Economics and Sociology* 51, no. 3 (1992).

Artigiani, Erin. *Revitalizing Baltimore's Neighborhoods: The Community Association's Guide to Civil Legal Remedies.* Baltimore, MD: Community Law Center, 1996. A guide to self-help legal remedies available to neighbors and community organizations.

Black, Karen. *Reclaiming Abandoned Pennsylvania.* Glenside, PA: Housing Alliance of Pennsylvania, 2003.

———. *Reclaiming Abandoned Pennsylvania, II: From Liability to Viability; A Technical Resource Guide for Action.* Glenside, PA: Housing Alliance of Pennsylvania, 2004. A guidebook with a good deal of useful technical information. While much of it is specific to Pennsylvania, some is more widely applicable.

Burton, Cynthia. "Want to Buy an Eyesore? In Philadelphia, It Takes Years." *Philadelphia Inquirer,* 18 March 2001.

Chicago Crime Commission. *Guide for Communities: Strategies and Options for Dealing with Problem Properties.* Chicago: Chicago Crime Commission, 1997.

City of Boston Department of Neighborhood Development. *2002 Abandoned Building Survey.* Boston, 2002. This survey, done annually by the city of Boston, is a model for detailed property information.

City of New Orleans. *Blight Busters: City Attorney's Guide to Acquiring and Rehabilitating Abandoned and Blighted Properties in the City of New Orleans.* New Orleans, LA: City Attorney's Office, 2001.

Community Design Center. *Affordable Housing Development Opportunities: Site Acquisition Assessments in Four Atlanta Neighborhoods.* Atlanta: Community Design Center, 2002.

Cornell Cooperative Extension Program. *City of Buffalo, New York: Vacant Land, Buildings and Facilities Asset Management Project.* East Aurora, NY: Cornell Cooperative Association of Erie County, 2004. A detailed management plan for a city's efforts to deal with abandoned properties, containing useful information for other cities dealing with similar issues.

De Wit, Jessica. *Revitalizing Blighted Communities with Land Banks.* Available online at http://www.umich.edu/~econdev/landbank/

Empty Homes Agency. *Joined Up Thinking: A Directory of Good Practice for Local Authority Empty Property Strategies.* London: Empty Homes Agency, n.d.

Fairmount Ventures, Inc. *Managing Vacant Land in Philadelphia: A Key Step Toward Neighborhood Revitalization.* Philadelphia: Pennsylvania Horticultural Society, 2000.

Fischer, Rebecca. *A Neighborhood in Jeopardy: Abandoned Buildings in Lawndale.* Chicago: Neighborhood Training and Information Center, 2003.

Governor's Growth Planning Council. *Vacant and Abandoned Property: Effective Solutions for Rhode Island.* Providence, RI: Governor's Growth Planning Council, 2003.

Keating, Larry, and David Sjoquist. "Bottom Fishing: Emergent Policy Regarding Tax Delinquent Properties." *Housing Facts and Findings* 3, no. 1 (2001).

Kelly, James J., Jr. *Project 5000 Tax Sale Foreclosure Legal Manual.* Baltimore, MD: Community Law Center, 2002. A step-by-step guide for attorneys and paralegals.

———. "Refreshing the Heart of the City: Vacant Building Receivership as a Tool for Neighborhood Revitalization and Community Empowerment." *Journal of Affordable Housing and Community Development Law* 13 (Winter 2004).

Kildee, Dan. "Bringing Flint Back to Life." *Getting Smart!* 6, no. 4 (2003).

Kraut, David T. "Hanging Out the No Vacancy Sign: Eliminating the Blight of Vacant Buildings from Urban Areas." *NYU Law Review* 74 (October 1999).

Kromer, John. *Vacant Property Policy and Practice: Baltimore and Philadelphia.* Washington, DC: Brookings Institution and CEOs for Cities, 2002. A good discussion of strategies and activities.

Krumholtz, Norman, and Brian Lloyd. *Land Banking and Neighborhood Revitalization in Cleveland.* Washington, DC: AICP Planners Casebook, Issue 41, 2002.

Metropolitan Planning Council. *An Analysis of Chicago's Property Acquisition Tools, with Recommendations for Improvement.* Chicago: Metropolitan Planning Council, 1998.

Office of the Deputy Prime Minister. *Empty Homes: Temporary Management, Lasting Solutions.* London: Office of the Deputy Prime Minister, 2003.

————. *Empty Property: Unlocking the Potential; An Implementation Handbook.* London: Office of the Deputy Prime Minister, 2003. Even though the legal and policy climate is very different in the United Kingdom, this valuable guidebook offers useful insights for United States practitioners.

Pennsylvania Horticultural Society. *Reclaiming Vacant Lots: A Philadelphia Green Guide.* Philadelphia: Pennsylvania Horticultural Society, 2002. An excellent technical resource for any organization dealing with vacant lot issues.

Regan, Charleen. *Back on the Roll in Massachusetts: A Report on Strategies to Return Tax Title Properties to Productive Use.* Boston: Citizens Housing and Planning Association, 2000. This book, although specific to Massachusetts law, offers an excellent model for analyzing the provisions of relevant state law and framing recommendations.

Temple University Center for Public Policy and Eastern Pennsylvania Organizing Project. *Blight Free Philadelphia: A Public-Private Strategy to Create and Enhance Neighborhood Value.* Philadelphia: Temple University Center for Public Policy, 2001.

Fostering the Sustainable Reuse of Abandoned Properties

3

CHAPTER 14

Laying the Groundwork for the City's Future

Thinking Strategically about Reusing Abandoned Properties

A. Believing in the Future

The ultimate goal of any abandoned property strategy is to reuse properties in ways that enhance and improve the properties, the neighborhood, and the community as a whole. In many cities where abandoned properties represent a major part of the land and building inventory, these properties are a critical asset for their future, and how they reuse them will largely determine what that future will be. Reuse must be taken into account as decisions are made about acquisition, disposition, and demolition of every abandoned property.

Not all reuse alternatives are created equal. Sadly, as American cities have been redeveloped over the past half century, innumerable sites have been reused for buildings that are inappropriate in use or scale, poorly designed, or cheaply constructed. Such structures have often been approved by local officials who could imagine nothing better or were so desperate for new development and rateables of any kind that they accepted proposals they knew to be inappropriate or second-rate. These projects add little to the city's quality of life or economic base and block appropriate development opportunities from emerging in the future.

Poor short-term decisions represent long-term missed opportunities. The mistakes of one generation of public officials and developers will haunt their successors for the next century. Conversely, the bold steps made by one generation become their gift to the future, like the Olmsted parks that grace cities such as Buffalo or St. Louis, the legacy of public officials and planners of the late nineteenth century. The legacy of today's public officials will come from the choices they make about the reuse of vacant and underutilized land in their cities. As they make those choices, every mayor, council member, development director, and city planner should be asking one question: *What will this choice leave our children and grandchildren?*

A sound reuse strategy is about making good choices, based on a few simple principles. First and foremost is that properties should be reused in ways that are appropriate and sustainable.

Appropriate reuse means reuse that is suitable for the site and its surroundings, taking into account the long-term plans for the area. It means not only that the use itself is appropriate but also that the project is designed to improve the area, reinforcing its positive qualities, such as its historical or architectural fabric. *Sustainable* reuse means reuse of properties in ways that will support and enhance the long-term social, economic, and physical vitality of the community. While the term *sustainable* is most often used in the context of husbanding environmental resources, we use it here to reflect the importance of building a stable, thriving economic and social, as well as physical, environment in our cities and neighborhoods.

A community's decision to foster the sustainable and appropriate reuse of its abandoned and underutilized properties reflects faith in the future of the city and its neighborhoods. This faith is not always present. In many distressed cities, the pervasive lack of hope among the citizens and their leaders has deep roots. Without a conviction that the city has a bright future, a mayor or city planner has little motivation to act in ways that value long-term sustainability over short-term expediency. Public officials must not only believe in their city but also show their constituents that a better city is more than an empty slogan.

Faith in the future is only a beginning. To understand what reuse alternatives are appropriate and sustainable, and to make sound reuse decisions, those decisions must be grounded in thoughtful revitalization planning, a solid understanding of market constraints and opportunities facing the community, and a strategy to overcome those constraints and use those opportunities as a basis for revitalization.

B. Understanding the Market

In a market-driven economy such as the United States, the market drives key decisions that determine the future of a city or a neighborhood. The market is made up of economic actors making decisions, *based on the choices and information available to them,* about where they should spend their resources. The decision-making process is basically the same whether the actor is a young family looking to buy their first home, a young woman deciding whether to stay in the town where she was raised or move elsewhere to begin her adult life, an entrepreneur trying to decide where to open a retail store, or a Fortune 500 company planning to open a new distribution center. While many factors go into these individual decisions, the central one is whether a choice makes economic sense for the individual or company.

Economic sense can mean many different things. For the young woman, it may have to do with job opportunities available in one community rather than another. For a home buyer, it may reflect a property's monthly carrying costs, the potential of future appreciation, or the cost of sending a child to private rather than public school. To the large corporation, it may include the cost of buying or renting a building, the availability of skilled workers, and proximity to the interstate highway system.

Except for the most disadvantaged, most people and businesses making these decisions have a variety of choices. Within a city, they can choose among different neighborhoods, commercial districts, or industrial areas. Within the region, they can select the central city, an inner or outer suburb, or the rural edge. Some people and businesses may even choose to leave the region for another part of the country or leave the country for another part of the world. *A city's growth and prosperity hinge on the extent to which people and businesses conclude that it makes economic sense to settle in that city rather than any of the many available alternatives.*

Put differently, a city's economic success depends on the strength of the market demand for what the city has to offer. The central issue with respect to reuse of a city's abandoned or underutilized property is the demand for the city's real estate—its land and buildings.

In a strong market, few properties are abandoned, and those that are rarely remain vacant for long. The presence of large numbers of abandoned buildings and vacant lots in a community, whatever else it may signify, reflects low demand for those buildings and lots. Successful reuse strategies depend on creating a demand for the properties, or for new uses to which the properties can be adapted. Since local government cannot manufacture demand out of whole cloth, creating demand usually means redirecting demand to affected neighborhoods from elsewhere in the region.

Redirecting demand means increasing the share of regional demand that is attracted or retained by the city, or by a particular neighborhood. Just as a manufacturer may seek to increase market share for its product, the city must seek to build its market share of home buyers and other users of real estate. *Cities are competing for those buyers and users with other communities in the same region, with other regions, and even with other cities around the world.*

A city that recognizes that it is in competition with other areas for its share of market demand must examine its physical assets—its properties, its neighborhoods, and its commercial districts—from a market standpoint. This process includes asking a number of separate questions:

- How competitive are the city's physical assets with those of its competitors?

- What factors make different properties, neighborhoods, or commercial districts in the city more or less competitive than others?

- What can the city do to make its various parts, and thus the city as a whole, more competitive?

Cities are not homogenous environments. Nearly all older cities contain some highly competitive areas, often historically upscale residential neighborhoods. These are areas of strong demand, reflected in relatively high property values, high levels of maintenance and improvement, few vacancies, and little or no abandonment. While such neighborhoods may not require any effort to create market demand, they may require intervention to sustain that demand and protect the civic asset they represent. Other parts of a city may be at the opposite end of the spectrum. These include severely distressed residential, commercial, and industrial areas experiencing little demand, low property values, and widespread abandonment. In some areas demand is so low that the market has effectively ceased to function. Such areas clearly require public intervention to create demand. Most of a city's neighborhoods fall somewhere between these two ends of the spectrum.

A city must understand the particular market dynamics of each of its parts if it is to build an overall strategy for revitalization and a specific strategy for reuse of abandoned and underutilized properties. Such information is essential if the city is to identify its opportunities, accurately diagnose and address its constraints, and target its limited resources most productively. This is not simply a matter of prioritizing resources. It requires an understanding that *the particular public investment strategies and priorities must be tailored to the market features of each area, and that those strategies and priorities must focus on those activities that sustain or enhance each area's competitive position.* Chapter 17 discusses tools for characterizing neighborhood market dynamics and tailoring strategies to those dynamics.

The public sector's legal and financial tools can have a significant impact on the market. Subsidies and financial incentives can reduce costs in the hope of leveling the playing field—that is, making urban locations more competitive with suburban or rural sites. Incentives can compensate for what may be perceived as the disadvantages of an urban location. The city can create facilities, such as a park or a magnet school, that will be seen as assets by prospective home buyers and enhance market demand in the neighborhoods where these assets are located.

In each case, the purpose of the intervention is to influence the choices of people whose financial means allow them to choose whether to live in the city or elsewhere. Distressed cities already have a captive market in the form of the region's poorest residents and the social agencies and marginal businesses that serve them. Investments that serve that population, such as low-income rental housing, are an essential part of the community's civic responsibility. They do not address the need to increase market demand, however, and, if not carefully managed, can even hinder a city's efforts to attract a more diverse population and a more substantial economic base.

The city's task is made more complicated by the need to both build its economic strength and diversity and address its civic responsibilities. Cities cannot turn their backs on their present residents or try to replace them with more affluent residents. At the same time, a city that fails to attract an economically diverse population or build a strong economic base is unlikely ever to be able to provide the services or the economic opportunities that its less affluent citizens need.

The quality of the city's planning process, at both the city and the neighborhood level, largely determines its ability to carry out the task of reconciling and balancing these concerns. Without a strong planning process, decisions are made on an ad hoc basis, often driven by short-term political or property-owner concerns to the detriment of the city's long-term revitalization and the interests of its citizens.

C. Building Capacity

It is not enough to accept that the marketplace must play a central role in a city's revitalization. Communities must build their capacity to turn that proposition into a reality. Decisionmakers in local government, CDCs, and elsewhere must become far more sophisticated in their understanding of how the marketplace operates and how they can influence the marketplace in order to build their community. They need to understand the factors that can make their city or neighborhood more competitive regionally and nationally, and how the development decisions they make will affect both its present market conditions and future market potential. They must understand what economic stimuli will lead individual homeowners, buyers, developers, and investors to put their money into one neighborhood rather than another, or into the city rather than an outlying suburb. They need to be able to use resources efficiently to influence the market so that scarce discretionary funds are not wasted and do not inadvertently provide windfalls for unscrupulous developers.

Understanding the market to this extent requires skills in planning, economics, and real estate that are not always available in the governments of many large cities and are even scarcer in smaller communities, where municipal planning and development offices are often severely understaffed. It may also require a change in the fundamental philosophy that individuals bring to their work. Many municipal officials and CDC staff regard the marketplace with either antagonism or excessive reverence, neither of which is a sound basis for building effective market-based revitalization strategies. They must not see themselves as passive victims of the market but as actors with power to channel its direction. Local officials who are excessively deferential to developers serve their community's interests no better than those who are hostile to them.

Not every mayor or CDC director needs to become an expert in every aspect of the property market. Much of the salient expertise, particularly when it comes to market analyses or feasibility assessments, is likely to come from consultants or a small number of specialized personnel. In some communities, assistance may be available from local universities, research centers, or corporations. Key staff must understand these areas well enough, however, to understand the information they receive from experts and make rational decisions based on that information. At the same time, both local governments and CDCs need to recruit more staff with real estate development skills and provide existing staff with training and educational opportunities to deepen their skills in these areas.

The next three chapters explore the ways cities can develop and implement market-based strategies, the use of market-oriented incentives to further community investment, and the role of neighborhood revitalization plans in the reuse of abandoned and underutilized properties. The final three chapters address the process of developing reuse strategies for those properties, from the neighborhood level to the individual site.

CHAPTER 15

Making Markets for Abandoned Properties

Any plan to reuse abandoned properties must ensure that there is a market demand for the proposed use. As cities and towns have learned, the maxim "Build it, and they will come" does not always apply to urban revitalization. Demand has to be created before or along with the reuse process. While in some cases market demand may emerge with little or no intervention, in other cases the public sector must take the lead in creating the conditions under which demand will emerge. Intervention is typically necessary in weak market cities generally and in neighborhoods in strong market cities that have yet to benefit from the market strength of the rest of the city.

Demand is not generic. Families who want rural McMansions are not the people looking for lofts in the city center. Young families with small children make choices that are very different from those made by empty nesters or foot-loose singles. Creating market demand for urban properties must begin with understanding the regional as well as the local market and then identifying targets—categories of buyers or investors whom the city has the potential to attract and who exist within the region. Targets include demand that may already exist inside the city, as well as demand that may be drawn from outside. Once those targets have been identified, strategies must be developed to reach them and convince them that the city's neighborhoods or developments are right for them.

This chapter introduces the process of identifying and attracting such targets, beginning with a description of potential target markets and concluding with a discussion of specific strategies that communities have used to build market share and find markets for abandoned properties. It provides only an introduction to this complex, multidimensional subject, offering thoughts on how to build a strategy in this critical area rather than laying out step-by-step procedures. When it comes to building market demand, each community is unique, and each strategy must be thoroughly grounded in local assets and constraints.

While some of the material in this chapter may seem remote from the specific question of how one finds ways to put abandoned properties back to use, it is directly relevant to that question. Markets are not about individual properties but about the neighborhoods and cities where they are located. *The way to build demand for abandoned or underutilized properties is by changing the market dynamics of the neighborhood or the city.* Successful reuse strategies for abandoned properties must be based on strategies to build the market for the community where they are situated. For this reason, the discussion of building market demand precedes the discussion of reuse alternatives—or creating supply to meet the demand.

A. Maximizing Internally Generated Demand

Cities are incubators of upward mobility. Struggling individuals and families move to cities, develop their skills and education, seek out opportunities, and prosper. Small manufacturers, retailers, and service firms start out in modest storefronts and lofts and grow into substantial companies. For decades, however, cities have seen these families and businesses move out once they can afford to do so, seeking greener pastures either in the suburbs or in other regions. Moving from a city row house or apartment to a "real" house in the suburbs has come to be seen as a marker of upward mobility. As a result, the city has lost households and businesses that, had they stayed, would have strengthened its neighborhoods, adding valuable social and economic assets. In consequence, cities have become steadily poorer relative to their suburbs, with an ever-smaller share of the regional economic pie.

The demand for better housing or business locations among families and businesses within the community is known as *internally generated demand*. While populations and businesses today are highly mobile, and no city can hope to retain all of the demand generated internally, any increase in the share that the city does retain will help it maintain its economic base, reducing the number of abandoned units and preventing future abandonment.

A broad strategy to build internal demand is made up of many separate elements. While this chapter focuses on market-based strategies, other strategies are equally important. Cities need to increase the earning power and assets of their lower-income residents through better education, job training, and other workforce development programs. The internal market for home ownership can also be increased by home buyer–oriented strategies such as housing education and counseling or by reducing barriers to homeownership.[1] Both of these strategies are important to the community's future and should be pursued along with more directly market-driven strategies. The most important *market-based* internal strategies, however, are those that are designed to retain upwardly mobile potential outmigrants.

---

1. While such strategies are sound in principle, in some communities overzealous efforts to broaden the base of potential home buyers may be counterproductive, planting the seeds of future defaults and abandonment. Strategies to promote homeownership must be pursued judiciously to ensure that participating families truly benefit.

GOOD PRACTICE

St. Joseph's Carpenter Society, a CDC in Camden, New Jersey, initiated a comprehensive strategy to rehabilitate abandoned houses in the Stockton section of East Camden for homeownership, combined with a strong homebuyer education and counseling program. Over nearly ten years, it rehabilitated more than 250 units, capturing as much as 80 percent of the total homeownership demand generated internally in the city of Camden. Abandonment in the neighborhood has been dramatically reduced, and house values in the neighborhood have risen significantly relative to the rest of the city.

Building a Strategy to Keep Potential Migrants in the City

Every year, in every city, numerous urban households reach the point where they can afford to improve their housing conditions by buying their first home, upgrading their current home, or replacing that home with another. Local government and CDCs should work hard to keep these households in the city, by influencing their choices in one of two ways:

- If they are committed to buying a new house, to buy inside rather than outside the city

- If they are choosing between improving their current home or buying a new house outside the city, to invest their funds in improving their current home

The decision of a family to buy a home in the city or improve an existing home there depends less on their assessment of the homes themselves than on their assessment of the neighborhood in which they already live or in which they might buy a home. The more positive a homeowner feels about her neighborhood and its future prospects, the more likely she will be to either buy in that neighborhood or improve her house in that neighborhood. In East Camden, New Jersey, a CDC that embarked on a long-term neighborhood improvement strategy was able to convince a large number of prospective home buyers that the area was a sound investment. As a result, many buyers who might have left the city bought homes in that neighborhood (see box).

The best way to hold on to upwardly mobile families is to make their neighborhoods better. Residents who feel their neighborhood is improving are more likely to stay and invest there, and residents elsewhere in the city who perceive that a particular neighborhood is on the rise may buy in that neighborhood instead of leaving the city. Neighborhood revitalization planning, discussed in chapter 18, is an important part of that process. Not only does it provide a road map of the actions that should be taken to rebuild the neighborhood, but it can also reassure the residents of the area that there is a larger strategy for their neighborhood, that improvements are not sporadic, one-shot measures, and that their own investment is not being made in a vacuum.

While revitalizing the neighborhood should be the heart of any effort to maximize internal demand, such a strategy may also have to provide incentives for individual home buyers or homeowners (see chapter 16). Incentives, even modest or symbolic ones, are important for another reason. Many city residents, particularly upwardly mobile ones, feel neglected and ignored by city government. Faced with the daily stresses of urban living, they feel unsupported—justifiably or otherwise—by what they often perceive as a distant, time-serving bureaucracy. *Any city government seeking to build internal demand must convince its upwardly mobile residents that the city actively wants them to stay.* Financial incentives by themselves will not send that message. They can, however, be a valuable part of a larger strategy to change people's feelings about the community and how they fit into it.

A strategy to maximize internal demand for new and rehabilitated houses, particularly in a severely distressed city with a large inventory of abandoned properties, has limitations and risks. The pool of potential buyers may not be large enough to utilize more than a part of the total available supply. As a result, even an effective strategy may only slow down the overall trend of outmigration, not reverse it. Moreover, if such a strategy is pursued unevenly, it runs the risk of cannibalizing demand, undermining other transitional neighborhoods in the city by drawing families that would otherwise have stayed in those neighborhoods and helped sustain them.

In the final analysis, a strategy that maximizes internal demand without also attempting to draw on regional demand is unlikely to lead to fundamental change in the community's economic vitality. It is a critical first step, however, valuable both in itself and as a proving ground for the larger strategy of increasing market demand.

Retaining Commercial and Industrial Operations

A strategy to maximize internal demand may also help cities hold nonresidential users, particularly manufacturers. Despite the overall decline in manufacturing, America's cities are still home to hundreds of small industrial firms, usually with fifty or fewer workers, operating well below the radar of most planners and economic development specialists. In the absence of a strategy to retain these firms, the successful ones typically relocate outside the city, and often outside the region entirely, as they grow. A number of cities have found that by focusing on existing, growing firms and creating locations for them through the reuse of vacant or underutilized buildings, or new construction on vacant lots, they can simultaneously achieve three separate, important, results:

GOOD PRACTICE

In the mid-1990s the city of Trenton, New Jersey, initiated an industrial retention strategy designed both to retain firms that had outgrown their current quarters and needed to find new space and to find uses for vacant industrial buildings or land. The city developed two industrial projects on brownfield sites, the first utilizing fifteen acres of cleared formerly industrial land, and the second an abandoned nineteenth-century manufacturing complex originally containing roughly 800,000 square feet on twenty acres. The city reconfigured the manufacturing complex into a modern facility with on-site parking and loading areas. After five years, the two areas contained fifteen companies, ranging from corrugated cardboard manufacturers to food processing firms, employing more than five hundred workers in all.

- Growing firms stay in the city, preserving jobs and creating more jobs for city residents in the future.
- Vacant buildings and lots are productively reused.
- New firms are attracted to the city.

Strong informal networks often exist among small manufacturers in the same or related fields. In Trenton, New Jersey, firms that were helped by the city to find good, affordable space shared their experience with their peers. The city was then approached by firms located elsewhere that were looking for similar space. Many of these firms ultimately moved to Trenton.

This strategy is likely to be less effective for retailers, whose facilities tend to be much more location-constrained. Unlike a manufacturer, who may need little more than good transportation links to the firm's market area and access to a suitable workforce, the retailer needs a direct relationship to the consumer. Where the problem is lack of suitable affordable space rather than limited market demand, however, or where retention is part of a larger strategy which involves building the consumer base as well, similar strategies can be applied to retail facilities.

B. Targeting Regional Demand

To understand a city's market potential, one must understand its region. The region is the larger area surrounding the city, linked to the city by economic, housing, and transportation connections. Because the different parts of a region are interconnected, much of the growth that takes place in one part of a region could easily take place in another part if it made economic sense for it to do so.

As a result, much of the regional demand, which usually represents a much larger pool of households and businesses than internal demand, could at least potentially be captured by the central city. Before World War II, cities typically captured a large part of total regional demand. If they are truly to thrive again, they must once again capture more of that demand. To do so, they must understand regional trends.

An analysis comparing growth trends between 1990 and 2000 for eighteen weak market cities with populations over 100,000 and their surrounding regions makes two important points:

- While the central city was losing population, seventeen out of eighteen of the metropolitan areas gained population outside the central city.

- In many cases, a small shift in suburban growth could have reversed the population loss of the central city.[2]

If Louisville had captured only 14 percent of its region's growth, or Cincinnati captured 21 percent of its region's growth, those cities would not have lost population during the 1990s. The bottom line is straightforward: *cities can dramatically affect their population dynamics even if they capture only a modest share of the growth in their suburbs.*

For that reason, cities do not have to target every economic, social, or demographic group in the region. Since a shift in a relatively small number of households at the regional level represents a much larger shift for the central city, cities can concentrate on those households which, for reasons of age, family composition, or other demographics are most likely to choose city living. Some cities may want to concentrate on attracting new migrants into the region—who will be less settled and more open to what the city has to offer—rather than try to convince settled suburbanites to relocate; whereas elsewhere, if the city contains facilities, such as concert and theater venues attractive to an older, more affluent population, a pool of settled, suburban empty nesters may be the city's best bet.

In recent years, some of the groups that have been increasingly drawn to urban centers include:

- Young singles and couples
- Gay individuals and couples
- Artists
- Empty nesters
- Immigrants

2. These eighteen cities were selected on the basis of two criteria. All had lost 25 percent or more of their population since their peak (usually in 1950 or 1960), and all continued to lose population between 1990 and 2000.

USEFUL RESOURCE

Many market researchers have identified demographic segments, or clusters, based on lifestyles and settlement patterns which cities can use to match with their assets and attractions in a process known as "target marketing." Perhaps the best known of these systems is the PRIZM model for segmenting the American population based on demographic and lifestyle characteristics developed by Claritas, a private market research firm. PRIZM divides the population into fifteen different groups and, within those groups, sixty-two different segments, with what it refers to as "catchy cluster nicknames." One group, of particular interest to urban planners, is known as the Urban Uptown group. Another, known as the Young Literati, is described by Claritas as follows:

> Although less affluent than "Money and Brains" [a different segment in this group], it is more educated. Young Literati executives, professionals, and students live in apartments, condos, and town houses near private urban universities. They have few children, leaving them free to pursue active lives filled with travel, art and fitness.

Claritas provides annual updates and five-year projections of household distributions down to the level of the census block group for the segments in the PRIZM model. This information is widely used by the real estate industry for marketing purposes. A case study on how the PRIZM model is used for target marketing can be found in Robert E. Lang, James W. Hughes, and Karen A. Danielsen, "Targeting the Suburban Urbanites: Marketing Central-City Housing," *Housing Policy Debate* 8, no. 2 (1997).

These groups are attracted to certain cities or neighborhoods because of the particular assets of those cities or neighborhoods, such as the employment base, entertainment facilities, or a distinctive or affordable housing stock.[3] Other cities have found assets that attract other population groups, such as the revitalization of a long-established but deteriorated African American neighborhood that draws middle-class African American families with roots in the city back from the suburbs.

Turning this analysis into tangible outcomes involves three basic steps:

- Identifying the demographic target groups to which the community is potentially attractive

---

3. They are also less affected by one of the greatest weaknesses of most older cities, the quality of the public education system.

- Identifying the assets that make the community potentially attractive to those target groups

- Developing strategies to utilize those assets to attract the target groups

This process is simple in concept but difficult in practice. Not every city can equally use regional demand as a basis for growth or for the reuse of abandoned properties. Not all weak market cities are surrounded by growing regions. Little growth is taking place around Pittsburgh, Buffalo, and Syracuse, where center city population loss exceeds suburban growth by a substantial margin. In other cases, even if regional demand is relatively strong, it may be difficult to match any part of that demand with central city assets because of either the demographics of the suburban population or the city's limited assets. This is the case in many small cities under 150,000 population in slow-growing regions of the old industrial Midwest.

Neverthless, regional target marketing should still be pursued in slow growth or no-growth regions. Although there may be little or no net growth outside the city, there are still target markets, such as young people and empty nesters, who may be drawn to the city's downtown or to neighborhoods with distinctive housing stock. This is not a zero-sum game between the city and its suburban neighbors. Making the city stronger and more attractive will ultimately enhance the competitive position of the entire region.

C. Marketing to Regional Demand

Cities must increase their share of regional residential demand in order to attract a larger, more diverse, population to live in the city or in targeted neighborhoods. From the standpoint of reusing abandoned properties, building residential demand can have far greater impact than building demand in any other sector. Although for many decades cities have focused on attracting industry or drawing tourists, with uneven results, until recently few cities have thought of making a systematic marketing effort to building residential demand. Today, more and more cities and neighborhoods have come to realize that if they are going to become "communities of choice," places where people *choose* to live, they must market themselves to the people they want to attract.

The first part of this section provides an overview of the elements that go into a marketing strategy; the second and third parts offer suggestions and examples for building effective citywide and neighborhood marketing strategies.

Laying the Groundwork for a Marketing Strategy

A marketing strategy must be grounded in two elements:

- Identifying the target population or populations to which one markets the city, community, or target neighborhood

GOOD PRACTICES

In the early 1990s, the Azalea Park neighborhood of San Diego had serious crime and drug problems. Its houses were old and architecturally interesting but small, with many lying vacant or abandoned. In 1993 a neighborhood association was established, which began to market the neighborhood to gay individuals and couples. The association identified gay-oriented events and venues at which they could set up booths, distribute literature, and promote the neighborhood. After five years, the effort was highly successful. Over one hundred homes had been acquired and improved by gay households, and the neighborhood was seeing a revival of retail activity and an increase in public sector investment. By January 2003, the association newsletter could brag that "in the past 10 years our neighborhood has been transformed from a high crime/low rent district to the beautiful peaceful community we all love."

The restoration of abandoned or underutilized mill buildings has fueled the revitalization of Pawtucket, Rhode Island, a small, older industrial city. In addition to having historically and architecturally distinctive mill buildings, the city has benefited from state tax laws friendly to artists, good interstate transportation connections, and proximity to the city of Providence. As the cost of space in Providence has gone up, Pawtucket's lower rents have become a major asset. Adding part of the downtown to the National Register of Historic Places made federal tax credits available for rehabilitation.

- Identifying the assets of the city or the neighborhood(s) to which one wants to attract demand

Assets that go unmarketed have only limited value; but marketing not supported by bona fide assets—whether in place or being created—has little meaning. *If the marketing effort is not part of a larger effort to bring change about through the creation of solid community assets, it is unlikely to succeed or bring about long-term, sustainable change.*

Assets must relate to the target markets. A vibrant downtown entertainment scene can be marketed to young professional singles and couples; this effort may in turn trigger market demand for rehabilitated late nineteenth-century industrial and commercial buildings, such as those in Portland's Pearl District or Cleveland's Warehouse District. A neighborhood with a distinctive housing stock, even if it has few other amenities, may be successfully marketed to a region's gay community, as in Azalea Park in San Diego. The relationship between assets and marketing, however, is a dynamic one. While it is hard to begin marketing a community without assets to market, the community must continue to build its assets as the marketing effort unfolds. If the effort is successful, the growth in new households will lead to the creation of still more assets, thus gradually making the marketing effort easier and ultimately self-sustaining.

The first step in building a marketing strategy is to determine what is being marketed. Marketing a city as a whole is different from marketing a neighborhood or a new development. Each requires a different emphasis and strategy. A multilevel strategy in which individual neighborhoods are marketed by neighborhood associations or CDCs within a citywide or regional marketing framework is likely to be the most effective. When such efforts are effectively coordinated, and all contribute to getting a consistent message across, they complement one another.

The focus of the marketing strategy is to increase demand and prompt people to come to the city to buy houses, rent apartments or commercial space, and redevelop abandoned or underutilized properties. A feel-good marketing strategy, one that appears to be creating favorable impressions but does not translate into economic decisions by buyers or users, is not only ineffective but harmful, because it gives the impression of activity without substance.

Marketing Cities

If the city is perceived negatively by the rest of the region, it may be necessary to change the image of the city. While neighborhoods and specific properties must be promoted—since the neighborhood and the property are the loci of consumer choice—negative perceptions of the city must be overcome before neighborhoods can effectively communicate their assets to target markets. A successful citywide marketing strategy is more than the marketing campaign itself. Promotional activities must be linked strategically to three other efforts, all essential to creating sustainable property reuse and neighborhood revitalization:

- Building further assets on the city's existing base, including promoting construction of new residential developments targeting specific markets; improving the visual environment through streetscape, greening, and other efforts; and improving community services

- Supporting existing and new home buyers by providing information and informal encouragement, as well as technical assistance and financial incentives

- Strengthening the city's neighborhoods by supporting the growth of strong neighborhood associations and CDCs, and by fostering effective neighborhood revitalization planning efforts

The ambitious strategy of Norfolk, Virginia, focuses on building market share. In addition to external marketing, the city's strategy tackles many related issues in a systematic and creative fashion. Norfolk has pioneered in designing specific new housing developments around target marketing strategies.

GOOD PRACTICES

In Norfolk, Virginia, Collins Enterprises, working with the Norfolk Redevelopment and Housing Agency, designed a new development for downtown Norfolk based on a detailed target market analysis developed by Zimmerman/Volk Associates. The analysis indicated that the market was both larger and more heavily skewed toward young singles and couples than either the city or the developer had expected. As a result, the type and layout of the units was changed and oriented more toward the street than initially planned. The development, Heritage at Freemason Harbor, has been highly successful. Nearly all the units were leased or sold well before construction.

Norfolk has also initiated a comprehensive effort to increase the city's share of regional growth by attracting families and individuals to the city. Under the banner of "Come Home to Norfolk, Now," the strategy is designed "to encourage and maximize investment in Norfolk's neighborhoods and to spread the word about the breadth and quality of the city's housing." It includes many different elements and activities, including

- organizing promotional material, events, and festivals on both the citywide and neighborhood levels;
- promoting new residential developments designed to appeal to a variety of different target groups;
- opening a one-stop center where people can learn about the city's neighborhoods and obtain technical and financial assistance with home improvement and rehab projects;
- conducting the Norfolk Neighborhood Planning Initiative, a way for neighborhood stakeholders to participate in planning the future of their neighborhoods.

Another city that has made a major commitment to marketing itself is Baltimore. In contrast to Norfolk, where the marketing effort is led by city government, in Baltimore the city partnered with private stakeholders to create a new entity, the LiveBaltimore Home Center, to manage the marketing effort. Employing five marketing professionals and support personnel and based in a high-profile downtown storefront location, LiveBaltimore carries out a dizzying array of activities that promote Baltimore's neighborhoods to prospective residents. It works closely with city government, which sponsors a variety of neighborhood improvement programs and offers a mix of financial incentives, ranging from Smart Commute incentives which encourage people to live close to transit lines to historic rehabilitation

GOOD PRACTICE

A public-private partnership led to the creation of the LiveBaltimore Home Center, an organization that promotes the city of Baltimore and its neighborhoods as a place to live. The organization runs a wide variety of promotional activities, including

- publishing and disseminating a "Baltimore Relocation Kit" for people interested in moving to the city;

- maintaining a web site, www.livebaltimore.com, with extensive information on neighborhoods, home-buying incentives, and other matters of interest to potential residents;

- targeted marketing, including advertising in Washington, DC, media, with particular attention to publications oriented to that city's gay market;

- sponsoring home-buyer fairs and house tours and offering financial incentives for buyers recruited through the fairs;

- providing information on financial incentives offered by the city, which works closely with LiveBaltimore to mesh incentives with the marketing strategy;

- designating real estate brokers and agents, title insurers, and others as "preferred real estate professionals," who are promoted by LiveBaltimore's web site in return for taking a course and paying a fee;

- sponsoring city "ambassadors," lay people who act as informal promoters of the city, to foster positive word-of-mouth advertising;

- distribution of promotional materials, including hats, bumper stickers, and license plates with the theme "I ♥ City Life."

The LiveBaltimore web site offers a great deal of useful information, including worksheets that neighborhood organizations can use to walk through the process of planning their own marketing strategy (see www.livebaltimore. com/nmi/market_sessions.htm).

tax credits. Although it is impossible to know how much of the appreciation is due to the marketing campaign, the average home sale price in the city of Baltimore increased from $64,000 in 1998 to nearly $105,000 in 2002, an increase of 64 percent over five years.

Smaller cities may not be able to support a marketing campaign comparable to the Baltimore effort. Rochester, New York, has focused directly on increasing the number of homes sold in the city, leveraging the city's resources by enlisting other stakeholders, including Realtors, home builders, historic preservation advocates, and neighborhood organizations to play active roles.

While city government plays a leading role in organizing and supporting these campaigns, their effectiveness is enhanced when other partners can be engaged not only to support the effort financially but also to carry out key activities, as in Rochester. Potential partners include organizations with a direct stake in the outcome, such as Realtors, as well as organizations with a more general commitment to the city, such as local foundations and corporations, neighborhood associations, historic preservation organizations, and civic groups. The campaign itself should be multidimensional, utilizing a variety of media and providing many layers of outreach to the groups—both within and outside the city—being targeted for attention. Table 15.1 outlines the principal features that should be part of a campaign.

It is just as important to market the city to those who already live in it as to those whom the city hopes to attract to it. The city and its partners must never lose track of the interests and concerns of the people who already live there. The Rochester program is a good model in that it reflects a conscious effort to balance and integrate the needs of the city's residents with the effort to draw in others.

Government and its partners must make a long-term commitment to the marketing effort. The effect of a campaign to change the public perception of a city is gradual, and, if successful, cumulative. If the campaign is closed down or significantly cut back after less than three years, it risks having been largely a waste of time, money, and energy. To remain effective over time, it should, however, be regularly fine-tuned to reflect changing market conditions and opportunities.

Marketing Neighborhoods

Neighborhoods can market themselves either within the framework of a citywide effort, such as Baltimore's, or independently. Azalea Park in San Diego was able to market itself successfully on its own, but it would have had a much harder time had it been located in a city that was perceived less favorably than San Diego.

Marketing a neighborhood is very much the same as marketing a city, except that the effort must be tightly focused on the particular assets of the neighborhood and the particular target groups that are likely to be most interested in those assets. The neighborhood may have to rely on residents to carry out the marketing effort, often on a shoestring budget. For this reason, the marketing plan should emphasize activities likely to have the greatest impact for the smallest expenditure of time and money. The marketing plan is a road map that not only guides the work of the neighborhood council or CDC but also makes it possible to enlist other stakeholders in the marketing effort. The elements of a neighborhood marketing plan are presented in table 15.2.

The table sets forth suggestions for *what* a neighborhood should do to market itself; the following pointers are helpful for considering *how* it should be done.

TABLE 15.1 Principal Elements in a City Marketing Campaign

Web site	The campaign should establish a web site that can be easily accessed through typical search keywords (e.g., "Living in ——"). The site should include descriptive and informative material about the city and its neighborhoods, as well as links to relevant sites, including neighborhood organizations and CDCs. The web site, advertisements, and print materials should be professionally designed around a single, distinctive, and readily recognizable theme.
Advertisements	Advertisements should be professionally designed and placed in media serving targeted geographic areas and demographic segments.
Media outreach	The campaign should develop relationships with local media—newspapers, magazines, radio, and cable and broadcast TV—to encourage greater coverage of positive events in the community as well as to provide greater visibility for the campaign itself.
Printed materials	Pamphlets, flyers, and guides conveying the theme of the marketing campaign should be made widely available. They should be disseminated where they are most likely to reach potential targets (e.g., in the human resources offices of local employers, popular restaurants, and entertainment facilities).
Connections to key marketing partners	The campaign should establish close relationships with partners who share the mission of the campaign and enlist them as active participants, including real estate brokers and agents and area homebuilders. Other key potential partners include local foundations and civic organizations and major employers in the city and region who share a commitment to the city's future, particularly universities and medical centers.
Connections to neighborhood partners	The campaign should establish close relationships with neighborhood associations and encourage them to create complementary campaigns, including neighborhood web sites, promotional materials, and events. The campaign should publicize neighborhood activities.
A highly visible base	A high-profile, welcoming physical location for the campaign should be established, ideally in a high-traffic downtown location, as a center where present and prospective residents can get information and access to technical and financial assistance.
Events	Events such as home-buyer fairs and seminars should be held to add visibility to the campaign and focus buyer interest. The campaign should participate in appropriate events sponsored by others as well as sponsor its own events.

GOOD PRACTICE

The city of Rochester, New York, has initiated a marketing strategy to increase the number of homes sold in the city. Operating within the framework of the city's comprehensive neighborhood planning and revitalization process, the city has built partnerships with other organizations to maximize its efforts:

- The city underwrites the cost of the Home Store, a one-stop center administered by the Urban League of Greater Rochester that provides credit and home-buyer counseling.

- With the Landmark Society and the Greater Rochester Realtors, the city cosponsors the Rochester City Living Center, which provides information on neighborhoods and home-buying opportunities in the city. The information is also available on the center's web site, www.rochestercityliving.com

- The city carries out many small-scale marketing activities, including buying ad space in the local newspaper for Realtors to list homes selling for under $30,000.

- The city partnered with area home builders to sponsor a "Parade of Homes," for which builders built a series of model homes on a 6.6-acre city-owned parcel in a transitional neighborhood.

Because Rochester is located in a slow-growth region, the city's efforts focus as much on maximizing internal demand as on attracting regional demand.

1. Seek help in developing the plan. Reach out for as much practical assistance as may be available. People who live or work in the neighborhood may have relevant skills, such as advertising, marketing, and graphic or web site design.[4] Large organizations such as hospitals or colleges located in the neighborhood may have professional marketing or design staff who can be enlisted to help. Similarly, many people in other fields, such as media workers or real estate agents, may be flattered by an invitation to help plan and execute the strategy.[5] Many outside sources of technical information, including web-based sources of information,

---

4. Far more people may consider themselves expert in these areas than truly are. Those running the campaign must be able to distinguish high-quality work and also be prepared to make decisions based on those distinctions, not on the basis of friendships or neighborhood ties.

5. If there is an effective citywide marketing campaign which uses a distinctive design to convey its message, neighborhood marketing materials should harmonize with that design scheme in order to link the neighborhood with the citywide effort.

TABLE 15.2 Elements in a Neighborhood Marketing Plan

Define the neighborhood product	Identify all aspects of the neighborhood relevant to the marketing strategy, including assets as well as liabilities.
Define the property product	Assess the type, price, and availability of housing in the neighborhood, and the availability of incentives and other assistance for new home buyers.
Identify the target market	Based on the assessment of the product, identify the type(s) of households that are potential prospects for the neighborhood and where they are most likely to be found.
Define the message	Decide what information should be conveyed about the neighborhood and its housing opportunities that will best influence the target market. Assess what messages are currently being communicated about the neighborhood, and how they must change for the neighborhood to present itself effectively.
Identify partners and outreach targets for the marketing strategy	Identify partners inside and outside the neighborhood who can help the neighborhood reach its target audience, and outreach targets such as real estate brokers and agents and media through which the target audience can be reached. Partners can include neighbors as well as neighborhood-based institutions, such as area employers, institutions, and churches, that reach wider audiences.
Determine future marketing and communication activities	Identify in detail every planned marketing or communication activity (see activities suggested in table 15.1).
Establish a budget and timeline and assign respon-sibility for activities	Make sure that no activities are planned unless a specific individual or group of individuals has explicitly taken responsibility for carrying them out.

published guides, and consultants, are also available. All of these can be useful in helping a neighborhood organize its marketing plan.

2. Be realistic. Wishful thinking has no place in a marketing plan. The plan must be objective and dispassionate in its assessment of several factors:

- *The neighborhood.* Focusing on assets does not mean overestimating them or sugarcoating real problems. A park may be a potential asset, but not if it is currently crime-ridden and drug-infested. Grand Victorian houses may appear to be an asset, but if they are in serious disrepair, it may be expensive and difficult to restore them. Real problems that

A neighborhood planning process in the West Side of Buffalo, New York, led to the creation of an umbrella organization, the West Side Community Collaborative (WSCC). The Buffalo Niagara Association of Realtors, which was seeking an opportunity to contribute to the revitalization of a city neighborhood, joined with the WSCC under the slogan of "Catch the Spirit" to market the West Side neighborhood. The Realtors have sponsored a neighborhood web site, tours, special events, an art poster contest, and promotional flyers.

affect the neighborhood's ability to market itself successfully must be confronted.

- *The target market.* A strategy aimed at households who are not realistically potential buyers is a waste of effort.

- *Available resources.* A neighborhood marketing strategy is a sustained multiyear effort. A sustainable plan must take into account the amount of money that can realistically be raised and the number of people available and willing to commit to the effort.

Only if the plan is realistic in all of these respects is it likely to succeed.

3. Fix the problems. Most neighborhoods undertaking a marketing effort contain both positive and negative features. The more the neighborhood and its partners can do to visibly address the negative features, particularly those most likely to affect the perception of the neighborhood by its target markets, the more effective the marketing strategy will be.[6] While particular attention should be given to tackling problems that are most likely to influence the decisions of the buyers the neighborhood is trying to attract, problems of concern to the residents who already live in the neighborhood must also be addressed.

4. Build partnerships. Partnerships are always a good idea, but they are particularly important for building a neighborhood marketing strategy. The residents of a struggling neighborhood may have limited time and money to devote to the strategy and have little access to many of the means through which the neighborhood can reach its target markets. By building partnerships with others who have either greater resources or better access to the region, the neighborhood can maximize the impact of its efforts.

---

6. The southwest Baltimore open space strategy (see chapter 13) is a good example of action taken by a neighborhood organization to address a specific obstacle to its ability to market itself.

Although a number of potential partners have already been noted, a list may be useful:

- City government, both elected officials and key personnel in the areas of community development, code enforcement, public safety, sanitation, and parks and recreation
- Major community institutions, such as hospitals and colleges, particularly those in or close to the neighborhood
- Neighborhood-based small and medium-sized businesses
- Larger city-based employers
- Religious institutions, including neighborhood-based churches with citywide or regionwide memberships
- Citywide or regionwide historic preservation, environmental, and open space organizations
- Organizations linked to specific potential target markets, such as artists' or gay organizations
- Print and broadcast media, including individual reporters and editors, particularly media targeting the neighborhood's particular target markets
- Local advertising and marketing firms
- Financial institutions

Partners can contribute financial and staff resources, technical assistance, assistance in solving neighborhood problems, and access to target markets.

5. Focus on present residents as well as future residents. It is easy for a marketing plan, having identified potential target markets, to focus on the issues of greatest interest to that market and neglect the concerns of the people who already live in the neighborhood. That is a dangerous mistake, since the present residents not only form the base of support for any neighborhood association or CDC but also represent a significant marketing opportunity in their own right. Failure to address their concerns can not only undermine the credibility of the plan as a neighborhood effort but also miss the opportunity they represent. The marketing plan should aim to motivate current residents to stay in the area and buy or upgrade their present home as well as appeal to people outside the community.

Marketing Specific Properties

Ideally, no city government or neighborhood association should need to get involved in marketing individual properties to buyers and users. In most places and at most times the real estate industry does this job well. Where, however, the job is not being done effectively, it may be necessary to step in and support or supplement the activities of existing real estate organizations.

Unfortunately, it is in the urban neighborhoods most in need of effective marketing that the real estate industry is often at its least effective, for a number of reasons:

- Active, full-service real estate firms are severely underrepresented in many urban and lower income neighborhoods. As a result, few firms may be knowledgeable about real estate opportunities in those areas.

- As a commission-based industry, the real estate industry has an inherent tendency to concentrate on selling more expensive properties, which usually require no more time or effort to sell than lower-cost urban properties but bring far higher commissions.

- Much of the urban property inventory is older, distinctive, and in need of major improvements, while real estate salespeople tend to be most familiar with newer properties in good condition. Only a small number of specialist Realtors and agents are confident in their ability to value and market such properties.

- Despite years of effort by the real estate industry and others to overcome historic barriers based on racial and ethnic differences, these differences still affect the marketing of many neighborhoods with substantial African American or immigrant populations.

Cities and neighborhood associations should work with the real estate industry and make them partners in the community's efforts to market itself to home buyers. Possible strategies include

- educational programs, seminars, and tours for real estate brokers and salespeople;

- a "preferred Realtor" program such as that initiated in Baltimore and Norfolk;

- financial incentives, such as increased commissions, or, as in Rochester, free advertising for low-priced properties for sale;

- outreach to the local Board of Realtors or Realtors Association to encourage "adopt-a-neighborhood" programs similar to that of the Buffalo Niagara Association of Realtors in Buffalo's West Side.

Where such efforts are not effective, however, neighborhood associations and CDCs may want to complement the real estate industry by creating an information center or a specialized brokerage firm to market properties within the city or in one or more target neighborhoods. Short of actually going into the real estate business, a CDC or other neighborhood-based entity can create an information center or clearinghouse that operates in tandem with a city's or neighborhood's marketing efforts. Such a center can have either a physical presence or a virtual presence on a community web site. It can also distribute printed information about

GOOD PRACTICE

In Pittsburgh, Pennsylvania, three CDCs formed a joint venture called Cool Space Locator. CSL is a nonprofit real estate brokerage firm that helps small businesses find affordable office and work space in underutilized or abandoned buildings in Pittsburgh's struggling neighborhoods. The company was established because the CDCs realized that while there were many underutilized buildings suitable for reuse in their neighborhoods, and companies—particularly design-oriented and high-tech firms—looking for space, the real estate industry was doing a poor job of matching users with spaces. The firms they have placed are typically small companies who need less than five thousand square feet of space.

available houses and home-buyer incentives, and sponsor events such as home-buyer fairs and house tours. The more active it is, and the stronger the relationships it can build with real estate firms, the more it is likely to motivate them to more aggressively market real estate in the neighborhood.

Creating a brokerage firm enables an organization to engage in the real estate market and act directly on behalf of buyers and sellers. It is not a step to be taken lightly. Nearly all states require that anyone who sells or leases property belonging to others must be a licensed real estate broker or a licensed salesperson working under the supervision of a licensed broker. In many states, the licensing requirements are substantial and can require many years of experience and coursework. One way of satisfying this requirement may be to find a retired or semiretired licensed broker to be the responsible broker.

In addition to satisfying licensing requirements, the operation must be financially viable. Selling low-priced property and leasing small spaces, particularly if it cannot be done in volume, is not inherently profitable and can become a financial drain on the parent organization unless outside support is available from a foundation or from the public sector.[7]

A good reason to develop community brokerages under CDC auspices is that they can combine the ability to market real estate with expertise in housing rehabilitation and the use of financial incentives from state and local agencies. If properties are likely to need work, the ability to package these incentives into a real estate transaction can make the difference between success and failure. Few conventional real estate firms can offer this expertise.

7. The Cool Space Locator (see box) received start-up assistance from the Pittsburgh Partnership for Neighborhood Development, a supporting organization of the Pittsburgh Foundation, and further operating support from the Richard King Mellon Foundation.

CHAPTER 16

Using Incentives to Further Community Investment

A. Thinking Strategically about Incentives

States and cities have become notorious for the generosity of the financial incentives that they offer large corporations to induce them to relocate. With far less fanfare, nearly all older cities, and some private institutions, also offer more modest financial incentives to households to buy a home or rehabilitate a property in the city or in one or more targeted neighborhoods. These incentives take many forms, including property tax abatements, state or local income tax credits, down payment and closing cost assistance, capital subsidies, grants, and even equity protection insurance.

Incentives are designed to influence the housing market in two ways:

- To assist people who might be unable to participate in the housing market without the incentives

- To prompt people to buy or rehabilitate properties that they would not consider without the incentives

The first category of incentives is typically directed at lower-income households, to increase their housing opportunities by enabling them to overcome barriers to their becoming homeowners. The second category, which is rarer, can be offered to households of any income level, but most often to middle- and upper-income households, to make properties in the city more attractive to individuals in a position to choose from a variety of options. From a market standpoint, the purpose of both incentives is to increase market demand.

While the underlying premise appears sound, it is not always clear whether the incentives that are offered actually increase market demand and, if they do, whether they do so efficiently. Grants or deferred loans for down payment assistance and closing costs, for example, are probably effective in making it possible for some lower-income households to buy a home. This assistance may benefit those households and has some effect on increasing both the internal market demand and the homeownership rate in a community.[1] As such, these incentives

---

1. The benefit to the buyers is highly uncertain. There is some evidence that the pressure to maximize homeownership may push some families into home buying when they are not appropriate candidates for homeownership; moreover, in many struggling urban neighborhoods, the purchase of a home is not always a particularly good investment or life choice.

are beneficial, but because they target households in need of financial assistance who are often not in a position to buy houses outside low-cost urban neighborhoods, their effect on the local housing market is limited.

The ultimate goal of a market-building strategy is to make the city or neighborhood attractive to households who do *not* need assistance to buy a home, prompting them to buy in a particular city or neighborhood rather than elsewhere. Whether those incentives have that effect is doubtful. Financially strapped cities spend millions of dollars, or forgo millions in tax revenues on market demand incentives, with little idea of whether they are effective. Cities would benefit significantly by being able to reduce their expenditures for incentives, redirect them to other areas, or target them more effectively. Little research has been done, however, to shed light on the extent to which the incentives being offered actually affect home-buyer choice, and whether they are an efficient or cost-effective way of influencing home buyers' decisions.[2]

A few principles can help design incentives that are more likely to be both effective and efficient. The two premises likely to influence the home buyer's decision are, first, that it must make economic sense for her to buy a particular house, and, second, that *economic sense* reflects the buyer's perception of the city and the neighborhood as much as it does the purchase price and carrying cost of the house. These premises suggest two key points:

- Incentives are likely to be more effective where neighborhood revitalization activities and an active support network for people buying homes and improving properties exist.

- Within that framework, incentives are likely to be most effective in encouraging people to invest in the neighborhood *beyond the level perceived to be supported by current market conditions.*

If a prospective buyer has already been "sold" on an urban neighborhood and intends to buy an existing house, in good condition and at a price comparable to that of similar houses in the neighborhood, the availability of incentives is unlikely to be a significant factor in her decision. If, however, she is contemplating buying and rehabilitating a house in poor condition where *the combined cost of acquisition and rehabilitation is likely to exceed the market value after rehabilitation,* incentives may well be a critical factor in her decision. In such cases, however, incentives may not be effective unless they are large enough to materially affect the economic sense of the decision.

Symbolic incentives do have a place in a market strategy. While they may not materially affect the buyer's bottom line, modest incentives, such as those offered

---

2. The fact that home buyers utilize the incentives says very little; even if a buyer would have bought a particular house without a particular incentive, she is unlikely to refuse an incentive if it is available.

The LiveBaltimore Home Center and the city of Baltimore offer a special incentive to home buyers who attend one of LiveBaltimore's home-buying fairs, which target a large part of the city rather than a specific neighborhood. The first fifty buyers who close on a house in that part of the city within ninety days after attending the fair and a house tour receive a grant of $3,000 toward their down payment and closing costs.

by the city of Baltimore (see box) may be seen by prospective buyers as reflecting the city's commitment to the neighborhood and its desire to encourage buyers there. Nevertheless, because their effect is uncertain, the amount of money a city allocates to symbolic incentives should be limited.

This brief discussion suggests some policy directions for local governments and others engaged in providing home-buyer incentives:

- Cities should make a clear distinction between incentives designed to remove obstacles to home buying by lower-income households and those designed to increase market demand on the part of higher-income households, or *market demand incentives.*

- Market demand incentives should be geographically targeted, based on the strength of the market of different neighborhoods.[3]

- Substantial market demand incentives should be carefully targeted at those investments—particularly rehabilitation of vacant properties—that improve neighborhoods and that entail improvement costs which potentially exceed current market value.

- Informational materials dealing with market demand incentives should not only describe the incentives but also show that the incentives will result in a particular investment's making economic sense.

- Incentives should be regularly reevaluated and adjusted over time to reflect assessment of their effectiveness as well as changes in market conditions.

- Symbolic incentives should be targeted in ways that generate the greatest possible visible impact over and above their effect on the economics of the home-buying decision.

3. Indicators of neighborhood market strength and weakness are discussed in chapter 17.

The Baltimore program is a good example of a symbolic incentive that generates extra impact by its visibility and its ties to a larger marketing strategy. The $300,000 per year that it costs the city of Baltimore (two fairs per year, resulting in one hundred total grants) is likely to be money well spent. Not only because of the money but also because of the limited and time-sensitive nature of the offer, the program might well motivate some families to buy in the targeted area sooner rather than later. Baltimore also offers larger, more substantive incentives, which can complement the symbolic incentives described above.

The bulk of market demand incentives should be directed toward transactions in which the economic sense of the transaction depends on the incentive. In areas with large numbers of vacant or abandoned properties, but with a functioning market in habitable houses, incentives should be targeted toward getting people to buy and rehabilitate the vacant properties rather than to buy houses in move-in condition. Incentives should be layered to bridge the "market gap," or the difference between the cost and the market value of the property, and can take the form of tax credits, tax abatement, and cash assistance. The incentives must be combined with a supportive environment for the people carrying out the rehabilitation, including offering technical assistance and fostering a constructive attitude on the part of the city's building officials. The process of applying for and obtaining the incentives, as well as the process of carrying out the rehabilitation work, should be made as simple and user-friendly as possible.

B. A Typology of Home-Buying and Rehabilitation Incentives

Table 16.1 describes seven different types of home-buying and rehabilitation incentives. The structure of incentives varies widely depending on state statutes and local policies. Tax abatements on new construction can range from five to fifteen or more years and can abate any part of the taxes up to the full amount otherwise due. Municipalities are often constrained in their ability to tailor incentives to their particular needs by two factors:

- State laws regarding permissible incentives vary widely. New Jersey permits municipalities to offer only types of tax abatements provided on a short "menu" in the state statutes. Other states give municipalities greater discretion to tailor incentives to local objectives.

- Many funding sources are reserved for households whose incomes are below federal or state limits. While such restrictions are important to ensure that needy families benefit from these resources, they can severely limit a municipality's ability to use these funds for market demand incentives.

Many programs are targeted to particular groups, such as

- municipal employees;

TABLE 16.1 Categories of Home-Buying and Rehabilitation Incentives

Tax abatement for new homes	Provides for the abatement (reduction) of property taxes to the buyer of a newly constructed or substantially rehabilitated home built in the city or in target areas. The number of years of abatement and the percentage of taxes abated varies widely among jurisdictions.
Tax abatement for rehabilitation	Provides for the abatement of all or part of the taxes arising from the increased value of the property resulting from rehabilitation; may also include some reduction in the preimprovement taxes due. The number of years of abatement and the percentage of taxes abated varies widely.
Down payment and closing cost assistance	Provides financial assistance to the home buyer to cover all or part of down payment and closing costs on the purchase of a home in the city or in target areas. Funds can be provided as a grant, a deferred or forgivable loan, or a low-interest loan. This assistance is usually offered only to income-qualified buyers.
Mortgage loans	Provides mortgage loans that may offer a lower interest rate, a smaller down payment, and/or more flexible credit and lending criteria than conventional mortgages. Such loans are often offered to income-qualified buyers or to specific target groups, such as police officers or schoolteachers, and sometimes targeted to specific areas, such as "transit-friendly mortgages" on properties in locations accessible to public transportation.
Rehabilitation assistance	Provides financial assistance to property owners to rehabilitate property. Some programs are targeted to buyers of vacant property, while others are targeted to owner-occupants—particularly low-income senior citizens—of homes in need of repair. Funds may be offered as grants or forgivable or deferred loans but are most often made as conventionally structured loans below the market interest rate. Some programs target specific rehabilitation activities, such as roof repair, lead paint abatement, or the installation of heating systems.
State historic preservation tax credits	Many states offer tax credits against state income tax liabilities for rehabilitation of historic properties or properties in historic districts. Unlike the federal tax credit, which applies only to income-earning property, many state tax credits are also available to individuals rehabilitating homes for owner occupancy. Programs are generally capped at a certain percentage of rehabilitation costs and a dollar amount and require a minimum amount in rehab expenditures.
Equity protection programs	Equity protection is an insurance-oriented approach under which the buyer's equity in her home is protected against a decline in property values in the area (see text).

Yale University, in New Haven, Connecticut, has assisted Yale employees to buy homes in designated neighborhoods in the city of New Haven since 1994. Yale currently pays buyers $25,000, of which $7,000 is provided at closing and the remaining $18,000 in nine annual payments of $2,000, as long as the buyer remains in the home. The program, which is available to any permanent employee of the university working more than twenty hours per week, has led to nearly six hundred employees buying homes in the city, resulting in a significant effect on the housing market in the targeted areas.

- police officers;
- schoolteachers;
- artists, often within specified arts districts;
- employees of companies participating in incentive programs.

While most employer-assisted housing initiatives have focused on making housing more affordable for their workers in tight housing markets, some urban employers have used their resources to help build housing markets in distressed areas in their backyards. Yale University's program is an outstanding example of a program that benefits the employer, the employee, and the community. Because of its scale and the generosity of its benefits, the program has had a significant impact on the New Haven housing market (see box).

Cities and neighborhood organizations should explore developing housing incentive programs in tandem with major employers in the area, particularly hospitals and universities, designed to complement other incentive programs and targeted to specific geographic areas to maximize their impact.

The concept of *equity protection insurance* is a new approach to building market demand that has been developed by a nonprofit organization in Syracuse, New York. While conventional market demand incentives address what a transaction needs to make economic sense in the present, this program tackles one of the thorniest aspects of economic decisionmaking—the prospect of appreciation balanced against the risk of loss over time. It recognizes that many prospective buyers are reluctant to buy in distressed neighborhoods, however promising the signs of revitalization, because of the fear that the property will lose rather than gain value in the future.[4] This is a legitimate concern in many areas, such as upstate New

4. This is not an irrational fear, even in areas showing some improvement overall. Between 1998 and 2002, despite strong appreciation in the housing market in many areas, property values in over one-third of Baltimore's neighborhoods declined either in absolute terms or in constant dollar terms:

GOOD PRACTICE

Home Headquarters, Inc., a nonprofit housing organization in Syracuse, New York, started a program in 2002 to protect homeowners and home buyers from declines in property values in their area. The organization tracks house prices by zip code. Under the program, in return for a fee of 1.5 percent of the amount protected—which can be either paid at closing or financed over three years—the insured value is protected against a decline in property values in the same zip code. Both new buyers and existing owners are eligible to participate, but they must remain in the house for at least three years after buying the insurance to be able to collect on resale. By tying the payout to a specific amount insured and the value change in the area, the program avoids the need to confront complex, judgment-prone issues such as the quality of the owner's maintenance or the value of improvements made to the property. The program was initiated with a $5 million special federal appropriation.

For example, if the buyer of a $100,000 house decides to insure its entire value, and the average price in the zip code in which the house is located drops by 10 percent between the time she bought the house and the time she sells, she will receive a payment of $10,000 (10 percent of $100,000) from the equity protection program, whatever the actual selling price of the house.

York, where the overall regional market is sluggish. Since there is little likelihood of dramatic appreciation even in the best case, a prospective buyer feels the risk of depreciation even more strongly.

An equity protection insurance or similar program is a legitimate option in communities where fear of losing value discourages people from buying or rehabilitating property.[5] It clearly requires adequate capitalization, and even if well capitalized it remains a risky venture. In fact, the long-term success of the Syracuse program depends on its success as a strategy to increase market demand and actually change the trend in house prices in the community, thus reducing the amount that the program will have to pay out. If this credible but uncertain scenario is not realized, the program may exhaust its capital in payments and go out

---

that is, they appreciated less than the Consumer Price Index rose during the same period. In more severely depressed Flint, Michigan, the average selling price of houses citywide declined by 4.2 percent in constant dollars from 1998 to 2001.

5. As interpreted by the state of New York, the Syracuse program does not fall under the state legal provisions governing insurance contracts. Other states, however, might view such a program as an insurance program and require that it comply with state insurance regulations.

of business. *Such programs must be seen not as an alternative to other revital-ization and market building strategies but as a supplement to such efforts.*

C. Bridging the Market Gap: Using Incentives to Foster Abandoned Property Rehabilitation

One by One: Rehabilitating Scattered Abandoned Properties

Perhaps the most important use of market demand incentives is to encourage the rehabilitation of abandoned properties, particularly scattered one- to four-family residential properties. This is especially important in the many neighborhoods where abandoned properties are present but not pervasive—blocks that may have one to three abandoned properties on them, rather than ten or more. Most cities have far more blocks containing only a few abandoned properties than blocks dominated by abandoned properties.

There are powerful reasons to devote public resources to these blocks, many of which are in transitional or revitalizing neighborhoods. Scattered abandoned structures affect far more residents and occupied properties than do those on the blocks where abandoned properties predominate. Each vacant house that can be rehabilitated on a largely occupied block is likely to have a dramatic impact on its neighbors' quality of life and on the value of adjacent properties.

Rehabilitation of these houses is frustrated by two factors. First, few developers, even CDCs, are attracted to scattered properties, preferring to work on large numbers of contiguous properties for reasons of efficiency and economies of scale. Second, rehabilitation costs are substantial and hard to estimate accurately. Moreover, in many neighborhoods the abandoned properties are subject to a market gap, so that small builders or developers are not motivated to acquire and fix up these houses for resale.[6] As a result, many such houses sit vacant for years and are ultimately demolished, leaving gaping holes in the neighborhood's fabric.

Where a market gap exists, local governments have two options for fostering rehabilitation of scattered abandoned houses:

- Work with CDCs to package scattered properties for the CDC to rehabilitate, providing the CDC with capital subsidy funds to cover the market gap.

- Create an environment, through a combination of financial incentives, technical assistance, and supportive regulation, to motivate

---

6. In some neighborhoods where the market gap is relatively small, speculative builders or owners buy abandoned properties and rehabilitate them to the lowest legally acceptable standard for short-term rental occupancy or sale to unsophisticated buyers, often using subprime financing. This practice provides little long-term benefit to the neighborhood. While local government cannot always prevent such transactions, it should discourage them and avoid practices which implicitly support such speculative transactions, such as selling municipally owned abandoned properties by auction, without strict performance requirements.

private individuals to undertake the rehabilitation of individual abandoned properties.

Where the city contains a CDC with the will and the capacity to tackle scattered-site rehabilitation, the first is a legitimate option. Many cities, however, lack even a single CDC with that capacity; elsewhere, the productive capacity of willing CDCs is far smaller than the supply of suitable properties. The city can try to recruit for-profit developers for such projects, but few developers other than CDCs are interested in pursuing scattered-site rehabilitation.

Even where CDC capacity exists, there are many drawbacks to using it for subsidized rehabilitation. First, it requires the city to commit large amounts of scarce public funds up front, which ties up the money for years as the rehabilitation moves forward. This is particularly true if a substantial number of scattered units have been assembled into a single funding package. Moreover, because of the cost uncertainties associated with rehab, the city may find itself having to provide additional public funds to the project as it progresses. There is always a risk that the project may fall through and substantial public funds be spent without tangible results.

Second, most sources of public funds for housing rehabilitation require that the units be sold to or occupied by lower-income households. While this is often desirable, it can be a barrier to carrying out a neighborhood strategy oriented to attracting a more economically mixed population. Thus, even under the best circumstances, CDC rehab with public funds is likely to be only part of the solution to the problem.

The second strategy, which can be either an alternative or a supplement to CDC rehab, is to motivate private individuals to rehabilitate individual abandoned properties. Most regions contain many households with the will, the energy, and the financial resources to rehabilitate urban properties. Many cities have found that when a neighborhood becomes "hot," hundreds of people come out of the woodwork to buy properties and rehabilitate them. There are many reasons why a city may want to bring about this effect through a combination of incentives and other actions:

- The expenditure of public funds per unit is likely to be far less than with subsidized CDC rehabilitation.

- The funds that *are* spent, rather than having to be provided entirely up front, can largely be provided after the rehab has already taken place, in the form of tax abatements, tax credits, rebates, or annual grants tied to continued owner occupancy.

- The occupants of the units are likely to be more economically diverse and more strongly committed to their houses and the neighborhood.

- A larger share of the subsidy can be provided through taxes forgone than through cash outlay.

The reason that the public expenditures can be deferred is that this strategy targets middle- and upper-income households that already have the disposable income or the ability to borrow to undertake the rehabilitation. The public sector does not need to front them the money to rehabilitate the property.

Incentives are a critical part of the strategy to motivate individuals to rehabilitate scattered abandoned properties, but they are not enough. *The municipality must first create an environment in which individuals will see the opportunity to rehabilitate these properties as a desirable personal choice.* Incentives must be offered within a larger program framework that includes

- an effective marketing strategy to make potential rehabbers aware of opportunities;

- visible revitalization efforts or commitments in targeted neighborhoods;

- technical assistance and a supportive atmosphere for individuals undertaking rehabilitation.

If a prospective buyer is being asked to put her money into an abandoned building in a neighborhood containing problems as well as assets, she must be confident that she has access to technical problem-solving support when she needs it and that she will not be harassed by overzealous inspectors or held up by bureaucratic rituals.

While building officials should not look the other way at inadequate rehab work, the inspection process should focus on the essentials, with officials maintaining the flexibility to accommodate the individual circumstances of the people involved, rather than adopting a "gotcha" attitude to *de minimis* issues and procedural violations. A city eager to promote individual scattered-site rehabilitation should designate specific inspectors, selected both for their detailed understanding of rehabilitation and their customer relations skills, to work with individual rehabbers on a citywide basis.

Putting Incentives to Work for Scattered-Site Rehabilitation

Incentives to encourage individuals to rehabilitate scattered abandoned properties have two purposes:

- To bridge the gap between the cost of rehabilitation and the resulting market value of the property

- To reflect the city's commitment to the individual undertaking the rehabilitation of the property

In order to achieve these purposes, the package or menu of incentives offered must meet the following criteria:

The incentives must be substantial enough to bridge a significant part of the market gap. They do not have to equal the projected gap dollar for dollar. The size of the gap can only be estimated. Furthermore, the rehabber is likely to anticipate some increase in market values between the point when she buys the unit and the point—usually a year or more down the road—when rehab is complete. The incentives must be substantial enough, however, to make the prospective buyer feel that the gap is being meaningfully addressed.

The incentives should contain a symbolic up-front element. Up-front support, however modest, reflects the municipality's commitment to supporting the rehabber's efforts. Typical up-front incentives may include a modest grant at closing or a waiver of building permit fees for the rehabilitation.[8] The city may also want to offer, either directly or through a community design center, free architectural or engineering services. Such assistance can be particularly valuable when the city is using a historic rehabilitation tax credit as an incentive.

Information about the financial effects of the incentives must be readily available. The most widely used incentives, in addition to up-front assistance, are tax abatements and, in some states, historic rehabilitation tax credits. The federal historic preservation tax credit is of no value to people rehabilitating houses for their own use, since it applies only to income-producing properties. Nearly twenty states, however, have stepped into the breach and enacted laws providing for tax credits against state income tax or other liabilities for rehabilitation of owner-occupied residential structures. *These tax credits, which are typically available for both individually designated historic structures and structures located in a historic district, are a powerful incentive for rehabilitating abandoned properties meeting the historic qualifications for the tax credit.* Table 16.2 illustrates the provisions of a few of the states offering historic rehabilitation tax credits.

Using historic rehabilitation tax credits can be complex. Not only must the property meet the eligibility standards, but the rehab work may also be required to meet the Secretary of the Interior's standards requiring use of historically appropriate materials and preservation of historic building features. Some states require prior approval of plans before a project is deemed eligible. If the city's strategy relies on historic rehabilitation tax credits, the city *must* take steps to assist property owners through the approval process so that it does not become unduly burdensome and a disincentive to their efforts.

Table 16.3 illustrates the benefits of the historic rehabilitation tax credit under the provisions of the South Carolina Historic Rehabilitation Incentives Act for a middle-income household with a state tax liability ranging from $2,000 to $3,500 per year. This example is for a house with a total cost of $150,000, including $120,000 eligible rehabilitation expenditures and $30,000 acquisition and other costs. On that basis, the total tax credits are $30,000. Credits must be taken over five years, but the law permits a carryover of unused credits for an additional five years. In this case the owner will receive a total of $27,000 in state

---

8. The grant may be structured so that it can be recaptured if the beneficiary lives in the property for less than some minimum number of years.

TABLE 16.2 Representative Provisions of State Historic Rehabilitation Tax Credits for Owner-Occupied Residences

State	Percentage of rehab cost eligible for credit	Maximum tax credit ($)	Minimum rehab cost ($)	Number of years credits can be carried forward	Comments
Colorado	20	50,000	5,000	10	Tax credit program sunsets in 2009
Connecticut	30	30,000	25,000	4	$3 million/year statewide cap
Delaware	20	20,000	NA	10	$3 million/year statewide cap
Indiana	20	NA	10,000	15	$250,000/year statewide cap for owner-occupants
Maryland	20	NA	5,000	10	$3 million/year statewide cap
New Mexico	50	25,000	NA	4	Tenants with leases of five or more years can qualify for tax credit
South Carolina	25	NA	15,000	10	
Wisconsin	25	10,000	10,000	NA	

TABLE 16.3 Effect of Historic Rehabilitation Tax Credit
(Based on South Carolina Historic Rehabilitation Incentives Act)

Year	State tax liability before credit ($)	Total tax credit eligibility ($)	Tax credit taken ($)	Net state tax liability ($)	Tax credit available for carryover ($)	Carryover in years 6–10 ($)	Tax credit amount not used
1	2,500	6,000	2,500	0	3,500		
2	3,000	6,000	3,000	0	3,000		
3	3,500	6,000	3,500	0	2,500		
4	2,500	6,000	2,500	0	3,500		
5	2,500	6,000	2,500	0	3,500		
6	3,000			0		3,000	$500 from year 1
7	2,500			0		2,500	$500 from year 2
8	2,000			0		2,000	$500 from year 3
9	2,500			0		2,500	$1,000 from year 4
10	3,000			0		3,000	$500 from year 5
Total	27,000	30,000	14,000			13,000	$3,000

Note: The South Carolina Historic Rehabilitation Incentives Act provides a tax credit of up to 25 percent of the rehabilitation cost, which can be carried forward for a maximum of 10 years.

income tax credits over ten years as a rebate of a portion of her rehab costs. $2,700 per year equals the amount needed to carry $37,500 in a 6 percent thirty-year mortgage.

Historic rehabilitation tax credits are a powerful incentive, but they are available only for properties meeting historic building criteria and, in many states, are constrained by statewide caps on the dollar amount of all tax credits issued each year. Local governments should consider creating similar incentives where no state tax credit exists or for properties not eligible for the state tax credit. Such programs could take the form of a new state tax credit, if enacted by the state legislature, or a direct rebate program using municipal funds or a combination of municipal and private funds. A city using such a program as a part of a larger revitalization strategy might be able to find a partner in a local foundation, or a corporation willing to support such an initiative for its employees.

The value of incentives can be calculated in three ways:

- Cash value, or the face dollar value of the incentive, whenever it is provided

- Present value, reflecting the discounting of future incentives on the basis of how many years from the present they will be provided

- Long-term capitalized value, representing the amount of debt that could be carried with the revenue stream from the incentives, not necessarily limited to the period during which they are provided

The $27,000 tax credit yield described above has a net present value, at 6 percent, of roughly $20,000 but can carry a thirty-year mortgage of $37,500. This last calculation may appear to be somewhat disingenuous, since the revenue stream is ten years and not thirty years, but is actually quite appropriate, since few buyers think in terms of a thirty-year personal horizon.

Table 16.4 presents four different models showing how incentives can be combined for a property, including:

- various property tax abatement options;
- historic rehabilitation tax credit, as shown above;
- 10 percent three-year rehabilitation rebate in lieu of historic rehabilitation tax credit;
- $5,000 rehabilitation grant;
- waiver of building permit and related fees.

The rehabilitation grant, which the buyer receives at closing and which is to be used for initial costs, reflects the city's commitment to the household undertaking the rehabilitation. In each of the combinations of incentives, the present value of the incentives represents between $35,000 and $45,000, an amount likely to compensate for a perceived current market gap of $50,000 to $60,000.

TABLE 16.4 Alternative Incentive Models for Rehabilitation of Abandoned Single Family House
(Total cost of property $150,000, of which $120,000 is rehabilitation expenditures eligible for incentives)

Incentive	Model 1	Model 2	Model 3	Model 4
Abatement on full value of improvements (rehab)	$25,200 over 10 years			$25,200 over 10 years
Abatement on 50% of value of improvements (rehab)		$12,600 over 10 years		
5-year phase-in of all property taxes (rehab and acquisition)*			$10,800 over 5 years	
Historic rehabilitation tax credit[†]	$27,000 over 10 years	$27,000 over 10 years	$27,000 over 10 years	
Rehabilitation rebate (10% of rehab amount paid over 3 years)				$12,000 over 3 years
Total phased incentives	$52,500	$39,600	$37,800	$37,200
Present value of phased incentives (rounded to nearest $100)[‡]	$38,400	$29,100	$29,500	$29,200
Rehab grant at closing	$5,000	$5,000	$5,000	$5,000
Value of fee waivers (equal to 1% of rehab cost)	$1,200	$1,200	$1,200	$1,200
Total value of incentives	$44,600	$35,300	$35,700	$35,400
Capitalized value of phased incentives treated as mortgage payment (6%, 30-year term)	$72,600	$55,000	$52,500	$51,700

*Assumes property pays no taxes in year 1, 20% of full taxes in year 2, 40% in year 3, 60% in year 4, 80% in year 5, and full taxes in years 6 and beyond.
[†]Based on South Carolina Historic Rehabilitation Incentives Act as shown in table 16.3.
[‡]Present value based on 6% interest rate. Five-year phase-in tax abatement considered three years for present value purposes.

The actual outlay by the municipality, even if it offers the rehabilitation rebate in lieu of a historic rehabilitation tax credit, is modest, far less than would be required to subsidize the rehabilitation of the same property by a CDC for a lower-income home buyer. The effective cost of the rehabilitation rebate, moreover, is reduced inasmuch as it is deferred until completion of the rehabilitation and then paid over three or more years.

CHAPTER 17

Building Reuse Strategies around Neighborhood Market Dynamics

Every neighborhood is different, with its own particular strengths and weaknesses, and no single reuse strategy works for all neighborhoods. Reflecting the growing importance placed on market demand issues, a growing number of cities are looking at their neighborhoods from a market perspective, asking how well the real estate market is functioning in each part of the city, and how government can most effectively stimulate market forces in each area. From that perspective, nearly every weak market city shows a similar pattern, with neighborhoods ranging along a continuum from those which are regionally competitive to those experiencing widespread population loss and abandonment, where the real estate market is functioning poorly, if at all.

This chapter briefly discusses some of the factors that illustrate the workings of the market at the neighborhood level. It then examines how to use this information to develop strategies that foster neighborhood revitalization and the reuse of abandoned properties. It is not a tool for making value judgments about the quality of life, assets, or other features of a neighborhood but rather for guiding the choice of strategies to rebuild the market and restore neighborhood vitality.

A. Indicators of Market Activity

A wide range of indicators are available to assess the workings of the real estate market at a neighborhood level. While some, such as the price of houses or the trend in house prices over time, are more or less self-evident, others may be less obvious. One indicator used in the Flint, Michigan, study discussed below was a disproportionately large number of elderly homeowners, which reflected the small number of younger families buying houses in the area. Depending on the availability of information and of sophisticated analytical tools, the analysis can range from a simple tallying of indicators to more complex cluster analysis, which seeks to identify patterns (clusters) reflecting relationships between the indicators.

In a study of Flint, Michigan, conducted by the author in 2003, the focus was on identifying factors largely derived from 1990 and 2000 census data that reflected

TABLE 17.1 Housing Market Weakness Indicators Used in Flint, Michigan, Study

Variable	Indicator
Population trend	Population loss >10% between 1990 and 2000
Age of homeowners	>25% of homeowners aged 65 or over
Single-family, owner-occupied housing trend	Single-family owner-occupied units declined >10% between 1990 and 2000
Vacant properties	Vacant units >10% of total housing stock
House value	Median owner-occupied house value <$40,000 (<80% of city median value)
House value trend	Median value increase lower than Consumer Price Index increase between 1990 and 2000 (net loss in constant dollars)
Homeowner vacancy rate	Vacant units offered for sale >2.5%
Absorption rate of houses for sale	Absorption rate >1 year
Homeowner replacement rate	Replacement rate <.67 (2 new homeowners for every 3 lost)
Tax foreclosure	Properties foreclosed as percentage of citywide average (higher levels of foreclosure were given up to triple weight)

neighborhood market conditions.[1] Since Flint lacks recognized geographically defined neighborhoods, the study used the census tract as the unit of analysis, with each tract containing on average roughly three thousand people, or one thousand households. The variables used as indicators, and the measurement used to define weak housing market conditions, are shown in table 17.1.

The indicators of market weakness were then aggregated for each census tract, and tracts were clustered into four categories (denoted as A through D) on the basis of the number of indicators.[2]

1. Census data is all but universally used by analysts for neighborhood studies because of its comprehensive nature and its availability for small areas, including census tracts and block groups within tracts. It must be used with care, however. First, it is time-bound. By 2006, data for the year 2000 is already obsolete in many areas, particularly those undergoing rapid change. Second, much of the data may be inaccurate, particularly with respect to small areas, partly because the census relies on a sample (generally one out of every six households) for all but the most basic information, but also because some questions are being asked of individuals who cannot realistically know the answer; for example, tenants in a multifamily building may be asked when the building was constructed. The Flint study relied heavily on census data because much other data, including Multiple Listing Service data on real estate sales activity, was not available at the census tract level, and the time and money constraints on the study did not allow for the amount of data manipulation that would have been needed to make that data useful.

2. To check the credibility of the analysis, the typology was compared against two other types of data available by census tract: Home Mortgage Disclosure Act (HMDA) data on mortgage originations and Flint Police Department data on selected crimes. Both data sources correlated highly with the market analysis, except that the variation between C and D areas was substantially less than the

TABLE 17.2 Two Philadelphia Neighborhood Types from TRF Market Typology

Steady	Distressed
High housing values, but not as high as Regional Choice and High Value markets	Home values well below other markets
Price appreciation during 1990s not strong	Some price appreciation, but based on a substantially lower base amount
Very little commercial presence, and high owner-occupancy rates	Housing stock old and in deteriorating condition
Substantial portion of the homes built after 1950	Demolitions, vacancies, and dangerous property counts are elevated
Resident credit scores are generally high but showing signs of erosion	Resident credit scores are on average low, meaning that mainstream financial credit is not likely to be readily available

Source: TRF web site, www.trfund.com/policy/policy.rema.methodology.htm

Another approach was used in Philadelphia by the Reinvestment Fund (TRF), which carried out a cluster analysis to elicit the market characteristics of Philadelphia neighborhoods. The variables used in the TRF analysis are given below:

- Housing tenure (whether a unit was owner- or renter-occupied)
- Age of housing (percentage of units built after 1950)
- Percentage of units demolished
- Percentage of properties vacant
- Percentage of properties deemed dangerous or imminently dangerous
- Percentage of properties categorized as commercial
- Year, value, type, and price of most recent sales
- Total count of residential units
- Percentage of households surveyed with high- or very high-risk
credit scores

The analysis was used to create a six-level market typology of Philadelphia neighborhoods, characterized as Regional Choice, High Value/Appreciating, Steady, Transitional, Distressed, and Reclamation areas. A comparison of the variables used to define two of these categories is shown in table 17.2.

---

variation from A to B, or from B to C+D: that is, areas exhibiting more than six indicators tended to show similar dynamics, suggesting that there is considerable redundancy in the indicators used and that they could be substantially refined in the future.

Other variables that can be used, depending on their availability, are sales transactions from the local Multiple Listing Service, including price and days on market, and mortgage originations from HMDA data.[3] County records of real estate transactions, including price and mortgage financing, if any, are widely available and represent another potential data source for market-based analysis.

Although some of the findings of a data-driven neighborhood market analysis may appear intuitively obvious to local officials and CDC personnel, others may surprise even experienced observers. For any city seeking to initiate strategies to rebuild the local housing market, such an analysis is a valuable tool for identifying problems and opportunities and targeting resources more effectively. While, in some cases, the analysis can be done in-house by a municipality or CDC, other cities will often have to find someone else, such as a research consultant or university team, to conduct the study. In either case, it is critical that the individuals using the analysis to frame strategies be closely involved in the process, so that they fully understand the premises and assumptions being made and the findings derived from them.

The most valuable aspects of a market-oriented neighborhood analysis are the analysis itself and the ability to accurately characterize the market dynamics of each neighborhood for purposes of adopting effective revitalization strategies, not the process of sorting a city's neighborhoods into categories. While some cities find the process of creating a typology, and classifying neighborhoods accordingly, to be a useful planning tool, others may not. Furthermore, the process of creating neighborhood typologies, although in itself value-neutral, risks being used in ways that are inconsistent with good planning and social equity, if the typology becomes an implicit vehicle for neighborhood "triage"—making decisions that certain neighborhoods are less worthy of attention than others.[4]

B. Neighborhoods and Neighborhood Typologies

Any effort to divide neighborhoods into categories is inherently somewhat arbitrary. Even so, many cities find that most neighborhoods do tend to fall into broad categories and that creating a typology—such as the one developed for Philadelphia, discussed above—is a useful planning tool. Minneapolis found that a break-

---

3. These data sources may underestimate the level of market activity, since they may not capture the activity in the informal market that exists where licensed brokers are less active and transactions take place with seller financing or other sources of credit.

4. Many of the cities that have adopted neighborhood typologies are concerned that they may be seen in this light. This concern is reflected in the careful choice of words used to characterize the neighborhoods at the more distressed end of the continuum, such as *reclamation* or *redirection*. While it is undoubtedly better to use descriptors without inherently negative associations, this show of sensitivity does not eliminate the risk of misuse.

TABLE 17.3 Baltimore Neighborhood Housing Market Typology

Category	Features	Strategies
Preservation	Healthy, attractive areas with high owner-occupancy rates, high property values, and low vacancy and abandonment rates	Low need for public intervention in real estate market; minimal public investments except for improved public infrastructure and parks
Stabilization	Homeownership rates and vacancy rates similar to Preservation areas, but much lower property values and scattered problems of deterioration	Need for targeted intervention in real estate market, including intervention buying, code enforcement, and selective demolition
Reinvestment	Moderate values and home ownership rates, and high vacancy rates	Need for targeted intervention to prevent widespread vacancies from developing
Redevelopment	Significant deterioration of housing stock and dense concentrations of abandoned buildings and vacant lots; market forces are not working in these areas	Need to stabilize target blocks, remove the surplus of vacant and uninhabitable properties, and create new units as well as recreational amenities and retail and employment centers

Source: Adapted from Baltimore city web site, www.ci.baltimore.md.us/neighborhoods/snap/typology.html

down of its eighty-one designated neighborhoods into three categories was most useful for its Neighborhood Revitalization Program:

- *Protection:* areas that are already stable and successful, where the goal is to maintain the existing housing stock and improve services

- *Revitalization:* areas with an aging but still viable housing stock, often close to declining industrial areas. The goal here is to invest strategically to enhance desirability of the housing and encourage stability.

- *Redirection:* areas with declining incomes and major social service needs, or whose housing stock cannot compete with housing elsewhere in the city or metro area. The goal here is to work toward major landscape transformation and attract much-needed new investment.

Baltimore uses a four-level typology for neighborhood planning activities, shown in table 17.3.

The Baltimore typology and the six-level typology adopted in Philadelphia are refinements of the three-level breakdown used in Minneapolis. The following discussion summarizes the key market-oriented neighborhood characteristics associated with the three levels suggested by the Minneapolis model.

Stable or Regionally Competitive Neighborhoods

These are the city's strongest neighborhoods from a market standpoint: areas where the housing market is working reasonably well, there is a steady demand for the housing, and prices are equal to or greater than replacement or rehabilitation cost. As a result, vacant properties are rare and generally restored or replaced quickly through private initiative. In these areas, the city's principal responsibility is to provide a high quality of public services and facilities, to ensure that they do not lose their edge.

While some typologies may place all stable neighborhoods into a single category, others distinguish between areas in which prices are clearly high enough to motivate private investment and prevent deterioration and those which, although equally stable at present, have lower house values, which may signal the potential for deterioration. These areas are characterized as Protection areas by Minneapolis, Preservation and Stabilization areas by Baltimore, and Regional Choice, High Value, and Steady areas by Philadelphia.

Intermediate Neighborhoods

Neighborhoods in which the market is still viable at some level but visibly under threat are common in older cities and inner-ring suburbs. In these areas maintenance may be slipping, traditionally high homeownership rates may be declining, and abandoned properties are beginning to appear on otherwise sound city blocks. As noted earlier, these neighborhoods usually cover much more of the city than do areas of widespread abandonment.

Such areas require carefully targeted strategies to reverse decline and strengthen the still-intact fabric. Housing investment is far more likely to take the form of small-scale infill and rehabilitation than large-scale construction, and it is likely to emphasize efforts to prompt existing homeowners to improve their properties and encourage others to move into the neighborhood, buying and restoring substandard or abandoned properties for their own use. These strategies, involving scattered properties and conducted on a small scale, rarely attract developer interest and offer few photo opportunities, yet they may represent a highly cost-effective use of discretionary resources available for housing investment.

There are different types of intermediate area, such as those in which the housing market is still relatively strong and destabilization appears to be just beginning, and those in which house values have fallen significantly below replacement or rehabilitation cost and evidence of destabilization is widespread, although not yet pervasive. These intermediate areas correspond to the Reinvestment neighborhoods in Baltimore and the Revitalization areas in Minneapolis.

Disinvested Areas

The third category is made up of the areas that have been most extensively disinvested. While such areas often have pockets of strength and assets that can serve as nuclei for redevelopment, deterioration and abandonment are so widespread that more ambitious efforts at rebuilding, either through large-scale development or through sustained and cumulative revitalization efforts over a long period, are needed to make them more desirable neighborhoods. Some such redevelopment efforts have included "rebranding"—giving the neighborhood a new identity as a marketing strategy, as Indianapolis did when it renamed King's Park as Fall Creek Place. Such an action may seem trivial, and perhaps offend some long-time residents, yet it may help build a market for the area in the face of long-standing negative perceptions.

C. Designing Strategies for Intermediate Neighborhoods at Risk

Viable but threatened neighborhoods are critical to any city's revitalization strategy, since further decline may lead to loss of property values and stable homeowners, and deterioration and ultimate abandonment will have a dramatic negative impact on the city as a whole. The cost of stabilizing such an area, moreover, may be substantially less than the cost of bringing back an area where abandonment is already endemic and the fabric of the community must be entirely rebuilt. Preventing further loss in the large number of blocks that are at risk will improve the lives of large numbers of existing residents as well as preserve a major part of the city's existing assets.

Prioritizing Vacant Houses

If the few vacant houses on a largely occupied block are left untended, they may gradually undermine the rest of the block. Effective strategies may require local government to take control through tax foreclosure or eminent domain and may involve subsequent rehabilitation by a CDC or by families who will rehabilitate properties for their own use with the aid of financial incentives, as discussed in chapter 16. These efforts can be tied to marketing activities to attract new owners, as discussed in chapter 15.

Scattered-Site and Small-Scale Strategies

Housing investment in transitional areas should generally take the form of small-scale infill and rehabilitation rather than large-scale new construction. A typical block in a transitional neighborhood may contain a large number of houses in good condition, a smaller number of occupied houses in need of repair, and a still smaller number of vacant properties, either boarded houses or vacant lots. Local government should work with CDCs and reputable local contractors and developers,

In Baltimore, the Patterson Park Community Development Corporation began a systematic effort to gain control of the vacant properties in that neighborhood in 1996. They rehabilitate the properties and either sell them to homeowners or maintain them as quality rental housing, depending on the market conditions of the immediate area and the needs of the community. The CDC has rehabilitated more than two hundred houses, leading to millions of dollars in private reinvestment, dramatic increases in property values, and higher tax revenues for the city of Baltimore.

In Orange, New Jersey, HANDS, Inc., has been carrying out a systematic strategy of identifying, gaining control of, and rehabilitating scattered vacant properties in troubled neighborhoods for homeownership. HANDS works aggressively to gain title to properties by using a variety of strategies, including buying tax liens, intervening in mortgage foreclosures, and buying U.S. Department of Housing and Urban Development properties. HANDS's strategy has stabilized three neighborhoods in the city and reduced the citywide abandonment rate by 71 percent.

providing financial and other incentives to encourage both neighborhood residents and newcomers to buy, rehabilitate, and occupy homes in the area. Occupied houses in need of repair should be addressed through assistance to struggling homeowners and programs to buy out irresponsible absentee owners and fix up properties for resale for owner occupancy.

Efforts to improve housing conditions should be combined with beautification activities to foster neighborhood pride and enhance curb appeal, such as facade grants, minimal landscape treatment of vacant lots, street tree plantings, and provision of attractive, uniform front yard fencing along each block.

Using Larger Projects as Anchors

While most activities in transitional neighborhoods will be small in scale and gradual in their impact, some neighborhoods contain opportunities for "anchor projects" which can stabilize the neighborhood and add a community asset, such as large apartment buildings, surplus school or institutional buildings, or vacant or underutilized commercial and industrial buildings. Many of these have been allowed to deteriorate or have been abandoned, becoming eyesores and sources of neighborhood blight. Converting such buildings into attractive housing or mixed-use buildings can provide a neighborhood with a much-needed shot in the arm, leveraging further investment in surrounding properties.

Finally, as noted earlier, any strategy to preserve or improve viable neighborhoods at risk must recognize that among an area's greatest long-term assets are the

The Circle F neighborhood in Trenton, New Jersey, grew up around a large factory built in 1880. When it closed in 1990, the neighborhood began to decline because of both the loss of jobs and the blighting effect of the vacant factory. The city of Trenton divided the property, converting part of it into a showcase senior citizen housing complex developed by a CDC, and the balance into light industrial space, which provided over one hundred jobs for area residents. Simultaneously, the city initiated a neighborhood preservation program in the area, providing home improvement grants and loans for owners and streetscape improvements.

many families who already live there and who are steadily improving their economic conditions. Holding on to these families while attracting new families to the area should be a priority for every neighborhood. That effort calls not only for physical improvements to the area, but also for strengthening the social fabric of the neighborhood through building strong community institutions and organizations.

D. Fostering Long-Term Change in Severely Disinvested Areas

Many older cities contain areas that have been disinvested and abandoned to the point where targeted small-scale revitalization strategies may no longer be relevant or adequate to address the area's conditions. These areas include not only heavily disinvested residential neighborhoods but also largely abandoned former industrial areas.[5] While they may occupy a small part of a city's total area, they contain a disproportionate share of the city's abandoned properties and are often seen as emblematic of the city's distressed condition. Such areas may be candidates for large-scale housing or mixed-use redevelopment projects, particularly where large amounts of vacant or underutilized land are available as a result of historic abandonment and demolition; or they may be more appropriate for a cumulative strategy of small projects, based on a comprehensive revitalization plan, under the leadership of a strong CDC.

Large-scale projects can create important opportunities for a city by

- changing the character of an area and the way it is perceived by the marketplace;

- responding to market demand by creating new housing products and settings not available elsewhere in the city's housing market;

5. For a discussion of former industrial, or brownfield, properties, see chapter 19.

- creating "move up" opportunities within the city to retain upwardly mobile residents;

- engaging regional and national developers and investors in the city.

Large-scale redevelopment projects are expensive and high-risk ventures that may demand large amounts of limited public resources up front. While a well-conceived redevelopment project can build market demand, demand itself is not unlimited. Overbuilding runs the risk not only of creating excess supply but also of cannibalizing demand from other parts of the community, destabilizing viable neighborhoods that are already at risk. The following questions can be used to identify and prioritize competing target areas and redevelopment schemes:

- What redevelopment resources are available to the municipality and its partners?

- How extensive is the market demand for new housing, and for what specific housing products?

- Which areas offer the best mix of assets and opportunities to respond to market demand?

- Which areas best complement other revitalization activities or priorities of the community, including strengthening viable neighborhoods at risk?

This assessment can help ensure that the areas with greatest potential for success are selected for action and that the scope of the city's undertakings does not exceed either the market demand or the available resources. The decision to commit the resources to plan, design, and carry out a successful large-scale redevelopment project should be made only after careful assessment of the opportunities and benefits of the project and the opportunity costs of using scarce resources on it. A number of large-scale projects under way as of 2005 are described in table 17.4.

A strategy designed to foster lasting change through the cumulative effect of smaller projects and activities over a long period, usually ten or more years, may be a viable alternative to large-scale redevelopment. Such a strategy is feasible where a CDC exists that not only has a long-term commitment to a particular neighborhood but also builds and sustains the capacity to carry out a long-term strategy, such as New Community Corporation in Newark or Slavic Village in Cleveland. Such CDCs represent valuable community assets. *Public sector and foundation funders should do their utmost to ensure that such CDCs have access to consistent long-term funding streams to enable them to sustain their neighborhood strategy.* Moreover, where such a strategy has been initiated by a CDC and appears to be a sound, potentially effective one, local governments should avoid undermining it by turning over large parcels of land to private developers for projects that are not coordinated with the CDC strategy or consistent with the neighborhood plan.

TABLE 17.4 Examples of Large-Scale, Market-Driven Redevelopment Projects

Project	Key area assets	Redevelopment focus	Special features
Fall Creek Place, Indianapolis	Adjacent to riverfront Historic Victorian housing stock	Residential development Mix of new construction and rehabilitation	Partnership of city, CDC, historic preservation groups, and private developers Utilized HUD Home-ownership Zone Grant
Fruitvale, Oakland	Adjacent to BART (Bay Area Rapid Transit) station	Mixed-use development New construction	Initiative came from neighborhood-based CDC Required creative financing partner-ship with city, BART, and private lenders
Brewerytown, Philadelphia	Adjacent to Fairmount Park Close to rapidly appre-ciating residential area south of redevelopment area Distinctive older industrial buildings	Residential development Mix of adaptive reuse and new construction	Partnership between city and major private developer

Whatever an area may offer in terms of location and other assets, its redevelop-ment is unlikely to be successful unless the community has a tightly and effectively focused, *market-driven* strategy for carrying out its redevelopment. The strategy should focus on the following questions:

- Which groups make up the market for this development?

- What types of housing products will be most attractive to the groups making up the market?

- What design and site planning features will render the products most attractive to the market and build a strong, sustainable community?

- What are the area's location assets, such as proximity to downtown, or to a major transit line, and how should the project be planned to take advantage of them?

- What other assets—such as parks, waterfront, and major institutions —does the area offer, and how should they be integrated into the area's redevelopment?

- What other amenities or features—such as open space and shopping— are necessary or desirable in order to draw the market and build the community?

- How should the development be phased for greatest success?

Any effort to transform a disinvested neighborhood must combine market success with community building. While a strong community cannot be built without market success, market success alone does not ensure a strong community that benefits the existing residents of the area as well as the newcomers drawn by new development. If the process is not grounded in a solid long-term strategy, it can be a transitory phenomenon, conferring few, if any, lasting benefits on the neighborhood or the city. This is particularly true if the market is artificially propped up with deep tax abatements and other subsidies, without a strategy to build true market value over time. Local governments cannot rely on developers, many of whom are thinking more of short-term gains than long-term stability, to ensure that a stable and sustainable community will come into being. Local government and its partners must make sure that a sound long-term strategy for each redevelopment area is in place from the beginning and is followed as the redevelopment process moves forward.

CHAPTER 18

Neighborhood Revitalization Planning and Abandoned Property Strategies

A. Neighborhood Revitalization Planning that Matters

Why Plans Are Important

A recurrent theme of this book is the importance of an overall strategy that addresses abandoned properties not only as problems but also as opportunities. To that end, there is no substitute for a plan that offers public officials, community residents, developers, and others a road map for creating opportunities that best reflect both market realities and community goals. A plan can:

- *Provide a clear direction for the neighborhood's future.* A plan can help ensure that investments are made in the most cost-effective manner and that the different improvements taking place in a neighborhood will complement and enhance rather than conflict with one another.

- *Balance market forces with other community objectives.* While market forces are critical to determining how an area will be redeveloped and abandoned properties reused, they are not the only factor. Uncontrolled, they can destabilize a neighborhood and undermine the quality of life of the area's lower-income families and individuals. A plan that addresses these issues can create a framework which allows market forces to work effectively while making sure that the outcomes reflect both short- and long-term community objectives.

- *Build a strong base of support for the community's future.* A strong plan is itself a statement of confidence in the community's future. Developing the plan can—and should—engage a broad spectrum of residents and other stakeholders, gaining their support not only for the plan but also for the actions that grow out of the plan.

- *Give credibility to the community's revitalization efforts.* The plan attests to the fact that the revitalization of the neighborhood is not a piecemeal or half-hearted effort and that a long-term commitment exists to rebuild the community. This commitment is critical not only for the residents of the neighborhood but for prospective home buyers and investors as well.

Not every plan accomplishes these goals. Every city hall holds shelves of plans for the revitalization of neighborhoods or for specific redevelopment projects that led nowhere. Some were tried and abandoned, while others were never implemented. In some cases, the plans themselves may have been unworkable; in others, political or financial considerations may have kept sound plans from being implemented. In either case, the outcome was much the same.

By trial and error over many years, good practices have emerged for neighborhood revitalization planning that provides a solid, realistic guide for the community's future. Good practices for an effective plan cover not only what goes into the document, but also who is involved in its preparation and who has a stake in its implementation.

Although successful plans may have important elements in common, there are many different ways they can be developed. This chapter describes some of the models that have been used in cities around the nation and discusses the financial and technical support of neighborhood planning. The final section discusses specifically how neighborhood planning can be applied to developing effective abandoned property reuse strategies.

What Is Neighborhood Revitalization Planning?

A neighborhood revitalization plan is prepared with the active engagement of the residents and other city and neighborhood stakeholders and provides both a vision and specific direction for the revitalization of the neighborhood.[1] It is defined by three separate features: the scope of the plan, the process by which it is created, and the process by which it is implemented.

Scope of the Plan. The plan should be both visionary and specific. A plan that lacks vision is unlikely to serve as a basis either for mobilizing residents or for building confidence in the larger community. A visionary plan without specifics is little more than a shared fantasy. The overall vision of the future of the neighborhood should be translated into broad revitalization strategies, which must then be grounded in clearly defined activities with specific dollar amounts and timelines. The state of Connecticut, in the guidelines for its Neighborhood Revitalization Zone (NRZ) program, boils it down to four questions:[2]

- What does the neighborhood look like today?
- What do we want it to look like?

1. A variety of terms are used to describe this or similar models, including *community planning, empowerment planning, participatory neighborhood planning, action planning,* and the like. Although the term *neighborhood revitalization planning* is used in other contexts as well, we use it here because it is a relatively neutral term.

2. The Connecticut NRZ guidelines, which include a good discussion of what should be addressed in each of these four areas, are available on the web at www.opm.state.ct.us/igp/POLDEV/nrzguide.HTM

- How do we get there?

- How can we measure our progress?

A more detailed breakdown is provided in table 18.1.

The strategies, activities, and budgets should be ambitious but realistic. A plan that simply lists all the projects everyone would like to see happen is a meaningless wish list. To be considered realistic, the plan's elements must meet two separate tests:

- They must be realistic in terms of the funds, technical, and managerial capacity available for activities or improvements in the neighborhood.

- They must reflect a realistic sense of what is feasible under current and likely future market conditions.

The plan must be closely attuned to the realities of the marketplace. Key elements, particularly retail and mixed-income housing, must be market-driven if they are to be successful. Unless the process includes an assessment of market conditions and trends and brings that assessment to bear on the choices being considered by the community, it is unlikely to be successful in the long run.

Participatory Planning Process. A fundamental principle of neighborhood revitalization planning is that it should take place with not only the participation but also the active engagement of area residents and other neighborhood stakeholders. Unless the people who make up the neighborhood play an active role in making the choices and framing the strategies that go into the plan, it will be far less effective as a vehicle for meaningful neighborhood change. This is particularly important in lower-income communities, where residents have become accustomed to being at best the beneficiaries and at worst the victims of decisions made elsewhere, with little input into their own future or that of the community.

Key principles should guide resident engagement:

- Residents are seen as a critical community asset, not only for planning but also for implementation.

- Residents have power in the process in relation to, and in balance with, other stakeholders.

- Residents participate in framing the plan, not just react to ideas put forward by others.

- Residents have substantive governance roles in the organization sponsoring the planning process.

- Professionals work cooperatively with residents and other stakeholders to serve the residents' agenda, addressing their ideas, hopes, and visions.

These principles demand a planning process, and specific outreach techniques, that go well beyond the traditional practice of holding occasional community

TABLE 18.1 Scope of a Neighborhood Revitalization Plan

Neighborhood definition	The neighborhood and its boundaries should be defined, and the reasons for selecting it should be identified. Key relationships between the neighborhood and other neighborhoods within the city, as well as other municipalities, if applicable, should also be identified.
Neighborhood conditions	A detailed description of conditions in the neighborhood, using both statistical and qualitative information, should be provided, adequate both to document the need for neighborhood revitalization and to establish the relationship between neighborhood conditions and the proposed strategies in the revitalization plan. This section should include maps, as detailed as possible, of existing physical conditions, with particular emphasis on problem conditions, such as abandoned or underutilized properties.
Concept or vision for the neighborhood	The plan should include a statement of the overall goals and objectives of the revitalization effort, as well as specific goals, such as improving housing conditions and increasing number of jobs and participation rates in preschool education. This section may include a description of the shared vision of what the neighborhood will be like ten or twenty years in the future, as a result of implementing the plan.
Strategies for fostering neighborhood revitalization	The plan should set forth specific strategies and, for each, a clear rationale showing how it addresses existing problem conditions and how it fits into the overall strategy, along with an explanation of how it will help realize the community's vision of its future.
Activities to be pursued to implement each strategy	Specific activities should be identified for each strategy. To the extent feasible, achievement measures of for each activity should be identified.
Financial requirements	Estimates of the funds that will be required for each activity, the nature of the funds (such as grants, short-term loans, and long-term loans) needed, and identification of potential sources, to the extent feasible, should be presented.
Timetable	A timeline for all of the activities that have been identified, including start and end dates, and, to the extent feasible, benchmarks for measuring progress of the activities should be included.
Monitoring and revising the plan	The plan should specify a procedure for monitoring the implementation of the plan, as well as changes in conditions within the neighborhood and city, and for reviewing and revising the plan on a regular basis to reflect changes in conditions and priorities.
Relationship to other plans	Any other plans that contain provisions for the future revitalization or redevelopment of the neighborhood, including master plans, urban renewal plans, and the like, and any inconsistencies or conflicts between the neighborhood revitalization plan and those plans should be identified.

Source: Based on criteria for neighborhood revitalization plans developed for the New Jersey Neighborhood Revitalization State Tax Credit program.

meetings. In many communities, development of neighborhood plans has been closely integrated with parallel community organizing efforts.

Engaging residents seriously in the neighborhood planning process is likely to create tensions between residents and professionals and between residents and other stakeholders, particularly local government. Many municipal officials, while often welcoming input, are reluctant to cede power over the process or its outcomes to nongovernmental partners. This issue must be addressed directly, because in many cities the process is initiated, and largely funded, by city government. The rules for the process must be clearly framed and understood by the parties in advance. If the governmental partners insist on maintaining excessive control over the process, the resulting plan may be less effective as a vehicle for neighborhood change.

Implementation and Monitoring. How the plan is implemented is as important as the process by which it is created. The plan should include an ongoing implementation strategy, identifying which organizations will be responsible for each element and how the overall progress of the effort will be coordinated.

The process must build the community-based institutions needed to implement the plan. If responsibility for implementation is centralized in city government, many of the benefits created by a participatory process will be lost. If residents and other community stakeholders have been engaged in framing the plan, they must also be engaged in implementing it. In many cities, neighborhood councils have been created for this purpose. Under a recently enacted New Jersey law, in order for a neighborhood revitalization project to be eligible for state tax credits, a nonprofit organization that has been engaged in community development activity in the neighborhood must have overall responsibility for preparing and implementing the plan.[3]

Monitoring is part of implementation. Traditionally, many plans have been prepared and adopted with little attention to implementation generally and even less to tracking and evaluating progress. Monitoring recognizes that neighborhood

3. The Neighborhood Revitalization State Tax Credit Act (see box on p. 258).

TABLE 18.2 Common Neighborhood Revitalization Planning Models

Model	Description	Examples
Citywide neighborhood revitalization strategy	Through city initiative, neighborhood revitalization planning is carried out in all neighborhoods—or all neighborhoods meeting threshold criteria—in city	Minneapolis, MN Rochester, NY Houston, TX Portland, OR Seattle, WA
Target neighborhood revitalization strategy	Through city initiative, neighborhood revitalization planning is targeted at selected neighborhoods on the basis of priority criteria	Richmond, VA Baltimore, MD
Neighborhood-driven revitalization planning	Individual neighborhoods initiate "bottom-up" revitalization planning strategies for their area	Camden, NJ East St. Louis, IL

revitalization is a dynamic process. Although a plan may have a five- or ten-year horizon, it must be designed to allow for modifications to reflect changes in conditions, address unanticipated problems, and take advantage of new opportunities. Neighborhood councils and CDCs implementing revitalization plans must also recognize the growing emphasis by funding agencies on accountability in the use of their funds and be prepared to respond accordingly.

B. Models of Neighborhood Revitalization Planning

While every neighborhood revitalization plan is different, the process of developing the plan tends to follow one of a small number of models. The three basic models are summarized in table 18.2.

Citywide Neighborhood Revitalization Strategies

Citywide efforts to promote neighborhood revitalization planning can be powerful vehicles for community change, as in Minneapolis, but they run the risk of becoming a diluted process that can potentially hinder more substantive efforts. Albeit with substantial variations from city to city, these strategies typically follow a parallel series of steps:

1. Neighborhoods or planning areas are designated. The city planning office typically divides the entire city into neighborhoods or planning areas, usually leaving out self-contained nonresidential areas such as industrial parks or rail yards and using widely accepted neighborhood definitions and boundaries where possible. Cities vary widely in the number and size of the areas they designate as neighborhoods for planning or revitalization purposes (see table 18.3), ranging from

TABLE 18.3 Average Population of Neighborhood Planning Areas for
Selected Cities

City	Total population in 2000	Number of neighborhoods or planning areas	Average population per planning area
Portland	529,121	8	66,140
Houston	1,953,631	88	22,200
Rochester	219,773	10	21,977
Seattle	563,374	38	14,826
Minneapolis	382,618	81	4,723

eighty-eight "super neighborhoods" for Houston's planning process to as few as
eight planning areas in Portland, Oregon, which combined many neighborhoods
into larger districts. The average population of neighborhood planning areas
ranges from more than 66,000 in Portland to fewer than 5,000 in Minneapolis.

The size of the neighborhoods or planning areas should reflect the nature of
the planning to be done, as well as the availability of resources.

2. Neighborhoods choose to participate in the planning process. Cities typically set threshold requirements for participating in neighborhood planning efforts.
Houston required the creation of a Super Neighborhood Council, while Minneapolis sought a more extensive demonstration of the neighborhood council's
capacity to organize and plan for the neighborhood. Typically, neighborhoods
that see the greatest need for revitalization strategies or which have strong organizations already in place will be quickest to participate. More stable or affluent
areas have also found it worth their while to participate in order to obtain better
access to resources for such things as street improvements and open space or to
utilize the process to gain a voice in reshaping city land use and other ordinances
affecting their areas to better reflect their concerns.

In citywide strategies, every neighborhood that meets the criteria becomes
eligible to participate, even though resource limitations may result in a phased
process. Minneapolis used a lottery to determine which neighborhoods would be
able to participate in its Neighborhood Revitalization Program (NRP) first. Neighborhoods selected for the NRP then entered into a participation agreement with
the city, spelling out how they would carry out their responsibilities under the program. Ultimately, every neighborhood in the city joined the NRP.

3. The plan is prepared. The next step is for the neighborhood, or the city and
neighborhood, to prepare the neighborhood plan, a process that includes community outreach and assembly of background information. The scope of the plans
and the nature of the planning process vary widely, depending on the city's reasons
for initiating the strategy and the strength of their commitment to citizen-based

GOOD PRACTICES

A number of cities have initiated citywide neighborhood planning strategies.

Minneapolis began the Neighborhood Revitalization Program (NRP), a large-scale effort funded through tax increment financing revenues, in 1990. Each of the city's eighty-one neighborhoods is engaged in planning and improvement activities under the NRP. According to the city's web site, "neighborhood-based planning and priority setting are at the heart of the NRP."

Rochester, New York, initiated Neighbors Building Neighborhoods (NBN) in 1994. The city was divided into ten planning sectors. Each planning sector has organized itself and has gone through a process of creating community vision statements, defining issues and priorities, and developing action plans. The action plans are used both to prioritize city investment and as the basis for the city's comprehensive plan, "Rochester 2010: The Renaissance."

Houston created its Super Neighborhoods program in 1999 with the goal of creating a neighborhood planning process directly tied to implementation. Each neighborhood creates an annual Super Neighborhood Action Plan (SNAP) that the city uses to prioritize investments in the neighborhood. Residents and others can track the status of SNAP elements through an online system.

planning. The scope of the Minneapolis and Rochester plans generally follows the description of neighborhood revitalization plans offered at the beginning of this chapter. In both cases the process has been strongly neighborhood-driven. In Houston, the Super Neighborhood Action Plans are much more focused on short-term actions than on long-term neighborhood change, whereas in Portland the preparation of plans was driven in large part by the city's comprehensive planning process.

The roles of the city and the neighborhood organization vary widely. The city usually provides at least some technical assistance, through city staff or consultants, or provides funds to allow the neighborhood council to hire its own. In Portland, the city's staff largely drove the process, reflecting the city's goal to develop small area plans as part of the city's comprehensive plan, rather than having a neighborhood-based impetus. Minneapolis's neighborhood councils had a strong support system available to them through the Center for Urban and Regional Affairs at the University of Minnesota, through the Center's Neighborhood Planning for Community Revitalization (NPCR) program (see page 260).

Adequate resources must be available to carry out the tasks that make up the planning process. Preparing a solid and well-documented neighborhood plan requires substantial time and commitment from professionals as well as lay individuals. A process that demands that neighborhood-based organizations do the planning, without providing access to adequate resources, is likely to fail.

4. *The plan is adopted.* Once completed, the plan must be formally adopted both by the neighborhood and by the city. Adoption at the neighborhood level is typically carried out through the neighborhood council responsible for developing the plan. If the plan is to be a part of the municipal comprehensive plan or land use ordinance, it must be adopted by the planning commission and sometimes by the municipal governing body. At that point, it becomes an official municipal document.

In Minneapolis, the plan is used as the basis for allocating large amounts of discretionary funds to neighborhood projects. It is first approved at the neighborhood level through a participatory process led by the elected NRP steering committee and then submitted to the city, where it is reviewed first by a management review team and then by the NRP Policy Board, a body made up of city and neighborhood representatives. It is ultimately approved by the city, county, and school district. Formal approval is essential to any city-driven planning process, since it provides the legal basis on which the city can build the neighborhood's plan into its land use regulations and use it to allocate public resources.

5. *The plan is implemented.* From the city's standpoint, neighborhood planning gives the city direction for public actions. From the neighborhood perspective, participating in the process should help influence city decisionmaking and gain resources for community needs. City actions growing out of neighborhood plans can include

- incorporating the plan into the city's comprehensive plan or land use ordinances and changing the city's zoning and other land use regulations to reflect the plan's strategies;

- using the plan to prioritize city activities, such as street or sidewalk improvements;

- using the plan to prioritize discretionary funds, such as CDBG, housing subsidy, and economic development funds;

- setting aside a pool of funds for specific projects and activities identified by neighborhoods in their plans.

An outstanding example of implementation is that of Minneapolis, where the city pooled a body of funds generated from tax increment financing districts to create the Common Fund to support NRP projects. The Common Fund was designed to generate $20 million per year for twenty years, or a total of $400

GOOD PRACTICES

Houston has established the SNAP Action Information System to track each action item in each Super Neighborhood Action Plan, along with the city's response. Once the city has accepted an action item onto its agenda, a projected start date is entered, and the project's progress is tracked from that point forward. The system is accessible online to neighborhood residents and other interested parties.

Seattle maintains an online Approval and Adoption Matrix to track implementation of each neighborhood plan. The matrix is divided into two sections: key strategies, usually complex projects or related activities that the neighborhood considers critical to the successful implementation of the plan; and additional activities, which are not directly associated with a key strategy. They are ranked on the basis of priority and time frame in the matrix.

million as seed money for the revitalization of the city's neighborhoods.[4] During the first ten years of the NRP, neighborhood allocations ranged from a high of $18 million in one severely distressed area to a low of $260,000 for another, more stable area.

Successful plan implementation is often the result of negotiation between neighborhood leaders and city officials. In Rochester's Neighbors Building Neighborhoods (NBN) program, a formal consultation takes place after the neighborhood plan is completed in draft and before it is finalized, when specific city commitments can be locked in, which are subsequently incorporated into the final plan. An NBN Priority Group, made up of senior officials from each city department and the school district and chaired by the mayor's chief of staff, meets quarterly to ensure that NBN priorities are reflected in each department's decision-making process.

How the plan will be implemented once approved, and the potential resources available for that purpose, should be clearly spelled out at the beginning of the process so that all stakeholders understand both the opportunities and the limitations of the plan. Implementing the plan should signify a formal commitment by the city and other participating jurisdictions to the neighborhoods engaged in the process.

4. Although the fund operated at that level for its first ten years, state legislation restructuring the property tax in 2001 had the inadvertent effect of significantly reducing the income stream into the Common Fund. This change resulted in a dramatic decline in subsequent funding for the program.

GOOD PRACTICE

Faced with concerns that the city was not using its community revitalization resources effectively, the city of Richmond, Virginia, initiated the Neighborhoods in Bloom (NIB) program in 1999. After an extensive planning process, the city designated six of the city's forty-nine neighborhoods as NIB neighborhoods. The city formed partnerships with neighborhood organizations and CDCs in those neighborhoods, developing strategies focusing largely on physical and public safety improvements. The city then assembled resources from many city departments and applied federal and state funding, aggressive code enforcement, public safety, and community empowerment to support those strategies.

The city initially committed its resources to these six neighborhoods for two years, a commitment that was subsequently extended for another two years. Crime rates have gone down in the NIB neighborhoods, property values have increased, and homeownership rates have gone up.

6. *Progress on implementation is tracked.* Implementation of a neighborhood plan is the sum of a host of separate actions. Without a well-organized system to track the elements of the plan and their progress toward realization, the implementation process may become disorganized and inefficient. Houston and Seattle have developed sophisticated systems to track implementation of their neighborhood plans. Such systems are most useful when they are Internet-based and thus easily available to neighborhood residents and other parties interested in knowing what is being contemplated and how it is moving forward.

Target-Neighborhood Revitalization Strategies

A hard issue in any citywide strategy is whether it is realistically possible for any city, given its operational and financial constraints, to foster meaningful revitalization simultaneously in all of its neighborhoods. If the city's discretionary resources for implementing neighborhood plans are limited, a strategy that attempts to spread those resources across the entire city may result in token activities incapable of bringing about meaningful change. Moreover, both the city and its neighborhoods may lack the planning, organizing, and project management capacity to pursue a large number of simultaneous strategies. These constraints have indeed limited some of the citywide efforts cited above.

Rather than attempt to address all of the city's distressed areas, an alternative approach is to target a smaller number of neighborhoods for revitalization. The advantage of such a strategy is that by concentrating both planning capacity and funds for implementation, the city can catalyze significant change in the targeted areas. Such a strategy, however, can also backfire if it is not sustained on a long-term basis. Experience suggests that targeted strategies should meet several criteria:

- A strong consensus should exist at both the city and neighborhood levels that targeting of resources is a sound strategy.

- The process of determining which neighborhoods are targeted should be open, data-driven, and participatory.

- The commitment to the targeted neighborhoods should be substantial enough, and extend over a long enough period, to create the opportunity for meaningful change.

- Some resources should remain available for priority activities in other parts of the city.

The elements of the planning and implementation process, including formal adoption of the plan and an effective tracking system for implementation, are essentially the same as in a citywide neighborhood revitalization strategy, described earlier.

Neighborhood-Based Revitalization Planning

The impetus for the planning strategies described above, although they engaged neighborhood residents, came from municipal government. Neighborhood-driven revitalization planning is fundamentally different. Here the impetus comes from an organization, coalition, or other body based in a neighborhood, operating independently of—and sometimes in conflict with—local government. Some of the most notable examples of effective neighborhood-based planning have taken place in areas where, for various reasons, municipal government was failing to address the need for change.

Neighborhood-driven revitalization planning arises from the desire by residents or neighborhood-based organizations to give community improvement efforts a tighter focus and clearer direction. The impetus may come from a CDC that realizes that it must go beyond a project-by-project approach to a more comprehensive rebuilding strategy, or from a neighborhood council or civic organization.

While the planning process itself is not fundamentally different from that described above, the dynamics of a neighborhood-initiated process are significantly different. Rather than having governmental approvals and resource allocation built into the process, neighborhood-based planners must sell their plan to the city and others in order to elicit the approvals and resources necessary to carry it out; such a process is as much about politics as about planning. Ultimately, the success of the plan may depend on the ability of the neighborhood's leadership to establish a sound working relationship with local government.

Neighborhood-based planning is usually much more about community empowerment, in the sense of building the ability of residents and other stakeholders to participate in decisions that affect their community and to act in an organized fash-

GOOD PRACTICES

The first neighborhood-based revitalization plan in Camden, New Jersey, was developed in 1993 by a number of organizations, including a community land trust, in North Camden. During the 1990s, a cluster of strong CDCs emerged in other neighborhoods of that city. Reflecting both the inability of the city to provide leadership for neighborhood revitalization and the growing capability and sophistication of the CDCs, a series of planning efforts began between 2000 and 2002 in five other city neighborhoods.

Residents of East St. Louis's Emerson Park neighborhood reached out to the East St. Louis Action Research Project (ESLARP) at the University of Illinois at Urbana-Champaign in 1990 for planning assistance. That initial request fostered a partnership between the neighborhood residents, the Emerson Park Development Corporation, and ESLARP that led to a five-year neighborhood stabilization strategy for the area. ESLARP subsequently broadened its efforts, working with three other neighborhoods and developing the Neighborhood College program to build the knowledge and skills of community activists.

ion to pursue their interests. This demands, in turn, greater emphasis on organizing, building leadership, and engaging residents in all steps of the planning process, as well as different behavior by the professionals assisting the community, as Ken Reardon has written:

> Empowerment planners actively involve citizen leaders, on an equal basis with practicing professionals, at every phase of the planning process. . . . Empowerment planners work to enhance the . . . knowledge and skills of local residents so they may maintain the community problem-solving and organizing processes initiated by the professional planner long after he or she leaves the community. Empowerment planners seek to reduce the dependence local citizen organizations have on outside experts and institutions by assisting local leaders in developing their knowledge, skills and power base.[5]

Neighborhood-based planning is more likely to recognize the inherent tensions between city governments and neighborhoods, which are often finessed rather than addressed clearly in city-driven planning processes. One tension is the competition for resources not only between neighborhoods but also between neighborhood revitalization and other competing government concerns. Another, even

5. Kenneth Reardon, "Community Development in Low-Income Minority Neighborhoods: A Case for Empowerment Planning" (paper presented at Association of Collegiate Schools of Planning annual conference, Phoenix, November 1994).

The New Jersey Neighborhood Revitalization State Tax Credit Act (C.52:27D-490 et seq.), enacted in 2002 and amended in 2003, provides for up to $10 million per year in state 50 percent corporate tax credits to generate $20 million in corporate support for community-based neighborhood revitalization efforts. As a result of the tax credit, the corporation can deduct 50 percent of its contribution from its corporate income tax or other state tax liabilities. Combined with its federal charitable tax deduction, the cost to the corporation becomes roughly 25 cents for every dollar contributed. For a neighborhood to be eligible for these funds, a revitalization plan for the neighborhood must be completed and submitted to the state for approval by a neighborhood-based nonprofit entity. The plan must be prepared through a participatory process, as outlined in table 18.1. While it must be submitted to the municipality for review and comment, municipal approval of the plan is not required.

more basic, may be the conflict between competing visions of the neighborhood's future and competing priorities for immediate action.

C. Building a Support System for Neighborhood Revitalization Planning

Neighborhood revitalization planning requires a support system, which should include financial resources tied to plan implementation, and access to the professional expertise needed to develop plans and to build the capacity of residents to plan for their community and direct the implementation of their plans.

Financial Resources

Important financial resources for neighborhood revitalization, such as CDBG or HOME funds, are not explicitly tied to neighborhood planning efforts. Successful revitalization efforts should link use of those funds to comprehensive revitalization strategies while leveraging those funds to generate additional dedicated resources.

Minneapolis's $400 million Common Fund is perhaps the largest sum explicitly earmarked by any city for implementing neighborhood revitalization plans. The New Jersey Neighborhood Revitalization State Tax Credit provides individual neighborhoods with up to $1 million per year, from a total of $20 million available annually statewide, with no limit to the number of years the neighborhood may receive assistance.[6]

6. The CDC that acts as the lead organization for implementing the plan must prepare an annual list of activities to be funded with tax credit assistance. The law requires at least 60 percent of the tax

The Philadelphia-based Wachovia Regional Foundation, established as a result of the 1998 acquisition of CoreStates Bank by First Union (now Wachovia) Bank, gives high priority to neighborhood revitalization planning and implementation. The foundation awards both planning grants ($25,000 to $100,000) and implementation grants ($100,000 to $750,000) to nonprofit neighborhood-based organizations in the Mid-Atlantic states. In 2003 they provided a total of $5.1 million to seventeen organizations.

Rhode Island Housing, a state agency, provides planning grants of up to $50,000 to fund community-based neighborhood planning, as well as small grants of up to $10,000 for targeted assistance to community groups.

The private sector is a growing source of support for neighborhood revitalization planning. Cities and CDCs have found that planning-based revitalization strategies are often attractive to corporations and foundations, which prefer to see their funds used in a strategic rather than an ad hoc fashion.

Technical Support Resources

Plans that create a challenging but achievable vision for a neighborhood's future, and that embody meaningful resident engagement, demand the support of planning and other professionals who have not only a high level of technical skill and knowledge but also the ability and desire to work with community residents and organizations, ideally playing the role of empowerment planner envisioned by Reardon. Such professionals are in short supply. Few cities have the planning staff to offer such support to their neighborhoods. While most planning consulting firms will readily take on neighborhood planning contracts, few bring the particular skills and philosophy needed to carry out such contracts effectively. It is arguably preferable to have no plan at all than to have a plan that, although glossy, fails to reflect community needs. University-based planning programs have filled some part of this gap. The University of Minnesota program (see box on page 260) is perhaps the outstanding example; the University of Illinois at Urbana-Champaign provided planning skills for neighborhood planning in East St. Louis.

Local officials, CDCs, and advocates should explore a variety of steps, both short- and long-term, to increase the extent and quality of neighborhood planning:

---

credit funds to be spent on housing and economic development activities; the balance can be used on other activities that benefit the neighborhood, including infrastructure improvement, community services, and community organizing and outreach.

Through the Center for Urban and Regional Affairs (CURA) at the University of Minnesota, a consortium of Twin Cities colleges and universities established a program called Neighborhood Planning for Community Revitalization (NPCR) in 1993 to help Minneapolis neighborhoods take advantage of the opportunities presented by the city's Neighborhood Revitalization Program. Over the first five years of the program, NPCR had carried out 161 projects, working with sixty-seven of Minneapolis's eighty-one neighborhood planning areas. NPCR considers the neighborhoods its clients, and faculty and students working on its projects are accountable to the neighborhood to produce a usable product, which can be a plan, a study, or an analysis of a particular issue, in a specified time period.

In 1999, CURA began to develop the Minneapolis Neighborhood Information System (MNIS), an interactive GIS system for use by the city and neighborhood organizations. In addition to making the system available to the community, CURA devotes substantial time and effort to training neighborhood residents to use the system.

- Work with state organizations to develop training and professional development courses in neighborhood planning skills for practicing planners and other professionals

- Work with graduate schools of city planning to add neighborhood planning to their curricula

- Encourage city planning and development agencies to hire individuals with the skills and motivation to be effective neighborhood planners

- Create neighborhood planning technical assistance centers, at the local, regional, or state level as appropriate, with qualified staff who can work directly with neighborhood organizations and CDCs and mentor less experienced planners

- Provide models, guidelines, and templates for use in neighborhood planning projects

- Build the capacity of neighborhood residents to work effectively with planners and other consultants and to carry out information gathering and dissemination activities

Building Resident Capacity

The essence of a neighborhood revitalization plan is that it belongs to the residents of the neighborhood. Enabling residents to participate fully in framing the

GOOD PRACTICES

The city of Rochester, New York, created the NBN Institute as a part of its Neighbors Building Neighborhoods (NBN) initiative. The institute provides citizens with training in community planning and revitalization. The city actively solicits community input regarding topics, time frames, and training formats. During 2000, three hundred citizens participated in sessions that included leadership training, local self-reliance and ownership, planning and land use, and the use of GIS tools.

Rochester's NBN initiative also includes the NeighborLink Network, a community technology initiative designed to improve communication among NBN partners and provide access to information and planning tools. A site is established in each of the ten planning sectors: each has a computer that provides access to the NBN Information Management System, GIS mapping, and other software applications, along with a printer. Residents can use the sites to track and report NBN activities, create customized maps for their communities, and access web-based resources.

Norfolk, Virginia, created the Neighborhood University in 1999 to train citizens to become effective advocates for their communities and work to improve housing conditions, strengthen neighborhood organizations, and build the quality of community life. Spring 2003 programs included twelve course offerings, ranging from leadership skills to grant writing, board development, and understanding environmental codes.

plan and directing its implementation, becoming more than passive consumers of planning services, is critical to realizing that outcome. A number of cities have responded to this imperative by structuring opportunities for capacity-building within the neighborhood planning process, beginning with East St. Louis's Neighborhood College.

As geographic and management information systems become more widely used, enabling residents to have access to and use those systems becomes a critical part of any planning and implementation process. The training the University of Minnesota provides in using the Minneapolis Neighborhood Information System makes that system a particularly valuable tool for neighborhood revitalization.

D. Using Neighborhood Revitalization Planning to Address Abandoned Property Issues

Neighborhood revitalization planning is a particularly effective way to build a neighborhood-based strategy to address abandoned property issues. A neighborhood focus is particularly useful because different neighborhoods may vary widely in several respects:

- The nature and extent of abandoned property problems

- The dynamics of abandonment and the types of abandoned property that are most problematic

- The priority given to abandonment as a neighborhood issue

- The specific strategies that can be developed to address the abandonment issue

These issues can often be addressed more effectively through neighborhood-level planning than through a centralized approach. Neighborhood residents trained to identify and assess properties can integrate that information into the planning process at a level of detail and specificity that is hard for city officials to match.[7] In addition to identifying properties, residents can provide information on their condition, their level of maintenance, and whether they are being used for illegal or inappropriate purposes.

The neighborhood planning team should also investigate the dynamics of abandonment in the neighborhood to identify strategies to prevent future abandonment. Increased predatory lending activity that could trigger future homeowner abandonment or a trend in disinvestment by landlords on a particular block can be spotted by trained neighborhood-level observers well before such problems become apparent to local officials.

Where abandoned properties are a significant issue in the neighborhood, the plan should address the issue explicitly, either as a distinct planning element or as a separately identified subset of the land use or physical redevelopment element of the plan. The plan should address all three dimensions of the abandonment "life cycle" described above—abandonment prevention, controlling abandoned properties, and developing productive reuse strategies for those properties.

We have selected two issues associated with abandoned property to illustrate how such problems might be addressed by a hypothetical neighborhood plan:

- An increase in predatory lending, triggering an increase in foreclosure and abandonment by homeowners

- Large numbers of abandoned properties in the neighborhood that could be used productively but which are not being adequately maintained or secured by their owners

7. This information can be integrated into a GIS system by providing the neighborhood residents with inexpensive handheld computers. If that is not feasible, they can complete paper forms from which data can be entered into the GIS system at a central location.

TABLE 18.4 Examples of Abandoned Property Strategies in a Neighborhood Revitalization Plan

Issue	Increase in predatory lending triggers increased foreclosure and abandonment by neighborhood homeowners.	Large number of abandoned properties that could be reused productively are held by absentee owners who are not adequately maintaining or securing their properties.
Goals	Reduce use of subprime mortgages and home equity loans in neighborhood. Reduce rate of foreclosures associated with existing subprime loans outstanding.	Improve condition and maintenance of vacant lots and vacant buildings. Reuse abandoned properties for productive purposes.
Strategies	Provide counseling for prospective borrowers (both new buyers and existing owners). Disseminate anti–predatory lending information and information on alternative borrowing options. Make competitive, affordable home improvement loan products available. Establish foreclosure prevention program.	Get vacant lots in neighborhood cleaned, fenced, and greened. Get owners or city to secure and maintain abandoned buildings. Press owners to transfer abandoned properties into hands of city or other entity capable of reusing properties productively.
Activities	Open storefront home-buyer and homeowner counseling and information center in neighborhood. Carry out anti–predatory lending "sweeps" at six-month intervals, using "Don't Borrow Trouble" and other materials. Get bank with neighborhood branch office to offer better home improvement and home equity loans. Obtain city funds to write down interest rate on home improvement loans to lower-income homeowners.	Create community greening program to take over vacant lots, clean and fence them, and plant trees or use space for mini-parks or community gardens. Get city to strictly enforce codes against illegal dumping on vacant lots and governing maintenance of vacant buildings, securing buildings and placing liens on properties as needed. Get city to undertake tax foreclosure of all eligible properties in area.

continued

		Purchase tax liens on selected abandoned properties to gain direct control of those properties for reuse.
		Obtain city consent to use vacant property receivership authority to gain control of abandoned properties.*
Potential funding and in-kind sources	CDBG funds Local lenders	CDBG funds Other city funds, including department of parks and recreation City staff, including tax office, city attorney, and maintenance crews CDFI predevelopment loan fund† Pro bono legal services
Potential responsible entities	NeighborWorks organization Other CDC or community service organization City department of housing Lenders	Neighborhood-based CDC City departments, including housing, tax, attorney, parks and recreation, and public works Local or area horticultural society or environmental organization Local youth employment or training program

*Assumes that statutory authority for vacant property receivership is available in the jurisdiction.
†A number of community loan funds as well as public agencies maintain predevelopment funds from which a CDC may be able to borrow funds for buying tax liens or properties at tax foreclosure sales.

The issues are presented in table 18.4. Both demand a multifaceted strategy. In the case of absentee-owned abandoned properties, attention must be paid to two issues:

- Improving the maintenance of the properties

- Establishing a process by which properties can be acquired and placed in the hands of entities capable of reusing them productively

Each of those strategies, in turn, has many different features and will require more than one step to execute. Improving the maintenance of abandoned buildings and vacant lots might involve many different activities:

- A campaign to curb illegal dumping
- Cleaning, landscaping, and fencing vacant lots
- A community gardening program
- Targeted code enforcement by the city
- Nuisance abatement activities

In some cases, a local entity, such as a youth training program or a locally based CDC, may be able to carry out one or more of these activities. Elsewhere, the neighborhood organization may be able to reach out to some entity, such as a horticultural society, providing services in another part of the city. Many of the necessary activities, however, can be performed only by the city or must be formally delegated by the city to a nongovernmental entity. As a result, the neighborhood must have, or build, the ability to persuade the city to allocate resources to those activities. Finally, funds must be found for each activity. While none of the examples listed above is particularly expensive as revitalization strategies go, funds will be required for each, including municipal funds for nuisance abatement.

CHAPTER 19

Principles for Abandoned Property Reuse

A. Thinking about Reuse

However problematic abandoned properties may be today, they represent a major opportunity to build a brighter community future by creating new uses that strengthen the community, enhance its quality of life, and improve its position in the marketplace. Whether that future is realized depends on a series of reuse decisions: not only the nature of the reuse—whether housing, open space, or a shopping center—but also the planning and design decisions that determine how it will look, how it will fit into its surroundings, and how it will mesh with the community's long-term strategy for the area.

The purpose of this chapter is to suggest *how* reuse decisions should be made, not to recommend specific reuse alternatives, which must be determined by those most familiar with the community and the features of each property. Finding the most appropriate and sustainable reuse, however, involves much more than deciding whether a building should be used for a store, a single-family residence, or an apartment building. Decisions must be made at three separate levels, of which the question of use is not the first but the third.

1. Scale. The scale of the reuse can range from an individual building or vacant lot to many acres. Scale is often an issue in cities such as Baltimore or Philadelphia, which contain large areas where vacant properties exceed the number of occupied buildings. To what extent these areas should be assembled into larger parcels and on what scale that assembly should take place, as well as the extent to which occupied properties should be taken in order to create suitable redevelopment sites, is a critical issue for public officials, planners, and CDCs.

2. Character. The character of the reuse project is established by the site planning and design that define the manner in which the site is used, and the relationship of new buildings and open spaces to existing buildings and to their neighborhood setting. Some projects may be designed to blend into their setting; others, such as many recent large-scale residential projects, may be designed to create a new environment contrasting with that setting. A fundamental issue in defining the character of a reuse project is the density of the development, in light of the growing trend to use abandoned property redevelopment as a strategy to reconfigure inner-city neighborhoods at lower, more suburban densities. A closely related question, discussed earlier, is when and whether to demolish abandoned buildings or preserve them for rehabilitation.

3. Use. Ultimately, within the framework of scale and character, decisions must be made about specific uses for specific properties. The most appropriate uses are often more a function of the location than of the physical features of the property. In some cases the reuse is obvious, but often it is not. An abandoned row house on an otherwise intact residential block should clearly be reused as a single-family home, but the vacant industrial building on the next block might lend itself to many uses, including multifamily residential, commercial or institutional, or continued industrial use—or a mixture of uses. The use or uses most appropriate in a given situation are the sum of many considerations:

- The long-term vision for the area
- Policy goals for the area, such as increasing the number of jobs or the homeownership rate
- The preferences and desires of the residents of the neighborhood, such as a need for more affordable housing or a desire for convenient retail facilities
- The present or future market demand for various uses
- The public sector cost for different uses and the availability of resources
- Developer interest in pursuing specific uses for the property

The weight given to each consideration will vary with each project. Developer interest, which is often allowed to drive redevelopment, is only one factor among many. The larger the development, the more complex and varied the choices are likely to be. Particularly for large-scale projects that could potentially change an area's character, a thorough evaluation should be carried out before making any decision. The quality of such an evaluation depends heavily on the quality of the planning, at both the city and neighborhood levels, that precedes it. If neither the city nor the neighborhood have a coherent vision of their future, decisionmakers will have no framework within which to evaluate alternatives.

B. Quality Matters: Establishing Design Principles for Reuse Projects

Any community seriously attempting to become more attractive to home buyers with the ability to choose where they live should make sure that all new development, rehabilitation, and reuse projects meet the highest standards of planning, design, and construction. While cities have little control over larger regional forces, they *can* control the quality of what takes place within the city. By following simple principles of good planning and design, cities can use design quality as a means to improve the city's quality of life and competitive position within its region.

How well a project is planned and designed, whether it is a single house or a new development with hundreds of units, will determine in large part whether it enhances the quality of the neighborhood and fosters its regeneration or merely perpetuates an unsatisfactory status quo. Off-the-shelf modular houses on infill lots, cheaply constructed speculative townhouses built on vacant lots, and seas of asphalt parking all send the message that the community has no aspiration to become a better place to live. By respecting the community's architectural heritage and making sure that every new development adds quality to its environment, cities can not only fuel revitalization but also increase the likelihood of long-term, sustainable change.

Design means far more than the architectural treatment of building elevations. It encompasses many interrelated considerations:

- The density, intensity, and massing of the development
- The relationship among the different uses on the site
- The relationship between the buildings and the open spaces on the site
- The relationship between the character of the site and its surroundings

Design subsumes the work of not only the architect but also the urban designer, urban planner, and landscape architect. Design in the urban context is a vast subject with its own extensive literature; this section highlights key design principles for successful reuse projects.

Reuse of abandoned properties can take the form of infill on small or large sites, rehabilitation of one or more buildings, or a combination of new construction and rehabilitation. With rare exceptions, it takes place within an existing environmental context. That context is generally an urban neighborhood, often a long-established built environment. The design will determine how the reuse project relates to that context. The design can consciously seek to blend the new development into its context, or it can consciously seek to create a positive contrast with that context. Finally, as has happened all too often in urban redevelopment, reuse projects can be designed so that they appear utterly indifferent to their context. In such situations, new projects not only fail to enhance their surroundings but can actually undermine their viability.

Two broad themes are central to the design process: respecting the past and respecting the future.

Respecting the Past

Few areas, even in the most distressed cities, have been undone to such an extent that the context for reuse projects no longer matters. Every older American city has a distinctive character and vernacular housing types central to its history and identity, such as the Philadelphia row house or the Chicago bungalow.

The typical urban neighborhood has a certain overall character, although it may vary in degree in different parts of the neighborhood. A Philadelphia row house neighborhood, for example, may have some blocks of two-story row houses and others of three-story buildings. On some blocks the houses may be set back from the sidewalk; on others, the front door sits on the sidewalk line and the front steps protrude onto the sidewalk. In cities like Detroit or Buffalo, where many neighborhoods consist of detached one- or two-family houses, the size of the houses and yards will vary from one block to the next, as will the features of the houses, such as front porches or gables. Variation generally tends to follow two general rules:

• Variations within a neighborhood are usually differences of degree rather than fundamental differences in housing type or character.

• Individual blocks, or clusters of blocks, tend to have a consistent character.

The characteristics of a neighborhood or a block can be categorized and defined in ways that provide direction for future development. The Lower West Side design study in Buffalo identified ten key design features that were characteristic of the area:

• Density, reflected in lot size and frontage patterns

• A mix of new and old housing

• Continuous sidewalk and streetscape amenities

• Landscaping and fencing

• Porches

• Construction materials

• Garages

• Roof pitches and elevation elements

• Window proportions

• Details

These features were used as the basis for developing detailed guidelines for infill housing in the area.

Where the existing pattern is still well established and where it satisfies contemporary market preferences, it may be appropriate to come up with reinterpretations of existing patterns that closely follow the vernacular. This is particularly desirable where new buildings are going to be added to a block on which existing buildings remain, as was the case in the Lower West Side project. Great sensitivity must be shown to design features and addressing the following concerns:

- Maintaining a consistent setback line, or a consistent pattern of variation in setbacks

- Maintaining a consistent ratio between building volumes and the space between the buildings

- Maintaining a consistent pattern of building height

- Replicating key design features, such as porches, stoops, and gables

Being consistent does not mean making every house identical, but rather ensuring that the new and the old exist in a harmonious relationship. The lack of visual harmony which arises when these principles are ignored can be jarring and unpleasant to laypersons as well as professionals. A space between two buildings that is substantially wider than the spaces separating the other buildings on a block feels like a missing tooth; a building that is substantially lower or taller than the general pattern of buildings on the block looks equally out of place.

In some cases, traditional patterns may have already been compromised by incompatible development or by abandonment and demolition, and redevelopment is likely to involve entire blocks or clusters of blocks rather than individual lots. In many such areas, much older housing may also be incompatible with contemporary preferences, as in some of the modest row house neighborhoods of Baltimore or Camden, New Jersey. Here the reinterpretation of traditional pat-

GOOD PRACTICE

The city of Rochester, New York, developed a series of context-sensitive design guidelines for the Atlantic-Woodstock redevelopment area, defined as "simply relating proposed development to surrounding development to ensure cohesive neighborhood character." The guidelines provide a wide range of options grounded in the principles underlying the local single-family residential vernacular architecture.

terns can and should be freer but should still reflect awareness of the history and traditional development pattern of those areas. New developments should be seen as "belonging" to the community, reflecting—through materials, the quality of the streetscape, or distinctive details—the positive features of that community.

Respecting the Future

The principle that redevelopment should respect the past is generally understood and widely accepted, albeit more in theory than in practice. The principle that redevelopment must also respect the future is less widely understood and even more rarely pursued. Simply stated, it is the recognition that each reuse or redevelopment project taking place within a community is part of a cumulative process of neighborhood change. The design choices made on one project affect not only its own character but the character of all those that follow. *The use each project makes of its site and its relationship to its surroundings simultaneously creates and closes off reuse and redevelopment opportunities in the rest of the neighborhood.*

Egregious examples of projects that foreclose future opportunities are the residential and commercial projects in urban neighborhoods where the buildings are set behind a sea of parking, or where they are oriented away from the street, often separated from the street by a high fence or wall. Whatever the justification for these design choices, which is often the desire to foster a perception of greater security, their effect is to severely limit the future potential of the street and ultimately the ability to make the development a meaningful part of a revitalized neighborhood. Other design choices, including excessive setbacks or the use of unattractive or incompatible building materials, can have a similar effect, although at a more modest, and sometimes fixable, level.

How best to respect the future depends to some extent on the scale of the proposed reuse. Where the neighborhood fabric is largely intact and reuse is largely a matter of rehabilitation or small-scale infill, respecting the future is largely the same as respecting the past. In those situations, the goal of reuse strategies is to restore the existing fabric, rather than create a new vernacular for the neighborhood.

In areas with widespread abandonment, where demolition has created large open areas or the existing housing is unsuitable for rehabilitation, design guidelines in themselves are likely to be inadequate. There is no substitute for a strong neighborhood plan to provide a framework to re-create the neighborhood on the basis of new design principles consistent with rebuilding the neighborhood housing market to create an economically diverse community of choice.

In order to provide strong direction for future development, a plan should set forth the following:

- Basic siting principles, including parking treatment, for all new developments, which may vary from one part of the neighborhood to another

- Delineation of areas suitable for rehabilitation and preservation, and design and siting standards for infill development in those areas

- Design guidelines for model housing types, identifying which types are most appropriate for which locations

The plan should specify the location and conceptual layout of future major facilities, where appropriate, including the following:

- New or substantially reconfigured schools or other community facilities

- New or substantially reconfigured parks and recreational facilities

- Open space nodes such as plazas or monuments

- New commercial facilities or substantial reconfiguration of existing commercial areas

- Changes in street patterns and reconfiguration of existing streets, where appropriate, such as widening, creation of green medians, and major changes to parking patterns

A plan formulated with attention to these issues provides a strong framework to ensure that the design of each site will contribute to a whole that will be far more than the sum of isolated, unrelated parts.

Enforcing Design Standards

Design standards and neighborhood plans are only as effective as their enforcement. Enforcing design standards, neighborhood plans, and other tools to ensure consistency with community design objectives depends on two critical elements:

- Establishing a legally enforceable basis for the standards or guidelines
- Establishing an effective review and approval procedure

A legally enforceable basis for design guidelines or a neighborhood plan can take many different forms. The principle that reasonable and fairly enforced design standards are legally valid is widely held, although specific standards vary from state to state. While design regulation for historic preservation has been firmly established since the 1978 Supreme Court *Penn Central* case, the power of local government to enforce such standards through land use regulations is not limited to historic properties or districts. Design standards often form a part of a redevelopment plan and may be treated as an intrinsic part of the municipal zoning or land use ordinance.

In redevelopment areas, detailed design standards may also be enforced in development agreements executed between the municipality and redevelopers. Similarly, if a developer is receiving any discretionary assistance from the municipality, including public land, rezoning, tax abatement, or HOME funds, the municipality can and should impose design standards in return for that assistance. Based on the provisions of state law and the particular conditions under which the design guidelines are to be applied, each municipality should determine the most appropriate legal basis for enforcing them locally.

The provisions of a neighborhood plan are typically enforceable through the municipal regulatory power, either by making it a part of the municipal master plan or by designating the area as a redevelopment area and using the neighborhood plan as the basis for the redevelopment plan.[1] In areas with widespread abandonment, it is usually a good idea to designate all or part of the area as a redevelopment area to enable the municipality to use the powers granted to it under state redevelopment statutes.

A legally enforceable framework for the design standards or the neighborhood plan must include a mechanism for enforcement. This is often more difficult than it may seem. Design standards must be enforced firmly but sensitively. Successful enforcement requires clear legal authority melded with technical expertise and thoughtful judgment. Enforcement must permit architects to work creatively and avoid forcing them into mindless repetition of existing patterns, while still respecting the character of the community.

A municipal ordinance typically designates a body responsible for enforcement. If the standards are a part of the zoning ordinance, their enforcement may fall to the planning commission or city council. If they are part of a redevelopment plan, they may fall to the planning commission or the redevelopment agency. These bodies, however, may lack the technical expertise or the will to administer design guidelines effectively.

Each city should create a design advisory board to review and make recommendations, including specific changes to the applicant's submission, to the body, which may be the planning commission or city council, with ultimate legal authority to approve or reject the submission. That board should include individuals with design expertise as well as residents of the affected neighborhoods. *Where guidelines have been designed to apply to a single neighborhood, the municipality should consider creating—or working with an existing—design advisory group made up of neighborhood residents.* Both the advisory board and the ultimate decisionmaking body should have access to staff or consultants with appropriate design expertise.

Educating and engaging those involved at the neighborhood and at the city level is critically important. Where design guidelines are neighborhood-specific, residents should be involved in framing the guidelines, both to elicit their sense of what neighborhood features are valuable and should be preserved and to build their support for enforcing those guidelines. Similarly, the local officials who ultimately approve or reject redevelopment proposals must understand the importance of maintaining consistency in their enforcement of design and planning standards to make possible the rebuilding of the neighborhood as a sound, sustainable community. *By enforcing strong standards from the beginning rather*

---

1. In different parts of the country, a master plan may be termed a *comprehensive plan* or a *general plan*. While some state land use statutes, such as that of California, explicitly provide for incorporating detailed small-area plans into the overall plan, we are not aware of any state which bars similar practices.

than adopting a laissez-faire attitude toward developers' proposals, local officials are building value for the future that will ultimately translate into significantly greater property values and tax rateables for the municipality.

C. Density

Recent years have seen a growing trend in older cities to reduce the density of urban neighborhoods, either through demolition to "thin out" such neighborhoods or through rebuilding strategies that deliberately seek to replace the traditional fabric with a new, lower density development pattern. While the now-famous single-family subdivision built on Charlotte Street in the South Bronx in 1985 found few imitators at first, its premise is now being emulated to varying degrees by planners and developers in cities across the United States. Despite its popularity, this strategy should be approached with caution.

The case for density reduction begins with two premises: first, that the typical land use patterns and housing stock in many urban neighborhoods, the result of late nineteenth- and early twentieth-century industrialization and immigration, are no longer seen as optimal, or even desirable, today; and, second, that the population losses that many cities have experienced during the past fifty years are largely irreversible. Although cities such as Baltimore or Philadelphia may hope to reverse the pattern of decline and perhaps even see small population gains in the future, a return to their peak population is unlikely.

These are legitimate points. Much older workers' housing in industrial cities was shoddily constructed or too small to be desirable to home buyers with even the most modest aspirations today. Many Northeastern cities contain blocks of tiny row houses with no more than eight or nine hundred square feet of living area, postage stamp yards, and no off-street parking, built corner to corner along narrow streets with narrow sidewalks, lacking even room to plant shade trees along the sidewalks. It makes sense to reconfigure such areas and create larger houses with the amenities sought by today's home buyers.

There is nothing sacrosanct about a neighborhood's historic development pattern, particularly if that pattern has been vitiated by years of neglect and abandonment. Few people will dispute the proposition that America's cities are well rid of the high-rise public housing projects that once disfigured their neighborhoods. At the same time, density reduction strategies should be approached with care. Before embarking on a major initiative, those involved should address two critical questions:

- Should the density in this area be reduced?

- If so, what are the most appropriate planning and design strategies to achieve that objective?

The discussion below is intended to help practitioners think through the questions and arrive at answers that work best in their communities.

A strong body of opinion holds that the entire idea is ill conceived. Laurie Volk and Todd Zimmerman, astute analysts of urban housing markets, have written:

The urge to suburbanize should be avoided. Knowledge of the characteristics of households that have the potential to populate urban neighborhoods provides a final important insight: they will be attracted to appropriate urban design, not to an urban re-interpretation of low-density suburban forms. Good urban design places as much emphasis on creating quality streets and public places as on creating quality buildings.[2]

This assessment is most probably valid for the creative classes, the young professionals and empty nesters who are likely to be the focus of regional marketing strategies. It may not be equally true of the households that represent a city's internal demand, particularly the upwardly mobile working-class households that make up the market for many of the projects being developed in urban neighborhoods under programs such as the Homeownership Zone and Hope VI, two HUD programs that have been used in recent years to foster redevelopment of urban neighborhoods, and the replacement of obsolete public housing projects with more appropriate residential configurations.

No city can be made up entirely of upscale neighborhoods. Cities need healthy, stable working-class neighborhoods as well. The issue is, then, whether an "urban reinterpretation of low-density suburban forms," as Volk and Zimmerman put it, is a sound and sustainable strategy for creating such neighborhoods. Buyers who truly yearn for the suburban lifestyle may buy a subsidized unit in an urban infill development because they cannot afford a suburban alternative, but they are likely to depart for suburbia as soon as they are able to do so.

It is important to distinguish between providing specific amenities that home buyers may be seeking and specific ways to provide those amenities, such as

- more interior space and features in the houses;
- adequate and appropriately located parking;
- more open space and a greener environment.

These are all amenities provided by suburban subdivisions. At the same time, they can all be provided—although perhaps not to quite the same extent—through careful planning within an urban environment. How the urban environment can be reconfigured to address reasonable parking concerns, and the desire for a green environment, is discussed further below.

The suburban environment, however, often lacks amenities more likely to be found in urban areas:

- The social interaction created by proximity and street life

2. Laurie Volk and Todd Zimmerman, "Confronting the Question of Market Demand for Urban Residential Development," presentation to Fannie Mae 2000 Annual Housing Conference, Washington, DC, 26 September 2000. Available online at www.zva.cc/zva_FNMA.pdf

- Pedestrian-accessible neighborhood shopping
- Pedestrian-accessible parks and playgrounds
- Convenient public transportation

High residential densities make possible the utilization of retail facilities, parks and playgrounds, and public transportation, sustaining their viability. Similarly, as Jane Jacobs pointed out more than forty years ago in her classic *The Death and Life of Great American Cities,* it is the area's density, along with the configuration of its buildings, that creates the opportunity for the interaction and engagement that are central features of urban life.

It is important to distinguish between two forms of density when discussing a neighborhood: the *overall or gross density* of the area as a whole and the *net density* of an individual block or residential development.[3] The two are very different.

A neighborhood strategy, for example, may seek to reconfigure an area that had a population of 12,000 in 1950, and, as a result of widespread abandonment, only 4,000 today to accommodate a population of 6,000 after redevelopment. This represents half of the area's peak population, or a decline in *overall density* of 50 percent. It does not follow, however, that it is either necessary or desirable to rebuild each residential block at a *net density* of half its historic density. Indeed, a plausible strategy in some cases might be to rebuild half of the residential blocks at net densities consistent with their historic pattern and convert the other half to open space or a mixture of open space and nonresidential uses. Using urban space wisely need not involve cutting it up into little pieces to create small and often unusable private yards, as discussed in the next chapter.[4]

Planners must ask, What is the most appropriate density (and reuse) for *this block* in the framework of the overall density goal for the neighborhood as a whole? For residential blocks, some of the relevant considerations include

- the existing fabric and texture of the block, and the extent to which that fabric has value and should be reflected in reuse strategies;
- the proximity of the block to key neighborhood facilities, such as retail space, schools, and parks;
- the proximity of the block to public transit and the nature and extent of the public transit available;
- the needs and desires of the households likely to live on the block;
- the extent to which complementary nonresidential facilities, such as open space, are planned for the vicinity.

3. These terms are used here descriptively, not according to their specific legal meanings under state land use codes.

4. The private yard has considerable symbolic significance for many people. Incremental additions to yards, however, when they take the form of relatively unusable space, particularly in side yards, are likely to add little or nothing to either their symbolic value or their practical use.

One outcome of such an assessment might be a *density gradient* strategy within a neighborhood or area, where densities are maintained—or even increased—in close proximity to key nodes or hubs and reduced as distance increases from those central points.

Once these issues have been thought through, the next step is to determine how best to provide the amenities the prospective market demands at the density most appropriate to the location. Creating units that are large enough and contain desired features—such as a second bathroom or a family room—can clearly be addressed in many ways that may be compatible with a wide range of densities and site configurations. While parking and open space issues are directly related to density, they, too, can be addressed in a variety of ways.

Dedicated, secure parking space is an amenity nearly every American household seeks and which planners typically want to provide in redevelopment projects. Many infill or redevelopment schemes provide each unit with a private driveway alongside the unit. This provides a dedicated parking space, easily visible from the house, at relatively little expense. It breaks up the block, however, by creating a quasi-suburban separation between houses, and it discourages pedestrian use and sidewalk activity. The large number of curb cuts, moreover, can create hazards, particularly for small children. On a block originally developed with row houses, redevelopment that includes individual driveways is likely to result in a density less than half the historic density of the block.

Parking in amounts and configurations acceptable to home buyers can be provided while still accommodating a larger number of similarly sized units. One alternative is to utilize an existing alley or create an alley behind the houses; another is to reconfigure or widen the street to create angle parking in front. Yet another is to create common parking "pods" behind each group of units. All offer a comparable or greater ratio of parking spaces per unit while permitting a substantial increase in the number of units along the block face; these options are also more readily adapted to a scheme that preserves all or most of the existing buildings. Such alternatives, of course, have disadvantages. They are more expensive and may involve acquisition of land—either for the alley or for street widening—that would not be needed for driveways. That cost, however, may be offset by the greater number of units accommodated on the site.

Open space alternatives are discussed in detail in the following chapter. The main point to be made here is that a continuum of open space and community greening strategies are available. The private yard represents one end of the continuum; the large community park represents the other. Many intermediate options are possible, such as tot lots and playgrounds, community gardens, plazas, mini-parks, and landscaped streetscapes. These can be designed as semiprivate spaces for the residents of a block or a residential cluster or as public spaces for a larger area. They all represent alternatives that should be considered in designing reuse projects.

In exploring these alternatives and determining suitable densities and building configurations, there is no substitute for eliciting the desires and preferences of those making up the potential market for the development, whatever their income levels. The fact that a project is intended to sell at affordable prices is never an excuse to cut corners on the quality of planning, design, or construction. The more a project reflects the desires of its buyers, the more it will engender their loyalty and their long-term commitment.

These approaches are appropriate for areas where active redevelopment or reuse is taking place. Some communities are pursuing another option, sometimes called "thinning out"—reducing density through selective demolition without reconstruction. The vacant plots created through demolition are typically sold as side lots for a nominal sum to adjacent owners or used for low-intensity open spaces.

While thinning out may be an appropriate expedient for a situation where scattered buildings in an otherwise intact fabric are unsuitable for rehabilitation, it is not an effective strategy for an entire neighborhood. The thinning is likely to create visible holes and breaks in the neighborhood fabric. Unless it is part of a concerted improvement strategy for the area which addresses the underlying reasons for abandonment, and unless the design issues associated with creating side yards are addressed, a thinning strategy may do little to change the dynamics causing disinvestment and abandonment in the neighborhood.

D. Integrating Brownfield Sites into the Abandoned Property Strategy

The United States Environmental Protection Agency defines brownfields as "abandoned, idled, or under-used industrial and commercial facilities where expansion or redevelopment is complicated by real or perceived environmental contamination." While the typical brownfield site is an industrial property, many other historic uses also leave environmental contamination behind after the property has been abandoned, including service stations, retail establishments such as dry cleaners, and even some residential properties.

Because of the issues arising from real or perceived environmental conditions, many states, counties, and municipalities treat brownfield sites separately from other abandoned or underutilized properties. Many local governments have been reluctant to engage with brownfield properties; some have done so only under special circumstances, as when a private buyer is ready to assume the cleanup responsibilities. The agency responsible for brownfields is often in a different administrative unit or level of government from the agency responsible for abandoned properties or neighborhood revitalization. In many cases, brownfields are seen as part of a city's or county's economic development activities, not connected to the jurisdiction's planning or community development activities. This view often reflects preconceived notions about appropriate reuses for brownfield sites. Separating brownfield activities from other community revitalization efforts, however, not only blocks efforts to carry out comprehensive neighborhood revitalization strategies but often undermines achieving the reuse potential of the brownfields themselves.

Control and reuse of brownfields should be part of the larger abandoned property strategy with respect to both policy and procedure. The entity responsible for the overall strategy should have the expertise to address the technical issues specific to brownfields. To understand how best to integrate brownfields with the abandoned property strategy, it is necessary to demystify both the environmental remediation and the reuse issues associated with brownfield sites.

Environmental Remediation Issues

Both the state of the art and the legal framework for brownfield remediation have come a long way since site remediation became a public policy priority in the early 1990s.[5] At this point, statutes and regulations that actively encourage brownfield remediation and redevelopment are widely in place:

- Most states and the federal government provide legal protection for innocent parties acquiring brownfield sites against liability for environmental contamination caused by prior owners. This includes protection for cities taking such sites through tax foreclosure or eminent domain.

- Most state environmental regulatory agencies offer flexible or risk-based cleanup standards, adjusting the scope of the cleanup to the nature of the proposed reuse. Where the cost of removing contaminated soil may be prohibitive, cleanup standards often permit administrative or engineering remedies such as capping.

- Many states and the federal government offer financial assistance to local government for preliminary investigations and site assessments prior to remediation, and in some cases for the actual site remediation.

- Environmental insurance has become available to protect those buying and remediating brownfield sites against future environmental liability.

- A growing number of private firms are engaged in brownfield redevelopment, many of which take on sites requiring environmental remediation.

Brownfield redevelopment has also become more feasible in light of findings that the extent of environmental contamination on many sites has been significantly overstated.[6] Careful investigation often reveals that many brownfield sites do not need remediation; in other cases, the cost of remediation is often mod-

5. Brownfield site reuse has gone on since time immemorial. For a long time, however, brownfield remediation and reuse were not seen as a distinct regulatory or public policy issue. When they first became a regulatory concern in the 1970s and early 1980s, the focus was largely preventive, even punitive, to an extent that may have encouraged abandonment more than remediation. Current policies designed to foster reuse were shaped by a reaction against those counterproductive strategies.

6. Many individuals, professionals as well as laypersons, tend to confuse brownfields with Superfund sites, that small subset of brownfields sites causing significant health hazards and demanding major federal intervention. They are extreme cases and are not representative of brownfields sites generally. The United States Environmental Protection Agency explicitly distinguishes brownfields from Superfund sites.

est, even minimal, compared to the value of the property or the potential reuse investment.

These observations should not suggest that brownfield remediation is easy or that it need not be taken seriously by local officials and others. On the contrary, it remains a challenging task requiring technical sophistication and financial resources. The agency responsible must assemble a team of staff and consultants who have the necessary technical expertise and who can establish good working relationships with the United States Environmental Protection Agency and the state's environmental regulatory agency as well as with any brownfield financing programs available. Nevertheless, the process of screening, assessing, and remediating brownfields has become a manageable and predictable one which can—and often should—be integrated into the larger neighborhood planning process.

Reuse Considerations

In older industrial cities, manufacturing facilities were often located in the neighborhoods from which their workforce was drawn and surrounded by modest workers' housing. Other facilities were located along the banks of rivers and barge canals, often forming a narrow industrial band separating the rest of the city from the waterfront. Development similar to modern industrial parks, with large numbers of industrial buildings located in areas clearly separated from the rest of the city, was rare.

To the extent that brownfield sites form part of the fabric of urban neighborhoods, their reuse must be framed in that context. To assume, as many do, that brownfield sites should be reused as industrial sites or for related economic development activities because that was their historic use, or because environmental remediation standards for industrial use are generally less demanding than those for residential or community-serving uses, sells both the site and the neighborhood short. *With rare exceptions, the environmental remediation requirements of brownfield sites do not limit the reuse alternatives.* During the 1990s Trenton, New Jersey, a pioneer in brownfield reuse strategies, redeveloped over a dozen sites. The historical uses of these properties, their reuse—either completed or in process—and whether they involved adaptive reuse or new construction are shown in table 19.1. The historical uses of these properties vary widely, reflecting the diversity of Trenton's industrial base.

Trenton's premise was straightforward: the most appropriate reuse of the property was determined through neighborhood planning, in which great weight was given to residents' needs and concerns, in concert with real estate market and design considerations. The historical use of the property and the potential remediation issues were treated as irrelevant to the reuse decision. In theory, the city recognized that plans for housing or open space might have to be modified if the site investigation found that the cost of remediating to residential standards was prohibitive. In practice, this question never arose.

TABLE 19.1 Brownfield Site Reuse Projects in Trenton, New Jersey, 1990–99

Site Name	Former use	Reuse	Type of reuse	Status
Roebling I	Steel cable manufacturing	Retail and office complex	Adaptive reuse	Complete
Roebling II	Steel cable manufacturing	Senior citizens housing	Adaptive reuse	Complete
Roebling III	Steel cable manufacturing	Museum	Adaptive reuse	Complete
C. V. Hill Corporation	Refrigeration equipment manufacturing	Industrial park	Adaptive reuse	Complete
Millner Lumber	Millwork and furniture manufacturing	Multifamily housing	Adaptive reuse	Complete
Circle F	Electrical component manufacturing	Senior citizens housing	Adaptive reuse	Complete
Perry Street	Multiple uses	Central fire department headquarters	New	Complete
Woodbridge Potteries	Ceramics manufacturing	Single-family housing	New	Complete
Blakeley Laundry	Industrial laundry	Single-family housing	New	Complete
Warren-Balderston	Lumber yard and warehouse	Single-family housing	New	Complete
Crane Potteries	Ceramics manufacturing	Industrial park	New	Complete
Luzerne	Rubber tire manufacturing	Industrial building	New	Complete
Lafayette	Multiple uses	Hotel and conference center	New	Complete
Champale	Brewery	Single-family housing	New	Planned
Magic Marker	Storage battery manufacturing	School and housing	New	Proposed
Freightyards	Railroad freight depot and siding	Community park	New	Proposed
Thropp	Recycling/junkyard	Community park	New	Proposed

CHAPTER 20

Greening the Urban Environment

Open Space as a Reuse Strategy

A. Why Does Open Space Matter?

Greening and the creation of urban open space should be part of the reuse strategy for any area larger than an individual building or infill lot. Greening is the strategy by which urban communities can use abandoned properties to create an enhanced quality of life for residents, a point well summarized in a recent publication from the American Planning Association:

> Existing vacant land . . . can actually be an urban asset as older communities are reconfigured and new ones are built. This empty land can be converted into parks, community gardens, recreation areas, private yards, "commons" for new housing developments, managed fields, off-street parking, and other public open space. Some of these remade spaces may become permanent, while others may be "greened" in the interim until redevelopment occurs.[1]

Greening lies at the heart of the concept of sustainable reuse, reflecting the growing recognition that good planning does not demand that reuse projects develop every possible square foot, particularly in cities with a surplus of housing and commercial structures. Open space and greening address many individual, group, and community objectives, including the following:

- Enhancing a community's quality of life

- Enhancing a community's marketability and its attractiveness to new and current residents

- Building community cohesion and empowerment

- Providing active recreation opportunities for all age groups

- Providing opportunities for adult activities and passive enjoyment of open space

- Creating opportunities for economically productive activities

- Facilitating temporary land banking that is benign or even beneficial, rather than problematic, for the community

---

1. Blaine Bonham, Gerri Spilka, and Darl Rastorfer, *Old Cities/Green Cities: Communities Transform Unmanaged Land* (Chicago: American Planning Association, 2002).

TABLE 20.1 Matching Greening and Open Space Strategies with Community Objectives

	Lot stabilization	Green sidewalk strips, tree plantings, and street medians	Squares and plazas	Mini-parks and sitting areas	Playgrounds and tot lots
Enhance quality of life in the neighborhood	X	X	X	X	X
Enhance marketability of neighborhood	X	X	X		
Build community cohesion and empowerment			X	X	X
Provide youths and adults with active recreation opportunity					X
Provide opportunities for adult activity and passive use				X	X
Create economically productive opportunities			X		
Provide land banking or interim use opportunities	X				

Table 20.1 presents a matrix of open space and greening strategies, showing which of these community objectives can be served by each of the various strategies. Each alternative can simultaneously serve different objectives. Creating a community plaza as a central feature in a neighborhood can enhance the quality of life and marketability of the neighborhood while also helping to build community cohesion and neighborhood identity. A community garden or farm can offer economic returns, becoming a community asset in the present while holding land for future redevelopment.[2]

The importance of greening and open space goes well beyond utilitarian, short-term values. Public or civic open spaces give us the opportunity to experience beauty. A civic space enables us to feel that it belongs to us as members of a community, and that we share it with our fellow community members, whether the community is defined as the block we live on or the city as a whole. In addition, as Peter Rowe observes, a good civic space "reminds individuals of larger senses

2. There is a growing body of research that documents the positive effect on property values of proximity to parks and other green spaces. A recent study by Susan Wachter at the University of Pennsylvania of the greening strategies of the New Kensington CDC in Philadelphia established that proximity not only to parks, but also to sidewalk tree plantings and stabilized vacant lots, increased the value of nearby homes.

Greenways	Community gardens	Community greens or commons	Neighborhood parks	Community farms	Garden centers	Waterfront open space or water bodies	City and regional parks	Fields and forests	Gateways
X	X	X	X	X	X	X	X	X	X
X		X	X		X	X	X		X
X	X	X	X	X	X				X
			X			X	X		
X	X	X	X	X	X	X	X		
	X			X	X	X	X		
X				X				X	

of responsibility and presents something that could be passed on to subsequent generations."[3]

B. Elements in the Network of Open Spaces

Open spaces complement one another. A community greening and open space strategy should aim to create a network of open spaces and greening opportunities in which open spaces are both linked with one another and closely connected to the built environment—the houses, stores, and community facilities that make up the neighborhood.

Green Sidewalk Strips, Tree Plantings, and Street Medians

Many inner-city streets are too narrow for today's needs, while others, such as arterial streets that no longer carry much through traffic, are too wide.[4] Wide

3. Peter Rowe, *Civic Realism* (Cambridge, MA: MIT Press, 1997), p. 69. This book is an excellent discussion of the creation and use of civic space, with detailed descriptions of examples from the United States and Europe.

4. Others should not continue to be used for through traffic because the resulting noise, safety hazards, and pollution are incompatible with creating an enhanced quality of life in the neighborhood.

streets can be reconfigured to allow wider sidewalks, landscaped strips, and tree plantings. Landscaped medians planted with trees can be added and wide swaths of concrete converted to leafy boulevards. Where a block face is vacant as a result of abandonment, a narrow street can be widened by taking land from the block to create wider sidewalks, tree plantings, and a planted median. Shaded, green streets and boulevards not only make the area more attractive to its present residents but also enhance its "curb appeal" to prospective home buyers.

Side Yards

Many cities with widespread abandonment have offered scattered vacant lots for sale to adjacent property owners, generally limited to owner-occupants, either providing them with side yards or enabling them to expand narrow side strips into more usable areas. While they may be a minor element in a greening strategy, such programs are popular with many homeowners and are widely utilized by local governments to unload small vacant lots with limited reuse potential. While in most cases they are a "residual" strategy, in that the side yard program is used to deal with leftover isolated properties, a few cities, including Syracuse, use a side yard program more intentionally.

The advantages of a side yard program are clear. The owner gets a yard, which in some cases can also provide off-street parking. The city is relieved of the obligation to maintain a small parcel without obvious alternative uses. The principal issues are the aesthetic effect of the program on the area, particularly on row house blocks, and its relationship to any long-term or larger strategies for the surrounding blocks

Cities undertaking side yard programs should consider requiring that buyers of the yards follow yard design and treatment standards developed for the city by a sensitive architect or landscape architect. Moreover, the city should evaluate whether the side yard program enhances or potentially complicates its long-term strategy for the area. If the city's goal is ultimately to assemble a block which already contains a large number of abandoned properties, the city may be doing a disservice to the remaining homeowners by selling them side yards and may ultimately make its own task more difficult.

Lot Stabilization

Many cities hold numerous vacant lots which have no clear use at present or must be maintained for months or years until their ultimate reuse can take place. Cities must maintain these properties, keeping them clean and attractive for as long as necessary. Maintenance is particularly important when the lot is highly visible or located along a neighborhood gateway. Although in many respects a maintenance activity, vacant lot treatments should be seen as part of, and tied to, the community's larger greening strategy. See chapter 13 for a discussion of specific strategies for lot maintenance and stabilization.

Mini-parks, Tot Lots, and Playgrounds

Small vacant parcels or vacant buildings slated for demolition in suitable locations can be used for mini-parks or sitting areas, tot lots, or playgrounds, depending on the needs and preferences of the neighbors. In contrast to larger open space facilities, such amenities serve the needs of the residents of the immediate area, which may be no more than a block or block face. The choice must reflect a resident consensus and be seen as important by the residents so that they will share in the maintenance—and possibly the construction—of the open space. In addition to providing a desirable community amenity, developing a mini-park or playground can serve as a powerful vehicle to build community cohesion and leadership, either within a specific block or as a part of a larger community-building strategy.

It is relatively easy to obtain volunteer labor and materials for mini-parks and playgrounds. Many corporations see building such spaces as an appealing community relations gesture, and the nature of the work creates many opportunities for neighborhood residents to be involved.

Community Gardens

Small vacant parcels are well adapted to the creation of community gardens, which can be planted cooperatively by a group of neighbors, divided into small plots for individual families, or a combination of both. Successful community gardens require a neighborhood-based commitment to maintain, plant, and harvest the garden, along with a source of technical and start-up assistance. Nonprofit organizations in many communities, including Philadelphia Green and Boston's Grassroots Program, have provided neighborhood organizations and block groups with assistance to create community gardens. While some community gardens are principally decorative, most are partly or largely devoted to producing fruits and vegetables for home consumption, or occasionally for wider use or sale.

The cost of creating a community garden can be significant, particularly if the goal is to create a sustainable community asset. Many potential sites may be contaminated, which may require the construction of raised beds. A reliable source of water and attractive, durable fencing are essential. Still, the costs are modest compared to many other community improvements and can often be phased over time: thus a garden might initially be fenced with an inexpensive chain-link fence, which can be replaced with a more attractive fence when funds are available. Many cities provide CDBG or other funds for this purpose; elsewhere, foundation and corporate assistance is often available. The large-scale greening campaign mounted by Philadelphia's New Kensington CDC was supported in part through CDBG funds but also received substantial assistance from the William Penn Foundation and the Pew Charitable Trust.

Garden Centers and Community Farms

A few communities have gone beyond the small block-level garden to embrace larger, more commercially oriented agriculture. Such efforts are particularly appropriate where the amount of vacant land, or the size of the vacant parcels, substantially exceed what can realistically be utilized through small-scale efforts. The garden center in the Kensington neighborhood of Philadelphia is not only a going business concern but also a key part of the support system for the neighborhood's community gardens and an important community-wide resource.

Urban agriculture, or community farming, operates at a larger scale than community gardening and is oriented toward producing agricultural products for sale rather than individual consumption. Detroit, with its vast amounts of vacant land, is the epicenter of the American urban agriculture movement, but a report on its projects reveals the unique difficulties faced by such enterprises:

Urban farmers face a number of challenges, from finding water (renegades tap into fire hydrants) to eliminating broken glass, concrete, and unsavory contaminants like lead from the soil. Hayfields, mistaken for "ghetto grass," have been mowed down by the Department of Public Works just as they are ready to be cut and baled. Greenhouses are sometimes claimed by the homeless, and pilfering is a fact of life.[5]

5. Kate Stohr, "In the Capital of the Car, Nature Stakes a Claim," *New York Times,* 4 December 2003.

More than fifteen acres of vacant land in Detroit have been converted to urban agriculture. The largest farm, covering ten acres in seven locations, produces hay, alfalfa, honey, eggs, goat's milk, and produce. Other farms include one operated by the Capuchin Soup Kitchen, which plants, picks, packs, cans, and distributes more than a ton of produce a year.

Greensgrow in Philadelphia operates a three-quarter-acre farm and greenhouse in the Kensington neighborhood, on the site of a former galvanized steel plant. It produces lettuce, tomatoes, and herbs, selling much of its produce to upscale Center City Philadelphia restaurants. It also operates a Community Supported Agriculture project, selling shares to community residents who receive weekly boxes of seasonal produce.

Village Farms in Buffalo, New York, is an eighteen-acre greenhouse on a brownfield site that formerly housed a steel mill. It produces seven million pounds of vine-ripened tomatoes from 170,000 plants each year.

Urban agriculture demands a core of dedicated individuals and a source of start-up support. None of Detroit's community farms are profitable, and all rely heavily on volunteers, grants, or donations. Soil contamination is widespread in urban areas.[6] All urban agriculture sites, including informal ones worked by groups of neighbors or immigrants, should be carefully tested for contamination and growing practices carefully monitored to ensure that no toxic substances enter the food supply. Despite these drawbacks, urban farms are a valuable community asset, as they not only utilize vacant land attractively and productively but also serve as an educational resource and volunteer opportunity for local young people.

Community Greens or Commons

Community greens, sometimes called commons, are shared parks tucked away inside residential blocks, collectively owned and managed by the neighbors whose homes and backyards enclose the green.[7] A community green can enhance the quality of life for the families living on a block or in a development and build cohesion and stability in the area as a whole. Where redevelopment of a block, or a substantial park of a block, is being planned, adding a community green to

6. Urban sites often have elevated lead levels, the result of decades of use of gasoline with lead additives, particularly along streets with heavy vehicle traffic. Toxic metals from nearby heavy industry, as well as other contaminants resulting from illegal dumping, may also be present.

7. This is the definition provided by Community Greens, a nonprofit organization that encourages the use of this open space strategy.

Hope Community, Inc., redeveloped a crime-ridden block in a low-income area of Minneapolis with rental housing built around an internal commons, including walkways, a playground, a community garden, and a pavilion on a concrete pad left from an old garage. The spaces are open to observation by the residents, and the area is accessible from the outside so that neighborhood children can use the play areas. The executive director of Hope Community notes that although the community is both low-income and racially and ethnically diverse, "the family lives are stable because the kids are happy—the stability in family life translates to stability on the block—the renters never want to leave."

the plans can help create a stable, sustainable community. Where redevelopment is taking place in phases over time, the community green can take shape gradually as the project emerges.

Since most existing city blocks are completely subdivided into individually owned parcels, a new community green can be created only if all or most of the parcels on the block are brought into common ownership—either by the city or a CDC—and are then re-subdivided or consolidated to create the green. Baltimore, where many blocks contain interior lots fronting on alleys, is an exception. Because of their small size and lack of amenities, large numbers of alley lots have been abandoned, even where most or all of the larger lots surrounding them remain occupied. The Neighborhood Design Center in Baltimore has prepared model designs showing how clearing and consolidating alley lots can create interior greens on many Baltimore blocks without reconfiguring the surrounding properties.

A community green must be carefully designed to foster a sense of shared community and security among those who live around it and use it. Hope Community used the principles of Crime Prevention through Environmental Design (CPTED) as a basis for designing the commons, including such features as giving each house a screened back porch facing the commons.[8]

Squares and Plazas

A feature common to nearly all traditional societies, particularly in Mediterranean and Latin American countries, is the village square or plaza. Centrally located, often facing the village church or town hall, it is the focal point of the community's

---

8. The CPTED principles are a set of strategies developed by the International CPTED Association, building on the work of Jane Jacobs and Oscar Newman.

identity and the locus of community events and informal gatherings. Larger cities may also have smaller neighborhood plazas. Except where they have been allowed to become parking lots, they are prized by the city's residents and popular with visitors.

The commercial impetus behind the development of most American cities placed less emphasis on squares, although Copley Square in Boston and Rittenhouse Square in Philadelphia are among our most prized urban spaces. These squares were either centrally located or built in affluent neighborhoods. Few plazas were built in these cities' immigrant neighborhoods.

The reuse of abandoned properties provides an opportunity to reintroduce the plaza as an amenity for an urban neighborhood. A square is a very different space from a park or a garden. Although it may contain flowers or plantings, it is usually a paved area designed to permit large numbers of people to mingle comfortably and walk through it. Although it should contain artistic elements such as statues or decorative paving, it takes much of its character from the buildings that surround it.

Choosing the right location is critical. Properly located and designed, a square can provide neighborhoods with both a psychic center and a social gathering place, as similar spaces do throughout the world. In addition to fostering community identity, it can increase the viability of a commercial area by drawing foot traffic. The square should be in a central location in the neighborhood and close to buildings that are heavily used by area residents, such as stores, or major community facilities, such as a church or a school. To the extent possible it should be framed by those buildings, giving it a clear spatial definition. A square in the wrong place will not be used and is worse than no square at all.

Neighborhood squares should be smaller rather than larger. The size of a square should reflect its probable level of activity and pedestrian density. In a neighborhood built at typical American densities, that is not likely to be high, except during special events. Christopher Alexander and colleagues recommend that neighborhood squares be no more than forty-five to seventy feet across.[9]

Community Parks, Greenways, and Recreation Facilities

Communities need parks, which have been called the "green lungs of the city." The redevelopment of abandoned properties offers innumerable opportunities to create parks and recreation facilities, often in areas severely underserved by such facilities. Parks not only enhance the community's quality of life, but—well designed and maintained—they represent a tangible community asset to potential residents and investors.

9. This subject is discussed further in Alexander et al., *A Pattern Language* (New York: Oxford University Press, 1977), 311–14. Every individual involved in urban rebuilding should have a copy of this book.

Seattle's Gas Works Park is a 20.5-acre community park constructed on the site of a former gas works, which required extensive remediation. Many remains of the original industrial architecture were preserved, giving the park a distinctive character.

Pittsburgh, a city with rugged topography, has developed a program to designate areas that are wooded, steep, and environmentally sensitive as greenways, in partnership with neighborhood organizations. The city has partnered with the Western Pennsylvania Conservancy, which provides technical assistance. Since initiating the program, the city has designated 573 acres of greenways.

Parks are important both as passive green spaces and as focal points for recreational activity by older children, teenagers, and adults. Many urban neighborhoods, particularly those with large immigrant communities, suffer from a severe shortage of adult recreational space, especially for soccer. Greenways, which are in essence linear parks, can link neighborhoods and open spaces and provide opportunities for walking or jogging.

The use of a brownfield site for Seattle's Gas Works Park illustrates that such sites are particularly suitable as park sites because of their scale and the relative simplicity of land assembly, despite the environmental issues involved. Industrial features such as cranes or bottle kilns can be incorporated into the park, adding interest and visual variety. Remediation often does not pose undue financial or managerial burdens.

Parks can be designed at a variety of scales and contain a variety of features, depending on available land, user need and demand, and the geographic area from which they will draw users. Any park, however, requires a major commitment of resources for design, construction, and maintenance. Many cities are reluctant to commit substantial funds to new parks, given their limited and often inadequate resources for maintaining their existing parks. In some cases, larger bodies of government, such as the state, the county, or a regional agency, have been willing to build and maintain urban parks, and in a few highly publicized but atypical examples such support has come from the private sector.

Where parks can be integrated with other important physical, cultural, or community resources, their value is enhanced. A park or greenway that runs along or contains a body of water, such as a river or a lake, will be more actively used and valued more highly than one without water. Existing bodies of water should be incorporated, but new ones can also be created. An attractive waterfront setting will draw many outside users who might not venture into the community otherwise.

Parks are the legacy a city's leaders and citizens leave to the future. The Olmsted parks of the nineteenth century are among the most visible and important assets of many of the same industrial cities which are trying today to confront their problems of vacant land and neighborhood deterioration. Today's public officials should regularly ask themselves whether they are leaving a legacy for the next generations comparable to that which their predecessors left them.

Fields and Forests

Some cities are faced with concentrations of abandoned properties in areas where market demand is weak and likely to remain weak for some time to come. These areas are unlikely to be a focus of redevelopment activity in the near term. In the absence of redevelopment, it is equally unlikely that properties in those areas are suitable for park investment. Cities must face the issue of what to do with these areas during the many years that these properties are likely to lie vacant.

Where urban agriculture is not a feasible option, reforestation or the conversion of vacant land into low-maintenance meadows may be economical alternatives, with respect to both initial cost and ongoing maintenance. Reforestation of an area can be a benign interim use, creating a natural setting that in time becomes a significant asset in terms of both marketability and quality of life for future development. Planting fast-growing species can result in an attractive wooded setting within as little as ten years.[10]

Private partners may be available to support the creation of fields and forests. The city of Pittsburgh, which has established a task force to pursue these options, has found open space and environmental groups, CDCs, and the Penn State extension service all eager to participate.

C. Building an Open Space Reuse Strategy

Thinking Strategically

While strategic thinking should drive all elements of reuse planning and implementation, it is vital with respect to greening and open space. A central point of using open space in a reuse strategy is to create a different environment, to change the character of the entire area, whatever other uses may be planned. An open space strategy is inherently hierarchical in that different elements clearly lend themselves to being addressed at different scales, with cumulative effects. Table 20.2 illustrates the specific open space elements suited to projects at dif-

---

10. In any area where reforestation is a serious option, contracts for demolition of abandoned properties *must* specify that the entire site, including foundations and basements, be cleared and replaced with suitable fill. A forest cannot grow on a site made up largely of concrete, wood, rubble, and other debris below a thin layer of topsoil.

TABLE 20.2 Relationship between Scale and Open Space Elements

Scale	Elements
Block face or street	Street trees Green medians Tot lots Community gardens Sidewalk greening Mini-parks Playgrounds Side yards
Block	Playgrounds Community greens Small neighborhood parks Community gardens Community agriculture
Neighborhood	Greenways Fields and forests Neighborhood parks and recreation areas Squares and plazas Community agriculture Neighborhood gateways
City	City gateways Squares and plazas City parks and recreation areas Waterfronts

ferent scales. For example, elements such as street trees or green medians can be introduced along a single block of a street. Their effect is multiplied if they are provided along the full length of the street or used as recurrent elements on the streets of an entire neighborhood.

An open space strategy is not just a matter of integrating different open spaces into a coherent physical network, but should also integrate them into the educational, economic, and cultural life of the community. Open spaces should contribute to the economic development of the city by making it more attractive to home buyers and investors or by enhancing specific economic development strategies. Open spaces offer opportunities for educating a community's children and providing job training and work for teens and adults. Philadelphia's Green City Strategy is a good illustration of a multifaceted open space strategy which has already transformed vacant property and improved the quality of life in two of Philadelphia's most distressed neighborhoods. This strategy offers a number of

GOOD PRACTICE

The Pennsylvania Horticultural Society has taken the lead in developing a Green City Strategy for Philadelphia which has six principal components:

- Cleaning and greening of as many as possible of the city's 31,000 vacant lots

- Neighborhood greening, focusing on reusing vacant lots for gardens, sitting parks, play areas, and green spaces; beautification of gateways and planting of street trees

- Upgrading of municipal parks and public spaces and mobilizing of civic, religious, and institutional partners to help maintain public spaces in their vicinity

- Citywide education, training, and organizational development to build a constituency to support and maintain green spaces in the city's neighborhoods

- Open space planning, retrofitting the city to meet twenty-first-century standards of living

- The Green Campaign, a promotional effort to educate residents about the citywide greening movement and encourage them to participate

The Society, through its subsidiary, Philadelphia Green, has initiated open space and greening strategies in partnership with neighborhood-based organizations in Kensington and Northeast Philadelphia.

valuable lessons for local governments, CDCs, and environmental organizations developing local greening strategies:

Improve existing green spaces. Many cities have existing parks and open spaces that may be poorly designed, poorly maintained, or underutilized. It is unnecessary to create new green spaces if the same objectives can be achieved by improving or reconfiguring existing areas. Conversely, many cities have green spaces that may not be appropriate for their intended purposes, such as mini-parks in unsuitable locations. A comprehensive strategy should identify such spaces and make them available for other uses.[11]

11. Some such spaces, often those left over from urban improvement schemes of the 1960s and 1970s, may be subject to legal restrictions barring their use for other purposes. Depending on the specific state statute, procedures—albeit cumbersome ones—usually exist to remove a property from those restrictions. One possibility is a land swap, whereby another property of comparable size or value is dedicated for open space use in place of the original one. If federal funds were used to create the spaces, approval from the federal government may also be necessary.

Engage as many people as possible in the process. The success of any greening strategy hinges on people's ongoing commitment to it, reflected in their willingness to provide time and money to maintain green spaces and to use and respect them in their daily behavior. This engagement is achieved by involving people in planning, design, and creation of green spaces and through educational programs for all age groups.

Link the greening strategy to all of the planning and redevelopment activities taking place in the community. Urban green spaces exist in relationship to the built environment, not in isolation. Every design and planning decision that is made in an urban community both affects the greening strategy and is affected by it. The design of housing projects, commercial corridors and nodes, and in particular major educational and institutional facilities must be integrated with the strategy, to create synergy between the open space and the built environment. A plaza designed in conjunction with a major commercial development, so that it reinforces the economic potential of the development while retail traffic enhances the use of the plaza, is an example of synergy. Similarly, where a community school is being developed, the design of open spaces which can be used both by the school and by the community can enhance the school's educational and recreational programs and increase utilization of the open space facilities.

Building Partnerships

Building partnerships around open space is perhaps easier—and more important —than almost any other aspect of urban revitalization. Thousands of individuals and organizations who may be mystified by the complex social and economic issues involved in urban rebuilding can be engaged in those issues through greening and open space:

- Park and nature conservancies
- Gardening organizations, including garden clubs and community gardening associations
- Watershed, riverkeeper, and water watch organizations
- Environmental and conservation organizations
- Food and hunger organizations
- University extension services
- University forestry, agriculture, and environmental departments and research centers
- University student-based community service and environmental groups

Such organizations can provide local governments and CDCs with a wealth of technical knowledge as well as resources of people and—to a lesser extent—money to support the open space strategy. While these groups tend to have limited funds, they can offer substantial numbers of committed volunteers in lieu of money. In

In the mid-1990s, people from Detroit's community gardens and members of citywide and state environmental and hunger action organizations joined to create the Detroit Agricultural Network. The Network has built a coalition of health providers, emergency food providers, and others to develop a Food Security Plan linking urban agriculture, food cooperatives, and youth training. The network also provided the impetus that led to creation of Adamah (the Hebrew word for *earth*), an organization devoted to fostering a long-term vision of the city's future based on agriculture, open space, and sustainability.

some cases, rather than the city trying to pull the groups together, a single private organization—such as the Pennsylvania Horticultural Society in Philadelphia—can act as the strategy's lead organization and the city's principal partner and engage others to work alongside it.

While a network of environment and open space organizations can bring great strength to an open space strategy, few of these organizations have roots in the inner-city neighborhoods to which the strategy is often directed. An open space strategy that relies wholly on such groups' involvement is unlikely to engage the people and institutions in the neighborhoods. The network of relationships and partnerships must balance "inside" and "outside" partners.

Philadelphia's green neighborhood strategies have been based on partnerships between the Horticultural Society and strong local CDCs, particularly in the Kensington neighborhood, where the New Kensington CDC took the lead in designing the neighborhood greening strategy. A local CDC or neighborhood-based organization can in turn reach out to block groups and other smaller organizations, as the Warren/Conner CDC does on Detroit's East Side, building the strategy block by block. As the strategy emerges, a citywide network—bringing outside and inside partners together—should be developed.

State and county governments are also important partners, particularly with respect to large-scale open space initiatives, as discussed below.

Finding Resources

A greening and open space strategy has unique features that make it easier to fund in some respects, but harder in others, than other aspects of urban rebuilding. Unlike housing or commercial revitalization, for which even the smallest activity requires substantial capital investment, many greening activities require little money. Conversely, a major open space project, such as the conversion of a large brownfield site into a community park, may require a long-term capital and operating commitment comparable to the largest redevelopment projects. Key steps in assembling the resources to carry out the open space strategy are:

Identify and include projects that require only modest amounts of money and which can be carried out with help from nontraditional sources. These can include tree planting projects, mini-parks, and playgrounds. Sources of assistance for such projects are described below.

Assemble financial and workforce resources for small-scale projects from non-traditional sources. Open space and greening projects offer great opportunities to assemble small contributions, cash and in-kind donations, and volunteer labor. Many corporations will donate money or supplies for community open space projects or mobilize their employees to provide a day of intensive volunteer effort to create a mini-park or playground. Nurseries and paint manufacturers may donate stock or supplies. Block or neighborhood residents can also be mobilized to work on such projects, which are attractive because the work generally does not require specialized skills or experience. The support of small community and locally based family foundations, which may lack the resources to fund larger efforts, may be able to leverage CDBG or other public funds. These same groups can be mobilized to maintain open space facilities over time, whether by enlisting the help of block groups and neighborhood organizations or by obtaining outside commitments through "adopt-a-park" campaigns.

Assemble corporate and foundation support for larger elements of the open space strategy. While small local firms may support small projects, major corporations and foundations may be willing to support larger projects. DaimlerChrysler made a major commitment to greening work on Detroit's East Side, and two large Philadelphia-based foundations have provided ongoing support for Philadelphia's Green City Strategy. Greening is attractive to many foundations, including some whose focus may be more on environmental than on urban or community development issues. As with most other aspects of urban revitalization, *major foundation or corporate support is far more likely to be forthcoming if the funder sees it as part of a comprehensive strategy rather than an isolated initiative.*

Enlist state or county support for major open space initiatives. Financially strapped cities are limited in their ability to undertake major open space improvements. Although many states and counties have extensive open space networks, these tend to be concentrated in suburban and rural areas rather than urban areas. Despite being the most urbanized state in the country with an extensive network of state parks, New Jersey contains only one urban state park.[12] Municipalities, together with regional open space and environmental advocates, should press state and county park agencies to create new facilities in urban areas that will be developed *and maintained* by the state or county.[13]

12. Liberty State Park in Jersey City. A small part of a second state park is located in Trenton.

13. Alternatively, a city can ask the state or county to take over responsibility for operating existing municipal parks of regional significance. This is a sound approach but may raise issues of local pride and control.

Municipalities and their partners should seek state or county financial support for their greening strategies generally, as well as for specific projects. A number of states, such as New Jersey and Ohio, are currently financing all or a large part of the cost of new schools in their central cities. In such cases, the city and CDCs in the areas where schools are to be constructed should work with the school district and the state to create multiple use open space and recreational facilities, making maximum use of state funds, and promote green design and site planning in the new schools themselves.

Identify self-sustaining open space or recreational uses. While grant funds may be needed to create open spaces, every effort should be made to identify open space uses that can sustain themselves without public funds or which can generate enough income to cover maintenance costs over time. Some small open spaces can be sustained with few direct costs if a block group or neighborhood organization makes a commitment to maintain the space. On a larger scale, communities should investigate creating income-producing open space and recreational facilities, including urban agriculture and recreational facilities which an economically diverse user population will be willing to pay to use. The latter can include a variety of active recreational facilities, such as golf driving ranges or ice skating rinks, as well as concessions that can be rented to private entrepreneurs.

Reassess the community's commitment to greening and open space. Finally, local government must assess its own level of commitment to greening and open space within its overall priorities. In recent decades, as cities have had to repeatedly tighten their belts, open space has been widely seen as a "frill," less important than core services such as police, fire, or sanitation. As a result, little money has been put into open space development, and basic maintenance of existing parks has been cut back, often drastically. The parlous state of many once-great urban parks in America's older cities reflects this neglect. While in a few highly publicized cases, such as that of New York's Central Park, massive private funds have been raised to supplement public resources, such efforts are rarely feasible, particularly for inner-city parks which lack Central Park's wealthy constituency.

The fiscal conditions under which older cities operate are still difficult, and overnight change is not possible. Still, a city concerned about its future should recognize the importance of its open space and natural environment and consider how it can devote more resources to maintaining and even improving it, in order both to improve the city's quality of life and to enhance the city's competitive position and attractiveness to investors and economically diverse home buyers. Moreover, area foundations and corporations will be more likely to help fund an open space and greening strategy if the city demonstrates its own commitment to the strategy.

Interim versus Permanent Uses

Design and implementation of a greening and open space strategy, like any other effort to transform the urban environment, is a long-term process. Although a tot lot on a vacant parcel or the planting of street trees along a block can become a reality in less than a year, creating a major new open space, particularly if it involves extensive site assembly and brownfield remediation, may be a ten- to twenty-year process. A greening and open space strategy must also make clear to all parties involved that although some open spaces are permanent, some are interim uses.

Lot stabilization, for example, is generally accepted to be an interim use of a property, with the anticipation that the site will be converted to a permanent use within a relatively short period, such as five years or less. The situation is less clear-cut with respect to other uses. Local officials, who see community gardens as an interim use of city-owned property, may, therefore, choose to lease rather than sell the property to a neighborhood organization. The users, however, may see the garden and the property as part of their long-term vision for the community. A battle rupted in 2001 in the Lower East Side of Manhattan when the city decided to sell a large number of community gardens, some of which had been maintained by neighbors for decades. Even Detroit, with its thousands of acres of vacant land, is reluctant to commit even small tracts permanently to gardens or urban agriculture.

Clearly, the better the communication between local government and the neighborhood organization, the lower the likelihood of future conflict. The conflict in New York City was clearly exacerbated by the near-total lack of communication between the city and the gardening organizations. Even with good communication and clear rules, conflicts can still arise from a basic clash of priorities and from changes in agendas over time. A block group that may accept initially that its garden is an interim use may feel very differently five years later. The conflict could be even more severe with respect to a community farm, in which the operators' investment is likely to be quite significant after a number of years.

In terms of the city's long-term future, community gardens, farms and forests, and not just formal parks and recreation areas, are as valuable as housing or commercial developments.[14] The working assumption of many local officials, that these uses are acceptable only until a more "productive" use appears, is unsound. That does not mean that all such uses need to be permanent ones. Within the framework of solid neighborhood planning, the local government and its partners in each neighborhood should identify which gardens, farms, and forested areas contribute to the long-term future of the neighborhood and should be considered potentially permanent, and which should be seen as interim uses because an alternative use will clearly be more appropriate in the future.

The term *potentially permanent* is used because the nature of the agreement between the municipality and the users should provide that the site will remain as a community garden or similar use only as long as it is in active use for that purpose. If the individuals or organization using the property discontinue active use, and no qualified individuals or organization are found to continue the use, the municipality should be free to reuse the property for other purposes.

14. While these uses do not directly provide tax revenues to the municipality, they cost the municipality little or nothing in service costs and help maintain, and arguably even increase, the value of neighboring properties.

CHAPTER 21

Stabilizing Neighborhoods after the Foreclosure Crisis

The years from 2006 through 2009 saw the most precipitous collapse in American housing markets since the Great Depression. As house prices tumbled and millions of homes went into foreclosure, many of the nation's urban and suburban neighborhoods were plunged into a crisis for which neither local governments nor CDCs were prepared. The proximate cause of the crisis was the collapse of the housing bubble that had sent house prices skyrocketing during the first years of the new millennium. The bubble itself was the product of a complex combination of factors, implicating both the private and public sectors. With a growing number of postmortem reports on the housing bubble starting to appear, this chapter will not go into that subject in detail. Instead, it will concentrate on how the collapse of the bubble and the ensuing foreclosure crisis have affected America's neighborhoods, and how public and private entities can best pursue the arduous work of pulling their communities back from the brink of disaster.

Between 1999 and 2006, house prices in many parts of the United States rose faster and higher than ever before in American history, fueled by the easy availability of credit and unsustainable subprime and other "exotic" mortgages as well as by the conviction of millions of lenders, homebuyers, builders, and speculators that the rise in prices would never end. Millions of homebuyers were lured into buying homes they could not afford or taking out ruinous second mortgages on the homes they already owned, while more and more new homes were bought by speculators seeking a quick flip rather than by homebuyers looking for a place to live. A collapse was inevitable. House prices could not continue to rise year after year forever while family incomes stagnated and economic growth was limited and uneven.

When the collapse came, it was particularly catastrophic since the bubble had gone on for so long and pushed prices so high. Between 2006 and 2009 house prices fell sharply and millions of homes went into foreclosure. As houses were foreclosed upon, owners or tenants were evicted or left their homes well before the inevitable end. Vacant, abandoned houses began appearing not only in hardpressed inner-city areas but also in prosperous urban neighborhoods and newly built suburban subdivisions.

Two parts of the country were most severely affected by the foreclosure crisis. One was the Sunbelt, where surging prices and overbuilding in California, Arizona,

Florida, and Nevada led to a particularly hard fall. The second was the older cities and inner-ring suburbs of the industrial Northeast and Midwest. Unemployment and economic instability were already high in cities like Cleveland and Detroit before the foreclosure crisis, and collapsing house prices reflected the continued loss of population and jobs. Few areas, however, were immune. Even in places like Boston, Chicago, and New York City that had seen sustained economic growth, foreclosures rose sharply in many urban neighborhoods and older suburbs, including communities that had shown significant signs of revival during the years preceding the collapse.

Foreclosures devastated the families and individuals losing their homes while setting off a vicious cycle of vacancy and price declines in their communities. As properties moved from default into the foreclosure process, owners often cut back on maintenance. As owners or tenants were evicted or walked away, their former homes became vacant and abandoned. As they became vacant, properties were often stripped and vandalized, their copper pipes and appliances bringing good returns on the black market. Neighboring homeowners saw their property values decline, while crime increased and their quality of life deteriorated.

Many of the neighborhoods that were hit first and hardest fell into a consistent pattern. In the Northeast and Midwest, they were often areas like Mount Pleasant in Cleveland or Vailsburg in Newark, where struggling working-class and middle-class families—more often than not African-American or Latino—had bought into the American dream of homeownership with subprime mortgages peddled by mortgage brokers who preyed on minority communities. Sunbelt cities like Phoenix and Miami had their share of affected urban areas, but they also saw an epidemic of foreclosures in the many modestly priced subdivisions and townhouse developments that had been built at the fringes of their metropolitan areas. These developments had been marketed to struggling young families as an opportunity to become homeowners and share in the suburban dream of clean air and open spaces, but they also contained large numbers of properties that had been bought by speculators looking for a quick profit.

As the crisis struck home, policymakers and practitioners first reacted by focusing on the crisis faced by the millions of homeowners and tenants at risk of losing their homes through foreclosure. It was not long, however, before the focus also turned to the destabilization of their neighborhoods and communities and to stemming the increase in vacant, abandoned properties. Since Congress enacted the federal Neighborhood Stabilization Program in the summer of 2008, stabilizing neighborhoods and dealing with abandoned properties have become a major concern of state and local governments, local CDCs, and other nonprofits. Yet in the course of this effort, some practitioners have tended to overlook the complexities of the process and the extent to which stabilizing neighborhoods needs to go beyond efforts, however important, to deal with individual abandoned properties. Indeed, strategies that have nothing to do with acquiring or rehabilitating vacant buildings may be even more important elements in the process of restoring neighborhood stability. The hard work that goes into rehabilitating fifty houses is likely to be in vain if, while that work is going on, two hundred more houses nearby become abandoned.

The first section of this chapter sets the stage by examining the federal Neighborhood Stabilization Program. The remaining sections address the central issue—how communities can put in place effective strategies to rebuild neighborhoods destabilized by foreclosure, vacancy, and abandonment. After an overview that looks at the principles involved in rebuilding neighborhood stability, the chapter includes extended discussions on reducing the link between foreclosure, deterioration, and abandonment; acquiring and reusing foreclosed and vacant properties; dealing with other property issues, particularly the role of investor-buyers of distressed properties; and finally weaving these elements together into a comprehensive approach to neighborhood stabilization.

A. NSP1 and NSP2: Neighborhood Stabilization Becomes a National Objective

By the beginning of 2008, after over a year of rising foreclosures, the accumulation of vacant REO (real-estate-owned, or bank-owned) properties had begun to affect urban and suburban communities across the United States and had become a major source of concern to local governments, CDCs, and neighborhood organizations. By early summer, with growing pressure on the federal government to address not only the foreclosure crisis but also the imminent collapse of Fannie Mae and Freddie Mac, the Housing and Economic Recovery Act of 2008 (HERA) was written in some haste by Congress and the Bush administration and signed by President George W. Bush on July 30.[1] Among its many other provisions, HERA included a section subtitled Emergency Assistance for the Redevelopment of Abandoned and Foreclosed Homes, which became the basis for the Neighborhood Stabilization Program. It was a major, although hastily formulated, federal initiative to deal with a rapidly emerging problem.

NSP1: Emergency Assistance

Under Sections 2301–2305 of HERA, $3.92 billion was appropriated to states, cities, and counties to be used for the following purposes:

(A) Establish financing mechanisms for purchase and redevelopment of foreclosed-upon homes and residential properties, including such mechanisms as soft seconds, loan loss reserves, and shared-equity loans for low- and moderate-income homebuyers

(B) Purchase and rehabilitate homes and residential properties that have been abandoned or foreclosed upon, in order to sell, rent, or redevelop such homes and properties

1. Public Law 110-289.

(C)   Establish land banks for homes that have been foreclosed upon

(D)   Demolish blighted structures

(E)   Redevelop demolished or vacant properties (Sec. 2301(c)(3))

The law further specified that the funds be allocated on the basis of a formula to be developed by HUD, which would take into account rates of defaults, foreclosures, and subprime loans, and that from the point that the funds were made available, state and local governments would have eighteen months in which to use them.

HUD published its fund allocations and guidelines for what it dubbed the Neighborhood Stabilization Program (NSP) by the end of September 2008. The two largest "winners" were Florida and California, which each received over half a billion dollars. States and local governments were required to submit spending plans for their allocations; once HUD approved their plans, they were then able to begin drawing down the funds. That point was reached in March 2009, when the eighteen-month clock began to run. By the end of January 2010, with only 30 percent of the funds obligated, it was already clear that spending the funds within the eighteen-month period prescribed by law would be a serious problem.

NSP 2: Economic Stimulus

Congress added $2 billion to NSP in the American Recovery and Reinvestment Act, better known as the "economic stimulus bill." While the ground rules for spending NSP2 funds were only slightly changed from those governing NSP1 monies, the process by which the funds would be provided was very different. Instead of relying on a formula allocation, the new HUD leadership convinced Congress to make NSP2 a competitive program and to allow nonprofits as well as state and local governments to compete for the funds. HUD issued its notice of fund availability (NOFA) in May 2009, with applicants required to submit their proposals by mid-July. Faced with more than $7 in requests for every $1 available, HUD announced $1.93 billion in NSP2 awards in January 2010. The balance was reserved for a technical assistance program that was the subject of a separate HUD NOFA. Again, Florida and California received the largest allocations; applicants in older industrial states such as Illinois, Michigan, and Ohio, however, received a substantially larger share of funds under NSP2 than they had under NSP1.

The Neighborhood Stabilization Program: Challenges and Opportunities

With only one year's experience with NSP1, and NSP2 projects just getting under way as of this writing, an evaluation of this major federal initiative is still premature. Some broad outlines, however, are already becoming clear. NSP has offered many localities and their nonprofit partners a critical opportunity to move forward with much-needed efforts to restore properties to productive use and stabilize their neighborhoods; at the same time, it is deeply flawed in important respects. The ultimate impact of the program remains uncertain.

Some of the problems that have arisen are external to the initiative itself. At the time the program was enacted, REO properties were accumulating far faster than buyers for them. As a result, it was widely assumed that acquisition, the linchpin of the program, would be straightforward. Policymakers expected local NSP grantees to have little difficulty finding lenders ready to sell them as many properties as they could use, and at deep discounts. That assumption turned out to be invalid, as private investor interest in REO properties grew steadily during 2009 and lenders' REO inventories shrank. Even with the creation of the National Community Stabilization Trust, an intermediary that has worked with lenders to make their properties available to local governments and nonprofits, many NSP grantees are still finding it difficult to put their funds to work.[2]

A second external problem is the difficulty grantees have experienced in finding non-NSP capital with which to leverage their NSP funds. In most NSP states and cities, the properties being acquired by grantees have a reuse value, either through sale to homebuyers or from rental cash flow. The most effective strategy in such cases is to use NSP money up front to acquire the properties, and then to find lenders to first provide construction loans for rehabilitation and then make take-out loans for the lion's share of the properties' appraised value, rather than use NSP money for the total project cost. In this way, the NSP money can revolve and be used to acquire and rehabilitate far more properties.

In theory, this seems simple and easily achieved. NSP's authors did not reckon, however, with the sharply reduced appetite for real estate lending on the part of America's financial institutions after their near-collapse in 2008 and 2009. With some notable exceptions, few lenders have been willing to partner with NSP grantees to enable them to leverage private funds. In a few states, community development financial institutions (CDFIs)—socially motivated nonprofit lenders with strong roots in many of the most affected communities—have filled part of the gap. Organizations such as New Jersey Community Capital, the Massachusetts Housing Investment Corporation, and the Greater Minnesota Housing Fund have developed loan products tailored to the NSP programs in their states. Most states, however, lack such programs, while those that have been established tend to suffer from severe capital constraints.

Other NSP problems have been internal, often reflecting the limited capacity of many grantees to carry out effective NSP programs. Many of the funds went to small county or city governments in the Sunbelt with few housing or community development professionals on staff and few if any CDCs or other nonprofits with whom to form partnerships. Many of these jurisdictions' NSP allocations were far larger than the amounts they had been receiving from the federal gov-

2. See page 324 for a description of the National Community Stabilization Trust.

The Neighborhood Stabilization Loan Fund (NSLF) is a $22 million fund established in 2008 by the Massachusetts Housing Investment Corporation (MHIC) to address foreclosure problems in distressed urban areas located throughout Massachusetts. MHIC also manages $13 million in federal NSP and state housing subsidies to support projects financed under the loan program.

The NSLF offers acquisition and construction loans to redevelop foreclosed residential properties; credit lines for deposits and predevelopment costs; federal NSP or state subsidies of up to $60,000 per unit; and receivership program loans for nonprofit receivership program administrators. Funds must be used in targeted neighborhoods in the cities of Boston, Worcester, Springfield, Lawrence, Lowell, Chelsea, and New Bedford.

ernment under the Community Development Block Grant program or other programs. Even in larger jurisdictions, capacity was still a problem. Many cities or CDCs had little expertise in negotiating property acquisition from private entities or in carrying out scattered site rehabilitation, and they had to learn new skills to make the program work.

The largest problem with NSP, however, flows from the nature of the program itself. Neighborhood stabilization is a complicated, multidimensional proposition in which acquiring and reusing foreclosed properties is only one part of a much larger picture. That, however, was the only activity for which NSP funds could be used. Moreover, given the magnitude of the problem and the number of foreclosed properties, NSP grantees could hope at most to gain control over only a small percentage of the properties in their communities. Given the scarcity of non-NSP resources, many grantees tended to focus narrowly on acquiring properties, rather than looking more broadly at the particular ways in which destabilization was taking place in their target neighborhoods and what combination of strategies would be needed to restore those neighborhoods to vitality. While some jurisdictions had developed thoughtful strategies for targeting key properties for maximum impact, those plans often ran afoul of the program's realities: acquisition was becoming more and more difficult, and the eighteen-month deadline loomed. It became increasingly difficult for NSP grantees to stick to a strategy in the face of these contrary pressures.

This leads to a larger question: how does NSP relate to neighborhood stabilization writ large? The short answer is that it is at best one tool of many that may be needed to restore vitality to an area undermined by foreclosures and vacant properties. The danger with NSP lies in the adage, attributed to Abraham

Maslow, that "if you only have a hammer, you tend to see everything as a nail." As will be discussed in the following section, effective neighborhood stabilization strategies need to link the activities permitted under the NSP statute to a cluster of other activities, with the specifics of the mix based on the neighborhood's particular features.

In framing the criteria for receiving NSP2 funds, HUD made a serious effort to address many of the concerns that had arisen under NSP1. The mere fact that it was a competitive program meant that all of the grantees would possess a minimum level of capacity. HUD went beyond that by requiring that applicants demonstrate that they had actually successfully performed activities similar to those they were proposing in their applications, at a scale consistent with that of the activities proposed. Even more importantly, HUD required that applicants provide a market analysis of their target areas and demonstrate how their activities reflected both an awareness of the market realities of their communities and a credible stabilization strategy based on those realities.

HUD's stiff capacity thresholds, coupled with minimum performance thresholds, had another positive effect on how local governments and nonprofits looked at the program. Many smaller cities, counties, and CDCs quickly realized as they read the NOFA that they lacked either the track record or the ability to operate at a scale that would make them credible applicants. As a result, they began to reach out to others—neighboring municipalities, county governments, other nonprofits, and for-profit developers—to mold collaborative efforts that would enable them to compete for the NSP2 funds. In many cities, this was the first time that many of the NSP2 partners had actually come together to work as a team. Although NSP2 activities have just begun, the program is off to a promising start.

Despite the obstacles and difficulties associated with the program, NSP funds have already unleashed powerful energy and creativity on the part of local officials, CDCs, and others in many American communities. As we turn to the central question of how to frame effective neighborhood stabilization strategies for distressed, destabilized communities, we will highlight many examples of creative initiatives from the nation's towns and cities.

B. Thinking Strategically about Neighborhood Stabilization

Understanding Neighborhood Stability

A single body of principles applies to any effort to restore stability to a neighborhood, whether the neighborhood has been destabilized by a wave of foreclosures, by long-term economic decline, by a plant closing, or by any other circumstance. The strategies may vary, but the underlying principles remain the same.

A stable neighborhood does not mean that everyone in the neighborhood stays in the same place. People are mobile, and few spend their entire lives in the same town or neighborhood. Neighborhood stability flows from how the residents of the neighborhood, as well as those of the larger city and region, perceive the neighborhood, and how they act on those perceptions. If people who live in an area perceive their neighborhood to be declining, they will not invest in their homes and will leave the neighborhood if and when they are able. People in the rest of the region who have enough income to choose between neighborhoods will not choose one that they perceive to be declining, or where they perceive that their investment—financial or psychological—will be at risk. *Simply stated, a stable neighborhood is a neighborhood where people feel that their investment is secure.*

People—both those living in the neighborhood and those who might consider buying there—are influenced both by an area's reputation and by a series of visual cues or signals that they pick up as they walk or drive through the area. Boarded houses are perhaps the most powerful such signal, but not the only one. The visible level of maintenance and cleanliness of an area is just as important. Dirt-covered front yards with scrappy, uneven fencing; sagging front porches and peeling paint; trash in vacant lots or gutters; and poorly maintained, dirty streets, sidewalks, and public spaces all send the same message: this is a neighborhood that lacks the stability that its residents crave and that prospective homebuyers demand.

Many things can destabilize a neighborhood. Destabilization can be seen as the cumulative effect of a series of *destabilizing events*. Every time a property is abandoned, a street crime is committed, a pile of trash is dumped on a vacant lot, or an occupied house is allowed to deteriorate, that is a destabilizing event. Some of these may be deliberate acts of vandalism and others the sad consequences of poverty, but their effect is the same. There is no way to prevent destabilizing events from happening. They take place in even the strongest neighborhoods. The issue is whether they are speedily addressed so that they have no long-term effect on the neighborhood, or whether they accumulate and drag the neighborhood down. As Jane Jacobs said in her famous book *The Death and Life of Great American Cities,* a stable neighborhood is one "that keeps sufficiently abreast of its problems so that it is not destroyed by them."

Successfully stabilizing a neighborhood or maintaining neighborhood stability from this perspective requires that the weight of stabilizing actions exceed that of destabilizing events. Restoring vacant properties to use, cleaning up vacant lots, and reducing street crime are all stabilizing actions. The more they happen, the more they can change the perceptions and behavior of the people in and around the area and reverse the area's downward trajectory. But if not enough stabilizing actions take place to outweigh destabilization, they are likely to have little effect, being nullified by the sheer weight of destabilizing events. While marketing efforts may also be needed to undo negative perceptions of a neighborhood, they are likely to be ineffective without a solid track record of stabilizing actions in place and under way. The role of government, CDCs, and neighborhood organizations is to foster the stabilizing actions that will ultimately restore neighborhood vitality.

Not Just about Buying Properties

These principles can be applied directly to neighborhoods being destabilized by foreclosures and to local governments and nonprofits using federal NSP funds. A city government or CDC that wants to stabilize a neighborhood must engage as best it can with a wide spectrum of destabilizing events to change the neighborhood's trajectory. If the dynamics that are leading to properties being abandoned in the neighborhood—whether through foreclosure or other reasons—are not addressed, programs that restore vacant properties, despite the expenditure of years of effort and millions of dollars, may not have a significant stabilizing effect.

In a destabilized neighborhood, decline can become a vicious cycle. While foreclosures may have triggered the process of destabilization in a neighborhood, tackling the vacant properties caused by foreclosures may or may not reverse that process, depending on the dynamics of change that have been set in motion. If more properties are still becoming vacant and abandoned than a local CDC is able to buy, rehabilitate, and sell, greater attention needs to be paid to reducing the flow of properties into vacancy. In some neighborhoods, the increase in vacant properties may have led to an increase in crime, which will have to be addressed before the neighborhood can regain health.

Furthermore, despite their best efforts, in most neighborhoods the number of properties that will be acquired under NSP—or other public or nonprofit initiatives—will represent only a small percentage of the distressed properties that become available during the course of the program, and an even smaller share of the total properties in the target area. What happens to the rest of the properties in the area may have a more powerful effect on the neighborhood's future than the outcomes of the relative handful of properties acquired under NSP.

Four propositions to guide neighborhood stabilization programs flow from the foregoing discussion:

- Focus on reducing the flow of foreclosures and vacant properties as much as on restoring vacant properties to productive use.

- Identify and address other forces contributing to the neighborhood's destabilization, such as crime or quality-of-life issues.

- Identify and target property acquisition and reuse activities to maximize the effect of available resources.

- Ensure that the trends and dynamics affecting the balance of the area's properties also further the stability of the area.

A comprehensive neighborhood stabilization effort should address all of these areas.

C. Prevention First: Minimizing the Neighborhood Effects of Foreclosure

Foreclosures are destabilizing events, but the problem is often not the foreclosure itself. Foreclosure is nothing more or less than a legal procedure being pursued by a creditor against a debtor. The problem is that foreclosure far too often leads to properties being neglected, disinvested, and vacated. Once a property has become vacant, it is at risk of being vandalized, particularly in high-density urban areas, and turning into a long-term blight on the neighborhood. This process can begin within days after a family receives its first notice of foreclosure and can continue for months or years, as the property is foreclosed upon, is taken back by the lender and becomes REO property, and is ultimately put up for sale. The longer the process, and the longer a property is vacant or is not being maintained, the greater the harm to the neighborhood.

The first steps a community can take to minimize destabilization and restore neighborhood health are to reduce foreclosures; reduce, to the extent possible, the connection between foreclosures that do happen and subsequent disinvestment and abandonment; and ensure that properties in foreclosure are occupied and—whether occupied or vacant—maintained. While both governments and lenders have begun to deal with these issues in the past two years, they still have a long way to go.

Keeping Properties Occupied

An occupied property is generally better than a vacant one. It does less harm to the neighborhood and is more likely to retain its value; from the standpoint of the owner or tenant, it is almost always better to be able to stay in your home than be forced to move. Despite this, lenders and servicers have, as soon as a foreclosure is final, routinely evicted not only defaulting homeowners but also tenants living in foreclosed properties. Tenant evictions have been a major problem: large numbers of foreclosed properties have been either absentee-owned properties—often bought by speculators at the height of the housing bubble—or two- and three-family houses, particularly in Northeastern cities like New Haven or Newark, with mixed owner and renter occupancy.

Preventing foreclosures. The first and often most important step in preventing vacant properties is to prevent foreclosures from taking place. This is really two separate processes: (1) trying to help owners keep their homes, by providing counseling, legal, and financial assistance and (2) where owners are unable to keep their homes, helping to bring about a process, such as a *short sale,* that will permit the ownership to change in a way that minimizes damage to both the homeowner and the neighborhood.

Most communities today have one or more organizations that work with borrowers facing potential foreclosure, along with hot lines and other resources for assistance. Many states have created mediation programs, pioneered by the city of Philadelphia, to ensure that before a foreclosure takes place, the borrower has an opportunity to meet with the lender in an effort to renegotiate the mortgage. Since early in 2009, the federal Home Affordable Modification Program (HAMP) has helped hundreds of thousands of distressed borrowers initiate loan modifications with lenders.

Despite these resources, the results are mixed at best. While HAMP has helped initiate large numbers of modifications, by early 2010 relatively few of them had turned into permanent loan modifications. Many modified loans soon redefault, particularly when they do not include a reduction in what is often a bloated principal amount or when borrowers have excessive amounts of non-housing debt. As a result, many distressed owners realistically will not be able to keep their homes. If their mortgage significantly exceeds the value of their home and their monthly payments are well above current market rents, they may not even want to.

A short sale is a sale by the current owner to a new end user—either a home-buyer or an investor—for an amount less than the amount of the mortgage. It can only take place if the lender is willing to accept less than full repayment of its mortgage from the sale, which requires the lender's approval. For "underwater" homeowners, a short sale is often the best route to avoid foreclosure and reduce damage to their credit ratings.[3] For the neighborhood, it is often the best route to avoid creating another vacant property. Although lenders were initially reluctant to approve short sales—despite the likelihood that they would end up with more money than if they went to foreclosure—attitudes have begun to change, and more short sales are taking place.[4] Many Realtors are becoming more sophisticated about negotiating short sales with lenders. Neighborhood organizations can work in partnership with Realtors to facilitate short sales in their community to homebuyers or to responsible investors, particularly in light of recent HAMP incentives being offered to encourage short sales.

Keeping tenants in their homes. The situation for tenants, often the innocent victims in foreclosure proceedings, has improved somewhat since the onset of the crisis. Before 2007 most states provided no security for tenants, who were routinely evicted immediately after a foreclosure sale. Although tenant protection has historically been a matter of state rather than federal law, facing widespread hardship and only scattered state action, in May 2009 Congress established a minimum federal standard to protect the tenants of foreclosed properties. The Protecting Tenants in Foreclosure Act requires the following steps:

- Tenants must receive a ninety-day notice before they can be required to vacate.

- Any tenants with leases must be allowed to remain in their homes until the expiration of the lease, unless the new buyers want to occupy

3. An "underwater" borrower is one whose mortgage amount exceeds the current value of the house. As of mid-2009, according to different estimates, 11–15 million mortgage holders were under water in the United States. In some states, most notably Nevada and Arizona, over half of all mortgage holders were under water.

4. Although short sales are increasing, a major impediment remains the large number of properties that have second mortgages or other liens in addition to the primary mortgage. For a short sale to take place, the interests of other lienholders must also be satisfied.

the property themselves, in which case the tenant must be given a ninety-day notice.[5]

This law is an important step, but it contains a major limitation. It is "self-executing"; in other words, no federal agency is responsible for seeing that it is enforced, and if it is violated, it is up to state and local authorities to take action within the framework of state law. Many tenants may not be aware of this law, and it contains no requirement that landlords or foreclosing lenders notify tenants of their rights. Many of those lenders may also be unaware of the law or may pretend to be, and may attempt to evict tenants immediately after foreclosure, as they have done in the past. Early in 2010, Connecticut's attorney general issued cease-and-desist orders to thirty real estate firms, lenders, and law firms accused of forcing tenants out in violation of federal law.

Local officials and neighborhood-based organizations need to make sure that tenants are aware of the law, and—in those few states where tenant protections are more extensive than the federal law—of the provisions of state law. They must also ensure that tenants have access to legal assistance if lenders or servicers attempt illegally to force them out of their homes. A recent New Jersey law requires lenders to serve tenants with a notice of their rights—which in New Jersey go beyond those in the federal law—within ten days of taking title at sheriff's sales. The law also provides civil penalties for anyone taking "any action placing pressure on a tenant to accept any offer to vacate the property."[6]

Keeping owners in their homes. While progress has been made in helping tenants stay in foreclosed properties, there has been less movement on the more knotty issue of whether homeowners should be permitted to stay in their homes as tenants after foreclosure. While this idea has found its advocates, most notably Dean Baker of the Center for Economic Policy and Research, it has only slowly begun to penetrate the political process and the consciousness of the financial community.[7] In November 2009, Fannie Mae announced a "Deed for Lease" program, under which certain owners would be offered one-year leases in return for the deeds to their homes. CitiMortgage announced a similar program, under which they would offer owners a six-month lease and at least $1,000 in relocation expenses in return for their handing the bank the deeds to their homes.

A more creative strategy is being pursued by an investor group buying properties in Phoenix. They buy houses from their owners through short sales, allow them to remain in place as tenants paying market rent, and after five years—when

5. Title VII of Public Law 111-222. These provisions will sunset, unless amended or re-enacted by Congress, on December 31, 2012.

6. Chapter 296, Public Laws of 2009.

7. Bills to permit owners to stay in their homes as tenants after foreclosure have been introduced in state legislatures in Arizona and New Jersey. The New Jersey initiative was broadly written, while the more narrowly written Arizona bill would have given the former owners of houses valued below the median price for their metropolitan areas who had lived in the houses for at least two years a one-year lease at market rent. Neither initiative was successful.

the investor group plans to sell the homes—give the former owners the option of buying their homes back. This is a win-win for everyone: the lenders benefit from the short sales; the former owners benefit from being able to stay in their homes and pay a rent that is far lower than their monthly payments were as home-owners; and the investors benefit from a responsible tenant, cash flow from rental income, and a high likelihood of appreciation at the end of five years. This model may not work in every community, but it works well in areas where the market prices of homes are low enough that they can be leased at a rent that provides a positive cash flow and where there is a realistic possibility of house prices going back up over the next five years.[8] This includes many Sunbelt areas, but fewer older industrial communities.

Keeping Properties Maintained: Who Is Responsible?

Chapters 5 and 12 of this book discuss the critical role that code enforcement and nuisance abatement play in addressing both vacant properties and properties at risk of abandonment, and the tools that local government can use to that end. Those tools are an important way of maintaining stability in areas affected by large numbers of foreclosures. Indeed, strong code enforcement and nuisance abatement, directed at neighborhoods that are also the focus of foreclosure prevention and property acquisition efforts, should be seen as an essential element within a larger neighborhood stabilization strategy.

Mounting an effective property maintenance strategy in a high-foreclosure environment raises new and difficult questions. The first arises from the extended periods in many states between the initial foreclosure filing, the foreclosure sale, and the ultimate resale of the property to an end user.[9] The duration of foreclosure varies widely from state to state; it can be as little as forty-five days in Georgia or Texas and well over a year in New Jersey or Ohio.[10] In states where the process is long and drawn out, the owner may often walk away from the property long before the foreclosure sale. After the foreclosure sale, the lender may not record the sale until many months later. As a result, for anything from a few months to two years or more, the property is in limbo—the borrower is still shown as holding title, but is no longer willing or able to take responsibility for the property and is all but impossible to find.

8. Prices, however, must also be high enough that the market does not draw too many bottom-feeders; that is, people who will buy properties for minimal cost, milk them for a year or two, and then walk away, as is the case in the most severely distressed markets, such as Cleveland or Detroit.

9. The foreclosure sale (also known in some states as a sheriff's sale or trustee sale) is the final step in the foreclosure process in nearly all states. At the foreclosure sale, title to the property is put up for sale and then taken back by the lender unless a third party bids an amount in excess of the amount owed the lender on the property.

10. Foreclosures fall into two broad categories: *nonjudicial* foreclosures, which tend to be expedited processes involving little more than a period of notice prior to the foreclosure sale, and *judicial* foreclosures, in which the foreclosing party must get a decree of foreclosure from the courts before the foreclosure sale can be scheduled. The latter is generally considerably slower than the former. Roughly half of the states have judicial foreclosure systems, and half have nonjudicial systems.

One emerging regulatory approach is to hold the lender or servicer responsible for the property if it becomes vacant—not from the point when the new title is formally recorded, but either from the date of the foreclosure sale or from the beginning of the foreclosure process. Such an approach was pioneered by the city of Chula Vista, California. Taking advantage of the broad "home rule" powers of cities under California law, the city adopted an Abandoned Property Registration Ordinance, which became effective in October 2007. The ordinance requires lenders, after the first notice of default, to register with the city and inspect the property. If a property is found to be vacant, the program requires that the lender exercise the abandonment clause within the mortgage contract and immediately begin to secure and maintain the property to the neighborhood standard.[11] The lender is not required to make interior repairs that are not visible, although it might be in its interest to do so. If the lender does not comply with the ordinance, the city may perform the needed maintenance or repairs, bill the lender, and fine the lender. During the first two years of the program, the city levied $1.5 million in fines. Many cities in California and elsewhere have adopted local ordinances based on the Chula Vista model. The state of New Jersey has adopted a statewide approach to this problem—the only state to have done so to date.

These statutes and ordinances can be controversial. Whether a municipality, or even a state legislature, has the power to compel a lender to maintain a property to which that lender does not hold title is not a simple legal issue. There are arguments on both sides, and little case law in most states to offer guidance. What is *not* in doubt, however, despite some misinformed claims to the contrary, is the lender's *ability* to do so. The standard mortgage documents used throughout the United States give lenders all but unlimited authority to enter onto property on which they hold mortgages, if the property has fallen into disrepair or become vacant, to maintain the property and protect their investment.[12]

In states like Georgia or Texas that have speedy nonjudicial foreclosure systems, making the lender take responsibility prior to the foreclosure sale is desirable but less important, since the property is likely to be vacant only briefly, if at all, prior to the sale. What is important everywhere is that the lender be held responsible for the property *immediately* after the foreclosure sale, rather than only after the lender records the deed or resells the property to a third party. Most states do not set a deadline to record a deed; as a result, to avoid responsibility for the property, a lender may not record the deed until literally the day before it is scheduled to sell the property to a new owner, which may be many months

11. For more details, see www.chulavistaca.gov/City_Services/Development_Services/Planning_Building/Building/Code_Enforcement/AbanResPropertyProg.asp.

12. The key language (which generally appears as Section 9 of the standard Fannie Mae mortgage) reads "[If] Borrower has abandoned the Property, then Lender may do and pay for whatever is reasonable or appropriate to protect Lender's interest in the Property and rights under this Security Instrument, including protecting and/or assessing the value of the Property, and securing and/or repairing the Property."

GOOD PRACTICE

Under a state law first enacted by the New Jersey Legislature in January 2009 and amended in January 2010, the following rules govern all foreclosures initiated in the state:[13]

• The lender must give the municipality notice whenever it initiates a new foreclosure. Along with the notice, the lender must provide contact information for an entity that will receive complaints about property maintenance and for an in-state entity that will accept service on behalf of the lender.

• If the owner abandons the property, even if it still has tenants living in it, the lender is deemed to have responsibility for maintaining the property. If there is a code violation on the property, the city "shall notify the creditor, *which shall have the responsibility to abate the nuisance or correct the violation in the same manner and to the same extent as the title owner of the property.*"

• If the municipality expends funds to correct a violation or abate a nuisance on the property, it has the same recourse against the lender as it would have had against the title owner.[14]

This is particularly important in New Jersey, which has among the longest periods of any state from initial filing to foreclosure sale.

after the foreclosure sale. California Senate Bill 1137, enacted in July 2008, requires the entity acquiring title at a foreclosure sale to secure the property, maintain its exterior, and correct any health hazards, such as mosquito infestation, that may become a public nuisance.

The need for code enforcement does not end once a property goes through the foreclosure process. In many cities, particularly those, like Cleveland or Detroit, with extremely low property values, distressed or REO properties are often sold by lenders to unscrupulous investors, who may attempt to rent or sell them in deplorable, often unsafe, conditions to the detriment of the property and the

---

13. N.J. Stats. Ann. 46:10B-51. Initially enacted as Chapter 127, Public Laws of 2008; amended by Chapter 296, Public Laws of 2009; signed into law on January 17, 2010.
14. Under New Jersey law, a municipality can not only put a lien on a property after it has incurred costs to abate a nuisance, it can seek a judgment against other assets of the owner as well; N.J. Stats. Ann. 55:19-100. While this can be a cumbersome process, it could be an effective tool in dealing with a lender unwilling to comply with the law.

neighborhood as a whole. As will be discussed later in this chapter, code enforcement is often a powerful tool that can be used to discourage this type of irresponsible and dangerous behavior.

Enforcement capacity may be a problem. Many cities' code enforcement efforts are constrained by limited personnel and weak internal management systems. With the foreclosure crisis and the recession triggering drastic reductions in municipal budgets, many cities have been laying off inspectors and support personnel even as the need for them has grown. Even cities with strong local ordinances have found it increasingly difficult to enforce them. As a general proposition, cities should consider code enforcement a higher priority than many do, and they should think twice before cutting their budgets in that area. Nevertheless, their fiscal constraints are real and likely to be long-lasting.

More than ever, cities should seek out opportunities to leverage their resources in this area with private resources. The greatest opportunities lie in partnerships with CDCs and neighborhood organizations, to create programs like Atlanta's Neighborhood Deputies program (see page 42) or the Cleveland Housing Court's code enforcement advocates (see page 45). Neighborhood residents can be trained to become the city's eyes and ears in areas experiencing large numbers of foreclosures, while inexpensive web-based systems can be used to allow neighborhood organizations, CDCs, and City Hall to share and act on problem property information.

The structure of a city-community partnership to ensure that properties are properly maintained can take many different forms, depending on the way city government is organized, the capacity and reach of CDCs and neighborhood-based organizations, and the magnitude of the problem. The important point is to recognize that *cities often lack the resources to tackle this problem on their own*. Overcoming traditional barriers and role definitions and reaching out to form partnerships with nongovernment entities has become not an option, but an imperative.

D. Dealing with Foreclosed and Abandoned Properties

Rightly or wrongly, the acquisition, rehabilitation or redevelopment, and ultimate reuse of vacant and foreclosed properties is an important, and often the principal, feature of most neighborhood stabilization programs. Not only are these the only activities for which NSP funds can be used, but they tend to be highly visible, and thus often important to the neighborhood's future vitality. Carrying out such activities in a fashion that will be both cost-effective and most likely to have a positive effect on the community, however, is not easy. Acquiring, rehabilitating, maintaining, and selling or renting properties demand a wide variety of skills. They also require a thorough understanding of the market conditions in which they are being pursued.

Market Conditions and Property Strategies

Housing markets vary by region, by town, and by neighborhood. While all communities experiencing high volumes of foreclosure are likely to be experiencing some difficulty in the marketplace, their conditions will vary widely. Those conditions will determine, more than any other single factor, which property strategies are most likely to be successful. In some cases, studying market conditions may lead a planner to realize that spending public money to fix up houses in a particular area may not be a good idea, either because the same houses are likely to be acquired and improved through private initiative or because there may be no market demand for them even after rehabilitation. In other cases, understanding market conditions will help the planner make a sound decision on what to do with a property that the city has acquired and avoid missteps that may end up costing the city time or money.

Although it is an oversimplification, it is possible to separate communities affected by foreclosure into three broad categories: *market correction, market destabilization,* and *market collapse.* Each of these three categories has important implications for property acquisition, reuse, and other strategies. A short definition of each is given in table 21.1.

In a market correction environment, private demand will gradually absorb available properties, including REO properties, as their price falls to realistic levels. A realistic price is that which is equal to or less than the capitalized value of market rent for the same property; in other words, a price at which a buyer can rent out the property and realize a positive cash flow.[15] In much of the Phoenix metro area, house prices needed to drop by roughly 60 percent before they reached that level; as they did, by early 2009, housing demand increased. By the end of the year, not only had the REO inventory declined sharply, but non-distress or traditional sales had also begun to rebound.[16] Despite the large number of foreclosures in Phoenix, one sees relatively few vacant, boarded properties in its neighborhoods.

This does not mean that there is *no* role for the public sector or CDCs in areas experiencing market correction. A disproportionate share of private market buyers may be absentee investors, and a CDC may wish to maintain a higher level of homeownership in a neighborhood than would come about without its inter-

---

15. In theory, this should be the price of a house absent buyers' expectation of appreciation. The difference between the house price and the capitalized value of the rent is attributable to those expectations. The greater those expectations, the greater the premium that buyers are likely to be willing to pay. The recent bubble, particularly in the Sunbelt markets, was based on wildly speculative assumptions about appreciation, which pushed prices to levels that were often two or three times the capitalized value of a realizable rental cash flow.

16. This does not prove that the Phoenix housing market is out of the woods. Continuing high rates of foreclosure starts, along with a marked decline in market rents during 2009, could herald future trouble. At the same time, it is clear that the market showed signs of at least short-term stabilization during that year, which cannot realistically be attributed to anything other than market forces.

TABLE 21.1 Categories of Markets Affected by Foreclosure

Category	Description	Typical of neighborhoods in:
Market correction	Demand increases as prices fall to affordable levels, and a balance between supply and demand is gradually restored.	Los Angeles, California Phoenix, Arizona Washington, DC
Market destabilization	Demand potentially exists but is constrained by lack of confidence or prices that are high relative to perceived value. It may need public or nonprofit intervention to be converted into effective demand.	Newark, New Jersey Stockton, California
Market collapse	Weak demand and a large oversupply of housing creates a surplus that cannot be absorbed by market demand.	Detroit, Michigan Cleveland, Ohio

vention. Alternatively, private market buyers may be shunning houses in need of major repair, which need to be addressed in the interest of long-term neighborhood stability. At the same time, rather than focus directly on acquiring properties—an activity that imposes significant direct and opportunity costs—a CDC may want either to provide assistance to individual homebuyers who want to buy in the area or to build partnerships with private investors to achieve its objectives.

The situation is the opposite in neighborhoods where the market has collapsed, and where many houses may literally have no value except to the occasional rapacious speculator who may buy houses for nominal prices in order to milk them for a year or two and then walk away. Many neighborhoods in distressed older cities like Cleveland or Buffalo, which continue to lose population, fit this description. There may be little point in spending public sector funds to acquire houses in many such areas except to demolish the structures and bank the land for some undetermined future use. In most cases, if the city and county have a well-functioning tax foreclosure and land banking system, many such properties can be acquired through tax foreclosure without public expenditure beyond transaction costs.

There are exceptions. Some houses may have historical or architectural value and be worth preserving, even if they have to be mothballed for some length of time before they can be reused. In other cases, a neighborhood—or part of a neighborhood—may have a reasonably intact physical fabric, or be close to an anchor institution or other important asset. In such cases, it may be appropriate to acquire properties as part of a strategy to revive market demand in such a neighborhood—although doing so successfully in a market collapse environment is likely to be an extremely difficult task.

It is the neighborhoods in the middle—where the market has been destabilized to the point that it may not be restored through private action alone, but where demand potentially exists if it can be effectively mobilized—where city or CDC action is most needed, and most likely, if well designed, to have the greatest impact. That demands that the city or CDC be strategic in choosing which properties to acquire and what to do with them. Resources will never be available to acquire all of the properties that may potentially be available. All properties are not fungible.

Local governments and CDCs engaging in neighborhood stabilization efforts should track market conditions in their target areas on as close to a real-time basis as possible, since markets are capable of shifting quickly and unpredictably. They should pay particular attention to changes in investor behavior, since both the level of investor activity and the strategies being pursued by investors will have powerful implications for neighborhood stability as well as market conditions. Tracking of market trends should be done through a combination of data monitoring—including such variables as the number of sales, type of sales (REO or traditional), type of buyers, and price levels—and regular contact with individuals with knowledge of local market conditions, such as Realtors and lenders.[17]

Acquiring Properties

Not all strategies to deal with vacant or distressed properties involve acquisition by a public or nonprofit entity. Property acquisition is expensive and time-consuming, and it imposes both direct costs and opportunity costs on the entity doing the acquisition. Before acquiring a property, a public or nonprofit entity should ask a critical question: *If we acquire this property, will we significantly change the outcome for this property, and by extension, for its surroundings?* If that question cannot be answered in the affirmative, the entity may want to reconsider acquiring the property.

Where a pool of available properties in fair to good condition exists and qualified homebuyer demand either exists or can be generated through marketing and outreach efforts, strategies to provide financial assistance to qualified homebuyers to buy houses directly on the market may be more cost-effective and less labor-intensive than acquisition strategies. Such programs should make sure that

---

17. Comparing sales prices in a small area over time can be problematic because of the likelihood that the nature of the properties sold will vary from year to year, so that changes in price may reflect differences in property characteristics rather than actual price trends. Economists use a methodology known as repeat sales modeling to correct for this factor; while this methodology is difficult to apply to small areas, techniques that can be used for this purpose have been developed by RW Ventures for Living Cities. A description of the Dynamic Neighborhood Taxonomy can be found at www.rw-ventures .com/download/DNT_project_description.pdf.

any homebuyer in the program (1) gets a sustainable mortgage and (2) moves into a house in good condition, unlikely to trigger unexpected repair or replacement costs. Both of these conditions can often be achieved for modest amounts, in the vicinity of $5,000 to $15,000 per house, although strategies for meeting these conditions are likely to be somewhat labor-intensive.

Most neighborhood stabilization efforts using NSP funds, however, will include some property acquisition by public or nonprofit entities. It is important that they be responsible buyers; in other words, they should understand their options, be able to evaluate the pros and cons of the different properties available, and negotiate prices and terms that further the public interest.

Properties can be acquired in many different ways. The most important options are illustrated in table 21.2. As the table shows, each has its advantages and disadvantages. Until recently, many of these options were not eligible uses of NSP funds. In April 2010, however, HUD substantially revised its guidelines, making many formerly ineligible properties eligible to be acquired or improved with NSP funds. This is particularly important with respect to short sales. Short sales make it possible for properties to change hands without an intervening period of vacancy and—as discussed earlier—can create an opportunity for the owner to remain in her home as a tenant and potentially buy it back in the future. Although for a number of years lender resistance tended to discourage short sales, lender attitudes have shifted since the beginning of 2009. Today more lenders are willing to negotiate short sales and respond to offers in a timely fashion, while the federal government has joined in with incentives to encourage them to do so.

In weak market areas, properties can often be obtained through tax foreclosure; that is, foreclosure by city or county government on properties on which the owners have failed to pay property taxes. This is discussed in detail in chapter 7. Tax foreclosure is the principal means by which most land banks acquire properties. NSP funds can be used to acquire tax-foreclosed properties from local governments or land bank entities. Using tax foreclosure to obtain property for neighborhood stabilization, however, is not without difficulties. Tax foreclosure is a slow and cumbersome process in many states, while county governments are often more concerned with maximizing tax revenue from foreclosures than with gaining control of properties for neighborhood stabilization.

Most neighborhood stabilization property acquisition activities tend to focus on acquisition of REO properties, if only because this is the most straightforward use of NSP funds. This approach poses its own difficulties, particularly where private investors are active, since the procedural and substantive requirements of NSP, along with the delays associated with property purchases by cities or CDCs, make quick cash offers from investors more attractive to lenders holding REO properties. Some large investors, furthermore, may have an inside track with some lenders, enabling them to get properties before they are offered to a wider market. They may also be in a position to make large-scale bulk purchases, which enable them to negotiate substantial discounts. Investor competition has significantly

TABLE 21.2 Property Acquisition Options

Option	Description	Advantages	Disadvantages
Conventional (non-distress) sale	Arms-length acquisition of property from owner	Negotiation likely to be straightforward and only involve property owner. Competition from other potential buyers likely to be limited.	Price likely to be higher than with other alternatives. Cannot use NSP funds for conventional arms-length purchases except under limited circumstances.*
REO sale	Purchase of property taken back by lender through foreclosure, either through Realtor or directly from lender	Price likely to be low. Can use NSP funds for REO purchases.	Property more likely to be vacant and in poor condition. Public or nonprofit buyers may face strong competition from investor-buyers.
Short sale	Purchase of property from owner at price that is below amount owed on mortgage	Price likely to be low. Property still occupied and likely to be in good condition. May be possible to structure deal to allow owner to remain as tenant and potentially buy home back in future.	Requires negotiation with both owner and lender—this can be difficult and time-consuming.

Method	Description	Advantages	Disadvantages
Purchase at foreclosure sale	Purchase of property at foreclosure sale by outbidding lender	Price may be low but bidding can yield unpredictable results. Property will usually still be occupied and is likely to be in good condition. May be possible to structure deal to allow owner to remain as tenant and potentially buy home back in future.	Requires bidding in potentially highly competitive and risky environment (not for the fainthearted). Little or no opportunity for due diligence.
Purchase of mortgage	Purchase of mortgage on property (rather than property itself) from lender	Price likely to be low. May be possible to structure deal to allow owner to remain as tenant and potentially buy home back in future.	Buyer must take property through foreclosure process in order to gain title, which may result in delay and high transaction costs. Cannot use NSP funds to buy mortgages.[†]
Tax foreclosure	Acquisition of property by city or county government through foreclosure for nonpayment of property taxes	Least expensive option—no cost other than transaction costs. Can use NSP funds for acquisition of tax-foreclosed properties.	Tax foreclosure process in many states is lengthy and cumbersome. May require cooperation of both city and county governments. Property more likely to be vacant and in poor condition.

*Property must meet HUD definition of abandoned property.
[†]But may be able to use NSP funds to take out other funds after the buyer of the mortgage has foreclosed on the property.

hindered both acquisition and homebuyer assistance initiatives under NSP programs in many communities.

A number of efforts have emerged to address this problem, the most notable of which is the National Community Stabilization Trust (NCST). The NCST was created by a coalition of national organizations as a vehicle to facilitate acquisition of REO properties by nonprofit entities.[18] The NCST's most prominent initiative is the First Look Program it has created as a result of negotiations with many leading lenders and loan servicers. Under this program, which was active in over a hundred communities by the end of 2009, servicers allow public and nonprofit purchasers a first look at properties as they enter their REO inventory. Fannie Mae operates a separate but similar program. These programs can be valuable ways for cities and CDCs to get access to properties. At the same time, they have serious limitations. Since properties become available a few at a time, and since the time frames for the first look programs are short, it can be difficult for a CDC to use the programs in a strategic or targeted fashion. Despite this, the NCST program has become a critically important resource for many entities stymied by investor competition in the marketplace.

Their financial and technical constraints place neighborhood-based nonprofits at a long-term disadvantage in property acquisition—a disadvantage only partially mitigated by NCST's activities. A new supportive infrastructure of centralized, better-capitalized entities is emerging to address this issue. In Chicago, Mercy Portfolio Services has developed an efficient property acquisition pipeline as part of their management of the Chicago NSP program, while in New Jersey, the Community Asset Preservation Corporation, a subsidiary of New Jersey Community Capital, was created to carry out bulk purchases of distressed properties and mortgages from lenders and servicers. These entities, and others like them, can continue to play a valuable role in supporting neighborhood revitalization efforts long after the immediate crisis has passed.

While HUD changed the NSP program guidelines early in 2010 to allow funds to be used for some other types of acquisitions, one can hope that Congress will design any future iterations of the program with the flexibility that local programs need. In the meantime, local governments and CDCs should actively seek out the resources to pursue other acquisition strategies. In many cases, such as short sales, the necessary funds can take the form of loan capital, rather than grant funds.

Reusing Properties

The purpose of acquiring properties is to reuse them in ways that will contribute to stabilizing the neighborhood, in the short or the long run. Local governments and CDCs have a finite menu of alternatives for reuse of the residential properties they acquire:

---

18. NCST sponsors are LISC, Enterprise Community Partners, NeighborWorks America, the Housing Partnership Network, the National Council of La Raza, and the National Urban League.

- Resale of the property to a homebuyer, either at market price or at a subsidized below-market price

- Rental as a short-term use, with the goal of selling the property to the tenant or a homebuyer in the near future (generally five years or less)

- Rental as a long-term use

- Demolition of the structure and construction of new housing, either for sale or rental use, on the property

- Demolition or mothballing of the structure and land banking of the property for undetermined future use

In rare cases, buildings or land may also be reused for nonresidential purposes.

While the choice of alternatives may be driven by neighborhood strategies or by a CDC's desire to address specific affordable housing needs that it has identified in its community, entities conducting neighborhood stabilization activities must be sensitive to market realities and maintain their focus on the goal of bringing about their neighborhood's market recovery. There can be significant tensions between current market realities and aspirations for the future of the neighborhood, as well as between affordable housing and market recovery strategies.

These tensions have powerful implications for the choice of reuse strategy. First, a *neighborhood stabilization strategy is not the same thing as an affordable housing strategy.* That does not mean that they are necessarily in conflict—they are not. A strategy that focuses exclusively or principally on meeting affordable housing needs, however, is very different from one that focuses on market recovery. An effort to stabilize a distressed neighborhood destabilized by foreclosure should be grounded in a market recovery strategy; the affordable housing effort needs to be pursued in the context of that strategy, carefully designed to ensure that it does not hinder achievement of market recovery goals.

The NSP rules, which specify that 25 percent of the funds be used to address the needs of households earning 50 percent or less of the area median income (AMI), reflect an attempt to find a balance. This requirement is a reasonable one. Households earning below 50 percent of AMI make up the great majority of those with significant housing needs in most communities, while using 25 percent of NSP funds to meet those needs is not incompatible with a market recovery strategy.[19] On the other hand, an NSP program that uses a significantly larger share of its funds for this purpose—however real the needs it is trying to address—may risk losing track of the goal of fostering the long-term economic health of the neighborhood.

19. The other income threshold in the law—that all other buyers or tenants must have incomes at or below 120 percent of AMI—is hard to justify from a policy standpoint. Few families at that income level in most metropolitan areas have difficulty meeting their housing needs in the marketplace, while requiring means-testing of any kind hinders market recovery. It is hard to escape the suspicion that the drafters of the legislation felt that *some* income ceiling, however arbitrary, was needed for political reasons.

A similar tension often exists between aspirations and current realities. Many (probably most) local officials and nonprofits strongly prefer to see properties sold to homebuyers. While increasing owner occupancy as a goal is consistent with a market recovery strategy, nonprofits have often discovered that finding prospective buyers who are both interested in their properties and able to qualify for mortgage financing can be far more difficult than they expected.

This problem has many dimensions. The buyer pool is smaller, while the competition is greater. The pool of potential buyers has been reduced by economic uncertainty coupled with increasingly stringent lender credit and down payment requirements. Many prospective buyers who might have easily qualified for a mortgage a few years ago cannot do so today or lack the funds to make a sufficiently large down payment to qualify. At the same time, market conditions in many neighborhoods targeted for stabilization are still weak, with an oversupply of houses relative to the number of buyers. Now that market prices have come down sharply in many areas, homes developed by nonprofits may no longer have a price advantage relative to the market; moreover, NSP requirements for counseling and for resale price controls or recapture requirements may place those houses at a disadvantage.

A nonprofit finding it hard to sell houses in a neighborhood stabilization project has three options. The least desirable may be to reduce the price further until the house sells, an option that not only requires more subsidization but also risks—if it is more than an isolated case—pushing prices in the area down and undermining market recovery goals. If the house is to be sold on a below-market basis, having the sale take place through a community land trust (CLT)—an arrangement under which the CLT continues to own the land and leases it to the homeowner—can be an effective way of ensuring that the house both remains affordable and contributes to neighborhood stability. The Northern Communities Land Trust in Duluth, Minnesota, is one of many CLTs participating in NSP programs.

Alternatively, if the houses are of high quality and the neighborhood has other desirable assets, the nonprofit may try to mount an aggressive marketing effort. The third option is to rent out the houses, on either a short- or long-term basis or through a lease-purchase model.

Rental and lease-purchase options. Under a lease-purchase model, the goal is for the tenant to become the owner within five years. Self-Help, a community development financial institution based in North Carolina, has developed a lease-purchase model in partnership with Fannie Mae specifically designed for neighborhood stabilization programs. An important feature of the Self-Help model is that the nonprofit developer receives a thirty-year mortgage on the property; thus, if the tenant-purchaser is unable to assume the mortgage and buy the house, the mortgage remains in place, and the nonprofit can find a second tenant-purchaser and try again. A lease-purchase program that relies on short-term financing and under which the financial status of the property is put in jeopardy if the tenant-

Self-Help (the Center for Community Self-Help and its affiliates) works with local nonprofit housing organizations that acquire and rehab vacant or foreclosed properties in neighborhoods throughout the nation. These nonprofits identify tenant-purchasers—renters who are likely to be able to assume the mortgage on the property in one to five years—and provide credit and homeownership counseling and property management services during the rental period.

Nonprofits can use any source for acquisition and rehab financing. Once rehab of the property is complete, the nonprofit pays back the financing by taking out a thirty-year lease-purchase mortgage on the property. This mortgage is originated by a bank partner and sold to Self-Help through its secondary mortgage program. Self-Help retains the credit risk and sells the mortgage to Fannie Mae. At the end of the rental period, when the tenant-purchaser can qualify for the mortgage under standard underwriting criteria, the tenant-purchaser assumes the lease-purchase mortgage from the non-profit and becomes the owner of the home. Self-Help has received approval to deliver $200 million of these lease-purchase mortgages to Fannie Mae and is seeking to partner with other nonprofits across the country to bring their lease-purchase product to scale.

purchaser fails to qualify for a mortgage within two or three years can be a very risky proposition for a developer.

An alternative is for the nonprofit to retain the property as a rental property, either as part of the community's long-term rental housing stock or with the goal of ultimately selling it to a homebuyer, but without a specific time frame or commitment as in a lease-purchase program. This has both advantages and disadvantages. The principal advantage is that it puts the property back to use in a timely fashion. A major disadvantage is that relatively few local governments or nonprofit developers have built the capacity to successfully manage scattered-site rental property.

CDCs should explore whether capable property management entities already exist in the community that may be willing to provide services under contract to the CDCs; if not, they may need to develop the capacity internally. It may be better, however, for one CDC or nonprofit developer in a city or county to develop rental property management capacity and then provide those services to other entities in the area with a rental property inventory. Among nonprofit developers that have built strong scattered-site rental housing programs are Beyond Housing in St. Louis, Missouri, and Chelsea Neighborhood Developers in Chelsea,

Massachusetts. Both are also engaged in multifaceted neighborhood stabilization efforts.

Holding and land banking. Finally, many neighborhoods, particularly in distressed older cities, have a long-term excess of housing supply over demand. Areas that are continuing to lose population—either entire cities or selected neighborhoods—may not have enough demand to use the available housing stock even as rental housing, let alone make it available for ownership. In such locations, cities and nonprofits may want to adopt a land banking strategy and assemble properties for long-term future use while removing them from the market for the time being.

A land banking strategy generally involves a combination of acquisition and demolition. While decried by some observers, large-scale demolition is often the only realistic strategy for areas experiencing long-term population loss. Demand will not absorb these buildings, even in the long run. The cost of maintaining them and the potential damage to the stability of their surroundings while they remain standing often substantially exceed the benefits of keeping them. This is generally, but not always, the case. *Some* properties should be preserved, even in the most distressed city. The principles for deciding when to demolish and when to preserve vacant buildings outlined in chapter 13 should be followed; buildings that contribute to a neighborhood's fabric or that have architectural or historical value may be worth retaining and mothballing for future reuse.

Another important piece of a holding strategy is having an entity capable of taking properties, maintaining them, and ultimately disposing of them in a cost-effective and responsible fashion. Chapter 11 offers a step-by-step guide to designing and operating land banks. The number of such entities has increased in recent years. As a result of land banking legislation it enacted in 2003, Michigan now has nearly thirty county land bank authorities as well as a statewide authority. The Cuyahoga County Land Reutilization Corporation in Ohio was authorized by state law and began operations in 2009. A 2010 Ohio law gave forty-one of the state's eighty-eight counties the authority to create land banks.[20] Although many land banking models can be effective, it is widely accepted that land bank entities, where possible, should be (1) government entities, so that they can take advantage of tax foreclosure and other public sector tools; (2) dedicated single-purpose entities, so that their ability to focus on their mission is not compromised by other agendas; and (3) countywide or regional entities, so that they can benefit from the larger scale as well as from the more diverse market conditions that exist across a larger area.

In contrast to short-term strategies, when land banking one does not necessarily know how and at what point properties will be used as they are acquired and taken into the land bank inventory. While the ten years that NSP regulations allow properties to remain in land bank inventories sounds like a long time, many properties may not be ready for reuse within that period. The nature of what constitutes an appropriate property reuse also needs to be carefully examined. In a city whose population is continuing to decline, redevelopment of many areas in the traditional sense, for either residential or nonresidential use, may not make sense either in the short run or for the foreseeable future. In those settings, the land bank, along with local governments and CDCs, should look at green land uses such as open space, stormwater management, and urban agriculture not as interim or temporary uses of vacant property but as long-term strategies for reuse of vacant land, as discussed in chapter 20.

Determining the uses for vacant property in a shrinking city should take place through a careful planning process that takes into account not only the aggregate need for land for various purposes but also a broader "reimagining" strategy for the city as a whole. This strategy must reflect the reality that such cities have far smaller populations than they once had, and that if and when they are to stabilize their populations, it will be at levels far below their one-time peak.[21] The strategy can identify which neighborhoods should be preserved and strengthened, and can distinguish between areas where greening may be a long-term goal and those—such as areas in close proximity to a major anchor institution or physical asset—where market demand may not exist at present, but where green uses should be temporary to keep open the possibility of future redevelopment.

E. Dealing with Investors and Other Property Issues

As was noted earlier, the properties that are likely to be acquired with NSP funds —or other public or philanthropic resources—in any given area typically make up only a small percentage of the distressed properties that come on the market

20. Substitute House Bill 313, signed by Governor Ted Strickland on April 8, 2010.
21. Of American cities that have had populations over 100,000 at any point, seven have lost over half of their peak populations: Buffalo, Gary, Detroit, Cleveland, Pittsburgh, St. Louis, and Youngstown.

GOOD PRACTICE

Cleveland, once a city of more than 900,000 people, today contains fewer than 400,000, with large numbers of vacant lots and buildings throughout many parts of the city. Recognizing this, the city of Cleveland, Neighborhood Progress, Inc. (a citywide community development intermediary), and the Cleveland Urban Design Center of Kent State University have collaborated on the Re-Imagining a More Sustainable Cleveland project, an effort to identify and explore the opportunities that can be created from the productive and strategic reuse of vacant land. In addition to framing broad strategies for reuse of vacant land, the project partners have developed a pattern book showing in detail how sites can be sustainably reused. They have initiated a series of pilot projects involving green reuse in partnership with CDCs, environmental organizations, neighborhood associations, and others; these projects include community gardens, market gardens, orchards, vineyards, native plantings, stormwater management, phytoremediation of brownfield sites, and vest-pocket parks.

while the program is under way, and a minuscule share of all the properties in the area. A neighborhood's occupied residential properties are likely to include both single- and multifamily properties, and to fall into three broad categories:

- owner-occupied properties;
- absentee-owned rental properties acquired or developed prior to the current crisis;[22] and
- properties—principally distressed properties—more recently acquired by investor-buyers.

While all three categories matter, the last one is particularly important.

Absentee Investors and Neighborhood Stabilization

For the first year or so after foreclosures took off in 2007, REO properties often went begging. By 2009, that was no longer the case. Private property investors—ranging from "mom and pop" investors buying one or two properties to large Wall Street firms buying entire portfolios—were buying thousands of REO properties in cities across the country. As the year went on, their number increased;

---

22. While in some urban areas this sector includes a substantial amount of subsidized low- and moderate-income housing, often owned by nonprofit entities, the majority are likely to be single-family or small multifamily properties, usually owned by "mom and pop" landlords rather than by large entities.

rather than wait for properties to come into lenders' REO inventories, they were increasingly buying houses through short sales, buying nonperforming mortgages, or even bidding against lenders at foreclosure sales. CDCs looking to buy properties with NSP funds found themselves regularly outmaneuvered by investors; if not for the National Community Stabilization Trust, many might have found it difficult to obtain any properties at all.

As investors became a major part of the picture, city and CDC attitudes toward them tended to fall into one of two equally undesirable camps. In some cases, investors were seen as a menace, and attempts—generally futile—were made to prevent them from buying properties in an area. In others, their presence was accepted fatalistically, with little thought to how public or nonprofit efforts could influence their behavior. Investors can have either a positive or a negative effect on a neighborhood's stability, but there are many steps that cities and CDCs can take to increase the likelihood that their effect will be positive. As with all other neighborhood stabilization efforts, however, those steps need to be attuned to both the constraints and the opportunities offered by the local housing market. Not only do the dollars spent by investors usually dwarf the amount being spent by cities and CDCs through NSP, but in most cases investors are not taking properties away from prospective homebuyers—they are taking properties that without their efforts would be at high risk of abandonment.

At the risk of oversimplification, people investing in distressed (foreclosed or pre-foreclosure) properties can be divided into four categories, as shown in table 21.3. Two of the categories—rehabber and holder—are more likely to have a positive effect on an area than the other two. Fostering neighborhood-benefiting investment, however, is not principally a matter of finding responsible investors who want to be rehabbers or holders. It is rarely the personal qualities of individuals that dictate whether the activities of investors as a group are beneficial or harmful. Investor behavior is largely determined by three key factors, all unrelated to individuals' moral compass. They are, in order of importance:

- market conditions in the area in which investment is taking place,
- the regulatory climate created by local government, and
- the nonmarket incentives offered by the public or nonprofit sectors.

Market conditions. Each community's market conditions largely dictate the mix of investors drawn to that community, and, in the absence of a concerted public and nonprofit strategy, their behavior. Rehabbers and holders tend to gravitate toward areas where market prices for distressed properties, while low enough to enable the investment to be profitable, are still high enough to discourage scavengers. For rehabbers to make a profit, the market price of a nicely fixed-up house in the area must be greater than the sum of their acquisition and rehab costs. This is likely to be true in many areas, but not everywhere. In many parts of Detroit, for example, a house that costs $10,000 to acquire and needs another

TABLE 21.3 A Typology of Distressed Property Investors

Category	Strategy	Investment goal	Time horizon
Rehabber	Buy properties in poor condition, rehabilitate them, and sell them in good condition to homebuyers or investors	Appreciation generated through ability to realize greater increase in value from rehab than the cost of rehab	Short (usually one year or less)
Flipper	Buy properties in poor condition and sell quickly (flip) to buyers in as-is or similar condition, often using unethical or illegal practices	Appreciation generated by taking advantage of buyer ignorance, providing misleading information or misrepresentation, or collusion with others	Short (usually one year or less)
Milker	Buy properties in poor condition for very low prices and rent them out in as-is or similar condition with minimal maintenance, often to problem tenants	Cash flow generated through disparity between low acquisition and maintenance costs and relatively high market rents; no expectation of property appreciation	Short to medium (usually one to three years)
Holder	Buy properties and rent them out in fair to good condition, usually following responsible maintenance and tenant selection practices	Sum of cash flow from rental income during holding period combined with long-term property appreciation	Medium to long (usually five to eight years)

$40,000 to $50,000 in rehab work is unlikely to appraise higher than $30,000 to $35,000. In such a market, a responsible rehabber would soon go broke, unless he or she had access to incentives in the form of public subsidies.

The same is true of holders. For an investor to justify holding a property on a long-term basis and devoting resources to maintaining the property while realizing a moderate but unspectacular cash flow, he or she must have a realistic expectation that the property will at a minimum maintain its value, and have a reasonable likelihood of medium- or long-term appreciation. The property must also fall within a narrow value range—it must be inexpensive enough that the investor can in fact generate a positive cash flow at market rent, but expensive enough that it cannot be fully amortized through cash flow in one or two years. From a pure investment standpoint, it is hard to justify a long-term holding strategy for a Detroit property, which can be bought for less than $10,000 and has little potential for appreciation, but can be rented—even in poor condition—for $600 to $700 per month. Such properties attract milkers, who spend little on maintenance, ignore property tax bills, recoup their investment in little more than a year, and walk away from the property—at this point most probably a total loss —after two years.

Whatever their business model, investors are likely to be an important part of the picture in many, if not most, neighborhood stabilization areas. Coming up with an effective strategy to work with investors is therefore likely to be an important part of any stabilization strategy. The first step is to learn as much as possible about their activity, by speaking with investors, Realtors, code enforcement officials, and others directly involved. The threshold question that should be asked is: *If there were fewer investors buying in the area, would the neighborhood be better off?* In most cases, the answer would be no. Investors are likely to be buying many houses that would not be bought by homebuyers, and in volumes that could not be matched by NSP grantees. Thus, in most cases, having fewer investors is likely to mean more abandoned properties.

While most of the time this would leave the neighborhood worse off, in some cases fewer investor purchases may not be a bad thing. In deeply distressed cities or neighborhoods, where the investors are flippers or milkers, a case can be made that their activities at most delay abandonment for a year or two, while perpetuating dangerous and unhealthy conditions. In such cases, it might be better to have less investment and to use public tools to discourage investor buying outright. These areas tend to be the exception rather than the rule.

Simply stated, good investor behavior makes the neighborhood better. Within the framework of what the market permits, cities should offer a combination of carrots and sticks to encourage good investor behavior and discourage bad, as a part of their neighborhood stabilization programs. This is particularly important where market conditions in themselves tend to encourage destructive investor behavior. To do this, public sector regulatory actions should be combined with financial incentives that will actively help further the community's stabilization goals. In weak market environments, while tougher regulation may discourage "bad apples," by itself it may do little or nothing to encourage the engagement of more responsible investors. This is a complex subject which requires far more space than can be devoted to it here; nevertheless a few points should be made regarding both carrots and sticks.

Enforcement strategies. Local governments have strong powers to compel property owners to maintain their properties. Failure to exercise those powers, including enforcement of housing codes and timely collection of property taxes, makes local governments de facto enablers of abusive investor behavior. Existing code enforcement and nuisance abatement tools are often the weapons of first resort for a municipality that is facing an increase in poorly maintained and neglected absentee-owned properties. Many municipalities have also enacted rental registration or rental licensing ordinances. While a registration ordinance typically requires that the owner register the property and provide contact information for emergencies, a rental licensing ordinance may require that before the property is licensed, it be inspected and found to meet reasonable health and safety standards.

As was noted earlier, the Achilles' heel of enforcement strategies is not the lack of legal powers at the municipality's disposal, but the lack of resources. Many cities that have rental registration or licensing ordinances in place readily admit that the great majority of rental properties are not registered and that they lack the personnel to do anything about it. While there is no simple solution to this problem, cities can leverage their limited resources through partnerships with CDCs and community organizations and by using technology to turn citizens into their eyes and ears on the ground.

States and local governments can also press loan servicers to avoid selling properties to known bad actors. Early in 2010 Fannie Mae announced that it would attempt to screen buyer histories before selling REO properties, yet purchases by irresponsible investors continue to be a major problem. The federal government, through the Federal Housing Administration, is a major offender. Proposals have been put forward for the federal government to offer servicers and lenders financial incentives to sell to responsible parties, along lines similar to the HAMP incentives they have offered, but no action has been forthcoming as of spring 2010.

An investor in Detroit who brought her properties up to a reasonable standard, maintained them adequately, and paid property taxes on time may still be able to realize a positive cash flow. Rents in that city continue to be high relative to the cost of buying distressed properties. The fact remains, however, that investors who do *not* adequately upgrade or maintain their properties or pay property taxes can make *much* more money, and in the absence of strong regulation they are motivated by the economics of the situation to behave irresponsibly. While effective enforcement may drive many of them out, incentives may be needed to replace them with responsible investors.

GOOD PRACTICE

Using a unique Utah state law that allows municipalities to impose a "disproportionate impact fee" on the owners of rental properties, many cities in that state have imposed such fees in conjunction with a good-landlord program.[23] Under these programs, landlords who participate in landlord training and then actively implement the objectives of the program by keeping their properties free of criminal activity and code violations receive a discount (usually around 90 percent) on their disproportionate impact fee. In the city of Ogden, over 1,300 landlords have participated in the program, which has led to visible improvements in maintenance and reductions in criminal activity in the city's rental properties.

Incentives. In some market environments, effective enforcement may in itself foster responsible investor behavior. In others, financial incentives are likely to be needed. While some incentives may be designed specifically for investors buying distressed properties, an incentive such as the good-landlord programs enacted by many Utah municipalities should be offered to any absentee owner of rental property in the community. These incentives can take a variety of forms:

- Preferential access to desirable properties
- Mortgage financing on desirable terms
- Capital subsidies
- Waiver of fees
- Assistance in finding and qualifying tenants or buyers

While their efforts are still in the embryonic stage, many neighborhood stabilization programs are exploring such programs, including using NSP funds to make loans or grants to investors; creation by a CDFI of a capital pool for investors in NSP areas; prequalifying investors to be eligible to purchase properties acquired by the municipality or a nonprofit through the NCST First Look Program or other programs; and partnerships between private investors and neighborhood-based nonprofits, in which the nonprofit can provide property management services or assist in selecting responsible tenants or qualified buyers as part of the investor's exit strategy.

23. Utah Code 10-1-203 (5)(a)(i)(C)(I), as amended by Chapter 189, 2009 General Session.

Supporting Neighborhood Homeowners

Finally, neighborhood stabilization programs need to pay close attention to the concerns of the area's homeowners—those who are not at risk of foreclosure but whose confidence level may ultimately determine the neighborhood's fate. They are likely to represent the majority of a neighborhood's long-term residents as well as those who are most engaged in neighborhood activities and most active in community organizations, and they are most likely to be seen by others as the voice of the neighborhood.[24] In many cases their confidence in the neighborhood has been undermined by the wave of foreclosures and vacancies in recent years. If the social fabric of the area was less than solid beforehand—which is often the case—they may completely lose faith in their neighborhood's future prospects. Should large numbers of existing homeowners choose to move out, or in the meantime defer maintenance or improvements to their homes, their decisions could undo any benefits of neighborhood stabilization programs.

Organizations pursuing neighborhood stabilization activities should make a concerted effort to connect with the homeowners in the area and take steps both to increase their confidence in the future of the neighborhood and to create ways in which they can gain tangible benefits from a stabilization program. Such efforts can take many different forms. At a minimal level, it is important to engage homeowners in the program, by making sure that they are aware of the activities going on—and of the fact that somebody is actually trying to do something about the problem—and actively consulting them about the program's priorities and direction. Beyond consultation and information, a stabilization program can help build neighborhood cohesion by devoting resources to strengthening the neighborhood's social fabric and organizational texture and by engaging residents in activities that both benefit the area as a whole and deepen their engagement with their community. Specific examples can include engaging residents in community clean-up programs, maintaining vacant lots, or creating playgrounds or community gardens.

Beyond outreach and community building, it is desirable to offer existing homeowners—as well as the absentee owners of small rental properties—tangible benefits. One such benefit is low-interest loans for improving their properties. Another is visible improvements to their blocks or the immediate vicinity; examples might include tree plantings or sidewalk replacements. An often inexpensive strategy is to provide grant funds for facade improvements, yard plantings, or fence replacement, all of which have the added benefit of enhancing an area's curb appeal for potential future buyers. Still another is to establish programs to guarantee the value of homeowners' equity. Under Illinois law, neighborhoods in

---

24. Even in neighborhoods that have a majority of tenants, homeowners are likely to constitute the great majority of long-term residents because of the rapid turnover of renters. The median tenure for urban tenants is rarely more than two to three years, while for homeowners it is often ten years or longer.

The Southwest Chicago Guaranteed Home Equity Program provides homeowners in the Greater Ashburn section of Chicago with home value protection by guaranteeing that their primary residences will maintain or increase their fair-market value for as long as they live in them. Homeowners who live in their homes for five or more years and remain current with their property taxes are eligible to sell their homes at a price guaranteed by the program. The program is financed by a levy on all one- to six-family properties in the district, which is one of three in the city of Chicago created under authority granted by the Illinois Home Equity Assurance Act (§ 65 ILCS 95/2) enacted in 1988.

Chicago can create special districts where a surcharge on the local property tax goes into a fund to support an equity insurance program.

F. Weaving the Pieces of the Neighborhood Stabilization Strategy Together

As was pointed out at the start of this chapter, the goal of neighborhood stabilization is to restore stability to an area. Any CDC or other entity carrying out a neighborhood stabilization program should have a clear sense of what that means, and how to translate it into a goal for its community—a goal that goes beyond a tally of the number of structures bought or the number of units rehabilitated. The goal should be a realistic vision of what the entity hopes its neighborhood or community, taken as a whole, will be like in three, five, or ten years. What that might be will vary greatly from one neighborhood to the next, depending on many different factors, especially

- market conditions in the neighborhood prior to the foreclosure crisis, and in many cases prior to a bubble that may have been created by subprime mortgages and speculation;
- the larger economic and market trends in the city and region; and
- the resources available to the city or CDC to foster change.

These factors define both the opportunities to build a healthy community and the constraints on that process.

In some cases, restoring neighborhood vitality and healthy housing demand within a relatively short period may be a realistic goal. In others, as in some deeply distressed cities, conditions three or five years down the road may be only incrementally different than they are today, as the city prepares the ground for

TABLE 21.4 Central Elements in a Comprehensive Neighborhood Stabilization Strategy

Element	Rationale	Representative activities
Foreclosure and vacancy prevention strategies	As long as foreclosures and abandonment continue to take place, they exert an ongoing destabilization effect, undoing the effect of stabilization efforts.	• Foreclosure counseling and mediation activities • Outreach to notify tenants of their right to stay in their homes • Programs to enable former owners to remain as renters after foreclosure • Efforts to encourage short sales in place of foreclosures • Partnerships with investors to ensure their properties are maintained
Vacant property strategies	Vacant properties are the single largest driver of destabilization in many areas and should be a priority in any strategy. Acquisition, however, is only one facet of a vacant property strategy.	• Ordinances making lenders responsible for maintaining vacant properties in foreclosure • Accelerated foreclosure for vacant properties • Vacant property registration ordinances • Acquisition of strategic vacant properties • Rehab or redevelopment of vacant properties • Targeted demolition of vacant properties • Efforts to monitor investor purchases of vacant properties and provide incentives for responsible rehab and operation of properties

Public realm/quality-of-life strategies	Neighborhood quality of life and "curb appeal" as reflected in the public realm are central to residents' confidence in their neighborhood and to the health of the housing market in general.	• Greening strategies, including park restoration and minimal treatment of vacant lots • Crime prevention strategies • School improvement strategies • Property improvement programs • Facade, yard, and fencing improvement programs • Street and sidewalk improvements • Building social capital and community engagement
Confidence- and market-building strategies	Depending on neighborhood conditions and the extent of destabilization, direct efforts to build resident confidence and market demand may be needed to overcome negative perceptions or past realities.	• Home equity protection insurance • Assistance for existing homeowners • Marketing and outreach to target homebuyer markets • Incentives for prospective homebuyers

long-term transformative change. While it is good to be ambitious, it is even more important to be realistic.

Having a goal demands in turn that one have a road map. Ideally, *one should be able to draw a compelling link between the activities that one is pursuing and the outcome one is hoping to achieve.* If the goal is broadly to restore neighborhood stability and housing market vitality, acquisition and rehabilitation of a number of scattered properties in itself may not achieve that goal, particularly if the area surrounding those properties continues to be plagued by foreclosures and abandonment. Acquisition and rehabilitation need to be part of a larger strategy that reflects the multifaceted nature of neighborhood stability. The major features of the road map—the elements that go into achieving neighborhood stabilization—as well as their rationales and some representative activities that can be pursued for each element are outlined in table 21.4.

Not all of these strategies may be appropriate for all areas. If the area is undergoing a market correction and demand is growing, many of the more far-reaching strategies identified in the table may not be needed. More effort may be needed instead in areas such as code enforcement and careful monitoring of investor-buyers to make sure that their activities contribute to, rather than detract from, the ongoing stabilization process. In a severely destabilized neighborhood that has realistic potential for revitalization, a more comprehensive approach may be needed if that potential is to be realized.

Three Key Themes

While many of the specific programs and activities involved in carrying out a comprehensive strategy have already been discussed, three key themes cut across strategy elements and have been shown to be fundamental to successful stabilization efforts:

- Leverage additional resources
- Engage additional partners
- Target limited resources

Leverage additional resources. NSP is a valuable but limited tool. It can be used only for a series of specific activities that rarely if ever represent the sum total of those needed to bring about neighborhood stabilization. To mount an effective strategy, other funds—public and private—will have to be found. This is particularly difficult today, as state and local governments are in the midst of severe financial difficulties and are forced to cut back on important activities and services precisely when the need is greatest.

Still, much can be achieved by improving the effectiveness of existing resources through targeted efforts and by leveraging private resources. Cities can often make their existing resources go further by adopting procedures or technology that allow their personnel to work more efficiently. Many cities and nonprofit organizations have been able to find local foundations willing to support neighborhood stabilization and improvement efforts, such as the George Gund Foundation in Cleveland or the Raymond John Wean Foundation in Youngstown. Partnerships with lenders, including CDFIs such as New Jersey Community Capital or the Massachusetts Housing Investment Fund, can also leverage valuable resources.

Other resources may be more indirect. Private real estate investors are directing a powerful stream of dollars into many of the neighborhoods that are the target of stabilization efforts. To the extent that the right combination of regulatory pressures and incentives can be devised, this can represent a potentially important source of resources for neighborhood stabilization. An additional strategy that has only rarely been explored is the creation of what amounts to a neighborhood "special improvement district," in which property owners agree to place a modest surcharge on their property tax bills to create a fund to support specific local improvements. One such district, the Southwest Chicago Guaranteed Home Equity Program described earlier, has been so successful in its primary mission that the district has begun to use its surplus funds to provide neighborhood property owners with low-interest home improvement loans.

Engage additional partners. No single government, nonprofit, or business entity is likely to have the financial resources or technical capacity to pursue a successful neighborhood stabilization program on its own. This is particularly true in a period of severe resource constraints affecting both the public and nonprofit sectors. The core NSP activity, the acquisition and rehabilitation of foreclosed properties, requires a mix of skills that are often in short supply in both government and CDCs in even the strongest cities. The task is even more difficult when the goal of the neighborhood stabilization program is to ratchet up the acquisition, rehabilitation, and resale of vacant units by CDCs well beyond historical levels. When the time comes to incorporate the other activities that add up to a successful stabilization effort, the need for multiple partners becomes inescapable. The potential partners that should be involved in the effort are identified in table 21.5.

The most successful programs are likely to be those that bring together government, CDCs, community residents, and the private sector in a cooperative effort. Within city government, getting the agencies involved in community development, code enforcement, public works, and policing on the same page is critically important. Getting neighborhood residents involved in areas such as policing or code enforcement can maximize limited public sector resources, while engaging local contractors and property managers can leverage the limited rehabilitation and scattered-site property management capacity that may be available to local government and the local CDC community. Realtors are important allies who share the overall goal of restoring neighborhood market vitality. They can be partners in many areas, including facilitating property acquisition and marketing the neighborhood. Sophisticated data and tracking systems, such as the Community Central system developed by Mercy Portfolio Services in Chicago, can enable a lead agency to coordinate the work of hundreds of separate partners.

TABLE 21.5 Neighborhood Stabilization Partners

Element	Partners
Foreclosure and vacancy prevention strategies	• Nonprofit counseling organizations • Legal services agencies • Tenant advocacy organizations • Realtors • Investors
Vacant property strategies	• Neighborhood residents and resident organizations • City code enforcement offices • City or county tax collectors or treasurers • County courts • Realtors • Appraisers • Contractors and developers • Property management companies • Investors
Public realm/quality-of-life strategies	• Neighborhood residents and resident organizations • Police department and crime watch organizations • School districts and parent-teacher organizations • City departments of public works
Confidence- and market-building strategies	• Neighborhood residents • Individual Realtors and Realtor boards • Local media • Major employers

Target limited resources. While the $6 billion appropriated for NSP1 and NSP2 seems like a lot of money, as it flows downward to hundreds of separate cities and counties, and thousands of neighborhoods, it dwindles rapidly. That reality, coupled with the existing financial constraints facing state and local governments, makes one thing clear. If one tried to address all of the areas that have suffered as a result of foreclosure—or in cities like Cleveland and Detroit, from foreclosure added to long-standing poverty and disinvestment—the money would be spread so thinly that it would have little or no visible effect. Individual houses here and there would be rehabilitated or demolished, yet the outcomes for the neighborhoods would be little different than if no NSP money had been invested in them.

As pointed out earlier, the only way a neighborhood can be stabilized is if the effect of stabilizing actions outweighs that of destabilizing forces. The corollary to

Mercy Portfolio Services, which administers the city of Chicago's NSP1 and NSP2 programs, has developed a property tracking and reporting system called Community Central, which allows them to manage property acquisition, rehabilitation, and reuse activity in nearly paperless fashion. In addition to being cost-effective, Community Central allows Mercy to coordinate the efforts of well over a hundred nonprofits, contractors, Realtors, appraisers, lawyers, and others to maintain a high, steady volume of property-related activities. By the end of 2009, Mercy was using this system to close on as many as fifteen properties per week. It is now licensing the system to other nonprofit organizations around the United States.

that statement is that *the only way stabilizing actions can outweigh destabilizing forces is if enough resources are directed to those actions.* That, in turn, dictates that funds be targeted to small enough areas in large enough amounts that they will indeed have an impact on those areas, even though such an approach will inevitably mean that other, perhaps equally deserving, areas will receive fewer resources or none at all. While this is a difficult strategy to implement—politically even more than technically—it is the only strategy that offers serious hope that any neighborhoods can be revived and brought back to health. As the experience in Richmond has shown (see page 255), where the political will is present, effective targeting is a realistic option, and can lead to highly productive results.

How much of the funds needed in a neighborhood will have to be public funds will depend on the area's market characteristics. In an area undergoing a market correction, private investors may be investing large amounts in properties, to the point that less public investment but more regulation—to ensure that investors properly maintain their properties—may be needed. Alternatively, while less public investment in property acquisition may be needed in such areas, other investments—in the form of crime prevention or improvements to the public realm —may be needed to ensure that the market recovery taking place is sustainable rather than transitory.

These differences do not affect the underlying principle of targeting resources, but they do point out that many different kinds of resources can have stabilizing effects, and these do not all come from the public sector. Market demand is a stabilizing resource, to the extent that it can be nurtured in an area that has been destabilized. That suggests another important principle: the stronger the market in the city or region as a whole, the more flexibility the public sector has to target resources more broadly to a number of different neighborhoods. In a city or region where market demand is severely limited, the number of neighborhoods that can realistically be stabilized and where strong private market demand can be fostered with the available resources may be very small.

Even within targeted areas, property acquisition should as much as possible be even more carefully targeted. Not all properties are fungible. Rehabilitating a property that is the only vacant house on an otherwise fully occupied block will have far more impact than rehabilitating a similar property that is one of ten vacant houses on its block. Within any geographic area, certain blocks or corners are likely to be more strategic than others; targeting acquisition efforts to those strategic locations is an important part of any program designed to have a significant transformative effect on a neighborhood.

Planning for the Long Term

The HUD NSP is a short-term initiative, designed to help communities address an emergency. While foreclosures have created emergency conditions in many neighborhoods around the United States, the immediate crisis should not obscure the reality that many of those neighborhoods were already suffering from serious social, economic, and physical distress, or were just beginning to see signs of revitalization.[25] While the many NSP efforts may help restore a measure of stability to these neighborhoods, those efforts are unlikely in most cases to be enough to put an area on a solid, long-term course toward restored health and vitality. For that to take place, more years, more resources, and more energy will be needed.

Today's neighborhood stabilization efforts can become the starting point for a true, sustained effort to rebuild the nation's distressed, destabilized neighborhoods, as long as cities and CDCs deciding how to spend their NSP funds see those activities as a beginning rather than an end—as long as they think about how to move from stabilization to sustainable revitalization. Those long-term strategies need to focus on building stronger markets, but they must also take into account the needs of lower-income residents, in terms of both preserving their housing opportunities and improving their quality of life.

Neighborhoods are dynamic systems and are constantly changing. As neighborhoods change, the strategies that are most effective and the interventions that are most needed also change. The hallmark of a successful neighborhood revitalization program is its ability to respond to change, phasing out old activities and replacing them with new ones. Effective programs constantly learn from their mistakes, adjust their priorities, change the ways in which they allocate their resources, and build new partnerships to reflect the changes going on in their neighborhoods, their housing markets, and their social and economic dynamics.

25. In retrospect, while one can point to many examples of sustainable neighborhood revitalization from the 1990s and early 2000s, many other seemingly "revitalizing" neighborhoods were not changing in fundamental ways during those years. Instead, they were seeing their housing markets propelled by speculation and the ready availability of subprime mortgages, with little or no change to their underlying social and economic conditions.

Resources for Further Information

Accordino, John, George Galster, and Peter Tatian. *The Impacts of Targeted Public and Nonprofit Investment on Neighborhood Development.* Richmond, VA: Federal Reserve Bank of Richmond, 2005. A detailed assessment of Richmond's Neighborhoods in Bloom revitalization strategy.

Adeyemi, Abiola. *Urban Agriculture: An Abbreviated List of References and Resource Guide.* Washington, DC: U.S. Department of Agriculture, 2000.

Alexander, Christopher, et al. *A Pattern Language: Towns, Buildings, Construction.* New York: Oxford University Press, 1977. An indispensable resource for neighborhood planners.

Beck, Nancy, and Lindley R. Higgins. *Building Neighborhoods of Choice: A Workbook on Marketing Neighborhoods and Affordable Ownership Housing.* New York: Local Initiatives Support Corporation, 2001.

Belmont, Steve. *Cities in Full: Recognizing and Realizing the Great Potential of Urban America.* Chicago: Planners Press, 2002.

Bonham, Blaine, Gerri Spilka, and Darl Rastorfer. *Old Cities/Green Cities: Communities Transform Unmanaged Land.* Chicago: American Planning Association, 2002. An excellent introduction to greening strategies for urban areas.

Bright, Elise. "Making Business a Partner in Redeveloping Abandoned Central City Property: Is Profit a Realistic Possibility?" Paper presented at Federal Reserve System's Third Community Affairs Research Conference, Washington, DC, March 2003.

Brophy, Paul, and Kim Burnett. *Building a New Framework for Community Development in Weak Market Cities.* Denver: Community Development Partnerships' Network, 2003.

Building Technology, Inc. *Smart Codes in Your Community: A Guide to Building Rehabilitation Codes.* Washington, DC: U.S. Department of Housing and Urban Development, 2001.

Ceraso, Karen. "Seattle Neighborhood Planning: Citizen Empowerment or Collective Daydreaming?" *Shelterforce* no. 108 (November/December 1999).

City of Rochester. *Neighbors Building Neighborhoods: Progress Reports.* Rochester, NY: City of Rochester, 1999, 2000, 2001. Contains good descriptive material about a model neighborhood planning strategy.

Crompton, John L. *Parks and Economic Development.* Chicago: American Planning Association Planning Advisory Service, 2001.

Frieden, Bernard J. *The Future of Old Neighborhoods*. Cambridge, MA: MIT Press, 1964.

Friedman, Eric. "Vacant Properties in Baltimore: Strategies for Reuse." Winning student essay, Abell Foundation Award in Urban Policy, 2003.

Garvin, Alexander, et al. *Urban Parks and Open Spaces*. Washington, DC: Urban Land Institute, 1997.

Gilliland, Ed, Larisa Ortiz, and Shari Garmise. *Real Estate Redevelopment and Reuse*. Washington, DC: Council for Urban Economic Development, 2000.

Goetze, Rolf. *Understanding Neighborhood Change: The Role of Expectations in Urban Revitalization*. Cambridge, MA: Ballinger Publishing, 1979.

Harnik, Peter. *The Excellent City Park System: What Makes It Great and How to Get There*. Washington, DC: Trust for Public Land, 2003.

Housing Design Advisory Board. *The Lower West Side Neighborhood Stabilization Demonstration Project*. Buffalo, NY: School of Architecture and Planning, State University of New York at Buffalo, 2002. A good model for developing and implementing design guidelines for urban neighborhoods.

Hughes, Mark Alan. *Dirt into Dollars: Converting Vacant Land into Valuable Development. Brookings Review* 18, no. 3 (Summer 2000).

International City/County Management Association. *Getting to Smart Growth, II: 100 More Policies for Implementation*. Washington, DC: ICMA, 2003. See particularly chapter 4, "Create Walkable Communities," and chapter 5, "Foster Distinctive, Attractive Communities with a Strong Sense of Place."

International Economic Development Council. *Converting Brownfields to Green Space*. Washington, DC: IEDC, 2001.

Kromer, John. *Neighborhood Recovery: Reinvestment Policy for the New Hometown*. New Brunswick, NJ: Rutgers University Press, 2000. A good practical discussion of neighborhood rebuilding issues, based on the author's experience in Philadelphia.

———. "Serious about Neighborhoods: Ten Success Strategies for Philadelphia's Residential Communities." Self-published paper, 2003.

Kromer, John, and Lucy Kerman. *West Philadelphia Initiatives: A Case Study in Urban Revitalization*. Philadelphia: University of Pennsylvania Fels Institute of Government, 2004.

Lang, Robert E., James W. Hughes, and Karen A. Danielsen. "Targeting the Suburban Urbanites: Marketing Central-City Housing." *Housing Policy Debate* 8, no. 2 (1997).

Listokin, David, and Barbara Listokin. *Barriers to the Rehabilitation of Affordable Housing*. 2 vols. Washington, DC: U.S. Department of Housing and Urban Development, 2001.

Mallach, Alan. *Flint, Michigan: An Assessment of Housing-Related Conditions, Resources and Programs*. Local Initiatives Support Corporation, Genesee County Treasurer's Office, and the Charles Stewart Mott Foundation, 2003. Available from Genesee County Treasurer's Office, Flint, MI.

———. *Building a Better Urban Future: New Directions for Housing Policies in Weak Market Cities*. Montclair, NJ: National Housing Institute, in conjunction with Community Development Partnerships' Network, Local Initiatives Support Corporation, and the Enterprise Foundation, 2005. A policy and practice guide to using housing investments strategically to foster neighborhood and citywide revitalization, available at www.nhi.org.

Martin, Judith A., and Paula R. Pentel. "What the Neighbors Want: The Neighborhood Revitalization Program's First Decade." *American Planning Association Journal* 68, no. 4 (2002).

Morrish, William, and Catherine Brown. *Planning to Stay.* Minneapolis, MN: Milkweed Editions, 1994. An excellent guide to understanding the physical features of a neighborhood and building rebuilding strategies around local realities.

National Trust for Historic Preservation. *Rebuilding Community: A Best Practices Toolkit for Historic Preservation and Redevelopment.* Washington, DC: National Trust for Historic Preservation, 2002. A good introduction to using historic preservation as a tool for vacant property reuse.

Neighborhood Design Center. *NDC Design Ideas: Creating Sideyards after Mid-Block Demolition.* Baltimore, MD: Neighborhood Design Center, 2001.

Northeast-Midwest Institute and Congress for the New Urbanism. *Strategies for Successful Infill Development.* Washington, DC: Northeast-Midwest Institute, 1999.

Northeast-Midwest Institute and National Association of Local Government Environmental Professionals. *Recycling America's Gas Stations: The Value and Promise of Revitalizing Petroleum-Contaminated Properties.* Washington, DC: Northeast-Midwest Institute, 2002.

Operation ReachOut SouthWest (OROSW). *Strategic Neighborhood Action Plan.* Baltimore, MD: OROSW, 2002.

Parks and People Foundation. *Neighborhood Open Space Management: A Report on Greening Strategies in Baltimore and Six Other Cities.* Baltimore, MD: Parks and People Foundation, 2000.

Proscio, Tony. *Smart Communities: Curbing Sprawl at its Core.* New York: Local Initiatives Support Corporation, 2002. Places neighborhood revitalization in a larger smart growth framework.

Rudlin, David, and Nicholas Falk. *Building the 21st Century Home: The Sustainable Urban Neighborhood.* Oxford: Architectural Press, 1999.

Schopp, Danielle. *From Brownfields to Housing: Opportunities, Issues and Answers.* Washington, DC: Northeast-Midwest Institute, 2003.

Schubert, Michael. "Revitalizing the Smart Growth Debate." *NeighborWorks Journal* 18, no. 3–4 (Summer/Fall 2000). A good "thought piece" about market-driven neighborhood revitalization.

Smart, Eric. *Making Infill Projects Work.* Washington, DC: Urban Land Institute, in collaboration with the Lincoln Institute for Land Policy, 1985.

Taylor, Roger. *Strategies for Restoring Vacant Land: An Analysis of Northeast Cities with Recommendations for New Haven.* New Haven, CT: Yale University Urban Resources Initiative, 2000.

Toups, Catherine, and James H. Carr. *Reimaging Distressed Communities: A Strategy to Reverse Decline and Attract Investors.* Washington, DC: Fannie Mae Foundation, Spring 2000.

Urban Design Associates. *King Park Area Homeownership Zone Urban Design Plan.* Indianapolis, IN: City of Indianapolis, 1999. Design guidelines and strategy for a model neighborhood revitalization project.

———. *A Pattern Book for Norfolk Neighborhoods*. Norfolk, VA: City of Norfolk, 2003.

U.S. Department of Housing and Urban Development *Urban Infill: The Literature*. Washington, DC: U.S. Department of Housing and Urban Development, 1980.

Volk, Laurie, and Todd Zimmerman. "Confronting the Question of Market Demand for Urban Residential Development." Paper presented at Fannie Mae Foundation 2000 Annual Housing Conference, Washington, DC.

von Hoffman, Alexander. *House by House, Block by Block: The Rebirth of America's Urban Neighborhoods*. Oxford: Oxford University Press, 2003.

Wachter, Susan. "The Determinants of Neighborhood Transformations in Philadelphia —Identification and Analysis: The New Kensington Pilot Study." Unpublished paper, 2004.

Wates, Nick. *The Community Planning Handbook*. London: Earthscan Publications, 2000. An excellent nuts and bolts guidebook to community planning.

Weber, Rachel, and Michael A. Pagano. "The Developability of Vacant Land: The Case of Chicago." Unpublished paper, 2002.

Wentling, James W., and Lloyd W. Bookout, eds. *Density by Design*. Washington, DC: Urban Land Institute, in cooperation with the American Institute of Architects, 1988.

Werth, Joel T., and David Bryant. *A Guide to Neighborhood Planning*. Chicago: American Planning Association, 1979.

Zielenbach, Sean. *The Art of Revitalization: Improving Conditions in Distressed Inner-City Neighborhoods*. New York: Garland Publishing, 2000.

Estimating the Number of Abandoned Properties
in American Cities

Estimating the number of abandoned properties in a city is a difficult and uncertain proposition. Few cities have either the resources or the inclination to carry
out comprehensive field surveys. Even when they do, uncertainty about which
structures can reasonably be considered abandoned and the difficulty of counting
dwelling units without access to the interior of the building result in a substantial
margin of error. That margin of error is increased by the fact that abandonment
is a dynamic process. Properties are constantly being abandoned, demolished, or
rehabilitated. Unless field surveys are performed regularly, the results soon become
obsolete.[1]

Despite these difficulties, a variety of estimates do exist. The table at the end
of this appendix provides estimates of the number of abandoned units, structures,
or properties for nineteen "weak market" cities.[2] These cities are likely to have the
largest concentrations of vacant properties of all American cities. The estimates
are derived from the following sources:

1. Burchell and Listokin 1978 survey (Burchell and Listokin 1981). These estimates come from the most comprehensive attempt to date to estimate the number of abandoned properties by city. The data was gathered through a telephone
survey of local officials in 150 cities in the summer of 1978, covering various
abandoned property issues as well as estimates of the number of such properties
by category in the municipality.[3] While this data is clearly too old to be relevant
to current conditions, it is included for purposes of comparison.

2. 2000 census estimates. Two estimates are drawn from 2000 census data.
The lower estimate is the number of "other vacant" units reported by the census;
the higher estimate combines the "other vacant" category with that part of the

---

1. One of the few cities that conducts regular field surveys of abandoned properties is Boston,
Massachusetts, which does so annually. Boston, of course, has far fewer such properties than typical
weak market cities.

2. These are cities with populations above 100,000 in 2000 which had both lost more than 25 percent of their population from their peak year (either 1950 or 1960) and continued to lose population
between 1990 and 2000.

3. It appears that 1978 was a much more patient time than the present. The survey instrument
(which is reproduced in Burchell and Listokin 1981) was long and complicated and clearly took a long
time to complete. It is hard to imagine many highly stressed municipal officials having the patience
to sit through such an extensive telephone interview today.

total of vacant units offered for sale or rent that exceed the number that are realistically in play in the housing market.[4] For the purposes of this estimate, vacant units in excess of 2 percent of the owner-occupied stock, and in excess of 8 percent of the rental stock, were considered abandoned.[5]

3. *Pagano and Bowman 1998 survey* (Pagano and Bowman 2000). This survey is based on responses from local officials, who were asked to estimate abandoned *structures,* rather than the total number of dwelling units in abandoned structures. The Pagano and Bowman survey, however, includes only a handful of the cities in the weak market cluster.

4. *Other sources.* A number of estimates have been compiled from a variety of other sources, ranging from newspaper accounts and interviews to surveys or other statistical data.[6]

All of these numbers are flawed; where they coincide, that is as likely to reflect luck as accuracy. The data provided by local officials to Pagano and Bowman, or twenty years earlier to Burchell and Listokin, is likely to be, in most cases, little more than guesswork. In the case of the 1978 survey, it is most probably second-order guesswork, in that the informants first estimated the number of abandoned structures and then the number of units in those structures. Moreover, as the low numbers Pagano and Bowman report for some cities might suggest, local respondents may be likely to understate the actual number of abandoned units out of civic pride or political expediency.

Defining precisely what is being counted further complicates matters. Field surveys are reasonably accurate at identifying the number of abandoned structures, although even a well-trained surveyor may miss some recently abandoned properties that have yet to show visible indicia of neglect. They are less effective at counting the number of units in those structures. The census, on the other hand, while it permits at least crude estimates of the number of abandoned dwelling units, is of little use in estimating the number of abandoned structures or properties. Finally, unless the questions are carefully framed, many estimates by knowledgeable public officials or other informants may conflate abandoned buildings with vacant lots. The information in table A.1, to the extent possible, excludes vacant lots. The number of vacant lots could easily exceed the number of vacant structures in some of the cities under consideration.

---

4. The census breaks down vacant units into five categories: (1) vacant offered for sale; (2) vacant offered for rent: (3) vacant awaiting occupancy; (4) vacant held for seasonal or occasional use; and (5) other vacant.

5. The flaw in this reasoning is that although these units can reasonably be considered *potentially* abandoned, many of them may not yet have been abandoned when they were counted by the 2000 census. Conversely, because of the lack of extensive field investigation in the census enumeration process, it is equally possible that these figures represent wishful thinking and that the "other vacant" category underestimates the actual number of abandoned units.

6. It can reasonably be inferred that figures in newspaper accounts come from some source such as a public official or real estate industry figure, but such sources are rarely identified.

TABLE A.1 Estimates of Abandoned Properties in Selected Weak Market Cities

City	Burchell and Listokin 1978 survey (DUs)	2000 Census (DUs)		Pagano and Bowman 1998 survey (structures)	Other recent estimates	Source (type of estimate)
		Low	High			
St. Louis	2,750	12,900	17,300	NA	13,073	1999 city survey (DUs)
Pittsburgh	5,500	8,100	9,300	NA	19,000	2003 estimate by PCRG staff member (structures)
Detroit	30,000	16,900	17,300	10,000	39,000	1999 newspaper article (properties)
					+12,000	2002 newspaper article (structures abandoned and deemed dangerous)
Buffalo	950	10,000	13,600	NA	8,684	2003 Comprehensive Plan (structures)
Cleveland	2,675	8,300	11,600	NA	11,642	2000 CANDO (vacant residential parcels)
Gary, IN	1,161	2,600	2,700	NA		
Newark, NJ	4,612	3,600	3,600	NA		
Dayton, OH	5,350	3,200	5,300	NA		
Flint, MI	2,836	2,100	3,500	NA	+7,200	2001 estimate by county treasurer (properties)
Louisville, KY	4,400	3,100	3,800	4,000		
Cincinnati, OH	4,500	4,600	6,600	1,000		
Rochester, NY	1,730	3,100	4,400	NA	2,500–3,000	2003 estimate by city officials (structures)
Syracuse	1,075	2,000	4,300	500	≥2,200	2000 newspaper article (structures)
Baltimore	6,815	21,000	23,100	15,000	26,000–40,000	2001 estimate by state official (properties)
					18,600	2003 estimate by consultant for BCDA (units)
Washington, DC	NA	9,400	10,300	NA	+4,000	2003 estimate by city official (structures)
Birmingham, AL	NA	4,000	6,300	NA		
Philadelphia	33,161	37,500	37,500	54,000	26,115	2000 city survey (residential structures)
Akron, OH	650	1,700	2,000	300		

Sources: See appendix text.

Note: Census figures rounded to nearest 100. Vacant lots not included in estimates.

Abbreviations:
BCDA   Baltimore Community Development Alliance
DUs   dwelling units
CANDO   Cleveland Area Network for Data and Organizing
PCRG   Pittsburgh Community Renewal Group

The distinction between the number of dwelling units and the number of buildings can be significant and may explain some of the disparities between data sources. For example, a 1996 survey by a civic organization found 571 abandoned residential properties in Hartford, Connecticut, while the census estimated 1,500 to 1,900 abandoned dwelling units. Since the average residential property in Hartford contains 4.4 dwelling units, the two data sources may be more consistent than they initially appear.

Despite these limitations, the data presented in table A.1 is, at a minimum, suggestive. The range of census data presented in the table offers a fair "order of magnitude" estimate, which—with substantially more reservations—may have been true at the time of the Burchell and Listokin data. A comparison between the two may suggest a broad outline of the trend in abandonment in the different cities, although without information on the extent of demolition activity by city it is not really possible to compare the data in meaningful terms.[7]

Over the coming years, as greater attention is focused on the issue of abandonment, attempts should be made to provide more accurate estimates of the extent of the problem, in order to encourage better strategic planning and program development.

7. Data from Philadelphia strongly suggests that during the past twenty years demolitions and continued abandonment were roughly comparable in number. A recent report from Detroit indicates that more than 28,000 houses have been demolished in that city since 1989–1990 (Jodi Wilgoren, "Detroit Urban Renewal without the Renewal," *New York Times,* 7 July 2002). It is not known how many were demolished in the prior decade, but it is clear that if the Burchell and Listokin and 2000 census estimates in the table are both at least moderately accurate, abandonment has continued to occur at a steady pace in Detroit.

Accordino, John, and Gary T. Johnson. "Addressing the Vacant and Abandoned Property Problem." *Journal of Urban Affairs* 22, no. 3 (2000).

Bailey, John. "Vacant Properties and Smart Growth: Creating Opportunity from Abandonment." *Livable Communities @ Work* 1, no. 4 (September 2004).

Brophy, Paul C., and Jennifer S. Vey. *Seizing City Assets: Ten Steps to Urban Land Reform.* Washington, DC: Brookings Institution and CEOs for Cities, 2002.

Burchell, Robert W., and David Listokin. *The Adaptive Reuse Handbook: Procedures to Inventory, Control, Manage, and Reemploy Surplus Municipal Properties.* New Brunswick, NJ: Center for Urban Policy Research, Rutgers University, 1981.

Center for Community Change. *National Survey of Housing Abandonment.* Washington, DC: Center for Community Change, 1971.

Cohen, James R. "Abandoned Housing: Exploring Lessons from Baltimore." *Housing Policy Debate* 12, no. 3 (2001).

———. "Abandoned Housing: Implications for Federal Policy and Local Action." Paper presented at Lincoln Institute for Land Policy conference, Ithaca, NY, September 2000.

Greenberg, Michael R., Frank J. Popper, and Bernadette M. West. "The TOADS: A New American Epidemic." *Urban Affairs Quarterly* 25, no. 3 (March 1990).

Greenberg, Michael R., Frank J. Popper, Dona Schneider, and Bernadette West. "Community Organizing to Prevent TOADS in the United States." *Community Development Journal* 28, no. 1 (January 1993).

Housing Association of Delaware Valley. *Housing Abandonment: The Future Forgotten.* Philadelphia: Housing Association of Delaware Valley, 1972.

Hughes, Mark Alan, and Rebekah Cook-Mack. *Vacancy Reassessed.* Philadelphia: Public/Private Ventures, 1999.

Lowe, Stuart, Sheila Spencer, and Paul Kennan, eds. *Housing Abandonment in Britain: Studies in the Causes and Effects of Low-Demand Housing.* York, UK: University of York Center for Housing Policy, 1999.

Pagano, Michael A., and Ann O'M. Bowman. *Vacant Land in Cities: An Urban Resource.* Washington, DC: Brookings Institution Center on Urban and Metropolitan Policy, 2000.

———. "Transforming America's Cities: Policies and Conditions of Vacant Land." *Urban Affairs Review* 35, no. 4 (2000).

Scafidi, Benjamin P., Michael H. Schill, and Susan M. Wachter. *An Economic Analysis of Housing Abandonment.* Philadelphia: Zell-Lurie Real Estate Center, The Wharton School, University of Pennsylvania, 1998.

Schilling, J. M. *The Revitalization of Vacant Properties: Where Broken Windows Meet Smart Growth*. Washington, DC: International City/County Management Association, 2002.

————. *Vacant Properties: Revitalization Strategies*. Washington, DC: International City/County Management Association, IQ Report, March 2002.

Setterfield, Mark. "Abandoned Buildings: Models for Legislative and Enforcement Reform." Unpublished paper, Trinity Center for Neighborhoods, Hartford, CT, 1997.

Tri-State Regional Planning Commission. *A Review of the Literature and a Summary of the Findings on Housing Abandonment in the Tri-State Region*. New York: Tri-State Regional Planning Commission, 1976.

U.S. Department of Housing and Urban Development. *Abandoned Housing Research: A Compendium*. Washington, DC: U.S. Department of Housing and Urban Development, 1973.

White, Michelle J. "Property Taxes and Urban Housing Abandonment." *Journal of Urban Economics* 20, no. 3 (1986).

Wilson, David, Harry Margulis, and James Ketchum. "Spatial Aspects of Housing Abandonment in the 1990s: The Cleveland Experience." *Housing Studies* 9, no. 4 (1994).

Page numbers followed by the letters *b, f, n,* and *t* indicate boxes, figures, footnotes, and tables, respectively.

apartments. *See* multifamily properties

APM. *See* Associación de Puertorriqueños en Marcha

appraisal gap. *See* market gap

appraisals, in inner-city areas, 36, 92–94

appropriate reuse, 191–92

Architectural Design Ordinance (Clive, Iowa), 273b

area median income (AMI), 325

Arizona: eviction after foreclosure in, 313n7; impact of foreclosure crisis in, 302–3; receivership in, 50t, 51, 52–53t, 60; underwater homeowners in, 312n3

assembly, property: acquisition for, 86; in decisionmaking about disposition, 108; by land bank entities, 133–34

assessment ratios: definition of, 145n1; for vacant properties, 145

assets, and marketing, 205–6

Associación de Puertorriqueños en Marcha (APM), 288b

Atlanta (Georgia): code enforcement in, 42, 42b, 317; land bank entity in, 129b, 136b, 141, 142t; Neighborhood Deputies program in, 42, 42b, 317

attorneys: in lien buying, 96; in tax foreclosure, 84

auctions, public, disposition at, 105, 111, 112–13

Azalea Park (San Diego), marketing of, 205b, 209

Baker, Dean, 313

Baltimore (Maryland): acquisition strategies in, 132b; agency reorganization in, 123b; "Believe" campaign in, 192b; demolition *vs.* preservation in, 176; eminent domain in, 89, 90b; intermediate neighborhoods in, 240b; LiveBaltimore Home Center in, 37b, 207, 208b, 219b; market correction in, 37b; marketing city of, 207–8, 208b; marketing neighborhoods in, 213n; neighborhood typologies in, 237, 237t, 238; number of abandoned properties in, 351t; open space in, 291; Project 5000, 132b; property disposition in, 105; property values in, 222n; receivership in, 98, 99b; self-help nuisance abatement in, 155b, 155n6, 156; side yard program in, 286b; symbolic incentives in, 219b, 220; vacant lot

maintenance in, 170b; vacant lot size in, 166; vacant property receivership in, 158b, 159, 161n, 162–64t, 165

banks, buying liens from, 96–97. *See also* lenders

bargain sales: acquisition through, 94–96; definition of, 87n, 94; use of CDCs in, 87

beautification activities, in intermediate neighborhoods, 240

"Believe" campaign (Baltimore), 192b

Berman v. Parker, 88

Beyond Housing, 327–28, 328b

Birmingham (Alabama), number of abandoned properties in, 351t

blight: in eminent domain, 89–91, 89n; use of term, 91n

boarding, of vacant buildings: aesthetic, 175; alternatives to, 174; by CDCs, 126; problems with, 174–75; protocol for, 172–74

boards of directors, in land bank entities, 140–41

Bon Secours of Maryland Foundation, 170b

Boston (Massachusetts): antipredatory lending campaign in, 35b; elderly owners in, 39b; field surveys in, 349n1; impact of foreclosure crisis in, 303; open space in, 288, 291–92

Brewerytown (Philadelphia), 243t

brokerages, community, 37–38, 215–16

brokers: in low-income neighborhoods, 36, 37; market correction and, 37–38; in neighborhood stabilization strategies, 341; as partners in marketing strategies, 209; in short sales, 312

Brophy, Paul, 13

brownfields. *See* industrial properties

bubble, housing, 302, 318n15

Buffalo (New York): demolition *vs.* preservation in, 176; design principles for reuse in, 269–70, 270b; market conditions in, 319; marketing neighborhoods in, 213b, 215; number of abandoned properties in, 351t; population decline in, 329n21; urban agriculture in, 290b

Buffalo Niagara Association of Realtors, 213b, 215

Burchell and Listokin 1978 survey, 349, 349n3, 350, 351t, 352

Bush, George W., 304

commercial properties: internally generated demand for, 201; as major type of abandoned property, 2; reasons for abandonment of, 7, 7t; training and technical support for owners of, 30

Common Fund (Minneapolis), 253–54, 254n, 258

common law: receivership and, 51; self-help nuisance abatement in, 155

commons, 290–91

Communities United, 173b

Community Asset Preservation Corporation, 324

community brokerages, 37–38, 215–16

Community Central system, 341, 343b

Community Development Block Grant program, 307

community development corporations (CDCs): acquisition strategies of, 87, 99–102; cooperation with local government, 15, 87, 99–100, 127, 341; disposition of property to, 113; financial resources of, 100–102, 242; foreclosed properties as rental properties under, 327–28; incentives for, 224–25; investors in competition with, 331; lending patterns and, 14; lien buying by, 96–98; loan programs of, 35; long-term strategies of, 242; in management system, 123–27, 124–25t; market conditions in approach of, 318–20; in marketing of neighborhoods, 215–16; in Neighborhood Stabilization Program, 306, 307; and owner accountability, 150; in prevention strategies, 14, 15; in receivership, 51, 60–61, 65; scattered-site rehabilitation by, 224–25; small buildings rehabilitation by, 110; in vacant lot maintenance, 126, 167–68; in voluntary conveyance, 96

community development financial institutions (CDFIs): CDC acquisition financing by, 101, 101n; in competition with predatory lenders, 35; in neighborhood stabilization, 306, 341

Community Greens, 290n

community land trusts (CLTs), 326

Community Law Center (Baltimore), 158b, 165, 170b

Community Planning Handbook (Wates), 249b

Community Preservation Corporation (CPC), 25b

Compton (California): illegal dumping in, 172b; securing vacant buildings in, 174n6

computers. *See* information systems; tracking systems

condemnation, 88. *See also* eminent domain

confidence-building strategies, 336, 339t, 342t

Congress, U.S. *See specific laws*

Connecticut: eviction after foreclosure in, 313; neighborhood revitalization planning in, 246–47; property disposition in, 105; receivership in, 50t, 52–53t; tax foreclosure in, 77

consideration, monetary, in terms of disposition, 113–14

Constitution, U.S., and eminent domain, 88–89

control of properties: and conditions for reuse, 73–74; costs of, 74; duration of abandonment and, 72–73; harm minimized through, 73. *See also* acquisition; disposition

conveyance: by land bank entities, 135–37; procedures for, 112–13; terms of, 113–15, 136–37; voluntary, 94–96. *See also* disposition

Cool Space Locator, Inc. (CSL), 37, 216b, 216n

cooperation. *See* public-private cooperation

Copley Square (Boston), 291–92

corporations. *See* businesses; community development corporations

courts: in code enforcement, 44, 46; in eminent domain, 91–92; housing, 44, 46; landlord training in, 29; in nuisance abatement, 98; in receivership, 49, 60, 62–64; in tax foreclosure, 85; in vacant property receivership, 158. *See also* Supreme Court

Covington (Kentucky), 4; voluntary conveyance in, 95b

CPC. *See* Community Preservation Corporation

CPTED. *See* Crime Prevention through Environmental Design

creative classes, 276

credit-line financing, for acquisition by CDCs, 101, 102

Crime Prevention through Environmental Design (CPTED), 291, 291n criminal activity: in foreclosure crisis, 303; nuisance abatement and, 46–47; role of abandonment in, 8–9

CSL. *See* Cool Space Locator

CURA. *See* Center for Urban and Regional Affairs

Cuyahoga County Land Reutilization Corporation, 328

DaimlerChrysler, 288b, 299

Dayton (Ohio): number of abandoned properties in, 351t; owner accountability in, 149b

Death and Life of Great American Cities, The (Jacobs), 277, 309

debris removal, from vacant lots, 167, 169–72

deductions, charitable, 87n, 94

"Deed for Lease" programs, 313

Delaware, receivership in, 52–53t

demand, 193–94, 197–216; competition and, 193–94; identification of targets and, 197, 201–4; incentives and, 217–18, 219; internally generated, 198–201; intervention for creation of, 197; in large-scale redevelopment, 241–42; in market collapse, 319, 319t; in market correction, 318, 319t; marketing to, 204–16; redirecting, 193; regional, 201–16

demographics, and demand, 202–4. *See also* population decline; population growth

demolition, 175–82; costs of, 175; and estimating number of abandoned properties, 352, 352n; fast-track, 180, 181f, 182, 182b; land bank entities and, 135, 135n, 328; large-scale, 73; in nuisance abatement, 156–57, 177; *vs.* preservation, 175–79, 177t, 178–79f, 328; pros and cons of, 73; protocol for, 179–82; *vs.* rehabilitation, 156–57

density, of development, 266, 275–79

density gradient strategy, 278

design advisory boards, 274

design principles: enforcement of, 273–75; for neighborhood revitalization planning, 272–75; for reuse projects, 267–74

Detroit (Michigan): code enforcement in, 45b; cost of abandonment in, 9; demolition *vs.* preservation in, 176; impact of foreclosure crisis in, 303;

investor behavior in, 331–33, 334; number of abandoned properties in, 4, 351t, 352n; open space in, 288b, 289, 290b, 298, 298b, 299, 301; population decline in, 329n21; urban agriculture in, 289, 290b, 298b

Detroit Agricultural Network, 298b

differential taxation, 145

disinvested neighborhoods: in neighborhood typology, 239; reuse strategies for, 241–44

disposition, property, 103–16; at auctions, 105, 111, 112–13; competitive selection process for, 112–13; of individual lots, 106–7t, 108–10, 109f; by land bank entities, 135–37; of large parcels and buildings, 106–7t, 111; monetary consideration in, 113–14; by non-municipal government entities, 115–16; policies for, 103, 105–11, 106–7t; politics in, 103–4; procedures for, 105, 112–13; reuse linked with, 74; of small buildings, 106–7t, 110–11; terms of sale in, 104–5, 112–15

disproportionate impact fees, 335b

"Don't Borrow Trouble" campaign, 35b

driveways, 278

Dudley Street Neighborhood Initiative (Boston), 88n

due diligence: by CDCs, 100; in voluntary conveyance, 95

Duluth (Minnesota), community land trust in, 326

dumping, illegal, in vacant lots, 169–72

Durham (North Carolina), 4

early warning systems, 17, 22–23

East Camden (New Jersey): design principles for reuse in, 272b; internally generated demand in, 199, 199b

East St. Louis (Illinois), neighborhood revitalization planning in, 257b, 259, 261

East St. Louis Action Research Project (ESLARP), 257b

economic development, open spaces and, 295, 301

economic reasons, for abandonment, 5

economic sense: incentives and, 218, 219; in market, 193

economic stimulus bill, 305

economic viability, of at-risk properties, strategies for improving, 15, 24–30 education: for home buyers, 198, 198n; for landlords, 28–30; open space and, 294–95, 299–300; on predatory lending, 34–35

elderly owners: as market activity indicator, 233; preventing abandonment after death of, 35, 38–39

Emerson Park (East St. Louis), neighborhood revitalization planning in, 257b

Emerson Park Development Corporation, 257b

eminent domain, 88–94; compensation in, 89, 91–94; conditions for using, 89–91; definition of, 88; land bank entities and, 131; legal foundations of, 88–89; in nuisance abatement, 47; principles of, 88–89; procedures for, 91–92; public purpose in, 88–89; quick-take, 91–92; spot blight, 89–91; state laws on, 88n, 89–92

employer-assisted initiatives, 222

empowerment planning, 257, 259

encapsulation, 182

enforcement: in abandonment prevention strategy, 40–48; of design standards, 273–75; goal of, 40; of nuisance laws, 40, 46–48. See also code enforcement

enforcement proceeding, single, in tax foreclosure, 75, 81

Enterprise Foundation, 101

Environmental Protection Agency (EPA), 279, 280n6, 281

environmental remediation, of brownfields, 280–81

EPA. See Environmental Protection Agency

equity protection insurance, 221t, 222–24, 337, 337b

ESLARP. See East St. Louis Action Research Project

evictions, after foreclosure, 311–14

exploitation, as reason for abandonment, 5

fair market value: in bargain sales, 94; in disposition, 104–5; in eminent domain, 89, 91–92

Fall Creek Place (Indianapolis), 243t

families, demand among, 197, 198

Fannie Mae: buyer screening by, 334; collapse of, 304; "Deed for Lease" program of, 313; first look program of,

324; lease-purchase program of, 326, 327b; lender authority over mortgaged properties, 315n12

farms, community, 289–90, 301

fast-track demolition, 180, 181f, 182, 182b

Federal Housing Act of 1949, Title I of, 88

Federal Housing Administration, 334

fees: registration, 145–46, 149; for vacant properties, 145–46

fencing: around vacant buildings, 174; around vacant lots, 167, 167n; for community gardens, 288

fields, 294

field surveys, 349–50

Fifth Amendment, and eminent domain, 88–89

financial institutions: buying liens from, 96–97; community development, 35, 101, 101n. See also lenders

financial penalties and incentives. See fees; incentives; penalties

financing. See funding; mortgages

fire risk, 9

first look programs, 324, 335

Flint (Michigan): abandonment in, 5; demolition vs. preservation in, 176; land bank entity in, 129b, 132, 133, 134b; market activity indicators in, 233–34, 234n1, 234n2, 234t; number of abandoned properties in, 351t; property values in, 223n5

flipping, property: definition of, 31, 331, 332t; by investors in foreclosure crisis, 331, 332t, 333; in reasons for abandonment, 6, 31–32

Florida: impact of foreclosure crisis in, 303; Neighborhood Stabilization Program in, 305

Food Security Plan (Detroit), 298b

foreclosure(s): duration of process of, 311, 314, 314n10; judicial vs. nonjudicial, 314n10, 315; for nuisance abatement costs, 47–48; in owner-occupied properties, 31–33; prevention of, 32–33, 311–12, 338t, 342t; of purchased mortgage liens, 96–98. See also tax foreclosure

foreclosure crisis (2006–): causes of, 302; regions most affected by, 302–3. See also neighborhood stabilization foreclosure sale: acquisition at, 323t; definition of, 314n9

forests, 294, 294n, 301

forfeiture, nuisance abatement and, 98

Freddie Mac, 35b, 304

Fresno (California), 4

Fruitvale (Oakland), 243t

Fulton County/City of Atlanta Land Bank Authority (LBA), 129b, 136b, 141, 142t

funding: for acquisition by CDCs, 100–102; for land bank entities, 141; for long-term strategies of CDCs, 242; in neighborhood revitalization planning, 253–54, 258–59; for neighborhood stabilization, 340–44; for open space, 288, 293, 298–300; for repairs in receivership, 49, 61–62, 64, 165. *See also* public funding

garden centers, 289–90

gardens, community, 284, 287–89, 301

Gary (Indiana): number of abandoned properties in, 351t; population decline in, 329n21

Gas Works Park (Seattle), 293, 293b

gay community, target marketing to, 202, 205b

Genesee County Land Bank, 129b, 132, 133, 134b

George, Henry, 145, 145n2

George Gund Foundation, 341

Georgia: duration of foreclosure process in, 314; land bank entities in, 123, 129b; tax foreclosure in, 79b, 80–81

gift property programs, 94–96

good-landlord programs, 335, 335b

government agencies. *See* agencies

grants, rehabilitation, as incentives, 227, 227n, 230–32

Grassroots Program (Boston), 288

grayfields, 5

Greater Minnesota Housing Fund, 306

Green Campaign (Philadelphia), 296b

Green City Strategy (Philadelphia), 295, 296b, 299

greening, community objectives met through, 283–84, 284–85t. *See also* open space

greens, community, 290–91

Greensgrow, 290b

green space. *See* open space

Greenville (North Carolina), nuisance abatement statute for, 156–57

greenways, 292–94

gross density, 277

Habitat for Humanity, 33b

HAMP. *See* Home Affordable Modification Program

HANDS, Inc., 97b, 240b

Hartford (Connecticut), number of abandoned properties in, 352

health, public, 9

HEMAP. *See* Homeowners' Emergency Mortgage Assistance Program

HERA. *See* Housing and Economic Recovery Act

historic properties: demolition *vs.* rehabilitation of, in nuisance abatement, 156; design standards for, 273; rehabilitation tax credits for, 227–30, 228t, 229t

HMDA. *See* Home Mortgage Disclosure Act

holding of properties: by investors, 331–33, 332t; by land bank entities, 132–35, 328–29

Home Affordable Modification Program (HAMP), 311–12, 334

Home Depot, 288b

Home Mortgage Disclosure Act (HMDA), 234n2, 236

homeowners. *See* owner(s)

Homeowners' Emergency Mortgage Assistance Program (HEMAP), 34b

homeownership: internally generated demand and, 198–200; strategies for increasing, 198, 198n

Homeownership Zone program, 276

home rule: and land bank entities, 138; and management system, 120; and vacant property receivership, 159, 161n

homesteading programs, 110–11

Hope Community, Inc., 291, 291b

Hope VI program, 276

Housing and Community Development, Department of (Baltimore), 123b

Housing and Development, Department of (Trenton), 123b, 137

Housing and Economic Recovery Act (HERA), 304–5

housing bubble: causes of, 302, 318n15; collapse of, 302

housing courts, code enforcement in, 44, 46

Housing Design Advisory Board (Buffalo), 270b

Housing Education Program (New York), 28b

housing prices: bubble in, 302, 318n15; collapse of, 302–3; in foreclosure prevention, 314, 314n8; in market correction, 318, 319t; realistic, definition of, 318, 318n15. *See also* foreclosure crisis; market value

Houston (Texas): acquisition strategies in, 132b; information system in, 154b, 254b; land bank entity in, 132b, 138; neighborhood revitalization planning in, 251–52, 251t, 252b, 254b, 255; nuisance abatement in, 154b; Super Neighborhood Action Plan in, 154b, 252, 252b, 254b; Super Neighborhoods program in, 154b, 252b

HUD: Neighborhood Stabilization Program under, 305, 308, 321, 324; in redevelopment of urban neighborhoods, 276

illegal dumping, in vacant lots, 169–72

Illinois: neighborhood stabilization in, 305, 336–37; receivership in, 50t, 54–55t, 99b; vacant property receivership in, 159, 162–64t

Illinois, University of, 257b, 259

Illinois Home Equity Assurance Act, 337b

immigrant neighborhoods, open space in, 292

improvements, neighborhood: in neighborhood stabilization, 336, 341; in prevention strategies, 14–15

improvements, property: to improve market, 38; in open spaces, 295–96; by owners, motivating, 26–27, 143–50; taxation of, 145

incentives, financial, 217–32; combinations of, 230–32, 231t; effectiveness of, 217–18; employers offering, 222; forms of, 217; historic rehabilitation tax credits as, 227–30, 228t, 229t; and internally generated demand, 200; and investor behavior, 335; market demand, 219–20; market gap bridged by, 220, 224–32; market influenced by, 194, 217–18; in neighborhood stabilization, 320–21, 335; for owners of vacant

properties, 146–47; principles for, 218; purpose of, 217–18; in reuse strategies, 194; for scattered-site rehabilitation, 224–32; symbolic, 218–20, 227; targeting of, 220–22; typology of, 220–24, 221t; value of, calculation of, 230–32

income thresholds, in Neighborhood Stabilization Program, 325, 325n

Indiana: receivership in, 50t, 54–55t; vacant property receivership in, 159

Indianapolis (Indiana): large-scale projects in, 243t; rebranding disinvested neighborhoods in, 239

individual lots, disposition of, 106–7t, 108–10, 109f

industrial properties (brownfields), 279–82; brownfields *vs.* Superfund sites, 280n6; definition of, 279; in disinvested areas, strategies for, 241; environmental remediation of, 280–81; internally generated demand for, 200–201; as major type of abandoned property, 2; as open space, 293, 298; reasons for abandonment of, 7t, 8; regulation of, 279, 280–81, 280n5; reuse of, 279–82; voluntary conveyance of, 95

infill development: in decisionmaking about disposition, 108–10; design principles for, 268

Inforent (manual), 29b

information systems, 17–23; in acquisition strategies, 87; boarding of buildings in, 174; code enforcement in, 43, 44, 45; critical data for, 18–21, 19t, 20t; definition of, 17; design of, 17–21, 23; in disposition policies, 108; early warning with, 17, 22–23; in neighborhood revitalization planning, 255, 261, 262n; property *vs.* neighborhood, 17; in tax foreclosure, 85; and training and technical support for landlords, 30; use of, 21–23; vacant lot maintenance in, 168–69

inner-city areas: correcting market failure in, 36; costs of abandonment in, 9; market values in, 36, 92; reasons for abandonment in, 6, 8; third-party purchasers of tax liens in, 77

in personam proceedings, 154, 154n

inspections: of rental properties, 42, 334; in scattered-site rehabilitation, 226; of vacant properties, 150 insurance: assistance for absentee owners, 27–28; equity protection, 221t, 222–24, 337, 337b; insurance pools, 28; liability, 149b

interagency coordination, in management system, 121–22

interim use: open space as, 300–301; of vacant lots, 168

intermediate neighborhoods: in neighborhood typology, 238; reuse strategies for, 239–41

internally generated demand, 198–201

International City/County Management Association, 176b

Internet, information system access on, 23, 255

intervention: acquisition as outcome of, 98–99; in market, 36–39, 194–95, 197; in preventing abandonment, 40–48. *See also specific types*

inventory, property, of land bank entities, 132–35

investors: incentives for, 335; lender screening of, 334; market conditions and, 331–34; in neighborhood stabilization, 330–35, 341; types of, 331, 332t

Jacobs, Jane, 277, 309

Jersey City (New Jersey), eminent domain in, 90–91, 91b

J-51 program (New York), 27b

judicial foreclosures, 314n10

judiciary. *See* courts

Kansas City (Kansas), vacant lots in, 166, 168, 169b

Kelo v. New London, 88, 89n

Kensington (Philadelphia), open space in, 289, 289b, 290b, 298

Kent State University, 330b

Kentucky, land bank entities in, 129b, 138–39

Land Bank Authorities (Alexander), 128n2

land bank entities, 128–42; acquisition by, 130–32, 131t, 328; definition of, 128n1; disposition by, 135–37; funding for, 141; governance of, 140–41, 142t; holding of properties by, 132–35, 328–29; legal power and authority of, 137–40; in management system, 123, 128–29; mission of, 128, 129, 132,

135–36; in neighborhood stabilization, 328–29; nongovernmental organizations and, 123; organizational structure of, 140–42; reasons for creation of, 123, 128, 130; scope of operations of, 129–37; staffing of, 141, 142t; state laws on, 128, 138–40, 328–29

Land Bank Fast Track Act (Michigan, 2004), 129b

Landlord Accreditation Scheme (Rochdale), 29b

landlords: code enforcement targeting, 42–43; incentives for, 335, 335b; insurance assistance for, 27–28; loan programs for, 25–26; preventing abandonment by, 24–30; registration of, 42–43; tax relief for, 26–27; training and technical assistance for, 28–30. *See also* rental properties

Land Redevelopment Authority (LARA) (Houston), 132b, 138

land swap, 296n

land use ordinances, design standards in, 273

LARA. *See* Land Redevelopment Authority

large parcels and buildings, disposition of, 106–7t, 111

large-scale revitalization: assessment of potential for, 242; examples of, 243t; opportunities created by, 241–42; strategies for, 241–44

Latinos, in foreclosure crisis, 303

law(s). *See* state laws; *specific laws*

lawyers. *See* attorneys

lead, in soil, 289n5

lease-purchase programs, 326–27

leases. *See* rental properties

lenders: approval of short sales by, 312, 321; buying liens from, 96–97; investor screening by, 334; maintenance of foreclosed properties by, 314–17

lending. *See* loan(s); mortgages; predatory lending

liability, in information systems, 21n

liability insurance, 149b

Liberty State Park (New Jersey), 299n11

licensing ordinances, rental, 334

liens: for boarding costs, 173; buying of, acquisition through, 96–98; in nuisance abatement, 47–48, 153–55; in receivership, 61–62; in short sales, 312n4; in tax foreclosure, 75–76, 77–78, 82;

Maslow, Abraham, 307–8

Massachusetts: eminent domain in, 88n; Neighborhood Stabilization Program in, 306, 307b; property disposition in, 105; receivership in, 50t, 54–55t, 61b; vacant property receivership in, 159

Massachusetts Community Banking Council, 35b

Massachusetts Housing Investment Corporation (MHIC), 306, 307b, 341

meadows, 294

medians, street, 285

mediation programs, in foreclosure prevention, 311

Mennonite Board of Missions v. Adams, 76, 84

Mercy Portfolio Services, 324, 341, 343b

MHIC. *See* Massachusetts Housing Investment Corporation

Miami (Florida): illegal dumping in, 173b; impact of foreclosure crisis in, 303

Michigan: land bank entities in, 129b, 132, 328; Neighborhood Stabilization Program in, 305; receivership in, 54–55t; tax foreclosure in, 79b

Michigan, University of, 134b

milkers, investors as, 331, 332t, 333

mini-parks, 287

Minneapolis (Minnesota): foreclosure prevention in, 33b; information system of, 22b, 23b, 260b, 261; neighborhood revitalization planning in, 251–54, 251t, 252b, 258, 260b; Neighborhood Revitalization Program in, 237, 251, 252b, 253–54, 260b; neighborhood typologies in, 236–38; open space in, 291, 291b; owner accountability in, 149–50, 151b

Minneapolis Neighborhood Information System (MNIS), 22b, 23b, 260b, 261

Minnesota: Neighborhood Stabilization Program in, 306; receivership in, 50t, 54–55t, 60

Minnesota, University of, 252, 259, 260b, 261

Minnesota Home Ownership Center, 33b

Missouri: receivership in, 50t, 54–55t, 99b; vacant property receivership in, 159, 162–64t

mixed-use properties: as major type of abandoned property, 2; reasons for abandonment of, 7t

MNIS. *See* Minneapolis Neighborhood Information System

monetary terms, of disposition, 113–14

mortgages: acquisition through buying of, 96–97, 323t; modification of, 311–12; subprime, 31, 31n, 302; underwater, 312, 312n3. *See also* foreclosure; lenders

multifamily properties: as major type of abandoned property, 2; owner-occupied, preventing abandonment of, 39; reasons for abandonment of, 7t; Section 8 vouchers for, 6

municipal liens: buying of, acquisition through, 96; in voluntary conveyance, 95–96

National Community Stabilization Trust (NCST), 306, 324, 324n, 331

National Vacant Properties Campaign, xi

NBN. *See* Neighbors Building Neighborhoods

NCST. *See* National Community Stabilization Trust

neighbor(s): adjacent, sale of property to, 110, 287; in demolition *vs.* preservation decision, 177; in nuisance abatement, 153, 155–56. *See also* owner(s); resident(s)

neighborhood(s): code enforcement targeting, 41–42; designation of, 250–51, 251t; design features of, 269–71; disinvested, 239, 241–44; foreclosure crisis impacts by type of, 303; improvement of, 14–15, 336, 341; in information systems, 17–23, 19t; intermediate, 238, 239–41; and internally generated demand, 199–200; long-term strategies for, 241–44; market activity indicators in, 233–36; market dynamics of, 233–44; marketing of, 206, 209–14, 212t; typologies of, 235, 236–39, 236n4; in vacant lot maintenance, 167–68. *See also* neighborhood revitalization planning; neighborhood stabilization

Neighborhood Deputies program (Atlanta, Georgia), 42, 42b, 317

Neighborhood Design Center (Baltimore), 170b, 286b, 291

Neighborhood Housing Services (NHS) of New Haven, 97b

Neighborhood Knowledge Los Angeles (NKLA), 22b

Neighborhood Planning for Community Revitalization (NPCR), 22b, 23b, 252, 260b

Neighborhood Progress, Inc., 330b

Neighborhood Reinvestment Corporation, 101

neighborhood revitalization planning, 245–65; abandoned property strategies in, 261–65, 263–64t; citywide, 250–55; design principles in, 272–75; failures in, 344, 344n; funding in, 253–54, 258–59; implementation of, 249–50, 253–55; importance of, 245–46; and internally generated demand, 199–200; long-term, 344; models of, 250–57, 250t; monitoring of, 249–50, 255; neighborhood-driven, 256–57; participants in, 126, 247–49, 251, 256–57; process for, 247–49; residents' role in, 247–49, 260–61; scope of, 246–47, 248t; target-neighborhood, 255–56; technical support for, 259–60; use of term, 246n1

Neighborhood Revitalization Program (NRP) (Minneapolis), 237, 251, 252b, 253–54, 260b

Neighborhood Revitalization Zone (NRZ) program (Connecticut), 246–47

Neighborhood Service Company, 176b

Neighborhoods in Bloom (NIB) program (Richmond), 255b

neighborhood stabilization, 302–44; acquisition options for, 321–24, 322–23t; code enforcement in, 314–17, 334–35; comprehensive strategy for, 337–44, 338–39t; destabilizing vs. stabilizing events in, 309–10, 342–43; goal of, 337–40; homeowner support in, 336–37; investor behavior in, 330–35, 341; long-term planning in, 344; maintenance of properties in, 309, 314–17, 334; market conditions in, 318–20, 319t, 325–26, 343–44; need for, 302–4; overemphasis on acquisition in, 307–8, 310, 320–21; prevention of vacancy in, 310–14, 338t, 342t; principles of, 308–10; resident perceptions in, 308–9, 336; resources for, 340–44, 342t; reuse strategies for, 324–29; road map for, 338–39t, 340. *See also* Neighborhood Stabilization Program

Neighborhood Stabilization Loan Fund (NSLF), 307b

Neighborhood Stabilization Program (NSP), 304–8; absentee investors and, 331; acquisition in, 306–7, 310, 321–24; allocation of funding in, 305, 308, 325, 342; establishment of, 303, 304–5; income thresholds in, 325, 325n; land banking in, 329; limitations of, 305–8, 340, 342, 344; REO sales in, 321–24; short sales in, 321

Neighborhood Transformation Initiative (Philadelphia), 180b

NeighborLink Network, 261b

Neighbors Building Neighborhoods (NBN) initiative (Rochester), 23b, 252b, 254, 261b

Neighbors Building Neighborhoods (NBN) Institute, 23b, 261b

net density, 277

Nevada: impact of foreclosure crisis in, 303; underwater homeowners in, 312n3

Newark (New Jersey): impact of foreclosure crisis in, 303; number of abandoned properties in, 351t

New Community Corporation, 242

New Haven (Connecticut): agency reorganization in, 122–23; incentives in, 222, 222b; lien buying in, 97b; Livable City Initiative in, 122–23, 123n, 126b; management system in, 122–23, 126b

New Jersey: appraisals in, 93b; CDC acquisition in, 101b; cleaning of vacant properties in, 173n; Community Asset Preservation Corporation in, 324; definition of abandoned property in, 2, 3b; eminent domain in, 90n5, 91, 93b; eviction after foreclosure in, 313, 313n7; foreclosed property maintenance in, 315, 316b, 316n14; foreclosure process in, duration of, 314; incentives in, 220; land bank entities in, 139b; landlord registration in, 43, 43n; loan programs for absentee owners in, 26b; neighborhood revitalization planning in, 249, 258, 258b, 258n; Neighborhood Stabilization Program in, 306, 324; nuisance abatement in, 47b; open space in, 299, 299n11; property disposition in, 104–5; receivership in, 50t, 56–57t, 62b, 63, 63b, 98; redevelopment in,

Olmsted parks, 293

O'Malley, Martin, 192b

open space(s), 283–301; community objectives met through, 283–84, 284–85t; density of development and, 276, 278; disposition for creation of, 110; funding for, 288, 293, 298–300; importance of, 283–84; improvement of existing, 295–96; interim *vs.* permanent, 300–301; in neighborhood stabilization, 329; partnerships in, 296, 297–98; restrictions on use of, 296n; scale of, 294, 295t; self-sustaining, 300; strategy for, 294–301; types of, 285–94

Open Space Management Program (Baltimore), 170b

Operation Brightside, Inc., 168, 169b

Operation ReachOut SouthWest (OROSW), 170b

Orange (New Jersey): intermediate neighborhoods in, 240b; lien buying in, 97b

Oregon, receivership in, 56–57t

OROSW. *See* Operation ReachOut SouthWest

owner(s): absentee, 24–30, 262–64; accountability of, 148–50; adjacent, sale of property to, 110, 287; defined in nuisance abatement, 48; eviction of, after foreclosure, 311, 313–14; financial penalties and incentives for, 144–47; foreclosure prevention for, 32–33, 311–12; motivating action in, 143–65; in neighborhood stabilization, 336–37; redemption for, in tax foreclosure, 75–76, 81–82; responsibilities of, 1; restoration of control of, in receivership, 49, 62–63; rights of, in vacant property receivership, 158–59; technical assistance for, 28–30, 149–50; tenure of, average, 336n; underwater, 312n3. *See also* landlords

owner-occupied properties: loss through inability to pay for, 31–35; loss through market failure, 35–39; multifamily, 39; preventing abandonment of, 31–39; reasons for abandonment of, 6, 31

Owner Services Program (New York), 28b

Pagano and Bowman 1998 survey, 350, 351t

park(s): community, 292–94; funding for, 299, 300; improvement of existing,

295–96; mini, 287; shared (commons), 290–91; state, 299

parking, 276, 278

Parks and People Foundation, 170b

partnerships. *See* public-private cooperation

Pattern Language, A (Alexander et al.), 292n

Patterson Park (Baltimore): vacant property receivership in, 158b, 165; vacant property rehabilitation in, 240b

Patterson Park Community Development Corporation, 240b

Pawtucket (Rhode Island): management system of, 122b; target marketing in, 205b

penalties, financial, for owners of vacant properties, 146–47. *See also* fees

Penn Central case, 273

Pennsylvania: differential taxation in, 145; elderly owners in, 39; foreclosure prevention in, 34b

Pennsylvania Horticultural Society, 296b, 297, 298

perceptions, resident, in neighborhood stability, 308–9, 336

permits, occupancy, for rental properties, 42

Pew Charitable Trust, 289

Philadelphia (Pennsylvania): boarding of buildings in, 175b; demolition *vs.* preservation in, 178–79, 180b; design principles for reuse in, 269; division of responsibilities in, 117, 118; illegal dumping in, 171, 171b; large-scale projects in, 243t; market activity indicators in, 235–36, 235t; neighborhood typologies in, 235, 235t, 237, 238; number of abandoned properties in, 4, 351t, 352n; number of vacant lots in, 166; open space in, 286b, 288, 288b, 289b, 290b, 292, 295, 296b, 298, 299; property values in, 8; urban agriculture in, 290b

Philadelphia Green, 288, 288b, 296b

Phoenix (Arizona): code enforcement in, 42b; impact of foreclosure crisis in, 303; market conditions in, 318, 318n16; short sales in, 313–14

physical obsolescence, 5

Pittsburgh (Pennsylvania): elderly owners in, 38; marketing of neighborhoods in, 216b; number of abandoned properties

Rochdale (England), training and technical assistance for landlords in, 29b

Rochester (New York): design principles for reuse in, 271b; information system of, 23b; market correction in, 37b; marketing city of, 208–9, 211b; neighborhood revitalization planning in, 252, 252b, 254, 261b; Neighbors Building Neighborhoods initiative in, 23b, 252b, 254, 261b; Neighbors Building Neighborhoods Institute in, 23b, 261b; number of abandoned properties in, 351t

Rochester City Living, Inc., 37b, 211b

Rowe, Peter, 284

rural areas: illegal dumping in, 170n; problem of abandonment in, 79n

sale of property: to adjacent owners, 110, 287; bargain, 87n, 94–96; in receivership, 63–64, 98; in tax foreclosure, 75–76, 82; tracking of, 320, 320n. *See also* disposition

San Diego (California): owner accountability in, 151b; target marketing in, 205b, 209

Save a Neighborhood, Inc., 158b, 165

scattered abandoned properties: incentives for rehabilitating, 224–32; in intermediate neighborhoods, reuse strategies for, 239–40

scattered-site rental properties, 327–28

schools: in neighborhood revitalization planning, 259–60; open space and, 299–300. *See also* education

Seattle (Washington): neighborhood revitalization planning in, 254b, 255; open space in, 293, 293b

Section 8 vouchers, 6

Self-Help (institution), 326, 327b

self-help nuisance abatement, 155–56

Senior Abandonment Prevention Program, 39b

short sales: barriers to, 312, 312n4; definition of, 312, 322t; in foreclosure prevention, 311, 312, 313–14; pros and cons of, 322t; rise in number of, 312

sidewalk maintenance, 135, 135n

sidewalk strips, green, 285

SIDE Watch, 173b

side yard programs, 110, 286–87

single-family homes: as major type of abandoned property, 2; reasons for abandonment of, 6, 7t

SkunkShot, 174n6

Slavic Village, 242

small buildings, disposition of, 106–7t, 110–11

small-scale revitalization, strategies for, 239–40

SNAP. *See* Super Neighborhood Action Plan

soil contamination, 289–90, 289n5

South Carolina, incentives for rehabilitation in, 227–30, 229t

South Carolina Historic Rehabilitation Incentives Act, 227–30, 229t

Southwest Chicago Guaranteed Home Equity Program, 337b, 341

special improvement districts, 341

speculators: in housing bubble, 302; in market collapse, 319

spot blight eminent domain, 89–91

squares, 291–92

stabilization: of neighborhoods (*See* neighborhood stabilization); of vacant buildings, 73, 175–82; of vacant lots, 287, 301

stable neighborhoods, definition of, 238. *See also* neighborhood stabilization

state laws: on brokerage, 37; on brownfield remediation, 280; on code enforcement, 41; definitions of abandoned property by, 2, 82–83; on disposition, 104–5, 116; on eminent domain, 88n, 89–92; on foreclosed properties, maintenance of, 315; on foreclosure, eviction after, 313, 313n7; on historic rehabilitation tax credits, 227, 228t; on incentives, 220; on land bank entities, 128, 138–40, 328–29; on nuisance abatement, 46, 47–48, 150–53, 152–53t; on predatory lending, 34; on receivership, 49–64, 50–51t, 52–59t; on tax foreclosure, 33, 77–83; on tax rates for vacant properties, 145; on tax relief, 27; on vacant property receivership, 159–61, 162–64t. *See also specific laws and states*

state parks, 299

State University of New York, 270b

St. Joseph's Carpenter Society, 199b

St. Louis (Missouri): cost of abandonment in, 9; land bank entity in, 142t; number of abandoned properties in, 4, 351t; population decline in, 329n21; rental property management in, 327–28, 328b;

transactional abandonment, 8

transitional neighborhoods. *See* intermediate neighborhoods

trash removal, from vacant lots, 167, 169–72

tree plantings, 285, 294

Trenton (New Jersey): agency reorganization in, 122, 123b, 137, 137n; anchor projects in, 241b; brownfield reuse projects in, 281, 282t; industrial retention strategy in, 201b; land bank entity in, 137, 137n; manufacturing in, 201, 201b; voluntary conveyance in, 95b

TRF. *See* Reinvestment Fund, the

triggers, abandonment, 6–8, 7t

Twin Cities Habitat for Humanity, 33b

underwater homeowners, 312, 312n3

universities, in neighborhood revitalization planning, 259–60

upward mobility, and internally generated demand, 198, 199–200

Urban Design Associates, 272b

Utah, incentives for landlords in, 335, 335b

utility bills, in tax foreclosure, 82

vacant buildings: boarding of, 172–74, 175; demolition protocol for, 179–82; demolition *vs.* preservation of, 175–79, 177t, 178–79f, 328; in intermediate neighborhoods, reuse strategies for, 239; securing of, 172–75; stabilization of, 73, 175–82. *See also* foreclosure crisis

vacant lots: estimating number of, 4; harm caused by, 2–3, 73; illegal dumping in, 169–72; individual, disposition of, 106–7t, 108–10, 109f; in information systems, 168–69; interim uses for, 168; maintenance of, 166–72, 287; non-governmental partners helping with, 167–68; open space created in, 285–94; size of, 166; stabilization of, 287, 301; as type of abandoned property, 2; *vs.* vacant buildings, 73

vacant properties, privately owned, 143–65; *vs.* abandoned properties, 1; demolition of, 180; financial penalties and incentives for, 144–47; harm caused by, 143, 144; motivating maintenance and improvement of, 143–50; nuisance abatement in, 150–57; owner account-

ability for, 148–50; receivership in, 157–65

vandalism, in foreclosure crisis, 303

Vey, Jennifer, 13

Village Farms, 290b

Virginia, eminent domain in, 90b

Volk, Laurie, 276

voluntary conveyance, 94–96

Wachovia Regional Foundation, 259b

Warren/Conner Development Coalition, 288b, 298

Washington, DC: eminent domain in, 90b; number of abandoned properties in, 351t; tax on vacant properties in, 145, 145b

Washtenaw County (Michigan), foreclosure prevention in, 33b

water, in parks, 293

Wates, Nick, 249b

Wayne County (Michigan), nuisance abatement in, 98

Western Pennsylvania Conservancy, 293b

West Side (Buffalo), marketing of, 213b

West Side Community Collaborative (WSCC), 213b

Westside Industrial Retention and Expansion Network (WIRE-net), 30b

Wichita (Kansas), illegal dumping in, 171, 171b

Wilkes-Barre (Pennsylvania), elderly owners in, 38

William Penn Foundation, 289

Wilmington (Delaware), fees on vacant properties in, 146, 146b

WIRE-net. *See* Westside Industrial Retention and Expansion Network

Wisconsin, receivership in, 58–59t

working-class neighborhoods, density of, 276

working groups, 121

WSCC. *See* West Side Community Collaborative

Yale University, 222, 222b

yards: density of development and, 277, 278; side, 110, 286–87

Youngstown (Ohio), population decline in, 329n21

Zimmerman, Todd, 276

zoning ordinances, design standards in, 273, 274